The Bo

Recovering from Two Brain Surgeries

My Daily Therapy Journal (12/31/12 – 8/15/13)

With A Detailed Introduction

Charles S. Caylor

Copyright © 2013 Charles S. Caylor

All rights reserved.

ISBN: 1492782807

Version Date: 11/16/2013

Dedication

To Those Who Look Beyond Their World...

Table of Contents

Acknowledgments 1
Introduction 5
   To Vanderbilt 18
      Cathy Tries To Keep Up 18
      I Worry About My Birds 19
      Smokey Joe and Christy 20
      Business Dreams 22
      Vanderbilt Students 24
      Benign Blob 24
      Vanderbilt Meals 25
      Brunettes 25
      Jamaican Surprise 26
      Brain Surgery Preps 27
      Bazaar Thoughts 28
      Gruesome Details 29
   Vanderbilt Mind Trip 31
      Triangle Briefcases 32
      Bowel Fun 32
      I Lose Everything But I Am Alive! 33
      "Saving The World For Democracy" 34
      Lack Of Energy 35
      Vanderbilt Walking 36
      Lost Money 36
   To The TN VA 37
      Seizure (Who Hit Ctrl-Alt-Del?) 37
      A Strange Healing Device 38
      Useless Cell Phone 38
      Real Eggs? 39
      Weird Nashville 40
      What Privacy? 41
      Belly Shots 42
      Falling Into Bed 42
      Swallowing 43
      Singing Opera 45
      Carnival Therapy 46
      Bar Fly Nuke Codes 48

Mary Returns 50
Franklin, Burger King, And Laxatives...............50
April Power...51
Balancing Act...52
Eye Patch..53
Window Wishes...54
Korean War Veteran..56
Weekend Escapes...56
VA Obstacles...57
Biting Tongues..59
Ray of Sunshine...60
WWIII When I Get Out?..60

I Leave Tennessee..61
Michigan Looks Familiar...61
Mom's Nightstand on Wheels..............................62
The Queen Sees Everything.................................62
One Item At A Time..64
Hand Dryers In Hell..64
Mail Call 64
Once A Nerd..66
Say What?..67
Numb Hair, Basketball, and Elevation...............68
I'll Pass Today, Thanks...69
Towel Holder Go Boom..71
VA Vision...72
Walk For Kate..72
Good Bye Eye Patch...73
Double Images...74
The Boy Who Lived..76
Drive To Recover...76
"Tridge" Bridge..77
Williams Township Park...79
Birds Gone Wild...80

Michigan and The Gamma Knife..................................81
Night Train...81
Morning Routine...82
Mall Walk Therapy..82

    Mornings At Burger King 84
    "Brain" Shirts 85
    Local Laundromats 86
    Baseball Games 87
    VA Medicine 88
    Casino Trip 90
    Painfully Slow Recovery 91
    Sloping Bedroom Ceiling 91
    "Quiet" Room 91
    Michigan Reunion 92
    Dow Coffee 93
    Gamma Knife 94
    Lake Michigan Shore 96
    Midland Symphony 97
    SSDI Success 99
    Michigan Fall Trips 99
More Michigan "memories" 100
    Talking To Strangers 100
    Right Leg 102
    Small Water Bottle 103
    VA Ann Arbor MRI Scans 104
    Saginaw VA Speech Therapy 105
    Saginaw Fashion Square Mall 106
    Saginaw Branch Library 107
    Saginaw Barnes and Noble 107
    More Store Selection 108
    Saginaw VA Neurologist 108
    Driving The Turnpike 109
    Hacking Mom's Lawn 109
2013 Michigan Therapy Continues 110
    Tinnitus 110
    Mental Distraction 112
    Bottle Returns 113
    In Their Own World 113
    Pierre Marquette 115
    "Waldo" Walk 117
    Less Shakin Goin On 119

- Hello Balance..119
- Grave Sites..120
- Mackinac Island Vacation..121
- Well Bite My Lip...122
- Mr. Gamma - Dr. Brian Copeland....................................123
- Beer And Tinnitus..124
- Irish Pub..125
- Mom's Pool..125
- Speech Recognition...126
- Introduction Wrap Up...126
- Daily Journal (12/31/12- 8/15/13)...128
    - CHAPTER 1 12/31/12 – 1/31/13 128
    - CHAPTER 2 2/1/13 – 2/28/13.......................................150
    - CHAPTER 3 3/1/13 – 3/31/13.......................................179
    - CHAPTER 4 4/1/13 – 4/30/13.......................................212
    - CHAPTER 5 5/1/13 – 5/31/13.......................................239
    - CHAPTER 6 6/1/13 – 6/30/13.......................................264
    - CHAPTER 7 7/1/13 – 7/31/13.......................................285
    - CHAPTER 8 8/1/13 – 8/15/13.......................................316
- Epilogue..325
- About The Author..368

Acknowledgments

It is hard to know where to begin to thank the many people who have played a role in my recovery from two brain surgeries. I am still alive and walking this planet thanks to the love and dedication of all of these amazing and tireless individuals. I may never be able to fully thank everyone for their efforts on my behalf but in a way I do that by being able to write and print this book of memories and daily reflections. I want them to know that I am and will always be grateful for my situation at this moment in time and for all of their help in getting me here. Many people played a part, some upfront and some in the background, and many continue to do so to this day in helping me to complete a most "miraculous" recovery.

The order that I mention these individuals does not necessarily reflect their importance to my story. Again, as I write about in my "memories" and journal, I hope I do not leave anyone out. There were so many and if I do, then my most sincere apologies.

My family, naturally, plays a very large role in my recovery and continuing therapy. My mother, Doris, continues to offer me her home, her automobile, her food, her hard work, and of course, her love and prayers.

My brother Dave, who has worked so hard on my behalf to get me the proper treatment, battling bureaucracy, bureaucrats, and the US government itself, played and plays a very large role. He not only did this behind the scenes with the authorities, but at the same time he valiantly struggled to run my business in Tennessee for as long as he could (bad plumbing and all), while I was mentally and physically "out of it". I learn more and more of his sacrifices on my behave each day. He truly has taught me the meaning of the phrase "doing the right thing".

My sister Sandra played a major role, and continues to do so in my life. She drove my mother down to Tennessee from Michigan and was there to visit me in the hospital. She was there also for my second brain surgery, the gamma knife procedure in Midland, Michigan. She has driven me to Detroit for my first follow-up MRI. Her husband Steve is someone to whom I will always owe so much for all of his efforts on my behalf. Their two daughters, Heather and Amy, continue to play important roles in my recovery.

My other family members, my brothers Tom and Bob and Bob's wife Marsha, have always shown me great support. I, of all people, know how difficult it is to get away, even for any unplanned "emergencies", and I realize that they would have been in Tennessee if they had been able. I appreciate their concerns and the good vibrations that they sent my way during the ordeal. They continue to offer me their best wishes.

All of Mom's other grandchildren, my other nieces and nephews, have given me great motivation to continue to get better. Ben, Emily, Bobbie, Sarah, Patrick, and Sarah's husband Josh, you all have helped me so much. A big thanks to all of you. A special treat it is to see that new smile of Brooklyn, Josh and Sarah's new daughter.

Of course, I will always be very grateful to my dear friend Cathy Lewis, who I had to leave back in Tennessee, for all that she did for me and for her wonderful companionship. I am thankful that she pushed me to finally get the treatment that ended up saving my life. A shout out goes to her two sons, Jessie and Josh, whom I got to see at the hospital before the "lights went out". Thanks guys! Someday, some way, I hope to see you all again (er, y'all).

Naturally, I thank the many neurosurgeons along the way for their knowledge and skill in getting me this far along the road back. A special thanks to Dr. Sills and Dr. Chambless, who both actually performed the craniotomy (my first brain surgery in Tennessee) and to

Dr. Singer for his embolization surgery before that. A shout out of thanks goes to the staff at the Vanderbilt ICU for their help in keeping me alive throughout the procedures.

I thank my doctors at the University of Michigan in Ann Arbor, Dr. Valdivia and Dr. Orringer who continue to be on the hunt for any remnant tumors. A special thanks to the late Dr. Copeland for his gamma knife expertise and especially for his patience and care in explaining the procedure before I underwent it days later. A big thanks to you too, Dennis, for all of your technical skills at the gamma clinic and to all the doctors who assisted in the gamma procedure.

My thanks to the wonderful and caring therapists whom I have met along the way, both at the Tennessee VA and here in Michigan. I am sorry that I do not remember all of your names, there were so many. A special thanks to April (I think her last name is Clark, but I am not certain), my physical therapist in Tennessee, for pushing me to the limit and a special thanks to Anita S. Wierda, my speech pathologist at the Saginaw VA, who helps me with my continuing speech therapy.

Thanks to all of the "good" nurses, students, and interns that I met in Vanderbilt and Murfreesboro who helped me to get to this point, cleaning me, medicating me, doing all of the everyday menial tasks that are so necessary for me to make it through all of this.

It is good to meet Jamie, Bobbie's [my brother Bob's son and my nephew] friend and James, Amy's [my sister Sandra's daughter and my niece now studying in Ohio] friend and I thank them for their good wishes. I guess the term now is BFFs, he he, but they will choose the correct word. A shout out to Amy in the UK also and may you and Emily have a wonderful life together. I also want to thank Rose, my Mom's friend, for all of her good wishes for my recovery. Thanks to my Aunt Betty and to Jerry, whom I get to visit with here in Michigan, for all of your support. You are both excellent role models. Thanks to their "kids", Mike, Pat, and Kathy and all of their clan for your support.

There were so many people and there continue to be many that are always there everyday. I'm sure I have left out someone important. You know who you are and the importance you have meant to me and again my apologies if I did not mention your name specifically. I will blame it on the "hole" in my head.

A special thanks to the "regular" people I come into contact with daily now, from the Starbucks coffee servers to the "kids" at the local Burger King here in Midland, Michigan. Thanks to the clerks at Walmart and Meijer who continue to listen to me mumble my story to them as they work. Thanks for the smiles and all the thumbs up from all of the people I see when I do my morning walking therapy at the malls. I want to thank the Midland Mall manager and his excellent cleaning crew for all of their smiles and encouragements.

I guess I am just so happy and amazed to be alive sometimes that I want to thank everyone I continue to meet along the way. The ending scene from "It's a Wonderful Life", as corny as it is, sticks with me now. It's the one when George can hardly contain himself as he sees his old world again and begins to appreciate every detail. I am George in "real" life.

So again, thanks to everyone for your part in my story, and now, as they say, on with the show...

Introduction

I started this daily journal entering into my second year of recovery from my "first" brain surgery on Dec 31, 2012. I am actually recovering from two brain operations but I will get into that at a later point. This is the first time that I have been able to get my thoughts into writing because of physical limitations of which I will discuss in this introduction. I record some of my recent life events that are the background to understanding these journal entries. The journal is word for word as I originally wrote it each day. I did not edit these entries except for minor grammar corrections or to explain something missing, as I want my original thoughts to be recorded as they were written. This journal introduction is an overall account of what happened from my viewpoint reflecting back on events that happened in 2010 and thereafter. This is the first time that I have been able to control my hands in order to type my account. I could not see clearly with both eyes until July of 2012, eleven month after my first surgery in Tennessee. I struggled to be able to communicate these stories to others or to document them for the record due to continuing speech and coordination problems. I still find it difficult to talk (I currently have speech therapy once a month as my words are still slurred and difficult for me to project outward as of this writing). For the first time I am able to slowly type what I wrote and recalled this year. In the summer of 2013 I was finally able to use speech-to-text software to help me transcribe this journal into a digital format. Before then the computer could not recognize my slurred speech. I apologize in advance if I miss anyone or mix up names and institutions. It was all such a blur that I am just glad that I can recall my name at all and I'm extremely happy that my brain is now allowing me to get this into writing and a digital format. I am still not fully back to "normal" but there are always small daily improvements.

As you read my journal, please realize that it was a spontaneous writing at the end of each day, a way to let off steam and for me to unwind and to freely write about what was on my mind. The primary reason that I wrote each day was for my own therapy, as that was about the only way that I could communicate "for the record". Many of the entries may be a bit personal, crude, or even illogical as read today but they were meant for personal use and growth. I certainly did not anticipate that they would be made public so soon, if at all. They may not necessarily reflect how I currently feel about a situation, event, or even the person or people involved. As I put these original writings into digital format and look at them now much later, I sometimes cringe and think "Did I really write that?". I have decided to let the original words stand, whether they embarrass me or not today, as a testimony to my mental development at the time. Anyway enough of the apologies and "legal" disclaimers. On with my introduction...

My full name is Charles Stephen Caylor. My friends in Tennessee and elsewhere know me as Charlie, whereas my family in Michigan always calls me Chuck. To tell you the truth I am more familiar with Charlie as I have lived away from family for most of my life, but now I answer to either name, as I am currently living and recovering in Michigan, where I was born and went to school. I write this from my mother Doris's living room on this warm May 2, 2013 afternoon. As mentioned earlier, this is the first time I have been able to control my left side shakes, particularly my left hand, enough to use the computer to communicate these stories. I relied heavily on the computer's spell checking ability for email or Facebook entries and could only write short, brief messages. I will cover more details of my recovery as we get into my story. I claim no great writing skill. I just want to get this story out as soon as I am able. I am very grateful to have survived intact enough to do so.

Beginning around Thanksgiving of 2010 I started having daily migraine headaches, mild at first but increasingly stronger and persistent. I noticed this during a visit of my mother and sister and her family and my niece Emily, by the way, who's birthday is today. Happy Birthday

Emily! I took some acetaminophen for the headaches and wrote it off to stress. After my visitors left, the headaches became stronger over the next few months and did not go away as normal headaches do. It was the fall before my 61st birthday (2011) when things really got "busy".

I lived in the small town of Benton, Tennessee where I ran a laundromat business (summer of 2003 until the fall of 2011) and lived above that laundry in my residential home. The home was on top of the one building while the laundromat was below the residence. I would go to my work by going down the hill from the residence to the laundry as there was no internal stairway between the two levels. The town of Benton is close to the Ocoee River which is a popular site for kayaking and river rafting. There is an annual summer influx of students and kayak folk ("river rats" as they are called) who come to challenge the river. There are several companies in the area that make their business offering tours and support to the rafters. They certainly helped my business in the summertime. I had accounts with several rafting companies where I would wash their sheets and towels for their guests. Many of these companies offered cabin rentals as well as rafting trips. I processed several hundred pounds of laundry during the summer for these companies.

In addition to the river traffic and my local customers, I had a commercial contract to do the residential laundry for the McMinn Memorial Nursing Home and Rehab Center about 15 miles north of me in Etowah, Tennessee. That was my biggest account and helped keep my business afloat. It was hard work and involved me doing the daily laundry for about 50 residents. I would pick up their dirty laundry every other day which would literally fill up my Jeep Cherokee Laredo. After washing and hanging up their laundry in my laundromat and office, I would drive back to the nursing home and distribute the clothing the following day, hanging up items in each resident's closet. I delivered on Tuesday, Thursday, and Saturday all year round, including most holidays. Though it was extremely hard work, (I did not get to take a vacation for over 7 years), it did help pay the bills as well as offered me a chance to meet and get to know the residents and those that worked at the nursing home. It was such a large amount of clothing to wash, dry, and hang up that I had to get up at 2 or 3 am in the morning, every other day, to process the load before my normal laundromat customers arrived. I had to use nearly every machine in the small laundromat so I would often lock the doors of the laundry very early in the morning and go to work. I would then hang up the clothing in my office while my customers came in to do their own laundry later in the day. The whole process at the laundromat took about 6 hours and then on alternate afternoons I would drive to the nursing home to distribute the clothing and pick up the next dirty load, always hoping that a customer did not jam up a machine or cause a flood while I was away (I kept the laundry open 24 hours). It took an additional 6 hours to deliver and hangup the clean clothing and return with my Jeep filled completely with soiled clothing. I had to use rubber gloves, as you can imagine, while handling the dirty nursing home clothing to prevent any infection. The smell was tough to get used to at first, but I adjusted to it in time.

One of the strangest things to me now is that I had to quit this way of life earlier than I had planned. Though it was a difficult life, it was my life and I was my own boss, and that had certain advantages. I was forced literally to retire (I had always planned to work till I "dropped" in my 70s or 80s)...but my story continues and I don't want to get too far ahead of myself. Back to the headaches... As I was dependent on the nursing home contract, the river companies, and my loyal laundry customers to survive, I kept doing my job, despite the headaches and the symptoms. And then things took a serious turn for the worse. I use the term "worse" as that is what it seemed like at the time and still does to this day in many ways, but things have a way of working out for the best, but I digress again.

The first event in Tennessee that I recall showed me that this was not just a series of normal headaches. One thing to be said upfront, and I now admit it in hindsight, is that I was stubborn and tried to overlook these occurrences. I knew I was so dependent on things to go just right, that when they began to "go south", I refused to believe or accept it. That first event was a morning in 2011 when I stubbed my small right toe on the corner of my bathroom shower stall in my residence. I stubbed it while quickly walking by, something I had never done before. I had a large bathroom, but after my divorce (2009) I had gotten used to using this smaller bathroom down the hall. I did not pay much attention to this event, even though my toe became black and blue for a few days, but I just wrote it off to clumsiness or "old age". Well little did I know it foreshadowed something much more serious.

A second incident occurred one afternoon in my residence while I was taking a break from my work. I usually got Sunday afternoons off to catch my breath after processing that day's nursing home load early in the morning. I would play my EA Sport's Tiger Woods 2010 Wii golf game up above the laundromat where I lived. I would monitor the Sunday customers on my security camera that played through my television as I played golf on the screen. My two little cockatiels would watch me as I played the golf game. One of my two cockatiels, Smokey Joe, squeaks each time I make a "golf" swing with the remote control. Christy, my other bird, and Smokey Joe had no idea what was happening to their "Dad" (and of course neither did I). I should note that I have always been a golf hacker, sometimes getting away to play some par-3 golf at a local range on Sunday afternoon. I hope to be able to do that again soon. Anyway I swung away with the remote control and lost my balance, spun around, and fell into a nearby recliner chair. At the time I laughed it off and did not think much of it. I did not know it was another early sign of a coming loss of balance.

Another foretelling event occurred at the local BP gas station in downtown Benton. While doing my nursing home laundry early in the mornings, I would occasionally walk over to this corner gas station/convenience store. They were one of the few places open that early. I would get a coffee and maybe a doughnut to start my day. One morning after I poured my coffee and got my doughnut I went to pay for them and spilled the entire cup of coffee all over their floor. The coffee was carried in my left hand. Again, this had never happened to me before and I was very embarrassed. I shrugged it off as just an accident. I now know that this was another early sign of my upcoming loss of left side control.

I noticed also about this time that I could not bend over to pick up dropped clothing or to load the laundry machines or to get any other items below my waist without my head seeming to split. There was intense pressure within my skull that only got worse when bending over. I ended up getting some "grabbers" or those devices that allow you to grip and pick up items without bending over for them. These helped me in my work and around the house but they were not that rugged and made me feel "over the hill". I wore out several and I could not find any "grabbers" tough enough for my laundry work.

I continued to do my job despite constant headaches. I had no one to delegate the work to or to fill in for me. It was a one-man shop and I was that one man and certainly not able to be sick and still keep things going. It was a matter of financial survival but I see now that physical survival was really at stake. The summer of 2011 was now in earnest with temperatures in the upper 90s during the day. I worked on my river loads and still managed to keep up with the nursing home laundry despite my physical problems. Looking back now I don't know how I managed to hold it all together. Truly I was slipping and did not realize it at the time or as I said earlier, I chose to ignore the signs.

I traveled to the nursing home in the heat of the afternoon in my Jeep without air conditioning. My job required that I go in and out of the buildings and into my vehicle frequently so I just decided to work in the heat for convenience and to limit the temperature changes to my body. After awhile this became routine but it really took a toll on me when I developed all of these physical symptoms.

I did not let anyone in on how serious my physical situation was becoming except my close friend Cathy, who works at the nursing home. A friend of hers introduced us because of our similar ideas and interests and we were both divorced. We immediately hit it off in our on-line conversations and during my visits to the nursing home. She ended up playing a huge role in the events that followed and in my personal life.

Now I knew things were getting serious as I was starting to hear noises inside my head. When I went to the Walmart in Cleveland, Tennessee (about 15 miles from Benton), the noises grew louder. It was a strange humming or buzzing sound. I thought they had left a large fan on or some machinery running. I realized then that it was inside of me and not in the store. As mentioned, it was at this time that my balance was weakening. I needed to rely on a shopping cart just to maintain my balance and make it through the store without falling. I was slightly dizzy and had difficulty walking across the store without a cart. I still hung in there and did the best that I could (out of stupidity and stubbornness I see now in hindsight). The symptoms were getting stronger and the headaches were continuous. I felt miserable all of the time.

I was trying then just to do my daily work and to keep things going. I was probably the only one who knew how poor my financial situation was and that to "literally" survive I had to go for as long as I could. I know now, as I write this and look back in time, that my decision nearly cost me my life. I want to mention that at this point I was taking what I thought was the maximum daily amount of acetaminophen, every four hours around the clock. I would take about 6000 mg (one 1000 mg pill every 4 hours) in a 24 hour period and that would allow me to continue with my work and try to get some sleep. I always thought I was under the maximum daily amount, but now I realize that I "pushed" that limit, but I was in such constant pain. The headaches were still there every day and night but they were not as bad after I took the medication. This was the only thing at the time that helped me endure but I now know how dangerous it was to absorb that many pain pills over that long of a time period. I did this for many months, always hoping that the headaches and other symptoms would die down on their own.

I was finally becoming convinced that I had to do something about the headaches and symptoms (I told you I was stubborn!). After years of running my business and doing everything by myself, I was used to doing things alone and not relying on others for help. That trait had me ready to go to the VA clinic in Chattanooga (some 40 miles away from me) on my own to find out what was happening. Fortunately, Cathy, my friend at the nursing home, has an independent and forceful personality and insisted that she take me there. I now know that she showed up in my life for several reasons and that this was one of them. We made a day of it and visited our favorite used bookstore in Chattanooga (we both love to read). We grew close over the years. She taught me to use a crock pot and to decorate my residence and many other things. We became very good friends. She was always checking out for my welfare.

The VA doctor in Chattanooga took my information and he thought that I had a sinus condition, maybe some sort of blockage. I thought about living above all of those laundry dryers over the years, so it seemed reasonable. I have always had the "white coat" syndrome at doctor's offices. The tension from having constant headaches and not knowing the reason, of course, added to this. My blood pressure readings were very high at the clinic and the doctor recommended a baby aspirin therapy and also prescribed some hypertension medication. Both drugs would play a major role in events to come.

When I was back in Benton I tried many sinus treatments. I bought a sinus treatment pot (a Neti pot). I flushed my sinus area out with tap water using this pot. It looked like a small tea pot with a long spout. You filled it with water, tipped your head to the side, and poured water into one nostril and out the other. It took some getting used to but it flushed things out. When using it I guess I forgot about my headaches for the moment but naturally they returned later. While shopping at Walmart I found a product that was called "Sinus Buster" and I had seen it advertised on television before. It was made of hot cayenne pepper, of all things, and you squeezed it up your nose. It sounded rather drastic at the time so I passed on getting it. I will admit that after a time I purchased the product and in desperation, as I was in such pain at the time, I sat down one night, braced myself, and took my shot. Of course it did nothing for the headaches long term but it certainly got my attention at the time.

The headaches continued and no sinus treatment was of any use. My kitchen was starting to look like a chemistry laboratory, as I would try vitamins, supplements, and what have you just to see if anything would help. As mentioned, only massive doses of acetaminophen seemed to have any effect. I ended up buying lots of Dolly Madison cakes and milk, as these helped calm my stomach and helped prevent any vomiting. That was the last thing I wanted to experience again. I had to avoid that at all costs.

Some of the details of my vomiting and violent head pain episodes are as follows: On the way back from my VA appointment in Chattanooga, my friend Cathy and I stopped for a Chinese buffet dinner, which we often did when out in that area of Cleveland, Tennessee. As the VA doctor had given me some new blood pressure and hypertension medication, I was anxious to try it out. During the meal I popped one of the pills.

All was fine until that evening back in Benton. I became very sick to my stomach and started to vomit early in the morning. When I did, it caused severe head pain as it forced me to rapidly bend down over the toilet. I would vomit, and I do apologize for the graphic details, and this would immediately cause me severe head pain as I rapidly bent down to the toilet and experienced the intense head pressure that came with bending down, which would lead to more vomiting, and then more severe head pain, and the vicious cycle would go on and on. It was probably the most intense pain and suffering I had ever experienced. I remember making it to the kitchen to try to drink some milk to stop the cycle. That helped some. By then I had the dry heaves and violent headaches going on continually. It was so severe that I remember dropping to my knees in the kitchen and literally screaming in pain. Looking back now, that moment could very well have been my last one, it was that bad. I managed to make it through that early morning. I remember at one point resting my face on a bath towel after the vomiting subsided. I was sitting in my favorite recliner, dripping with sweat, with my head buried in the towel, trying not to make a move to trigger another terrible cycle. I remember looking up at my two birds and both their heads were tipped toward me out of curiosity, looking down at me from their cage. They must have been thinking, "what's wrong with Daddy?" They had heard me vomiting, screaming out loud in pain, making quite a commotion and they had no idea what was wrong, and of course neither did I. After this incident I got extra milk and cakes so that my stomach would be filled with "bland" food, and that this type of episode would never happen again.

Soon after this incident, I had another "wake up call", though not as painful, but still very serious. It was a very hot Tennessee summer day and I was at the nursing home delivering my new load of clothes. I had my "grabber" to pick up laundry from the residence's laundry buckets and for any dropped items. The headaches were not as violent and went back to their consistent, dull quality. I thought things were fine or at least tolerable. I did have some loss of balance but as I held on to the laundry cart I used to deliver and pick up clothing, I could disguise my reliance on the cart from others. Cathy, however, was too smart and knew things were not normal. As I mentioned, she always kept an eye on me. She noticed that I did not return right away after I had delivered the fresh clothes and was ready to collect the new soiled ones. In several years of doing that job, I had never needed to rest or take a break between loads. This day I just had to take one. The combination of the heat and my physical symptoms were just too much for me. Between loads, I went over to the attached Woods Memorial Hospital lobby and sat down with a Pepsi. I should have let Cathy and the nurses at the nursing home know where I was but I was not thinking clearly then. I was close to passing out (and really, reflecting back on it now, I may have been close to a stroke or death, but maybe I'm being too melodramatic).

So my Pepsi break helped me but alarmed the staff at the nursing home. When I came back later they grilled me on where I was and what had happened to me. I really did not know they paid that much attention. I also alarmed them because my face was flushed and I was very sweaty. They told me they thought I was about to have a stroke. Being nurses and CNAs (Certified Nursing Assistants, which Cathy is), they checked my temperature, blood pressure, and other vitals with their equipment. They were all way high! I insisted that I was OK and I finished the job and drove back to Benton. This whole incident helped to finally wake me up that something was very seriously wrong with my health (well, duh!).

After the pains I experienced at my home and with the reduced abilities to do my job, I was able to set up a cat scan and to have the VA check further into my case. This was no sinus condition. The Chattanooga Clinic set me up for a scan there but at the last minute, I believe a day before the scheduled scan, they called and said I would have to wait. I practically pleaded with the lady on the phone that I really needed one fast. She said there was one opening the following Tuesday (I think it was a Thursday or Friday when I spoke with her on the phone) at the VA Hospital in Murfreesboro, Tennessee some 150 miles away. I said sign me up! (I knew I would find a way to get there). Now again, living alone, being divorced, and being very independent (or stubborn) I planned on driving myself up there. I would have to rearrange my schedule somewhat but I was prepared to have things looked at further and as soon as possible. Again my good friend Cathy intervened and insisted that she drive me to the cat scan. Again, we made a day of it. This was August 2, 2011 and I remember it was a nice warm and sunny day, however it was also a day in which my life would change very dramatically.

Now, as mentioned before, the events from here on out seemed to occur very rapidly and yet very slowly. I am looking back at them now from a period of nearly two years later (it is late summer of 2013 as I write this), so they may not be precisely in order, as to where I was delivered to, whom I saw, and so on. I am very lucky to have as good a memory as I do have of these events. My recollections from this point on in the story will be more in how these events appeared internally to me and what was going on in my mind. Readers that know my story may laugh at my use of the term "mind".

At the VA clinic in Murfreesboro, Tennessee I recall that Cathy and I were waiting in the reception room for the cat scan. When I was called, she had to stay in the waiting room while I went down the hall to the scan room. I recall taking the scan and then there appeared to be a lot of activity among the technicians there. They asked me to wait at a bench outside in the hallway. It seemed to take forever, a period of time with my life in suspension, so to speak, and then they called me back in and had me sit down for the results. One of the technicians said, and this was the very first time I had heard this, that the scan showed a "large mass" of "unknown tissue" inside my brain. I was then told, when I asked how serious it was, that they would have to call the neurologists on duty first for their opinions. The technicians were limited in what they could say to me. I was told to go back to the waiting room to see Cathy and that they would get back to me soon.

As the old saying goes, my life became as a movie or play at that moment, that is, I sort of withdrew to the theater seats and seemed to just be observing what was happening to me (or the play). When I went back to the waiting room to see Cathy, she probably sensed that something was wrong. I did not say much, as at that time I really didn't know what was happening myself.

At this point in my story, as I have mentioned, events became a series of memories and visions to me and now that a period of almost two years has passed as I write this, the events are even more a series of small plays and memories. As I often mention, or think of today, I am very lucky to have survived the ordeal with my mind "relatively intact". Again, it amazes me that I still have most of these memories and that I can now share them with others. On that note, let me explain how I will proceed with the rest of this introduction.

Because at this time I cannot be absolutely sure of the flow of events from this point on in the story and I could easily miss any important ones or important people (and there were so many) I stopped for awhile in the writing of this introduction and thought about all of the things that had happened to me and to others over those months. The idea came to me in contemplation of these memories, that I just sit down and create, what I call here and in my journal, "memory" pages. These are separate pages where I would just think of a memory and write down all that I could recall. I would then assemble them in a general order of occurrence and use them to help me finish this introduction. I was not concerned with exactly when in the flow that they actually occurred, but just in getting down in writing as much of the events that I could recall before (or if) they vanished from my mind.

In a way, these "memory" pages sort of simulate how my brain was processing things back then. They let the reader experience part of what I experienced, seeing events in a "piece meal" fashion. This technique allowed me to get the most memories down on paper that I can still recall at this late date. If they appear a little disjointed, I apologize. As I have said, I want to get them down in print before or if lose them, but somehow I think they will always be with me. So without further ado, as they say "in showbiz", I continue with the story using my "memory" pages.

I will add one more comment before we continue: In each "memory" page I have included all comments and recollections without any paragraphs. I took out the original paragraphs in order to compress the introduction somewhat. I noticed that there were so many memories flooding back to me that I just did not want this introduction to get too long. It's probably too late for that. Oh well, read a bit here and there and eventually you will get through it all. Or perhaps you will just want to select certain stories and just read those for now. Either way please enjoy my recollections.

To Vanderbilt...

The following "memory" pages cover my trip by ambulance after the brain tumor was discovered (in Murfreesboro) to the Nashville VA and then on to the Vanderbilt University Medical Center in Nashville where I was admitted to the ICU (Intensive Care Unit). I remained there until baby aspirin was out of my system and then they could go further with my case. The memories and worries occurred when I was taken away from my usual world: my life, my friends, my business, my home, my pets, and so naturally I laid in bed and worried about that world. I really could do nothing about my situation and I eventually came to realize that.

Cathy Tries To Keep Up

This is one of my first memories after being diagnosed with a brain tumor at the VA cat scan center. I was rushed by ambulance to

Nashville and was somehow able to see out the back window. I watched Cathy follow the ambulance. I wondered at the time why she had such a stern, concentrated look on her face. Later I found that the ambulance was racing down the expressway at nearly 80 mph, if I recall correctly. To me it all seemed like slow motion and I wondered why we were going so slow. Still I don't know how I was able to look out the window. Cathy later told me that she had all she could do to keep up.

I Worry About My Birds

I have two cockatiels and they have been with me for a long time. "Christy", my female yellow bird, I got in Sarasota, Florida in the 90s. Her original name was "Squeaky", due to the sounds she makes. I bought her in a pet store. I was married at that time. She was renamed in Tennessee after Christine from the "Phantom of the Opera". My other bird is a male gray cockatiel named "Smokey Joe". I got him from a pet store in Tennessee. He was very shy at first (I know that's hard to believe). Both birds have unique personalities. Smokey is very outgoing now, talkative, whistles and pounds on the side of his cage. He is always moving back and forth as he is a restless bird. He rarely sits still. Christy is very cautious, moody, and has "an attitude" but loves her "Daddy". She has a high shrieking voice and, being a female bird and unable to whistle much, she screams instead. She has a fit when I use the restroom, especially when she doesn't see me. Smokey is not cautious when anything new is around. He will go right up to fingers, people, dogs, anything, and he will whistle and carry on. Perhaps he is just friendly but I think he may not see that well. I used to let them out all of the time in Tennessee as they were my children and especially after my divorce in 2009 when I was mostly alone. When I divorced, my ex-spouse kept two other birds, also cockatiels, that seemed to like her the best. I kept these two that "liked" me the best. They have a huge cage now as I kept the original cage that once had four birds in it. When in the hospital I naturally was worried about them. My ex-sister-in-law, Barbara, who also lives in Benton, was kind enough to stop by my house and take care of them while I was gone. I told her where my key was hidden. After my family arrived, they took over the care of the birds.

Smokey Joe and Christy

Here are some more interesting things about my two birds. Christy is the older bird, moody, loves cookies, biscuits, pizza, cheese, and chocolate. She just loves to eat. I don't let her have too much chocolate. I still find it hard to believe that a bird could have a "sweet tooth". As mentioned, she is very attached to me, screaming (she can't sing, as I mentioned) if I leave the room. I always talk and whistle to her and Smokey when I am around. That is mostly habit from the past. She and Smokey are my kids and I admit that they are spoiled. My bird's ears are so powerful that they always hear things that I usually don't hear, especially lately due to my tinnitus. They will hear my Mom get up in the morning or the middle of the night to use the bathroom. Sometimes that or any other sound or sudden movement will startle them and one or both will react (even to each others actions) and fly off in a panic even if they are inside the cage. They usually have a "flight before fight" approach, as do most birds. If they are in their cages when this happens they can cut themselves, and cockatiels are notorious for having bleeding issues. As mentioned, Smokey is younger than Christy, full of energy and himself. He loves to sing and listen to noises and whistles. He can memorize tunes and was good at singing the theme song from the Andy Griffith TV show. Smokey thinks he is king of the castle and Christy will let him run the place to a point, typical male and female behavior you could say. If they are close to each other and their tail feathers touch then they both peck at each other or whoever is nearby. I think Christy thinks I am her "bird" Dad, as she waits for me to return from my morning walk or whenever I leave the house and will scream when the car turns back into the drive. I think she waits to see and hear me come back. She used to do that when my Jeep would return or she would see me walking up the hill from my laundry. I usually let both of them out in the morning, their "birdie break", while I have my coffee and watch TV. If Christy is calm enough, I will pet her head and sometimes she will relax and stretch out her legs underneath her and I will rub her head and cheeks while she lays on my chest. I think she hears my heartbeat. After Smokey sings to my toes and dances, he usually flies to the top of the entertainment center, his favorite spot because it is high and those type of birds go to the highest spot because they feel safe there. They both have their own habits. Both birds love to get their heads rubbed, especially under their chins. They will fly around or snack, generally get their "out of the cage" break early in the morning, usually around 6 am. Smokey also keeps an eye on me when I am nearby. He knows I occasionally work on puzzles for therapy in the living room. Mom sometimes helps. One day she was working on a puzzle and I let him out of his cage. He flew to the puzzle that was on a card table in the living room, as he often does, and he walked right up to Mom sitting there working on the puzzle and started sputtering at her, like he was cussing her out for helping. He knew I usually sat there and was trying to be "King Kong" as usual. Mom told him she was not scared of him but he got right up "in her face". It was cute and we took his picture as he was "lecturing" Mom. Smokey would often jump over to a half completed puzzle that I had left on a card table in the morning and turn over only some of the completed pieces. It's hard for those not around birds to understand, but he knows the difference in the pieces. He would always turn around and look at me after he did it and do his famous "laugh", or "ha, ha, ha" and I would tell him to stop it. I think it got to be one of his favorite routines. He would do this often in the morning when I let them both out for a break, the little "squirt". They both kept me company in Tennessee and are my "kids", as I have mentioned. We have a strong bond and we have shared many experiences together like any family. It's good that they are healthy and with me again. Smokey acts up at supper often as he did in Tennessee. He has restless energy, almost like he has "ADD" (Attention

Deficit Disorder) for birds. He runs back and forth on his soft perch, puts his nose inside a toy because it feels good, anything to burn up some energy. He now plucks at the side of the cage and makes a banging sound, mostly at night when we are playing games or we are at the table and naturally ignoring him. He will then stop and see if anyone is paying attention after he makes his noise. Long ago I taught them both to ring a bell if they wanted out of their cage. That was a big mistake! Living alone, I would let them have the run of the house so it did not bother me that much. Since I am a "visitor" here, I have not let them out that much, especially at night. That does not stop them from trying and ringing the bell. I can see the frustration in Smokey as I don't let him out when we eat. They just don't know what has happened to me of late. Christy, being older, is ready for rest at night early and goes to her corner and tries to ignore him. They are more mother/son or brother/sister than mates. Even after months without a dog in the house, Christy will still often bend her head down over the edge of the stand near my recliner in the living room in the morning, looking to be sure no animal will surprise her. It's funny how she always kept an eye on Mom's dog when she was around and would never go near her. Smokey, on the other hand, walked right up to the dog on the floor, got real close to her nose, as Mom and I watched them both very closely, and started doing his songs and whistling about an inch from the dog's nose. Either he has no fear or he can't see that well up close. He always does that to anything close, he sings, whistles and carries on. The dog probably thought that's the smallest dog I have ever seen and it has wings too! I should mention also that both birds hate it when people talk with other people in the room or on the phone. They just have to be the center of attention, as do most pets, and they will carry on until we acknowledge them. They are spoiled little creatures!

Business Dreams

I had dreams that my ex-sister-in-law Barbara had left my laundry doors open and that someone had stolen my newly purchased video arcade games. To me this was all very real. I knew it was only a dream later on but I believed it may have happened earlier while I was hospitalized and I worried about my business and if everything was still intact. I eventually came to the conclusion that I could do nothing about the situation, and like my cell phone, I just surrendered to fate, so to speak. I am grateful to Barbara for looking after my two birds at first until my family arrived. I worried very much about those birds while I was in the hospital. She would stop by and feed them and make sure they had fresh water. That was very important to me. Later on my family began to distrust Barbara and even Cathy, my close friend, and her family. It's a long story and I won't go into much detail here, but my family thought that they were spying on us (especially when I visited), most likely out of fear that my family would "kidnap" me away. They were naturally worried about me and did not realize all of the details that were involved. I decided to return to Michigan, as I was losing my business, my home, my physical abilities, my mental abilities, basically everything "me". I did have the sense to know what I had to do, but I think some of my friends were not so sure of that. Now in Michigan I deeply miss Cathy and my Tennessee friends but I had to recover and get better before anything else. Someday they may understand that. They never knew how much debt I had acquired and how precarious my financial situation was in Benton. I could not afford to stay in a private nursing home, as the one I did laundry for in Etowah. I only had the VA health plan at the time, of which I am most grateful, and had not yet received any Social Security Disability. In the end, I believe all things work out for the best. Someday I may visit with my friends back in Tennessee, who knows? Anyone who reads this, let it be known that in the end, I made the call to do what I believe was the only thing for me to do back then. I talk more about my decision later in this book.

Vanderbilt Students

As it is a university and teaching center, student shifts started at all hours at Vanderbilt. Unfortunately, many students had little consideration, ICU or not, for the patients there. Lights were left on all of the time. People were always talking loudly, especially at shift changes. My door was usually open with the shades up at night. Several times I had to ask the people there to close the door, lower the shades, hold it down and let me try to sleep. You wouldn't think I would have to do this, but it was a regular request. I had trouble giving blood while there. The students went by the book and always tried to do what they had been taught, but would usually give up several pokes later and let more senior staff try. I had little choice but to take the stabs and became a human pin cushion. Finally they found out I had better success giving blood on my hand area instead of my arms and they started doing that. This applied to IVs as well. I was always plugged into machines while I was there. They continually measured my blood pressure by machine and I remember learning to quiet my mind and meditate some to keep the readings in line. The blood pressure readings would always go up if family or friends visited. I always wanted to talk and my blood pressure would rise when I did and it would set off the alarms. I had a potassium IV once that really started to burn me. All other IVs were fine and I got used to them but this one literally hurt and was burning my skin. It was set up by a student and then she left for lunch. I had to yell for help and someone finally came by and lowered the fill level or something and then it was more comfortable. It sure did burn before it got better. Naturally, at that time, most people were at lunch and I had to flag someone on duty for help.

Benign Blob

My neurologist and chief surgeon, Dr. Sills (Allen K.) , gave me a piece of great news while I was waiting for baby aspirin to clear out of my system in the Vanderbilt ICU. He and his staff did a biopsy and other tests and found that nothing like the brain tumor had spread inside my body. They said the tumor was not malignant and was just a benign "blob" and only in my head. That, as you may imagine, was fantastic news to hear. What a relief! I did not have a spreading cancer.

Vanderbilt Meals

While waiting for surgery, scheduling was a bit mixed up. I think because it is such a large facility and that they have so many patients to schedule for surgery that there were several delays. The trouble is that you cannot eat prior to surgery so I was basically confined to my bed and not given any food to eat because they did not know exactly when my surgery would take place. This happened several times while I was there. One supper I had to ask for food. I got caught in a period of "limbo" with the surgery and food and they had not prepared me a normal supper. Luckily, I never had much of an appetite and I would rarely complain, but this one afternoon I just had to or I would have gone completely without food that night. When the staff noticed this they delivered food to my room on a tray and at that time it tasted great. Finally, I was scheduled for my brain surgery (craniotomy) the early morning of the 12th of August, 2011. I was admitted to the ICU on Aug 2nd so I was waiting there for ten days. Ironically my surgery was on my ex-wife's birthday. Awkward huh?

Brunettes

Vanderbilt had many student interns, especially in the neurology department. They had regular morning rounds with the neurosurgeons there. I could tell that student neurologists were assigned to me and had to check me out. They all asked me the same questions and shined their little pen lights looking into my eyes and had me follow and touch their fingers with my own. This was no big deal, in fact it got to be funny, as I knew the drill pretty well after awhile. I certainly remember Dr. Chambless (Lola B.), who ended up assisting Dr. Sills in my operation (and probably did most of the work).

She was always nice to me, checking on how I was, and I must say that she was very easy on the eyes too. She is a beautiful brunette neurosurgeon and always has a pleasant smile and personality. As I say, it's my guess that it was Dr. Chambless who actually removed the large tumor, using the microscope, piece by piece, but of course I don't know for sure. It could have been Dr. Sills but he probably directed her in the operation. My good friend Cathy Lewis, speaking of good looking brunette women (she will get a copy of this book), was there with her two sons, Jessie and Josh. Cathy may also have stayed on the first night I got there as they had a couch in my room and allowed one good friend or family member to stay there. Again, if I am wrong I apologize for not remembering the details at this late date. I am very fortunate to be able to remember anything at all now. You could say that I might have been a bit "preoccupied" back then.

Jamaican Surprise

Throughout this book and journal, I do get into bodily functions a bit, as they played a big role in my life then and I suppose that they still do, and I do apologize for the details and for bringing up some things that perhaps I shouldn't, but as I mention, I lay it out in the journal and in these notes mostly as they were written originally, "warts and all". So on that note, on with the details of this fun little episode...

At Vanderbilt while waiting for surgery I had trouble emptying my bladder or urinating. I knew that they would force it out of me with the "tube" (male catheter) in a most inconvenient spot for us guys, as they say, if I couldn't do it myself. They said there was a risk of poisoning my system if I could not go soon. It's funny now, but I remember pleading with the doctors on duty to just give me a little more time and I was sure I could go. I'm sure they heard that one before. They gave me some more time but not enough (in my opinion). Very early one morning it had to be done. I remember a male Jamaican accented nurse had the duty. "Hey, how's it goin, mon?". He was a big and strong young guy. I'm sure he'd done it before. He used the early hour and the element of surprise. I remember he had his tube and stuff and suddenly climbed up on my bed with his back towards me. He took charge, held me down, and did not waste time. I did not know at first what he was doing but then I figured it out, half asleep and all. He said I might feel some pressure. I felt more than pressure, mon! It hurt like hell, but then the relief was wonderful when my bladder was finally being emptied. Funny scene no doubt but it was quite serious to me at the time and it compared to the pain of my terrible headaches. Fortunately it was only a brief, terrible pain, followed by a great relief. I could say it was "tubular, mon" but that's a terrible pun and I won't go there.

Brain Surgery Preps

I have clear memories of being in anesthesiology (also it was the emergency room at Vanderbilt) and talking with the doctor in charge and the nurse there who was busy "prepping" me. She was setting me up with one final IV. I remember there was someone in emergency and I think she was a young girl in her 20s and something was wrong with her leg. Many family and friends were with her, all comforting her. I was thinking it's all perspective...wanna trade places? There was a lot of blue color in there, from gowns to machines. I remember all sorts of medical devices everywhere. It was early in the morning (Aug 12th) when they started my final preparations. That is my last memory before the lights went out, so to speak, and my whole world was changed. I was talking or trying to talk with the doctor and next thing I know I am back in my room at the ICU, looking pretty messed up (I'm told). But I was still on the planet! Everything was so bright but my eyes had double vision, oh no! It was an intense light everywhere but at least I could see the lights. My eyes still to this day, nearly two years later, squint to certain lighting conditions. I seem to have little voluntary control over this. They seem to squint on their own, most likely some sort of built-in body protection. At the dining table and near certain windows I still get this. It is also bright outside in the sun but I use sunglasses there, as I always have, and that helps protects my eyes from the bright light. At Vanderbilt, everyone told me how I squinted even more than now to any light source. The good news is that, like most of my symptoms, even this light sensitivity is getting better over time. I talk further about my double vision and how I fought it later on in this book.

Bazaar Thoughts

As mentioned, I waited ten days in ICU until the baby aspirin that the VA in Chattanooga had me on was out of my system. They can't operate as it could cause too much bleeding. They gave me steroids immediately when I got there to shrink the tumor and that got rid of my headaches almost immediately. Oh what a relief that was! After nearly two years of constant headaches, they were suddenly gone! My family and friends said I had a big smile on my face. I have had hardly any headaches since that time and that has been almost two years of being headache free. So I undergo the crainiotomy that early morning in August and I live through it, obviously, but one never knows what will happen. I understand later that my family was in the reception area awaiting word of my surgery results and no one called them when I was out of surgery. For all they know, I might not have made it. I guess I was back in recovery, resting, and naturally totally out of it. I found out later from my family that I looked pretty bad right after surgery. My head was swollen (my sister said it looked like a flat basketball), my Mom said I had a tube out of the top of my head to relieve pressure. You can see by reading the operation details that I have included in this introduction that it resembled a "Home Depot" project, as I like to call it. Later I found that this tube was still in my head to drain the fluid pressure when I was back in recovery and that it was monitored around the clock. Fortunately there were no complications. One day in Midland, while at my Mom's, I was reading some of the paperwork on the operation and I rubbed my head on top and felt the small indent where the tube had been. My Mom told me that the drain tube was there. I had no clue in the world that this had happened until that moment and in reading the operation details. I feel sorry that she had to see me that way but she is tough. She was also in the hospital years ago for major heart surgery and had a very close call. My brother Dave also has his own hospital history as I allude to in the acknowledgments to this book. If I ever feel that my surgery was all a dream, I can rub my finger on my neck just under the hairline and feel a rather deep indentation that is there at the base of my skull. There is some skull bone missing there. That is where the bone flap was made and the surgeon with the microscope did his or her thing. I have a running joke with my sister and mother. They have sales (called bazaars up here in Michigan, yard sales down south). They are always looking for ideas to make money at these sales. I had the idea of going with them someday (I have been to a few already), wearing a "brain" shirt (shirts I have received with the words "brain surgery" on them), and bringing a fruit jar. I would charge the people 25 cents to feel my brain indentation, or scar at the base of my skull. Tacky yes, but then again my weird sense of humor always cracks me up and I am sure I could get some money before the people that run the sales found out. I'm sure I could easily get us all kicked out of these events. Back to my story... As you have read, I wrote down some of my last memories of being in the Vanderbilt emergency room and operation "prep" room just waiting for that "first" surgery. The surgery did occur in Vanderbilt on the morning of August 12, 2011 and I include here the record of that surgery. This is directly from my medical records. Here are the details and I caution you that some of it is indeed graphic:

Gruesome Details

Vanderbilt University Medical Center
033230194 CAYLOR, CHARLES (12/16/1950 – then 60YO M)

Surgeon: Allen K. Sills, M.D.
1st Assistant: Lola B. Chambless, M.D.
2nd Assistant:

Anesthesia: General endotracheal tube.
Estimated Blood Loss: 800 mL.
Replaced Fluid: 2500 mL of crystalloid, 500 mL of colloid, and 2 units of packed red blood cells.

INDICATION FOR PROCEDURE:

The patient is a 60-year-old male who presented with dysmetria and headache and was found to have an extremely large posterior fossa tumor with compression of the cerebral aqueduct with some early hydrocephalus. He had the tumor embolized to reduce blood supply. After a discussion of indications, risks, and benefits, he elected to proceed with craniotomy for removal as detailed below.

DESCRIPTION OF PROCEDURE:

Patient was brought to the operating room and general anesthesia induced. He was initially placed supine, and a right frontal standard sterile prep and drape was carried out.

An incision was made at Kocher's point. A twist-drill hole was made. Dura was incised, and a ventriculostomy catheter was advanced down to cannulate the frontal horn of the right lateral ventricle. There was good return of clear CSF under significant pressure. The ventriculostomy was tunneled out through a separate incision and then connected to an external collection system. The initial incision was closed with nylon, and the catheter was secured.

The patient was then placed in the Mayfield head fixation device and turned prone into the Concorde position. The midline posterior fossa was again marked, and a shave and standard prep and drape were then carried out. An incision was made extending above the inion down to the superior aspect of the cervical spine. This incision was deepened down to the bone through the various muscular layers. Multiple burr holes were placed above and below the transverse sinus, and a craniotomy flap was developed, extending above the transverse sinus and down toward the foramen magnum. The dura was opened in a Y-shaped fashion based on the sinuses. At this point, the microscope was draped and introduced on the field and used throughout the reminder of the removal of the lesion.

Under microscopic visualization, CSF was again released from the ventriculostomy as well as from the cisterna magna. Using microscopic visualization with microdissection technique, the superior aspect of the cerebellum was gently retracted down, and the lesion was identified. Samples were cut and sent for frozen section analysis. This came back as consistent with a spindle-type neoplasm with no obvious malignant features but with obvious effects of embolization and disorganized-appearing tissue.

At this point, an extended microdissection was carried out to identify borders of the lesion where possible. The lesion was encapsulated and appeared to be separate from the investing cerebellum. The pieces were taken out, and the lesion was isolated away from the tentorium and completely encircled eventually. The tissues of the tectal plate were identified and preserved and protected. The lesion was completely removed from the deeper areas superficially with the areas along the tentorium being reserved for last. These were trimmed down to as thin as felt safe, and then the remaining tissue was coagulated extensively with the bipolar cautery.

An extended period of hemostasis was carried out. Once absolute hemostasis was guaranteed, the dura was closed with interrupted 4-0 Nurolon sutures. A piece of dura repair was used for additional dural supplementation and closure. The closure was augmented with the placement of DuraSeal polymer sealant material. A piece of dry Gelfoam was placed in the epidural space.

The bone flap was reapproximated with the micro-plating system. The wound was then closed in layers of 0, 2-0, and 3-0 Vicryl and the skin closed with staples. Needle and sponge counts were correct at the end of the procedure. The ventriculostomy was left in place, and the patient was transferred to the recovery room in stable condition.

Vanderbilt Mind Trip...

After and during the first brain surgery at Vanderbilt I experienced bizarre dreams, naturally, and was not my usual self, to use an understatement. I was still at Vanderbilt briefly after the operation, trying to recover and eventually I was sent to Murfreesboro, Tennessee, a few miles south of Vanderbilt, to the VA rehab facility and hospital (Alvin C. York) where I would spend a few months trying to find my way back to the world. On that trip from Vanderbilt to the VA rehab center, I write about having a seizure, and the beginning of my memories of the Tennessee VA rehab facility in Murfreesboro...

Triangle Briefcases

Probably the first dream I recall at Vanderbilt is the one where during surgery I seemed to be watching or "hovering" (as in the movies) above my operation and suddenly a neurosurgeon said "gather him up fast, put him in these briefcases and let's go" or something along those lines. I was being moved rapidly from one room to another or from one table to another but my body was cut up into triangle shapes. There was a panic of sorts or a hurry to move me. My mind obviously was all scrambled at that time but this was a strong dream or vision that I recall to this day.

Bowel Fun

In Vanderbilt I had a problem right after surgery and had a bowel movement all over the hospital floor (eewwh!). Panicked, as this had never happened to me before (this was my first time in a hospital as a patient; they always joked with me that I went for "the big" one when I did admit). I tried to clean it up before it was discovered and as I was very unsteady and out of it I did not get far. I could have hurt myself doing that and I got chewed out (appropriately) by the young black nurse that was on duty. She said climb back up on the bed and don't worry about it. Stern, but in a nice way, she put me at ease. She cleaned up my bottom as she had me roll over for that reason. That was my first experience like that, and as those having been in a hospital can tell you, it was a very embarrassing moment. I guess that's one way to cure shyness. She said not to worry and that it was her job to clean me up and also that I should never do that again as I could get very hurt. As I said, I had never been in a hospital before, so it was all new to me and, naturally, I was very disoriented at the time. This was a vivid memory but I was so out of it that I still am not sure of the exact location (I am pretty sure it was at Vanderbilt) or the time, except that it seemed to be late at night. It was hard to be embarrassed again in any hospital or rehab situation after that episode.

I Lose Everything But I Am Alive!

After the craniotomy in Vanderbilt, I was almost instantly forced to retire. I could no longer work as I could barely function. Fortunately, I won SSDI (Social Security Disability Insurance) on the first try in 2012 while in Michigan. That rarely happens except in severe cases, such as my own. I talk a bit about this later. I lost my home, my business, my rental cabin, all to foreclosure and due to non-payment of mortgages. I later assumed I had a "default" bankruptcy as I was not able to pay anything on any of my debts. I was taken by dishonorable lawyers in Cleveland, Tennessee. I was dumb enough to pay for a "legal" bankruptcy upfront and then leave the state (hindsight is a wonderful thing). Naturally, the lawyers never followed through with their promises and kept my money. Again, as I mentioned, my debts were cleared by default anyway. There have been no calls here in Michigan from creditors. Perhaps they got wind of what had happened to me and just wrote the debts off. They may have written me off as well. I had a lot more than debts to worry about after surgery. My mail was all forwarded to Hawaii, where Dave, my brother, lived and worked until recently. He came to Tennessee to help me battle for treatment. He is very familiar with bureaucracies and how the government works, having worked in government for many years himself. He has battled cancer so he has been on the inside of hospitals and knows of them and of pain firsthand. I was fortunate to have him help me get through this. My mother had open heart surgery a few years ago in Michigan, as discussed, so she knows of hospitals as well. She and my sister were able to drive down to Tennessee from Michigan. My mother has provided me a place to stay while I recover as well as the use of her car. My sister has helped me get to scheduled MRI scans in Ann Arbor and Detroit and has helped me walk around on sidewalks when I used a cane. I am very grateful for all of my family's help. While I was in the hospital and rehab in Tennessee, my brother and mother stayed at my residence and tried to keep up with my laundromat business as best they could. They drove to visit me some 150 miles from Benton to Vanderbilt and Murfreesboro several times. They stayed in a nearby motel in Nashville a few times. They spent many hours playing cards in Benton, discussing my situation late into the night. Dave especially played a huge role behind the scenes. He was my spokesman, my Power of Attorney, doing his best to figure out how I kept my business and finances above water for as long as I did and how he could continue that for as long as possible. Dave made sure I got the medical treatment I needed and did more for me than I or anyone may ever know. He battled my leaky, worn plumbing back at the laundry and did his best to try to keep the place open as long as possible for my customers. Occasionally I could visit Benton on a weekend while in rehab, but since I could not think that clearly, it was hard for me to help. Things that I normally did at the laundry, I could not remember. My mind obviously was not "all there". We all made some hard memories back then and they give me much to write about today.

"Saving The World For Democracy"

This was one of the more bizarre and realistic dreams or delusions I had while I was at Vanderbilt. Perhaps it was drugs, surgery, or both. It might have been parts of old movies that were stuck in my head also. Now that I think about it I believe it was right after surgery and I was naturally trying to recover. I thought that I was the President of the United States. I think I thought I was Barack Obama. Sean Connery

(James Bond—Agent 007), of all people, was inside a magic carpet (triangular shaped) helping me to "save the world for democracy". He was embedded in the carpet but upside down, similar to the Superman movie where the three villains are imprisoned in the triangular devices that swoop down from space and pull them in for all time. To me this was serious business. My brother Dave later told me that I broke up a conversation with him when I said I was busy now and that I had to go back to helping Sean. Very funny! I later thought that I should be able to chose my diet (or medicines?) because, after all, I was the President. I told this story to my family when I first arrived in Michigan in 2011. I told it to my brother Tom who on that Christmas got me a framed picture of Sean Connery as James Bond. Sean had his famous revolver with him. On the picture Tom had printed "I'm Sean...Sean POTUS (President of the United States). And Mr. Caylor, I'll see you in your dreams!". That's hilarious and I now have that picture next to my computer where I see it everyday.

Lack Of Energy

After surgery and even through rehab I noticed that I wanted to sleep or just watch TV more than usual even though there was not that much of interest on in the daytime. I rested lots of times between rehab appointments on my bed, mindlessly surfing TV channels, due to just being exhausted. It took lots of motivation and energy, but once up and going, therapy was fine. Perhaps it was the boredom of the place (this applied to Vanderbilt as well as to the TN VA). They had a nice reception area on my floor at the TN VA with a TV, books, and magazines but with the eye patch on (I had continuing vision problems that I write about later), I lacked motivation to read anything. At times while waiting for VA therapy I would wheel myself down the halls and go for a "spin". This was late in my therapy, when I began to get some of my energy back. I hear that after major surgery the body gets tired. I can testify to that. Even now in Michigan, nearly two years after surgery, I tire often, especially early evenings, but much of that is due to having a different sleep schedule than most people. Going to bed early is an old habit from my last job, from the early VA dining hours, and because I need to cover my right leg in the bed to ease the continuous pain.

Vanderbilt Walking

The staff had me walking around the Vanderbilt hallway outside the ICU right away after my brain surgery. They had to hold me up as images were double and blurry and I was very unstable. I had survived the ordeal and I had a big smile on my face. My Mom tells me that it took at least two people, one on each side of me, just to support me. I got polite nods from the people outside my room. I thought I was doing great and waving to staff there but I'm sure from what I hear later that I was in a delusional state, not fully back into my mind yet. The mind was, and is to this day, slowly coming back. I still have memory of this event and the smiles on the faces of those outside the ICU. And why was it so bright in there?

Lost Money

I had some cash on me during my time at Vanderbilt. I usually got some cash from an ATM before I went out of town. I was out of it mentally as you can imagine after the surgery. I may have left that money out or my wallet in plain view. I was not in a state of mind to know what exactly happened. Someone working there or a family member or a student took advantage of my mental and physical state and likely stole the money from my wallet. My brother reported it, but nothing ever came of it. As I said, I did not have the presence of mind to keep track of it so I lost it. It was a shame that there was someone that low who would steal from someone that just had brain surgery. Being a teaching university, with several staff changes and students and family coming and going, it could have been anyone. All I can say is that it was a really low thing to do and I hope that they really needed the money.

To The TN VA ...

Now I am headed back to the VA in Murfreesboro, TN for rehab and therapy right after my brain surgery ...

Seizure (Who Hit Ctrl-Alt-Del?)

This is typical of a big organization like the VA. They can work magic as they did in getting me the surgery so fast (with my brother's help, naturally). However, things don't always go so well as when they transported me very roughly from one facility to another. The memories are sketchy but I still have a basic recall of the event. I was coming out of brain surgery at Vanderbilt and transferring to the VA rehab in Murfreesboro, Tennessee. I remember being strapped to a gurney and being put into the back of an ambulance pretty roughly. I was just another patient who's name was on their clipboard that they had to deliver. We whipped around the highways, and I was riding rough in the back. Of all things my mind was somehow on MSDOS, the old computer operating system of Bill Gates and Microsoft and one that I worked with often in my past. I used to work in technology and I programmed computers for a living, and so my thoughts went back to those days. My mind was drifting, no doubt due to the brain surgery and the rough ride. I remember being delivered to rehab and then all went blank. It was at that time that they said I had a seizure and they rushed me to the emergency room there. Well I wonder why? This was when the VA did not know if I would have one again so they put me on an anti-seizure medicine. I took this medication during my whole therapy and it even got left on my list of drugs well into Michigan. Somehow I knew that the seizure was a one-time event, mostly caused by incompetence at the VA. In Michigan I mentioned the drug to my neurologist and I was able to phase it out. I have not taken this drug or any other VA prescribed drug in almost a year now (with the exception of a baby aspirin regimen that I chose to continue). The doctor said they normally prescribe seizure medication for about six months after brain surgery. Well it's been almost two years since my surgery so now I am safely off all VA drugs. Without my own and my family's intervention and initiative, I might still be on this or other now unnecessary medications.

A Strange Healing Device

After I was out of surgery and healing I had a dream or delusion of a strange healing device within my head. I think I was at the VA rehab with my mind spinning when this occurred. I had to be perfectly still when it came around into view inside my head. It made a steady circular motion inside of my skull. It would come into view every few seconds. It made very little noise, just a whirring sound. It was like a robot or automatic device that would fly inside of my head and heal or work on the surface of my skull. I was able to look on that surface and it was a copper floor with hieroglyphic symbols, very polished. It had great detail. The robotic device would shoot a jet spray or some sort of laser beam down to the surface (again as in the movies) and I would have to be real still and not move. That spray or beam would heal the injuries and look for more. It would fly around several times. I could not touch the device or the hieroglyphic "brain" floor. Maybe I was getting an MRI at the time and they told me to be still and don't move. It was all a fantasy/delusion/mix-up of memories then, but this one was quite vivid to me. I am almost certain that it occurred while I was resting in bed at the VA rehab facility.

Useless Cell Phone

Right after surgery in Vanderbilt and at the VA rehab facility I was unable to physically use my cell phone. I had it with me and it had all of my contacts. I was used to texting as I had often done with my good friend Cathy. When I tried to use the phone to call for help, as I was delusional at the time, or to let anyone know what had happened to me, I could only hit numbers instead of letters and it was all scrambled nonsense. I also could not see well after surgery and was not even able to read the keyboard. I once thought that the nurses were after me at the rehab center, so I was trying to get help on the phone. My mind, as you can imagine, was all confused. I remember being frustrated at not being able to use the phone as it was so much a part of my former life. At some point I just surrendered and realized I could not use it yet and I just set it aside. I may have even told Dave, Mom, and Sandra that they might as well take it back with them as it was useless to me. At Vanderbilt before the surgery I kept trying to keep it plugged in and charged but as I was losing control of my physical abilities, I kept losing it or could not reach the electrical plugs in the ICU. It was getting difficult to physically use it even at that point. I would drop it a lot or not be able to find the charger. It was getting harder to see and use it in my condition. And as I say, I just left it off and gave up on using it all together.

Real Eggs?

We ate at very regular times at the TN VA rehab facility. Breakfast was at 7:00 am, lunch at 12 noon, and supper at 5:00 pm. They had a special dining room for meals. We were all in wheelchairs with the exception of one older guy who made it to the dining room with a walker. I remember looking at him admiring that he was so "advanced", wondering if I would ever be able to use a similar walker someday. I giggle now looking back at this (as I walk now without even a cane) but I know that it is what I thought while in my wheelchair back then. Night nurses would come down around 6:00 am every morning to our rooms and turn on all the hall lights and the room lights to get everyone up. They were brighter for me than for anyone else of course. They would then go back to their breaks or whatever they were doing. It reminded me of the military and my boot camp days. I was pretty strong with the wheelchair back then so I would wheel myself all over and did not have any problem going down the halls and into the dining area. I was usually up and getting ready early anyway. Sometimes there would be talking in the dining room before they served us food but usually we were all quietly waiting for the meals like trained animals. I had a special diet that required I eat "bland" food with no chunks (I talk about this later and my difficulty in swallowing). I also had a special drinking cup that restricted liquids. When I had choking/coughing spells with my food they had me go slow, be "in the moment", and that helped. It was a bit annoying when they would send their staff down with their clipboards to watch me eat and make sure I chewed my food properly. When I was close to leaving the VA (a "short" timer) I smarted off a bit. I knew I wasn't long for the place and my mind was getting very far ahead of my physical abilities. I asked a guy next to me at breakfast, when we were served eggs one morning, if he knew how to tell if the eggs were real or not. He said no. In my most serious face I told him to pick the eggs up and sling them against the wall. If they stuck, they were real and then I burst out laughing. I easily amused myself back then and I guess I still do. Though I often felt like a prisoner there, I could see the humor in most situations I was in. A nurse was behind me at the time and did not look too amused. I think she told me to knock it off or something like that. I piped down and concentrated on just getting out of the place. I guess my humor would be wasted there. Several times at breakfast the nurses would have to go get someone's false teeth that they had left by their sinks. We would all have to wait for them to return. I still have my real teeth, so I felt out of place. I was considered the "youngster" back then at 60, go figure. I remember they served me lots of mashed potatoes in little Styrofoam cups and ground up turkey or some other "mystery meat" because of my swallowing problems. That may be a part of the reason I don't eat that much now. I simply stopped eating most of the food but I was never that hungry to begin with.

Weird Nashville

While in the dining room at the TN VA rehab facility they always played the local Nashville TV stations. In my confused mental state (before my mind started to wake up), I interpreted the TV programs strangely. I remember thinking that Nashville is an odd place. What do people here do for a living? I had delusions of people not working, of it being some kind of a welfare state, where people bartered or something like that to get by. It seemed like Nashville and the area surrounding it were small isolated areas or communities and that the people were limited to each area? I really don't remember many details except wondering how the people got by there, as I mentioned. My mind distorted the television background to where I thought Nashville and it's surrounding areas were very strange places indeed. There was obviously a mixture of local commercials and television programming with my mind interpreting things in ways that did not make sense. After I was becoming more awake, I remember a patient named Jackson that the nurses brought into the dining area. He had to be helped with his eating. He had to be hand fed and I remember thinking, that poor fellow. I didn't realize it at the time but I too probably needed that kind of help in those early days right after surgery.

What Privacy?

During rehab the showers were very hard for me to use because I was so unsteady. Toward the end of my stay I could clean myself much better but still I needed to use a seat in the shower for safety. I do that to this day as I am not fully stable yet but I can stand up if there is a rail or something for support. I took my first stand-up shower in about two years at a cabin in St. Ignace, Michigan that we rented on our Mackinac Island vacation in 2013. Fortunately that shower was small and I could hold on to the sides. At first I am sure that the nurses, and they were almost all women, had to bath me. At first I was embarrassed by this but I soon got used to it. They would eventually get me in and then leave me some privacy to wash. I would pull a string when I was done so they could come get me and help me out and back into my wheelchair. As I say, toward the end I could wash and take a shower myself but I went along with their help to not make any waves (bad pun). I wanted just to get out of the place as soon as possible. Help with the toilets was similar to the showers. They would get me in there, leave me to do my business, then I would use a pull string so that they would come and get me, making sure I was back in the chair and that I was cleaned up properly. I am sure they had to do everything at first but I have limited memory of that. Maybe that's a good thing, as Martha would say. I had some close calls with toilets during physical therapy. This was before I was aware that the VA still had me on laxatives. Physical therapy was always at 1:00 pm and I had just eaten lunch at noon. I had to get help to get to my toilet in my room from April, my physical therapist. Sometimes I would have to use a public restroom in her rehab office if there was no time to make it to my room. To make it worse I was usually doing stationary bicycles, balance tests, or trying to walk when the urge would come upon me. It was always so embarrassing but she took it all in stride. It's funny I could not go that regularly, particularly urination, at Vanderbilt around surgery time, but in rehab and now at Mom's place, as my diaries show maybe too many times, things are "regular" again. I guess I am lucky that I still have control over those bodily functions.

Belly Shots

Right after surgery I was given several shots in the stomach daily. It seems that these were administered very early each morning by the night staff, maybe at 3 or 4 am. They would wake me up for the shots, then let me sleep a bit more. I actually got so used to the shots that there was little pain. They eventually gave me most medicines orally. Most drugs were mixed up in applesauce. This may have been related to my swallowing issues. They tasted crappy either way.

Falling Into Bed

There was a reason why I was in the VA's "Falling Leaf" program. That is where the veteran is supposed to remain in a wheelchair or a bed unless someone is there to help him get up. I was disorientated one night at the VA. I tried to relieve myself as it usually took the night nurses too long to get to me. Eventually I stopped trying to ring for help. Again, I did not realize that the VA had me on laxatives. One night I made it to the bathroom in time, but the lights were off or dim and I left them off. I remember spinning or getting dizzy and fell to the floor in my room. I was OK and did not hit my head, fortunately. I just lost my balance and fell to the floor, bottom first. It happened a second time that night and this time I spun and landed into my bed. That got my attention, as you can imagine, and I rested just thankful that I was OK and happened to make it to my bed. I thought that I had fallen onto a bench seat in the bathroom but I had somehow fallen into my bed instead. I just laid there for a moment, breathing a sigh of relief, and thanking "the powers that be" for looking after me and thankful that I wasn't hurt.

Swallowing

This has been a persistent problem and still remains one, however there has been much improvement in this area. It first showed up at a Hardee's restaurant in Etowah, TN just outside of where I worked at the McMinn Memorial Nursing Home & Rehab Center. I had stopped for a lunch there and I choked while drinking a Sprite right after eating a hamburger. I was surprised and did not understand why this had happened. Due to the location of the tumor, the surgeons said that they expected that I would have swallowing difficulty a little while longer. It was a problem at the VA in Tennessee and again it got worse after my second surgery in Michigan a year later. There was a picnic for veterans down in the courtyard at the VA. It was a beautiful day, as most are in Tennessee. I think my physical therapist, April, was helping to put it on. I remember getting through a hot dog and hamburger slowly and safely without a problem but when I swallowed a Coke, it just expelled from my mouth all over my plate. I was embarrassed but now I know that I probably took the Coke straight down my throat which I now know I can't do. The nurses there said "don't worry" and they helped clean the mess up. To this day I cannot take food or liquid directly down the center of my throat as I could before surgery. I was put on a special "bland" diet at the VA for this problem. I had x-rays taken in the "swallowing lab" and an analysis of my swallowing was made and they found that food and liquids would not go all the way down but would get stuck in my throat, then go down on the second swallow. No wonder I was choking and coughing. I remember having to swallow samples of different foods while they examined me. They found a physical condition and this again was a symptom of where the tumor was located. To avoid choking I used to carry a small plastic bottle of water with me almost everywhere. I don't need this anymore unless I am on a long walk or a hike where there is no water. I stopped carrying this bottle with me in 2013 when I gained more control of my swallowing ability. As mentioned, I had to use a special drinking cup at the VA meals to limit the inflow of liquids. Back then they thought I was drinking too much fluid at one time when it was simply the angle of entry into my throat that was the problem. A funny memory I still have was when at dinner at the VA one night, all these old guys around me (or older than I was) all had beans and wienies. I was not allowed the wienies. Here they are with mostly false teeth and me being probably younger by ten years or more, and using a special drinking cup and having to eat special food. I wondered "what's wrong with this picture?" They often served me ground up turkey or who knows what "mystery meat". No wonder I never ate much there. I later learned to swallow by taking a small gulp and holding it in my mouth until I was mentally ready for the swallow to go down my throat, but at an angle, not straight down as one normally would do. This I learned in 2013 in Michigan on my own and after I gained more physical control of my body. Also being "in the moment" was required, as each and every swallow, even to this day, and especially with beer and soda products, could start a serious choking incident. I had difficulty at the drinking fountain there at the VA before I became aware of how serious my swallowing problem was. I would always choke on drinks of water and I wondered why. This has been a problem for two years but I can now control it much better. As I mentioned, the VA would assign lab techs, mostly young girls, to carry clipboards and sit with me during the meals and just watch me eat and swallow, noting when I rushed or would choke. I would always ask them if they wanted a bite. They always declined. I even saw nurses watch me closely, when they did not know that I saw them, so they were all probably helping to observe my swallowing ability. Cups of mashed potatoes, being easy to eat, were served to me all of the time. I think they were served at all meals, including breakfast of all things. I ended up not eating much of that food, especially the nasty ground meats. I did not have much of an appetite during those days.

Singing Opera

At first, naturally, I had poor cognition skills and this was right after surgery. I was pretty much out of it. I had regular speech therapy as I had difficulty speaking (I still do but it is much improved). Again, this was due to the location of the tumor, and even after it was removed, the brain has to relearn many of these abilities. My speech therapist in Tennessee was a young girl and I am sorry I do not remember her name. She would conduct her therapy in my room around 8:00 am. She would let me sit in my bed while she sat in a chair against the wall giving me my therapy lessons. She mostly gave me cognition tests at first as well as discussed methods to speak better, such as breathing, slowing down, enunciating, and so on. She would always ask me the day of the week, month, year and who was the President. After I started getting that right all of the time (my brain was rapidly improving) she stopped asking and concentrated on speech techniques. She let me use the calendar and clock in my room to come up with the answers to her cognition questions and she actually encouraged that. As I rapidly improved, I got a bit silly and ran an old joke past her one morning. This joke was older than she was. But thankfully I had my wits about me so I was ready to have some fun. In my most serious face, one day I asked her "if I could sing opera after all this was over?". She looked at me, thought for a bit, then said sure, probably. She must have thought, what a geek! After she answered, I was most serious as I delivered the punchline. Many of you may know what comes next. I said, "well I never could sing it before". I was roaring inside but kept a straight face. She was silent for a moment then burst out laughing. I joined in and told her that's an old gag, older than she was. She was probably 20 something. She really laughed and said she liked it, in fact she was going to tell her boss the joke. From that moment on, she knew, and so did I, that I would be OK.

Carnival Therapy

I had an occupational therapist at the VA in Tennessee. Unfortunately I forgot her name but not some of the things she and I did there. It seems to me that it was Diane or Denise, but I am afraid I do not recall. I wish I did. She was a bit older than most of the other therapists, perhaps in her 30s or 40s. She was cute, wore glasses, and yes she was a brunette, but she had a boyfriend. I knew this as she would text him after she gave me things to do such as log puzzles or regular puzzles. I was in a wheelchair but already gaining more physical and mental control each day. I was much better physically than she knew and she always treated me as if I would fall if standing near my chair. I just went along with it so I could get out sooner. I sat at a card table working on therapy tasks while she would text on her cell phone behind me. She probably did not know that I knew about that. I would break puzzle speed records after awhile according to her. At first I could barely do a large 10 piece puzzle but like everything, I advanced rapidly toward the end of my stay. She would start me on a puzzle, go into her office, and have me yell when I was done. She barely had time to sit and relax in there when I would say "I'm done!". She got less and less downtime as I healed. I remember that she had a big screen TV on in the room and as it was daytime she usually had "The Price is Right" game show on. I tried watching it with both eyes but could not see well due to the double vision. I wore the eye patch then to see fairly clearly with one eye. The room reminded me of a nursing home activity room, with sunshine coming in the windows, books and VCR tapes all around, puzzles and games all over, everyone in a wheelchair, just like the nursing home in Etowah where I delivered the clothes. All that was missing was the elevator music. There were usually other patients there doing occupational therapy at the same time as me. I tried my best to improve my skills as I wanted to leave rehab as soon as I could. As mentioned, I advanced rapidly so that I was aware of the environment and what was happening to me and others in that room. One day they had a veteran's carnival down in the courtyard. My occupational therapist wanted to attend and asked me to go there with her. At that time my control was better and I also wanted to go. It was almost like I became the "teacher's pet". I guess I made her job easy. She said the carnival visit would do as that day's therapy. Again it was a warm and sunny day, typical for Tennessee. I wheeled myself around the courtyard as I had strength returning. I also retained arm strength from my job in Tennessee. I was pretty strong overall for my age. She followed behind me. I remember winning several events and they would give out small prizes. I gave them to her. She enjoyed herself (why not, she was getting paid to take me there). We stopped for a snack at a picnic table and I had a hamburger for lunch. I remember that she got some cotton candy. It was a fun moment and I enjoyed soaking in the sun, even though it was bright for me. It almost felt like I had a girlfriend and it reminded me of the fun that I had with Cathy before the surgery. At times I felt somewhat normal, except that I was in a wheelchair. As I had swallowing issues then (and still have some now as I have mentioned) I had to eat very slowly to avoid choking. I stayed away from sodas as they were hard for me to swallow. She used to practice some line dancing while I worked back in the therapy room. I asked her once about it and I was told that she entered a competition and was going dancing with her boyfriend after work and wanted to practice. Apparently my hygiene was not that good back then and I must have had bad breath occasionally. I remember she mentioned that once. At first I was offended but then I thought about it and that she was probably right. Bad breath was at least better than no breath. I think she was a bit paranoid about cleanliness anyway, always washing her hands and wiping down the work table after each therapy, though she may have been told to do so. I do remember being sure that I bathed and brushed my teeth much more regularly before I went to visit her.

Bar Fly Nuke Codes

This is one of the more bizarre events that I experienced but like the air raid siren on my exit from the VA rehab, it really did happen. I was not imagining this one as I did so often back then. The VA would give us field trips on occasion to various dinners, picnics, and events. We were offered one to an air base where there was a dinner in honor of veterans. I always tried to go just for the break from sometimes monotonous therapy. We were in wheelchairs as always at the VA. We rode on a bus and the wheelchairs were lifted (with us in them) into the back of the bus using the chair lift. We would then ride in the regular bus seats as they folded up the chairs in the back. We stopped and picked up residents of the VA nursing home nearby. The party was on an air base about 50 miles down the expressway. I remember being let off the bus using the lift. As I wheeled into the dining room, there was a line of soldiers on both sides of the sidewalk, dressed in Desert Storm fatigues, all saluting us as we wheeled by. This was so funny to me as I felt like a wounded war veteran. I acknowledged them and waved back. Most likely they were just following their orders to show up there. They saluted to show their respect to all the veterans but to me it was a funny moment. I was laughing on the inside but did not let it show. There were many veterans there, many who had real war experiences, and I was told that the air force did this party once a year to honor all veterans. They put me in "the cold war" category. I should have told them I was in the gas wars of the 60s. We had hamburgers and hot dogs. I had to watch my eating, as always, paying attention to every bite and eating slowly. There were veterans from WWII and Korea there, many who came with me on the bus. I felt a bit out of place, but I guess I did serve in my own way. There were several speeches at the podium. The commander of the base stopped at our "VIP" table, shook our hands and talked with us "war veterans". Hey, I was out of the VA for awhile and that was nice so I enjoyed the moment. I certainly "fought" hard to live! Afterward we were wheeled and helped to go to an outdoor Karaoke bar they had set up. You had to go across a grass yard so we needed orderlies to help push us. They also had horse rides and boat rides available. It was quite a nice place. I remember there was a nice golf course right next to the outdoor bar. The sunshine felt warm on my face. I sipped on some water at the "bar". I remember looking at the golf course and thinking that one day I will be out on one again. There was a DJ playing tunes behind us. Some in my group went on a horse ride. I stayed back by myself in my wheelchair just enjoying the music and the sun. There were some veterans dancing with girls there on the dance floor. There were some ladies around the bar and that was nice to see. I felt strange in a wheelchair but I really could not walk or stand back then. I kept thinking some day! I watched several ladies dancing on the lawn in front of me. I was enjoying the moment and it felt nice to be in the "real" world, if only on a base. As I was relaxing, a lady, perhaps in her 40s, sat down by me and started talking. My first impression was that she had been there before (my "bar fly" feeling). She started asking me what branch of the service I had been in, when did I serve, what did I do, but then asked me if I ever worked with cryptography or anything secret. I thought I was in the middle of a bad movie. If I had been more alert I could have had some fun and pretend to give her nuke codes or something, but then my story would be over and you would never hear from me again. She said that she came to this event every year. I was talking as best I could (I had my slurring back then) but she listened intently. As soon as I said I had not worked with secret codes or equipment, she sort of faded into the crowd. I was certainly glad that my brain was intact enough to know that it was a suspicious situation. I guess I bored her as I did not reveal anything secret. As my brother Dave said, after I told him the story, maybe she was a plant by the VA to see if I could be trusted or would blab secrets after my brain surgery. Who knows? It was weird and almost surreal but it really did happen. Later the orderlies wheeled us back into the bus. I had to take a leak and being in a wheelchair made that difficult. No orderly asked us before we were loaded onto the bus if we needed to use the restrooms so I remember holding it for about an hour back on the bus. We were loaded up so fast I just did not say anything. They probably did not realize how difficult it is to be in a wheelchair and to try to use a restroom.

Mary Returns

I met Mary S., the physician's assistant (sorry I don't recall your last name Mary except that I think it started with an 'S'). She played a key role in getting me "released" and I feel bad that I don't remember her last name. After she returned to her job at the TN VA rehab, I found out that she also had a tumor operation on her brain but after meeting her and becoming friends she said that it was not as large as mine. She had made a quick recovery and was walking very well again. She had similar symptoms but to a smaller degree. She would stop by my room with two young interns (one had been to Benton of all things) and she would see how I was doing. I would always wave when I saw her. She was a good role model for me. Not only did my brother Dave play a big part in my release, but Mary did as well. She knew what I was dealing with and she knew I had a business and a life back in Benton (or so I still thought). Someday if she is still there I would love to <u>walk</u> into the VA and see her and apologize for not getting her last name in my book.

Franklin, Burger King, And Laxatives

While a patient in the Murfreesboro, TN VA, I was allowed to visit my neurosurgeon Dr. Sills's clinic in Franklin, TN for a follow-up visit. He said all was fine but that I would have a long and slow recovery ahead. I had some problems on the trip to his office. As it turned out the VA had me on laxatives still from the brain surgery and at that time I did not know it. Naturally, I had the urge to go all of the time. I had to take frequent trips to the restroom while waiting on the doctors at Franklin. I think it was during this trip that I had a problem at a Burger King pit stop. I was filled with laxative, without my knowing it, and did not make it to the restroom toilet at Burger King quite in time. I don't remember all the gruesome details (and maybe that's good), except that it was my brother Dave's Birthday that day. I told him that it would be a birthday he would always remember. I recall that my stability was so bad that the restroom looked very long and that the toilet was way on one end of the restroom and it had "slippery" white tile on the floor. The toilet on one end of the floor looked a mile away back then. They had me wearing something like "Depends" underwear and I ended up soiling these. Dave was kind enough to help me out. I had a spare pair but I don't think these were the right size. Again, it was a bit of a blur back then so I don't recall every detail but I am sure that some of the scenes will always stay with me.

April Power

I remember my very good physical therapist at the VA in Tennessee. Her name was April (Clark?). She always had lots of positive energy and optimism. She was perfect for her job. She was much younger than me. She was in her 20s most likely and she was very good at her work. She would come to our rooms and get us for her therapy sessions if we didn't show up in her therapy room on time. She helped me try to walk when I was very unstable and I had very little balancing ability. I kept leaning in one direction when trying to walk in the hallway. She used a waist belt and would stand behind me as I tried to walk. It was the one of the toughest things I have ever done but she was persistent and had a great attitude and tons of patience. She would always encourage me to keep going. A few times, as I have previously mentioned, I had to go to my room as fast as possible as we had just had lunch and I needed a restroom right away. I was still on the laxatives without my knowledge. She was helpful with me and waited until I was done with my business, still with an optimistic, smiling personality. I bet many are in her debt for all of her help and for her wonderful attitude. Though kind, she was tough on patients, insisting that they do their stationary bike exercises and all of their assigned therapy. I remember those stationary bikes and having to put up with Fox News blabbing on the TV in the background. There was another VA worker there, I think his name was Steven but I do not recall exactly, that loved that channel. He was a little "one-sided", a conspiracy, anti-government type from his conversation. Ironic that the government paid his wages, I thought, but I quietly did not make waves again as I wanted out. I never got the hang of walking that well there in the halls. They had me on the "Falling Leaf" program, as mentioned, where I was not even allowed "officially" to get to the toilet on my own, but I did it anyway. I HAD to go! I was always getting lectured. I never had the strength or balance and control that I do now. On my last day, April took me to the fire escape stairs. She held tightly as I maneuvered down the stairs. I felt like showing off that I could take bigger steps, but she did not let me and was probably right in her caution. I tried to take several steps (because I was rapidly getting better) down the stairs, but she said not yet, and that I should still be very careful. She was right, of course. I left later and thanked her for all of her help.

Balancing Act

In physical therapy April had me maintain my balance on a machine with a curved surface on which I would try to stand still and balance my weight. She would help me get on it and then I would try to balance myself by holding very still, then shifting my body weight in order to keep my balance. I was allowed to hold onto the side rails at the start but then I had to release my grip. It was hard back then but I was surprisingly good at it and no one came close to my scores, according to April. I got so good at it (when I didn't have to rush to my room to use the toilet) that she took me downstairs to another physical rehab room that had a better balance machine for me to try. She put me up on that machine and again I did very well, breaking all kinds of records. I think she said, "I don't believe it", or something like that. Obviously I was beginning to heal even way back then. I even had scores better than the "normal" therapists there. I know I was becoming aware of everything going on around me. I may not remember it all, but certain scenes and situations did make a lasting impression. I am lucky to be able to recall them at all. I was and still am more limited physically than mentally. I clearly remember the downstairs physical therapy room that April and I visited. There were a few other people using the room at the time. There was an exercise track where a young lady was jogging. I remember then thinking it must be nice to be able to jog. I saw a man in a separate waiting room. He looked like he had a leg injury and was waiting to get therapy.

Eye Patch

The idea of the eye patch to help with my double vision originated with April, my physical therapist. I knew her well and talked about many things with her. I also mentioned my vision problems to other nurses, mainly the head nurses and I asked for an optometrist to check me out. I never got one there but I did see one later, Dr. Hrywnak (Veronica), at the Saginaw VA in Michigan in 2012. I finally got an eye patch in Tennessee, thanks to my brother Dave's intervention and April's suggestion and I tried it out, alternating daily from right eye to left. It allowed clearer vision but with only one eye at a time. I was teased at the meals as I would come in there using it on different eyes on alternate days. That probably looked strange to everyone. They teased all in good fun and it added levity to our routine. One guy, who always was joking around, said that I should come in one morning with it in the center of my forehead to see what the nurses would say. That was funny to me and I probably would have tried it, but I think I was a "short timer" then and I did not want to "rock the boat" and be delayed in getting out. I remember listening to "horror" stories of other veterans being told a certain number of days that they had left of therapy and then they would be released and then they would get extended for some reason. I felt sorry for some as they were much older than me and I thought that some might never get out or would be sent over to the nearby VA nursing home. Most likely I was headed there without family and friends to intervene. The VA really had a prison atmosphere at times and I learned later that they got more money the more patients they had in rehab. Perhaps this is why they seemed to be dragging their feet on my release. As I mentioned, the eye patch worked because it limited my vision to just one eye so that there was no double vision, but of course I was only able to use one eye at a time. After awhile I got used to it but I always missed using both eyes. I remember thinking that there had been an error in my surgery and now I was stuck with double vision when using both eyes. May of 2012 in Michigan was a big turning point in my life and I certainly write a lot about it later in the book. I made the decision that I would try to force both eyes to work and I removed the eye patch completely. All was blurry and double vision everywhere but I was determined to force the eyes to get better. Fortunately, the two images (one from each eye) got closer and closer, very slowly each day. The vision "gap" between the images got smaller daily so I stuck it out. It took about two months to correct and by July 2012 I could see one image, even if a bit out of focus, with my two eyes open. I was getting better and shortly after that time I was well enough to drive, as hard as that is to believe. Images using both eyes became that clear. I have been able to drive since July of 2012.

Window Wishes

There was a small waiting room down the hall from me next to the elevator on my 4th floor at rehab. Occasionally I would wheel down there and check it out. I was motivated to do this toward the end of my stay as my energy levels increased. I recall wearing the eye patch then as it was the only way to see clearly. I recall looking out the window at the parking lots and sidewalks watching the VA workers come and go with my one eye. At that time I wondered when and if I would ever be out there in the "real world" again and seeing as I did before, even walking again as all of those workers down there. At times it felt like a prison or being, as I have mentioned, in a boot camp. Even the buildings in the courtyard only lacked gun turrets on top and armed guards, my family and I often thought. My brother and mother would occasionally take me out for a break and we would bring back some "junk" food and eat it outside in the courtyard. We would comment that the VA would make a great Federal or State prison. I would have loved to read books in that waiting room but my eyes were not ready for the strain. I had no close-up or reading glasses that worked back then. I may have had my old pair but they were not correct for my brain anymore. I remember an Arnold Palmer golf book that looked interesting on the shelf but it was always blurry. The TV was usually on. I could make things out on the TV but it too was a bit blurry to me and things obviously were not as sharp back then as they are now. However, I was happy just to be alive and to be able to see as well as I did. I was happiest that my brain and thinking were the same as always. What a relief! I could now take anything that happened to me. They had vending machines in that room and I used them toward the end of my stay. I think I got a Snickers candy bar once but I knew that I had to eat it slowly and carefully. I, like now, am rarely hungry, so I did not buy too many items. I think I bought only one Snickers bar and a water while there a few months. My mind awoke rapidly toward the end of my time there and when I got bored or restless waiting for therapy or dinner, I would wheel around that waiting room, look out the window, and try to read the staff lists posted in the hallway. Those images, like anything I can see now, were fun and fascinating to me and, as mentioned, I was very grateful just to see them at all. This book and my writings have helped me to recall some of these memories and have helped me to appreciate how far I have come. I will try very hard now to never take the little things, like walking, seeing, talking, and swallowing, for granted again.

Korean War Veteran

I had probably one of the more interesting and also one of the oldest guys living there across from my room. I talked with him on occasions, mostly on our way to dinner or therapy. I found out he was a Korean war veteran. I would have never guessed that. He was quite a colorful character. He had a full head of white hair, was thin, and very youthful looking and acting, for his age. He liked his smokes and he was always borrowing cigarettes from a nurse that smoked and he would be outside in the courtyard taking his smoke breaks for long periods of time. The therapists and nurses often would complain that he was missing his therapy appointments due to hanging outside smoking. He seemed to have pains, particularly leg problems, but I was not sure of his condition. He often wore a stocking cap, usually red, to meals. He sort of played to his "own drum beat", so to speak, and I remember him well. I regret not speaking to him more often, but I had a hard time getting any words out back then.

Weekend Escapes

If I was a "good" boy and basically kept my mouth shut, something usually easy for me, but increasingly more difficult as new personality traits were beginning to show toward the end of my stay, I could go back to Benton, where I lived, and stay with my brother Dave and my mother Doris, who were doing their best to keep my place running. On one "getaway weekend", and I treasured these as there was so much I wanted to do to help, but of course my brain limited me in that, Dave and I were in his car at the Tennessee VA parking lot. This time my Mom stayed in Benton. It was a tough 150 mile trip for her to endure. There was some last minute mix-up and a male nurse called my brother while he and I were in the car about ready to leave. They always wanted me back a certain time, usually on a Monday, but since this one was a holiday, I got official permission to extend my break through the holiday. No therapist would be there anyway. I couldn't believe there would be a last minute problem just then. There is and was then less of a "throttle" on my mouth and brain after surgery so I blurted out "bullshit" when I heard the male nurse say I had to be back earlier on that following Monday or that I couldn't go. I was so angry. I urged Dave to just take off. It was a funny moment. We told the male nurse it was approved with the "higher-ups" and then we headed out. When I returned I had dreams of that male nurse being angry at me and trying to do me in, so to speak, because of this event. He, in my mind, was literally seeking revenge on me and would kill me before I could get out. I truly believed he would be after me because he had heard my verbal reaction. Here was my action plan: As I was in a wheelchair, I was ready to tackle him if he came into my room that evening and started to attack me. I laid in my bed going over all sorts of contingencies. I had a plan that I might wheel down to the lower floor library they had for veterans and I would hide out there so that he couldn't find me. That evening I had a dream or delusion that he came into my room and offered me a tetanus shot. That is the one shot that I am allergic to and it says so in my record. I tried to explain this to him. He then politely asked me if I wanted a flu shot instead. I said no and go check my records. He left my room peacefully. Of course he was never really after me or ever offered me shots. In fact, he was one of the most polite nurses there. He was also nice to my brother when we checked out and even asked to crash on his couch sometime if he made it to Hawaii. Again it was my twisted mind that read more into the situation.

VA Obstacles

Though the VA did much for me, obviously, there were some tough moments, usually of staff just showing up for work, and not caring that much for the work that they did or the patients that they cared for. Most nurses were terrific. Most had great attitudes and were very friendly but there were a few that could use their position to control you or there were those that just showed up for the paycheck, as in any large organization. I had one particularly obnoxious nurse like that, and my family soon found out about her. One day I don't think she knew that my family was still there. She was nagging at me about going to the restroom without assistance or "permission". This was likely the time they had me filled with laxatives after my surgery. She said something like "get back in that bed" at the top of her voice from the restroom. I think my Mom heard that (and she is hard of hearing) because it was so shrill and loud. My Mom said she had all she could do not to say something to her. We all just held our tongues so that it would be easier for me there. To me that was just her normal nagging and I was pretty much used to it. Toward the end of my stay when I was really starting to wake up inside, I did observe something just incompetent or perhaps sinister, I don't know to this day. I was always having to ask for my plastic urinal bottle at night. It has always helped me if I had the urge to go in the middle of the night and if I did not have the time or did not want to disturb any night nurse, and after Vanderbilt, I usually did have to use it at all hours. Also it was helpful as I was not supposed to get out of bed myself. By the time the nurses got to my room, if I did call them, it would have been too late. I tested this out and it took them way too long to get to me. Well one morning I found a plastic urinal bottle high up on top of a desk near my bed, just out of my normal reach. I noticed it only at that moment because I was getting much more aware of my surroundings. I was not able to see it there before. I hope it was not put there on purpose, just out of reach like that. As of this moment, I think it was just incompetence or someone just putting in their time and not paying attention. To me it was a big deal back then. However I was "short" then and I only had a couple of days to go and I did not want to "rock the boat", so to speak, so I did not report it. This was the first time that I was alert enough to see and reach this bottle that was just out of my normal reach.

Biting Tongues

I recall an evaluation meeting that I was asked to attend with my family and friends to get permission to go back to Benton on a weekend. Now the VA did wonderful things for me, as I have written about, but I and my family and friends also had our run-ins with bureaucrats, red tape, people with a "better than thou" attitude, and just a general lack of respect for the patient. Being quite out of it for much of the time after surgery, I still had enough presence to know when things were going against me or when falsehoods were placed in front of me. I and my family and friends bit our tongues when this was going on. My family and friends all exercised amazing control because they knew it would be tougher for me had they said something. I might have ended up in a VA nursing home permanently. In that evaluation meeting, the head of speech therapy said I only took one shower a week, which was definitely not true, but we all let it slide. Much of what she said, no one ever spoke to me about, or I didn't recall it if they had. To me it all sounded made-up to make me look like a helpless bum. Later when my family and friends left, the staff psychologist sat down in my room and read some of my mental test results and cut me off in midspeech when I dared question them or the methods, rudely saying that she was the "brain" expert, not me. I tried to politely discuss the results as not being totally accurate based on my recent rapid developments (those tests were given to me weeks before when my mental state was much worse. I also knew a bit about psychology, having a degree in the subject but that did not seem to matter). She said the results would be about the same if I took the test again. I knew differently and I still think she is wrong to this day. I guess I was a bit impatient back then and may have interrupted due to my rapid mental improvements. She also heard my slurred speech and judged my mental ability on that first impression, something someone in her position should know better than to do. Right or wrong, she had a horrible "bed side" manner. I immediately shut my mouth and bit my tongue, as insulting as she was to me. I smiled and knew in my mind that I would have the last laugh by getting out of that place, as I listened to her belittle me. That was only a day or so before my "big escape" so I calmed down.

Ray of Sunshine

Almost all of the nurses were female at the VA in Tennessee. There were a couple of males. Ray, one of the best nurses in the place, occasionally had duty in my wing. He would give me medicine and work on the staff occasionally. I would always say hello to him. He had a real positive attitude and seemed to like his job and the residents, always smiling and being polite to his patients. He was funny and always seemed to enjoy the moment. He helped me in my last day there by wheeling me in my wheelchair downstairs to get my check-out medicines, to fill out my papers, to save my brother some time when he got there to get me. Ray was a bit of a "card" with the ladies. He wheeled me into one office downstairs and said watch this. He then proceeded to flirt with a female office worker there. She acted like she knew him or maybe was just taken with him. That worked to get me some needed paperwork quicker and I thanked him for it and admired his skills with the ladies.

WWIII When I Get Out?

A funny moment happened on my exit from the TN VA rehab facility. I am glad my brother Dave was with me, or no one would believe this one. They would think it's just another delusion of mine. I got officially released and I think it was maybe 9 or 10 am on a sunny, bright fall day. You couldn't wipe the grin off my face. Dave got me into the car. I was still in a wheelchair. When we were getting into the car we heard an announcement on an outside speaker off the hospital grounds to take cover and a siren was blasting. It was a clear day with no storms in the area. We didn't know what was going down. My first thought was that they had set the alarm off because of me leaving (how self-centered). That is funny to me now, like I could be that important!

Dave wanted to check the radio for news in the parking lot. I was so anxious to get off the VA property that I said let's go and play the radio on the road. Dave said OK and we drove out to the main road. What a feeling of freedom! I finally had "escaped" what to me felt like a prison for so long. I could care less about some siren or WWIII (that's how bad I wanted to get out of there!) and later on down the road we did not hear anything further. I am thinking now that they may have been running a drill or testing sirens in the area but it sure sounded like the real deal. We stopped at a nice restaurant for some breakfast, damn the "end of the world". If we were going to be nuked (I was thinking of all the luck, on the day I get out), we would be nuked in a nice restaurant.

I Leave Tennessee...

Michigan Looks Familiar

Now after I left the TN VA rehab facility in the fall of 2011, I was determined to continue my recovery. I had lost, as mentioned before, my home, my business, my cabin, basically everything I had in Tennessee, but I was alive and the headaches were now gone. I had not much choice but to take up my mother's kind offer to stay and recover at her home in Michigan. I was basically homeless, without any income source (at that time), physically and mentally drained, so my options were limited. I could not at that time afford to stay at a private nursing home as the one I did the laundry for (how ironic). The VA nursing home in Murfreesboro, TN is where I likely would have been transferred to, but I would be right back in the environment that I had tried to "escape" from. What a nightmare that would have been. I made the decision to go back to Michigan to heal. As I have said, I felt that I did not have much of a choice at that time. Time will tell if it was the right choice but as of now, I think it was. My rehab now becomes pretty much on my own as my recall will now show. It continues when I arrive in Michigan, thanks to my brother Dave driving me back there. My mother had returned earlier with my birds, thanks to my sister coming to get her. The story continues now back in Michigan....

Mom's Nightstand on Wheels

In the fall of 2011, right after I arrived in Michigan, I slept on my mother's bed. I was in my wheelchair when I arrived but very rapidly I was able to use a walker. One morning I dropped my glasses upon awaking and reached to support myself on a nearby nightstand as I bent down for the glasses. The nightstand had wheels on the bottom, which I did not know about. It moved on me and being very unstable I then fell forward and the corner of the nightstand hit my face just under my right eyebrow. It missed my eye, fortunately, but I got a small scar underneath one eye. I had the eye patch on back then, so I tried to hide the scar from Dave and Mom so that they would not worry. I finally told them about it later. It was a close call, nearly hitting an eye and it made me be much more cautious around Mom's house.

The Queen Sees Everything

Early at my Mom's house in Michigan I bumped my head, but not seriously, on a wooden house that was hanging in the hallway near her basement just outside of her kitchen entrance. This was in 2011 as I was just getting my bearings back while also adjusting to my new environment. Mom loves to hang things all over the place and this wooden house was high enough not to bother her. It was good for me to adjust to the real world but at the time it was a funny incident also. I rarely go down my Mom's basement except for weather emergencies. The elevation changes were hard on the brain, so I avoided it if possible. I once went down to try to help Mom with her fuse box and checked a few fuses when we lost power. At that time I was very happy to still have my mental abilities to check fuses and I carefully made it down to the basement. As I have talked about in my journal, it is almost all a physical recovery now, thankfully. I am also happy to report, as of this writing, that my brain is now better able to handle elevation changes. I once remember hearing lots of clocks ticking (before the tinnitus got too loud in 2013). My mother loves clocks everywhere (so much so that we kid her about it) and they are mostly battery operated. I started to hear them just after a "thawing out" of some of my head numbness and before the experience of tinnitus. Back in 2012 I did hear many in the dining room ticking along one morning and I laughed. She has three battery operated wall clocks on the dining room walls. I guess we all have to love something. One of the funniest moments at Mom's place involved a cardboard cutout of the Queen of England. This was in Mom's large "China" chest and I did not know it until someone pointed it out to me one night while we were playing games. It made me laugh so much when I first saw it. It still cracks me up when I look at it and if I had discovered it one morning while making coffee or getting something on my own, I probably would have lost it right there, spilling the coffee and who knows what. The Queen is holding a deck of cards, sitting on a bench, with a wide silly grin. It has to be one of the funniest things I have ever seen. She watches over us as we eat or play games. She was much better for me then the anti-depression medication I was once taking. We (Dave, Mom, and I) often play games (dominoes or Scrabble) after our supper. I am not a big fan of cards and right now I see a blur of things close-up at the table, including food, and if I switch to reading glasses I am not able to see the people at the table as clearly as before my surgeries (back when I had one pair of glasses for all vision). Lately I have been physically able to help Mom clean her swimming pool. Dave and I often put an umbrella in the center for shade when we have a heatwave, as in July of 2013. Now on the first of August, it has dropped to 68 degrees in the pool, a bit cool for swimming. As I write this we are back in the pool in the middle of August 2013 as it is hot again. It's been unpredictable weather here as always in Michigan. Yes I have been able to use the pool, of which I write about in this introduction and in my journal.

One Item At A Time

Before regaining some of my balance and stability in Michigan in 2013, I recall very clearly a time when I could carry only one item at a time and then very slowly and carefully. This was in 2011 and 2012, two very tough years for me. Those years were so difficult for me that just now in 2013 I am finally able to write about them. I still have to be careful that I don't try to do too much, as before the surgeries, but now I am able to carry two or more things on a trip, as silly as that may seem. I know to my "normal" readers this must sound unbelievable, but I assure you that this is the truth. Mom probably chuckles at this one, as I am always asking her not to try to take everything on one trip (into the basement or in and out of her van). Thankfully, those tough times are vanishing as the days advance.

Hand Dryers In Hell

This is not that big of a deal to most "normal" or "non-disabled" people. I was so unstable back in 2011 and the first part of 2012 that it was very difficult for me to dry my hands after washing them in almost any restroom. That is because most men's hand dryers or towel machines are opposite the sinks, across the room on a wall. It seems silly now but that was a major obstacle. I had poor basic balance and it was like walking on ice to get to one of these devices. I wondered why they designed the bathrooms that way and I was a bit angered by this. Now I understand that most are electric and they have to be wired that way but at the time I could have used an older mechanical one closer to me.

Mail Call

I remember this very clearly as the first time I did this it was in the winter months of 2011 with snow flurries in the air. I wore my eye patch and I think I was using a walker to get around or maybe a cane. I was and still am a bit "crazy" but I have a "make or break" attitude now and I am very determined to get better. Due to my physical condition and because of my recent experiences in hospitals, I am very fearless and was so back then in getting the mail. Even though I could get the mail early in recovery, for many months I was unable to walk up the small hill to the mailbox without holding on to the nearby railing. It is rather steep and of course it got slippery in the winter. Now it's easier and I routinely go up that hill with no cane. I still use caution but not as much as before. As I mentioned, I clearly remember that snow flurries were blowing almost horizontally on that first venture, as I was looking into the field beyond which was not sharply into focus yet, even with the eye patch. My memories were strong: I had fuzzy, out of focus eye sight, I was hardly able to walk, snow was blowing, there were times I questioned my own sanity, but I went forward anyway. It took every ounce of my bravery and fearlessness but I went for it. Without being in my shoes and having these physical limitations, it is very hard to imagine how difficult this "simple" task was back then. At that stage in my life I had nothing to really lose, as crazy as that may sound. I got better at this task with practice and even continue doing it while working without the eye patch in the spring of 2012. Those few months, as I discuss, were brutal and my vision for awhile with two eyes open was very blurry and double. The world was so bright. I had to wear sunglasses back then with my old out of focus glasses on. As I write this I am reminded of that old song by Timbuk 3 - "Future's So Bright, I Gotta Wear Shades", their one big hit. Now that's a shirt I need to find. I must have looked blind to the neighbors as I went for the mail. Nevertheless I continue to get the mail for my own training and recovery. I recall walking back looking at the garage door "squares", and noticing the blur on the edges. Everyday, like all images, they would get sharper and sharper and I could look at them and see the gradual daily improvements. As I have said, I knew it was risky to get the mail (especially in the winter) but I was determined to advance by "doing". I think I am where I am today because of that earlier bravery. I know I thought on some days, "Well here goes nothing!". I have always had a lot of faith that things work out for the best and a lot of positive energy. That has sure helped me get through all of this.

Once A Nerd

This memory still amazes me. Being out of it mostly in 2012, I still had the presence and skill to hook up my two computers into a home network with Mom's computer in her computer room. It took every ounce of balance and hard work to do it, even more than it would if I were "normal". I still don't know how I did it. Each time I had to bend down and run some wires under a desk I had to be very cautious. Elevation change, as mentioned, made me woozy and very unstable, especially back then. I succeeded in hooking everything up and getting it all to work. It was great that I retained all of that former technical knowledge. I began to re-learn C++ programming of all things and studied other areas of programming, being a former programmer in a past life. I wanted to see if I still remembered those skills. My mind was just as sharp, thankfully. As I write about, I have physical disabilities, not mental ones. People naturally think the opposite when they hear my slurred speech or see me try to walk. People that know me, know better. About midway through my work in programming, and it was great mind therapy, I realized that I did not want to go down that road again. I left for Tennessee from North Carolina to get out of programming and all the stress that comes with it. Now I was slipping back into it again. It was at that point that I stopped the studies and went on to other brain activities and therapy. I came to the realization that I needed to decide what to do with the rest of my life and to do what I wanted to do. I am very grateful that my mind is sharp enough to work on computers and that I had all the skills and memories that I had before the surgery. I just confirmed my previous life choice to stop the programming (except for "fun") and the related stress that always comes with it. I had that "t-shirt" and had been down that road in the past.

Say What?

Mom is in her 80s now. She is very hard of hearing. We have to repeat words and talk loudly. Lately she has been trying to use her hearing aid again. She does not like to wear this one much. She says it works too well sometimes and she hears too many sounds at once. The challenge has been, and as you can guess, in communicating with her, especially for me. It is very hard for me to speak at all and hard for her to hear so you can imagine how funny that can be. It makes for some strange situations. The gods have a sense of humor I guess. I try not to make fun of her hearing but it is an amusing situation at times. If I try to teach her something on the computer, for example, then I must talk loudly. It is so hard for me to just talk normally, let alone at a higher volume. I usually burn up lots of energy in trying to just talk. I suppose you can look on the bright side in that it is the best speech therapy for me. We were recently at a yard sale and I bought a cardboard tube for "older" people to improve their hearing. One is supposed to stick it up to an ear to help magnify the sounds. It was basically a gag birthday gift. I used it as a megaphone in the back seat of her van as we went to yard sales one day. We had some good laughs. I was not laughing at her condition but with it I suppose you could say. She was a good sport when I used it and it really did help her to hear me back there in the van. It has been hard for her in doctor's offices as things need to be repeated often. I have mentioned we do run across people now and then who seem to understand and take the extra time to help her understand them, such as the late Dr. Copeland at the gamma knife clinic here in Midland, Michigan (MidMichigan Medical Center). I write more about his high level of patience when we visited his clinic. As my brother Bob recently mentioned about my Mom, at 80 many people cannot even walk, let alone hear. Mom, like me, has a physical condition with her hearing problems and it is certainly not a mental issue. At 80 now (and soon to be 81 as I write this) and on Facebook and the Internet nearly everyday, she does very well for herself.

Numb Hair, Basketball, and Elevation

After surgery, mostly in 2012, I noticed that my hair was still numb. Now you would think that only the head would be numb but there was so much numbness back then that I could not even feel my own hair for the longest time. Slowly this changed to where I can now feel my hair but the head still remains numb in places. It may always be this way due to the loss of some nerves.

<u>SVSU vs. Cedarville basketball 2011 or 2012</u>:

My first Michigan outing was to go with Steve, Sandra, and Heather to a basketball game at the local Saginaw Valley State University (SVSU) campus. SVSU was playing Cedarville, Ohio, the school that Amy and Heather attended. Amy still goes there. It was in the winter time. I rode with Steve ahead of Sandra and Heather in a van. I remember it being cold with snow flurries flying. I still wore my eye patch and I used a cane. I remember looking at the ramp to the auditorium as a very long sloping upward ramp. Steve, who had not been with me after my surgery, took off as if with a "normal" person, so I said "well here goes nothing" and took off to try to catch up with him. To me the ramp looked much bigger than it was and it was a big challenge back then. The whole campus to me looked large. I immediately went towards the railings for support and made it inside the auditorium. I enjoyed the game and had lots of fun. It was all so big and bright. Steve went down to participate in a basketball shooting contest during halftime. I remember getting woozy when leaving and walking up the bleachers. A man in the audience saw me starting to fall backwards down the seats and offered me his hand. I took it and thanked him. I saw that hand coming toward me out of the crowd and his voice offering to help just as I was tipping back down the bleachers. Most likely I would have fallen. That was very nice of him and very symbolic of how the universe works, at least in my "mind". There will always be a helping hand when you need one. At that time I was not aware that I needed to wait a moment for my brain to adjust to elevation changes, especially after a long time sitting in one position. I found out about needing a time delay at Bob's (my younger brother's) place one time. We were invited for dinner, I dropped something under the table, and went down to get it. I held on to the table but the quick change in elevation got to me. I tried to get up too fast and I fell hard into the wall making quite a noise. I did not get hurt, I just made a large bang. I was more embarrassed than anything. It was at that point that I knew I needed to be careful of elevation changes and that my brain needed a few seconds to adjust. This has gotten better now but it still can be an issue. I really notice it at the movies, which I still like to attend now and then. When I sit for a long time there, I am really unstable, even to this day, when I get up at the end of the movie. I have to hug the rails when exiting the theater. I used to stand several seconds at my car before I dared start walking because of the elevation change from riding to standing. Even at my Mom's front steps this was an issue when I went up and down the steps on her porch. I do not have to delay as much now. I am also better able to bend down, but again I must use a great deal of caution, bend slowly, and balance myself carefully

I'll Pass Today, Thanks

I thought about leaving this memory out of the book but I have since changed my mind. This person, if she ever reads this or hears about it (I will leave her name out), may have moved on (or not) but I really don't care. Perhaps I won't even be around either, who knows, by the time these words are read. Either way, I thought it best to describe this meeting "for posterity". This was about my initial meeting with a heath care provider assigned to me at the Saginaw VA in 2011. Now don't get me wrong, I am very grateful to have had the medical help, the therapy, and all that the VA has done and continues to do for me. This meeting, however, was hard to take. It's a textbook example of how not to deal with a new patient and how to just "go through the motions". Now since then I have a feeling that my provider may have helped behind the scenes (after getting read the "riot act", and rightly so), and if that is the case, then my thanks go to her, but still how we were treated at our first meeting reflects a lack of professionalism and care at that time and should be mentioned in my writings. Unfortunately I could not talk that well back then, having just had the major brain surgery in Tennessee, so likely this practitioner did not even understand me that well as I attempted to mumble at her and try to answer her questions. My Mom who was with me and cannot hear that well, can agree that this lady treated us both very poorly and went beyond disrespect. Perhaps she had a bad day or something. I will try to replay the meeting highlights for the record, as best I can recall. I was transferring to the Saginaw VA from the VA in Murfreesboro, Tennessee after surviving my first brain surgery at Vanderbilt. At first it appeared that she had not even bothered to look at my medical records or to become familiar with my case. Maybe they don't get that many transfers into the VA in Saginaw from another state. It was like who are you? And why are you here? I had a letter from my brother, who has been helping me get my health care (and he was back working in Hawaii at the time) and it listed what I needed to have done, according to my neurosurgeon back in Tennessee. My brother knew that it would be hard for me to communicate so he had things written down for me to give to the provider. Again, it was like this was all new to her and she continued to ask me questions from a standard VA health form on my general health state, details she would have known, had she bothered to look at my case. It was beyond insulting but I was there to get back into the system so I let it go. I felt like walking out right then. I was burning up inside with anger (and I seldom get angry) at this person's unbelievable incompetence and lack of preparation, even a lack of concern. I even caught her yawning a few times like we were bothering her or taking up her precious time. Several times my Mom asked her to repeat what she said because she did not hear it properly. This women had no clue and was abusive to both of us. We muddled through the appointment and reluctantly she agreed to have me get the MRI appointments that I needed at another

VA clinic, questioning the letter, asking who this Dr. Sills was and who my brother was. She even asked, "well, what is my brother's medical background? "Is he a doctor?" Fortunately, I told my brother what had happened or he heard, and being a bureaucrat he went to her supervisor and things started happening in the right direction. It is a shame it had to be done that way. Recently my Mom reminded me of the funny way our meeting with the provider had ended. I had forgotten, as I was so mad at this woman. As part of her routine exam, she asked me on the way out, if I wanted a rectal exam (even after all that bad treatment). I said, "No thanks. I will pass on that today". My Mom thought that quite funny afterward and I also see the humor in it now. My first thoughts back then were, after the way this meeting went and how we were treated, I didn't want her probing around "down there".

Towel Holder Go Boom

In one of my early visits to the Saginaw VA, I went with my mother and sister to see my health care provider on a routine visit. I had to go to the blood lab and give blood. I stopped into the restroom outside of the lab. I used a cane at the time but was stable enough to use the restroom by myself. Mom and Sandra waited outside. A funny incident took place inside the restroom. After washing my hands I was drying them on some paper towels. It was an old fashioned (not the motion sensing) kind of towel rack. As I wiped, the top of the towel rack fell down and hit me on the top of my head. It was just a gentle bump and nothing serious but the irony of the situation made me chuckle. Here I am after major brain surgery, using a restroom at the VA, and what happens? The towel rack smacks my head, of all places. I had to share the story with my mother and sister. I did so afterward and I still giggle about it. I see that a lot now, in that I have more time to observe, that life has all kinds of ironic incidents or amusing situations. Usually we are so busy that we don't see them. I know I used to be that way. Now circumstances have given me more time to observe things, for which I am most grateful.

VA Vision

Upon my return to Michigan and my transfer into the Saginaw VA, I was able to see an optometrist, Dr. Hrywnak (Veronica). She has been very patient with me, despite my requests of her to order progressive lenses as I had worn in my former life. They were also transition lenses. I got spoiled before in using one pair of glasses for long and close-up distances. They originally took me awhile to get used to but they were worth it. I sure have missed them. The doctor said they could not yet make any progressives that would work for my brain. It still had to heal more. This was back in 2012. They did fit a prism lens to my original pair of glasses to try to correct for double vision. That helped somewhat but the best help was the brain healing. I think all along she knew that. My next appointment is a full year from my last, in February of 2014. I hope I can handle progressives by then. The VA did order two pairs of glasses for me and they have allowed me to read and to see while I await my appointment. The left lens on the reading pair was originally incorrect, as I write about in the journal, so I suffered for a long time with blurry vision, and double images, but part (and I thought all of it at the time) was my brain healing. The new pair of long distance glasses were slightly adjusted for brain changes. I see pretty clearly now but there is a slight double image under some letters. I notice it mainly on light letters with dark backgrounds or the opposite (in other words where there is contrast). I think it could still be related to brain changes but if it is still there at my next eye exam in 2014, I will mention it to the doctor.

Walk For Kate

I attended this event on a Saturday at the "Tridge" park in downtown Midland in 2012 (a place where three bridges come together). I had my cane. Sandra went with me. I still had a difficult time with stability. It was a pleasant and sunny day (I guess they all are now that I am alive). I could not go over the "Tridge" bridge then or join the runners and walkers further up the Pierre Marquette trail so I stayed behind and briefly chatted with the husband of Kate who puts on the annual event. Online and by email I found out that Kate has a brain tumor in the pituitary gland area and it is inoperable. I saw the tent there in 2013 but I did not go over to it as I was late and it was crowded. I probably should have. I have mixed feelings about the event, similar to when I wear my "brain" shirts. One is that I believe that the more we fight against something or think on it, the more that it appears in our lives. We tend to attract those frequencies and events into our lives that we focus on. Another is that you naturally want to support those causes, especially after having survived brain tumor surgery (twice), but again fighting something seems to give it more power and influence in your life. But maybe that is just my own way of looking at things. In 2012 I made a contribution to the fund raiser and that felt right at the time. I was glad that I could do it. They put up a tent near the trail each time for the event, but mostly young joggers and walkers are the only ones that turn out. I saw no other "disabled" people there but myself (there I go with the labels again). I'm sure many could not physically attend. I am one of the rare ones that could make it there.

Good Bye Eye Patch

In May of 2012 I did a very tough thing by removing my eye patch and literally forcing myself to start using both eyes. I did not want to end up with a patch and looking like some pirate for the rest of my life. I had to stop all reading for a two month period but I was determined to give both eyes a chance to heal. Each eye image was pretty clear independently but the two images did not line up together and I saw blurry and double images at all times. With the patch naturally I saw only the one image but I wanted to go beyond that. I remember looking at the entertainment center, the TV, plants, vases, anything in the living room and slowly and painfully watching those images focus and sharpen. This was over the period of a couple of months with very slow improvements daily. The point of focus would slowly get closer and closer so I did not give up, though it tempted me. When I rode with my mother in her car (I could not see to drive then), I remember looking at the roadway and seeing a double white line down the right side of the road but like all other symptoms, the combined image got better daily with the gap between the two images getting closer and closer. This gave me hope and I stuck it out. The months of May and June 2012 were very difficult and agonizing months, as I could remove the double images by wearing the patch but I forced myself not to do so, as mentioned. I was absolutely determined to "see" this through and to be able to use both eyes again. I could not see the outside trees clearly in my Mom's yard during this time. I could not see the pool deck clearly. Everything in my world was blurry and double but I refused to give up. Slowly images sharpened in the living room. I remember I could not read Mom's shawl with all of her grandchildren's names on it from my favorite burgundy recliner. By July 2012 the images finally aligned and I breathed a sigh of relief. Images got to the point where I felt safe and competent to drive the car for the first time in almost a year. This is when I began my walking therapy at the parks and malls. I was still not able to type like I do now and I had to wait until the summer of 2013 to work on digitizing this journal by typing. My left hand would shake too much before that time and would not allow me to type on the computer as I do now. Luckily I was able to write by hand in late 2012 so I started writing in my the daily journal book on the last day of December of 2012 but I was not able to start digitizing it until May of 2013.

Double Images

While trying to see again without a patch, the two eye images took a long time to align. They still are slightly off but pretty much back to normal except that I have to use separate reading (close-up) glasses and long distance glasses to see under different conditions. Every day vision is sharper but as of this date, August, 2013, the eyes continue to adjust. The variance between eyes and brain is quite close now as I write this but it is still not perfectly "normal". I refer often to this in my writings as "brain lock", for lack of a better term. One eye image was always slightly angled upward on the page or on my bedroom ceiling. This slowly cleared as I fought to regain normal site without the use of the patch. With either eye closed, or in wearing the patch, the vision was clear. Again I write more about this in the journal. After I got a pair of reading glasses from the VA, I later found out that it had the wrong left eye prescription due to an error at the labs. The left eye always seemed fuzzier and I could never focus that eye. I always assumed, like everything else, that it was my brain adjusting and healing. Well that was part of the story. They re-ordered new glasses, and I then received these two pair in the mail, and the images were much clearer. I still can't do progressives yet but I can read and do close-up work with the "Coke bottle" glasses, what I call my close-up (reading) glasses because of their very thick lenses. I remember always looking up at the ceiling in my bedroom at night and seeing the image, where the ceiling and wall meet, rise up at an angle to the right, never straight as normal. I talk about this later and in my journal often. Again I endured about two years of seeing this strange image. It cleared up finally in 2013. As I've mentioned, I have a follow-up eye exam in February of 2014 (a year after my last exam), so perhaps then I will be able to have one pair of progressive glasses. At the dinner table I use my long distance lenses so that I can see people at the table, however it makes the food I eat look slightly fuzzy (or the games that we play) and not sharp as in the time before my surgeries. I could use the close-up glasses to see the food better but then seeing people at the table would be difficult. I am quite sure that seeing blurry images like this causes extra strain on my eyes and makes me tire more in the evenings. I have noticed that there is a time delay currently when I switch between these two glasses and it seems necessary to let the brain and eyes adjust for a few minutes. I am sure this will improve over time. It currently takes about two minutes before I can see sharply. My brother Dave says he has this with his glasses and that age may have something to do with it. The new glasses, though better, are still an adjustment for the brain. I sometimes see a double image on certain words that are small and usually on bright backgrounds. I noticed this on the TV "crawler" often. Most words, signs, and mall windows are sharper now.

The Boy Who Lived

As I was struggling with my vision in 2012, I ordered the Harry Potter complete audio series on DVD as read by Jim Dale. It is excellent and I highly recommend it. I got this on the Amazon website. I could not read well at that time due to the double vision and my efforts to go without an eye patch, which I wrote earlier about. I was determined to stop reading and to let my two eyes work without a patch. I had read the complete set of Harry Potter books in Tennessee. They were loaned to me by my good friend Cathy. I really enjoyed them and I saw all the movies in the theaters. I think we both went to see at least one of the movies together. I ordered the audio set because I could not read the books and I listened to them on a player while my eyes recovered. It let my mind escape to the "wizarding world" while my vision healed. They were good for my brain and brought back lots of good memories. I started to use them later while I had to stop reading due to my bad left eye prescription. I began to rip them to my mp3 player but I found that one of the DVDs was warped and could no longer be used. It was at that time that I could finally read again due to my replacement pair of glasses arriving by mail. When my eyes improved I ordered the complete set of Harry Potter movies and watched them on television. I think I watched them twice again with gratefulness and enjoyment. My priceless vision was going to be fine!

Drive To Recover

This is one of the biggest factors in my overall recovery. It gives me a feeling of independence and freedom to be able to drive, to go to therapy appointments, MRI appointments, walking at the malls, browsing in bookstores, shopping, drinking coffee at Starbucks, in other words having an "almost" regular life again. As soon as my vision was clear after removing the eye patch last summer (2012), I was able to drive and I recognized it. I had to wait for all double images to clear, naturally. As mentioned, I remember riding with Mom down some country road and watching the double white line on the right side of the road. I had to close my eyes occasionally or at least not look at what was in front of me. Obviously it should have been a single white line. I did not see double images wearing the eye patch, but I was determined to rise above using a patch and had faith that the eyes would correct on their own if I took the patch off. As mentioned I did that in May 2012 and it took a "long" two months for this correction. Those were tough months but I stuck with it and did not resort to the patch. It was tough for this bookworm to stop all reading for a two month period but I had to think of the long term. I began to drive again in the summer of 2012 after the two images merged and I have been driving ever since then. I go to the mall to walk almost every morning. I have driven in heavy traffic in Saginaw and in Ann Arbor. I have driven on the Ohio Turnpike. I have driven back to Midland from Elkhart, Indiana. I have been over to Bay City. I have driven Mom's van. Mostly I drive her 1995 Oldsmobile in the mornings locally and am usually back around noon or 1 pm. Mom covers the registration and insurance. I fill it with gas and keep oil in it. I also check tire pressure and clean the car occasionally. I will get an oil change for her soon. Still having this skill always amazes me and I am most grateful for the opportunity to drive again.

"Tridge" Bridge

I had finally crossed the "Tridge" bridge in downtown Midland, Michigan early in my walks (2012). I wanted to see if I could do it back then and it took much bravery given my physical condition. It was always a challenge due to the steep incline of the ramps to the bridge. Early on I crossed over to the nature park and walked around the trail on the river banks (2012). I went back in 2013 and crossed the bridge again using a cane and then a hiking stick. I eventually went without a supporting device as before. All of this, of course, I discuss in my journal. I picked up a sliver one time crossing the bridge by tightly hanging on to the rail but no wood was left in my hand, just a slight cut. I did this in 2013. I believe, as I have mentioned, that the gamma radiation treatment (July 2012) had a delayed reaction, making me more unstable a few weeks later , so I went back to the cane. In 2012 a young man over near the Frisbee golf course across the bridge asked if I was OK as I was staggering a bit after taking a long walk. I said yes I was fine and thanked him for stopping and asking. I think this was when I was experimenting without a cane. I looked like I had one too many drinks or I had taken drugs. I used to walk the park sidewalks near the "Tridge". Sandra was with me then. I was unsteady and I had the cane with me. I later improved to where I could go without a cane but I was never that steady and I am still a bit shaky as of this writing (July 2013). In my "Tridge" park walks I would go down toward the Riverfront Retirement Center and stop for a break outside on one of their park benches. Several times it was a nice sunny day and I recall soaking up the sun and relaxing, amazed that I was still on the planet. I have rested at the pavilion area in the Chippewassee Park across the "Tridge" bridge many times. One day in the late spring of 2013 I noticed some young Asians coming out of the H Hotel in the park area downtown. As I walked by I said hello to them. As I walked on past them I heard them giggle behind me. They were trying to catch up with me, a "disabled" person using a cane. Again there is some irony there. They were trying hard but I kept ahead of them as I did not see them and that made them laugh. They asked me if I could help them find the nearby nature park. They had a good command of the English language. I did not have my reading glasses with me, but if I held my long distance glasses up I could make out close details, enough to read a map. What a sight, foreign students, lost, asking help from someone who just had brain surgery (twice) and who could barely read without using his glasses as a magnifying glass. I told you the gods have a sense of humor. I was able to direct them up and over the bridge to the other side and then to the nature park. All along I was thinking it seemed early for tourists to be here with the cool temperatures and the bare trees but it made for a great memory.

Williams Township Park

In 2012 during the summer after I could see without an eye patch, I was able to drive myself to the local park in Auburn [Williams Township], about 4 miles from my Mom's place. I would go there early around 7:00 to 7:30 am. I loved the fresh air and the park was never that busy that early. There would be an occasional jogger or someone walking their dog, but other than that it was pretty empty. I made a lot of progress walking there that year. At first I used a cane and then I got to where I could go without the cane but I was never totally stable. I usually played my mp3 player while I walked. I remember I played Mozart's Requiem Mass quite often that year. It is about the same distance around the park on the outside sidewalk as a full lap at the Midland Mall, or about 0.8 miles. Like the mall, I took a break after every lap, sometimes more than one break during a lap to sit at the benches and just enjoy life and also to ease my hot leg. I used to sit on a bench near some flowers half way around the park. I could smell them blooming. I really enjoyed the summer breezes and smells. The park and I go way back and there is a special connection there. I walked some in 2013 in the park and would play my hypnosis mp3 on a bench occasionally if my tinnitus grew too loud. I was not aware of any tinnitus early in 2012. That has been mostly a 2013 problem. One Saturday I stopped and watched a soccer game for awhile. I used a cane then. I remember sitting on a bench watching the game, needing to lift my leg every now and then due to the hot leg pains. I first noticed these in 2012. I would often wave or say hi to the attendants there at the park early in the morning as they emptied the trash or checked the restrooms. I would wear a "brain" shirt now and then so that any "lookers" would have some idea of what happened and might stop gawking at me. I remember that a robin looked like it was watching me walk, going from tree to tree spying on me. It was very amusing. It was quite a hike and it was very difficult at first with stability and vision but I did not give up. I am very determined to make progress (come "hell or high water" as they say) in my walking. That's the most dedicated I have been to anything but nearly losing your life, then having everything taken away, does that to a person. I have a whole new set of perspectives. I remember I did at least four large laps around the park toward the end of my walks there. I did not use the park that much this year due to the heat and I decided to go back to the mall for the flatness, the AC, and my long history with the malls. I have only taken a break from my walks to work on this manuscript.

Birds Gone Wild

I have always enjoyed feeding wild birds and animals (Cathy taught me to use bread and scraps of food for them and to not just throw those items away) back in Tennessee. I had several bird feeders on my porch there. I resumed feeding birds and other animals here in Michigan. It was a great challenge at first as I had difficulty using the hose (and taking care of it on the hose holder) for their water. I was quite unsteady but I tried to keep up with them in 2012 and I still do. Bending down to take care of their water was difficult and I would have to hold on to a nearby tree for support. I'm much better now. I can bend down more and keep my balance but I must still be careful. Dave put up some finch and chickadee feeders near our dining window. We put special seeds and suet in there and lately (summer of 2013) the little birds are going crazy for it. They all love the peanut flavored suet. We also have a hummingbird feeder and have seen one come around in the evenings. Now and then I throw out biscuits or bread on the ground and small animals will eat them up. We had some robins in the yard very early this spring. They were either early or winter was extra long or both. We see robins now and then looking for food in the back yard as we swim. Mom says there are less birds bothering the pool so maybe the seeds in the front yard are helping with that.

Michigan and The Gamma Knife...

In the following Michigan memories I talk about the gamma knife procedure which was my second brain operation. In 2012 in the summer during a routine MRI in Ann Arbor, a remnant of the original tumor was discovered and the next MRI showed that it was growing rapidly. It was found just in time to be treated the "modern" way, with powerful gamma radiation. I was fortunate to be offered the gamma knife radiation brain operation. I discuss this here and my memories of the procedure as well as other Michigan memories...

Night Train

Mom lives right next to a train track. It gets loud when the trains go by. They mostly go back and forth to Dow Chemical here in Midland. I am always glad that they go by quickly and safely and don't derail here. I should not even think of that possibility. They go by at all hours now, probably to prevent any possible terrorist incidents. The birds have adjusted well to the trains. They were here with my mother for awhile until I could join them in late 2011. As with all pet birds, we cover them up at night so that they can relax and sleep and feel protected. When the train goes by it blows it's loud horn at all hours but my birds are very well adjusted to it and don't react that much, even though it's very loud, especially when the windows are open in the summer or in warm weather. Usually anything can spook the birds, but they seem used to the train. If I hear it and am up I will say "here comes the "birdy" train" or "woo woo", anything to try to calm them down and to let them know I am around. I am usually in my bedroom when this happens and the birds have such good ears that they hear me and once in awhile they will chirp in acknowledgment. I am used to the trains too but occasionally they will come by after I awake due to the tinnitus. Then of course it is hard for me to go back to sleep. This was a real pain at first but I seem better adjusted to it. Now I usually am so tired that I sleep anyway despite trains or head noises.

Morning Routine

I usually have a regular routine that I do every morning. The birds are used to me doing this and I usually hear a peep in their cage when they hear me get up. I always answer back so that they know that it is me. Christy, as mentioned earlier, is still jumpy over the dog Mom used to have. I put on some coffee. I have a doughnut or roll or a banana. I usually let the birds out for a break around 6 am. Smokey whistles at my foot then flies up on the entertainment center. Christy eats doughnuts or rests on my chest while I pet her head gently. She likes to spread her legs out underneath. She completely trusts me like that, but she has to be relaxed and not on edge which she is sometimes because of sounds or darkness or dog memories. Sometimes the birds like to walk on the carpeted floor. I usually watch CNBC, the weather, or local news in the morning. Sometimes I turn on "Morning Joe" on MSNBC or will check "Sports Center". If it's nice outside and I am early or it's a Sunday when I usually don't walk, I might work on the patio to read or write in my books.

Mall Walk Therapy

My past job in Tennessee trained me to be a morning person. The early morning headaches added to this in 2010 and 2011. I used to get up very early to keep up with my work before my customers arrived at the laundromat. The headaches got bad enough that I could not lay on my side to sleep without experiencing bad head pain. They were so bad that I had to stay up. The VA in Tennessee continued that habit of early rising when I was a patient there for rehab. The nurses would turn all the room and hall lights on at 6 am. Breakfast was served promptly at 7 am so we had to wake up and get ready early every day, seven days a week. There was no sleeping in at that place. So now in Michigan when I get up early, and I do every day, I set out to give myself regular, daily walking therapy unless I am working on this book. I used to walk in downtown Benton when I could, mostly evenings and Sunday afternoons. It was about a three mile walk. So enjoying walking and being a morning person (I go to bed early still out of habit and to get extra rest for recovery as well as to help reduce the continuous pain in my right leg), I started walking in the Midland Mall in 2012 after I could use two eyes and had removed the patch. I could drive then and would not need a ride to walk. My mother and brother both stay up later than me and sleep later in the morning so it is easier for me to go out walking alone in the early morning. Of course that is also therapy that helps me to be more independent. In the early days I used a cane often. I got a setback after the gamma knife and became unsteady again. For safety and because it was winter, I went back to the cane at the mall. In summer of 2012 I used the local park in Auburn [Williams Township] in all of the days that had decent weather. I now am back to no cane and have better stability and balance but I still walk slowly and deliberately out of necessity. There is still a slight delay or distortion between my vision and my brain, but very little lately. I occasionally speak or wave to the "regulars" at the mall. I used to be very unsteady and would hug the walls closely and stagger like a "drunk" If only! One day I was stopped by the owner of a hair styling salon inside the mall. She was headed for work. I believe it was a Regis Salon. She saw me stagger and grab the wall for support. I was very unsteady back then and I was trying it without a cane. She asked if I was OK. I told her yes and that I was just getting over surgery and thanked her for asking about me. I told her a bit of my history but at that time in 2012 it was very hard for me to communicate with my slurred speech. It's all getting better now. I improve with practice and consistent training at the mall. I have hardly missed a day and do it "religiously". I still try to do it at a relaxed pace without "trying" too hard. I do not strive or push myself and have the time to stop when I need to or wish to. Just being there and doing it routinely really helps. It has been a big factor in keeping me healthy and increasing my energy. I do it six day a week and have done so since I could see in the early summer of 2012. I average about 3 to 4 miles a walk. I have taken a break lately in order to work on this manuscript. For variety I sometimes walk at the Fashion Square Mall in Saginaw. It is slightly larger than the Midland Mall and close to a larger Barnes and Noble bookstore, so naturally I go there on occasion. I am over there when I go to the Saginaw VA for speech therapy. I have returned to walking the local mall or the one in Saginaw in the summer due to the heat, dogs, and bear stories. It helps that the malls are level and air conditioned. I have a lot of history at both malls so I will likely make my full recovery in a mall.

Mornings At Burger King

There is a Burger King open each morning at 7:00 am near the Midland Mall. I often stop there before I start my morning walking, especially if I am up early. Their early opening is good for me as I am usually up that early and out there, whether because of loud tinnitus, or just because I usually start my walking when the mall opens at 8:00 am. When I went there, early in 2012 and 2013, I had a cane and it was hard for me to get around. I was very disorientated inside Burger King but OK enough to have a coffee or a small breakfast or cinnamon rolls and milk and just relax and wait for the mall to open. This was really good in the winter when it was too cold to wait in the parking lot at the mall. I remember watching snow blow by the windows inside Burger King on several winter mornings. I could gauge my recovery by how much images there would sharpen over time. I started talking (or slurring) some of my story to a worker there in 2012. She is a very pretty young girl (with dark hair, naturally) and sometimes I still see her working there. I talked to her once. I soon realized that they are very busy in the morning taking drive-through orders, especially if they have a headset on. Now when I am there I don't bother them that much anymore but just have my coffee or breakfast out front. As my journal talks about, one day when I was not thinking about it, and that could be a key to all of this (that is, not mentally dwelling on the symptoms, and just thinking as if things were OK), I stepped backwards while waiting for my order. I did not have a cane then and this was a new movement for me, as silly as that may sound today. The next day I went without the cane again because I knew it was time. My basic control was returning and I have not been using a cane since then. I am thrilled to have more control and a return of the ability to step backwards again.

"Brain" Shirts

I received my first "brain" shirt, as I like to call them, a dark blue one, from my brother Bob and his wife Marsha for Christmas. I think that was in 2011. It says "I had brain surgery, what's your excuse?" I always liked that one and often wear it out to the mall or dinner. I will wear a "brain" shirt on occasion, many times just for the fun reactions of people. That and my other "brain" shirts help when the looks get too annoying after awhile. I will throw one on and then when they look they have something to see and think about. I have a couple of others. My niece Sarah's husband Josh got me a one with a picture of a brain and it says "I had brain surgery and all I got was this lousy t-shirt". This is also a very funny shirt and I do enjoy wearing it often. I picked two others up online and they say "Brain surgery, it's not rocket science" The lettering is a bit blurry, most likely on purpose, as that is certainly what my eyes saw for quite awhile. I write more details in the journal section of this book. I had mixed feelings at one time over the shirts. I don't so much anymore. There was a risk, at least in my mind, of labeling yourself, perhaps subconsciously, as a victim (or in my case, a survivor) and taking a chance that you could get stuck at a certain level of recovery. The suggestion of seeing yourself as a "brain surgery survivor" and possibly not getting fully beyond that level has always been on my mind. I discussed this with my speech pathologist in Saginaw, Anita, and in her opinion, I should continue to wear them now and then as a symbol of being proud of what I have endured. She made sense and at this date I still will wear them occasionally. I am most fortunate and what she said about being proud struck a note with me.

Local Laundromats

As I got more control my balance and awareness slowly began to return. When I became more stable I went to some local laundromats for some real world therapy. I wanted to experience what it was like to simply be a customer and not an owner anymore. It is another of those ironies I mentioned. I was and am still amused to be on the other side of the fence, as they say. It also helps my Mom who faithfully did my clothes while I could not. I started visiting the small laundromat in Auburn [Auburn Cleaners & Laundromat], a little town close to my Mom. I believe a married couple run it. The wife was working the laundry that day. In my very first visit I was a bit of a talker, mainly because I used to be an owner and I have so many experiences to share. I still slurred my words but they were trying hard to come out that day and people do say they understand me better now, so I blabbed my life story to this lady. She patiently listened to my story as she continued to do her work. I don't know how much she believed. It is a rather unbelievable tale. I did my laundry there without problems, however I was a bit unstable. It was in the winter of 2013. I remember looking out the window and seeing snow flurries as I waited. I naturally wondered how the business made ends meet. To me it looks like all local laundries here have dry cleaning services, so that is probably how they pay the bills. I did not ask the owner. On that first visit I was playing a pinball game to kill time and also to give them some business. Of all things, the ball got stuck in the game. I had flashbacks of when I had to try to fix my own games in Tennessee. I was very far away from the pinball company in Chattanooga, some 40 miles. Like everything in Benton, I learned to fix things the best I could in an emergency. I think on my third visit to the laundry in Auburn I had a coin problem with a washer and I had to get the owner for help. Another ironic moment indeed. She did her best to fix it but I had to use another machine. I was too embarrassed to go back there again so I started using the laundromat in Midland on Waldo Street, maybe a couple of miles from my Mom's place. I think the name of the Midland laundromat is "Totally Clean". They also do dry cleaning and special washes. I get better every time I go there. I went there this morning as I write this and I was much more stable, able to walk all around and do my wash much easier. I have probably been there about four times as of this writing, all without a cane. They have a golf video game that I naturally enjoy playing. Today I was able to wash my bed comforters. They had not been done since I got here in 2011. Obviously I used to do them often in Tennessee since I owned my own laundromat. It's fun to just be a customer now, with a lot less worries. It is very strange how life is working out for me now. It's hard to predict what's around the next corner. Right now my mission is to just get better and to take the days one at a time.

Baseball Games

As part of my "therapy" I ventured to a couple of minor league baseball games here in Midland in 2012. Dave had not come back to Michigan at that time, else I would have asked him to go with me. I remember my first game very clearly. I had a cane then and I was very unsteady. I was recovering from my eye patch. I got to the new stadium for the "Loons", a local Dodger organization, I believe Class A. It was ironic because in Chattanooga they also had a Dodgers minor league team (Class AAA). I saw many games there, alone and with some friends. They were the "Lookouts", named after the nearby Lookout Mountain. I really enjoyed those Tennessee games so naturally I wanted to see how well I would do at the local "Loons" games. I wore a "brain" shirt at one of the games. I think I went to three games that year. I recall that my right leg started hurting badly that year (it was the year that I first noticed this) at the games. The leg was painful, as it was in the late evenings, or at least my awareness of the pain was there more than now. I had to lift my right leg up and down in the seats to put up with the pain during the games. Naturally that took away from the enjoyment of the game but I was also just happy to be there and to just be able to see baseball games again. Here is a funny story about the stadium entrance. My mind was better but still not fully back to normal yet. Many might say this is still the case. I was waiting at an entrance at one end of the stadium in line with all of the people and I wandered down to the other end of the stadium out of curiosity. In my mind why would there not be another way into the park. There was more than one entrance in Chattanooga. I made it to the other end of the stadium which was pretty neat with a cane. I remember walking into the stadium at that new entrance and noticed that no one was there to take tickets. That should have been a clue, but I saw the stairs inside and I was so curious that I hugged the rail and worked my way slowly up the stairs. It was like scaling Mt. Everest. I was pretty proud of my achievement, even if no one was there to witness it. I made it to the second floor of the stadium and was surprised when I found that the doors to the stadium seats were locked, again with no one around. Well I knew then that there was only one open entrance. I later read that attendance was down that year so they probably let some staff go and only had the one entrance available. I at least was able to make it up those imposing stairs so that was excellent therapy in itself. Even when I went into the park at the only open entrance I used the stairs and hugged the rail. There was an elevator but I think I am still alive in order to get better, so I pushed the limit, something I continue to do to this day. Several people went around me as they were impatient to get in but I didn't care about it. I was making progress and building up my confidence by just being there.

VA Medicine

I had the sense, thankfully, to see the weakness in a large organization like the VA with apparently no overall guidance on persons in transfer, particularly in checking their prescribed medications. Without me and my family questioning the drugs I was prescribed by the VA, some of those drugs I would still be taking here in Michigan. I was given anti-depression ("happy" pills) in case I needed them, which luckily I did not. I was given laxatives because of the troubles I had near surgery in Vanderbilt. I was able to shake them in the VA in Tennessee thanks to my family's intervention. I was given seizure medication routinely because of brain surgery and because of the one incident in the VA in TN when I was transported very roughly just after surgery, bounced around in the ambulance, and then I had the one seizure, so seizure medicine was "stuck" on my medication list. I document how I very slowly weaned myself from these drugs elsewhere in this introduction and in my journal. These and other medicines, although maybe important at the time, were, as I say, stuck to my record, without a physician going over them and saying he still needs this or that one (at least to my knowledge). I stayed on those medications a long time but I could see that they had followed me up to Michigan and many no longer served a purpose. When I did phase them out it was over a very long time and I was able to note any changes this caused. I probably took about six months to very slowly wean myself from those drugs. I am happy to say that I have not taken VA medications for over a year now. I still take a baby aspirin but that is my choice. I talked about my medications with my neurosurgeons and my health care provider and found out that the seizure drugs are routinely given to brain surgery patients for about six months following surgery and then they are usually phased out. I knew I was on solid ground. I knew and had faith in my body but I also followed my doctor's advice also. I still take a relaxant, GABA 750, in the evenings. I took that medication in Tennessee. Those drugs, combined with a sleep aid at night, help me to sleep despite the loud tinnitus that I currently have. The rest of the drugs I take are vitamins and supplements that I have taken many times prior to surgery. I may eventually phase them out and maybe just take a multiple vitamin and a baby aspirin. So I am a great believer in technology and the marvels that it can do, when it is the right course of action, but I also am a believer in the body's ability to recover and to self heal, with the help of supplements and a positive attitude. I think I am a walking example of how positive belief has it's place in recovery.

Casino Trip

Mom, Dave and I went to a casino in Standish, Michigan in 2013. I believe this was our second trip up there. We were also there in 2012. That first year we stopped at a gift shop on the way in Pinconning and I believe I had a cane or walker. I remember having a hard time getting around the store. The store floor is not quite level and it is wooden. They sold the famous Pinconning cheeses and Dave bought some both times we visited. This last time I was much better with stability, not using a cane but having to hold on to things for support now and then. On the trip there I could only look out one side of the car easily. I could see the other side but had to limit my head movements back and forth as my brain was just re-learning that trick. I still have some disorientation and a slight offset of eye images but not as bad as that earlier time. I also could not talk as well as I do now so I did not say much and limited my head movements in the car. I rode in the back so that Mom could hear Dave better. I did not want to be rude but I was just trying to adjust to my brain limitations. I remember seeing many seniors there at the casino, many with oxygen tanks, walkers, and canes. What struck me was that they all looked so serious. They were probably determined to win back their Social Security checks. The smell of cigarettes and smoke was everywhere, but we had fun. Mom and Dave like the video poker games. I do also but I like the ones that continue to go on their own if you win. I am not into betting as much as some people there, but I will admit it is entertaining. I am thankful that I am able to get around without a cane at places like this. I am also grateful that I have enough sense to walk away after I am done with the "entertainment". I would enjoy going back again sometime. I bring a certain amount of money to gamble with and when it's gone, it's time to head back.

Painfully Slow Recovery

Dr. Sills (Allen K.), my chief neurosurgeon in Tennessee, said it would probably be about two years for me to fully recover. That was not including the gamma knife operation which seemed to set me back for awhile. I have noticed that, despite my wishes, the pace of recovery is extremely slow with only small, daily increments of improvement. Sometimes I go back a bit, but overall it is in the right direction. I wish it were faster and I sometimes get impatient but it is headed in the right direction. The pace is very slow, especially in my vision, walking, and speech improvements. I have, fortunately, always been a positive and patient person. This has been the ultimate test of that patience.

Sloping Bedroom Ceiling

Where the ceiling meets the wall in my bedroom never was quite horizontal to me. It always rose up from lower left to upper right. The main reason for this image was my vision adjustments. I was seeing double images and they took a very long time to align. The second image would always rise from lower left to upper right, so I would never see a straight alignment of the ceiling to the wall. Day after day the improvements were very small so that now it is much better. Now when I have my reading glasses on in bed I still occasionally see this image but that is mostly because it is out of the range of these glasses. With my long distance glasses on, it is much improved. The image has become more horizontal of late (August 2013). The image was incorrect and I saw a rise in the ceiling for at least two very <u>slow</u> years.

"Quiet" Room

Before I started working on this book, I would often stop in the "quiet" room at the Dow Library and read magazines and newspapers. I would usually start out with the New York Times newspaper, then browse the New Yorker magazine and it's famous cartoons. I did this after my morning laps at the mall or outside in the park. I have to switch to my "Coke bottle" close-up glasses to read there (as I do everywhere). At one time in the library, I used my old eye patch to cover up my left eye in order to read. That was when I discovered that my left eye prescription was incorrect and that the left eye was always out of focus. Images in that "quiet" room also got sharper over time. I have just recently noticed the wall paintings and ceiling fans as I have a better ability to look upward. It has a very high ceiling and large glass windows. Outside is a Japanese garden which is beautiful with many lush trees. It is similar to my mother's back yard in the summer. I have also seen it in the winter with the snow flying. I have watched the seasons come and go there. It's a great room with a great view. Again I used to use a cane at the library but now I do not need one. I still (as of this writing) need to delay movement when I stand up (change my elevation) to give my brain time to adjust. I also need to hold onto the magazine racks or tables occasionally. This gets less and less necessary as time goes by. You can still tell something happened to me as I still have that "vacant" look. Fortunately, my brain is coming back, but very slowly. I enjoy libraries and I am very grateful to be able to keep up with happenings and the news. Just to be able to see and read again is a thrill. I often read entertainment magazines, computers (naturally), amateur radio, just about anything. It's all a treasure to me. I appreciate this more than you can imagine. Occasionally when tinnitus flares up, I have played my hypnosis mp3 in the "quiet" room and that always helps to reduce the head noise. I must (as of this writing) lift my right leg up and down occasionally, almost to force blood flow inside of it. This eases the constant pain in my right leg. Generally, as mentioned, that pain is much less than last year (2012). I have found that mental distraction helps with my right leg as it does with my tinnitus.

Michigan Reunion

I was able to attend the Chalker (my late grandmother Gertrude (Gertie) Rust's maiden name and family) reunion in August of 2012. I used a cane then as I was unstable and I also wore one of my "brain" shirts. It was nice to see my cousins again, Betty, Shirley, Nancy, and Mary(Lou). They were all older of course, like me, with full lives of children, divorces, and what have you. We all have a story. I am one of the lucky ones with time now to tell mine. It was held at a nice park near Corunna, Michigan, where my grandparents lived and where several of the Chalkers still do. We had an auction with my brother Tom as MC. Mary (we used to call her Mary Lou) helped Tom with the auction as did my other cousins. I bid and won a couple of Tennessee lamps and a golf wall hanging. We had a lot of fun. I was able to mumble my way through with my heavy slur but of course I am much better as of this writing. I look forward to the 2013 reunion which I will attend on August of this year in Corunna, this time with no cane. Mom was with me in 2012 and I remember looking out across the park as we sat on a bench. I thought we were looking at headstones or graves. I guess they were some kind of drying platform for some lawn game, a little like "Hacky-Sack (Footbag)". I guess back then I was still working on vision and basic recognition. We both had a good laugh as we walked out to investigate. I thought that maybe it was a park patron's grave site. It was a another beautiful sunny day and I thought how odd that I was physically there and not back in Tennessee killing myself on my job and how odd that someone would want to be buried at a park.

Dow Coffee

My improvements allowed me to visit the "Cup and Chaucer", a small coffee shop inside the Dow Library in Midland. It is the coffee shop with the clever name. Being inside the library, it is a great place for more therapy, as I am there usually every day. I read magazines and newspapers or work on my journal at the library after my walking. I usually take a coffee break around 10:30 or 11:00 am. Every time I go there my vision improves as does my speech. It is a good place to practice on my swallowing ability, especially with the hot coffee that they serve. I went there a few times using a cane as I needed one for stability. Now I am able to go without one but I still need to watch my step. I am still a bit unsteady but the images there continue to improve as does my walking. Many times I have worn one of my "brain" shirts so that the staff and patrons have an idea of what happened to me, but they probably don't know it happened twice. I remember looking at the backs of books near the vending machines as I drank my coffee. These got clearer on each visit even while wearing my long distance glasses. The coffee shop hires several "disabled" people to work there. I think that also attracts me to the place. I still must sip my coffee slowly as I work on my swallowing. At least one time I choked on the coffee and it exploded out of my mouth and all over the table. Fortunately, I don't think anyone saw that. This has not happened much lately as I have gained more control over my swallowing. I go there so much that I guess I am a "regular" now as the servers get my porcelain cup out for me when they see me coming. I usually have only a small cup of house coffee but sometimes if hungry I will buy a chocolate chip cookie. I try to drop change into their tip cup there when I can. I think they all do a terrific job with the shop.

Gamma Knife

I have been getting a routine MRI in Ann Arbor every three (now four) months. The first MRI I got in Michigan was at the John Dingle VA in Detroit. Sandra, my sister, drove me to the first two, the first one in Detroit and second one in Ann Arbor. Dave, my brother, drove me to another one in Ann Arbor but since then I have been able to go there on my own. I have driven to Ann Arbor at least four times as of this date in the summer of 2013. The neurologists there are looking for any missed tumors that might start to regrow which is common in my type of operation. As I talk about in my story, a remnant tumor was found in the spring of 2012. By summer it had rapidly grown and I was a candidate for the gamma knife operation to kill the tumor's DNA. This, though as in any brain operation, was risky but I did not want to go through another terrible round of headaches and vomiting and even another possible brain surgery a few years down the road. I was ready to take another chance and was very grateful for the opportunity. High beams of gamma radiation are directed at the tumor remnant. Where they intersect, the DNA of the tumor is damaged but if there is no intersection there is no harm. It was recommended by Dr. Copeland, chief neurologist and head of the gamma knife department at the MidMichigan Medical Center here in Midland. I understand there are only two of these locations in the whole state. Again I am in the right place at the right time. He said he would urge me to have it done if I were a member of his family. I chose to undergo the procedure. I had a helmet bolted into my skull with four screws so that I could not move during the operation. It took place inside a large machine similar to an MRI. I was awake during the whole procedure. After the surgery I had four red screw marks on my head for several weeks. I felt no pain as they anesthetized the skin first. I knew that this was part of the procedure. I had the operation on July 25, 2012. I had my first year anniversary just recently. I felt no immediate effects but there was a delayed reaction in that I lost a bit of stability that I was gaining from my first operation. I went back to walking with a cane. I felt more secure with it. My speech and swallowing also seemed to slip back some. I think I have now recovered from most of that second operation as it has been a year now, though it does not seem that long ago. The tumor remnant was just under the limit of 3 cm so it was caught just in time and the VA approved the operation, thankfully. Dennis, the technician there, knows Mom from church and also my sister Sandra. Mom and I were there to get an explanation of the procedure from Dr. Copeland a few days before I had the operation. Sandra drove me there on the day of the procedure and stayed in the waiting room. We had a secret code of "Roosevelt School" that I was to say afterward if all went well.

We both went there as kids (in Owosso, Michigan). One never knows what will happen and when I came out I joked with her, "Roosevelt School, just down the road from Chestnut Street where we used to live..." I kept rattling on and when I mentioned the ball field where we played catch as kids she knew I had made it through and was just continuing on to be a "smart mouth". Sandra said she watched me in the machine on a TV screen that they had for guests in the waiting room and thought that I died or had burned up in there, I was so still. Well I told her, they purposely bolt you in there so you can't move if you wanted to. You don't want to move when those beams of radiation are blasting at your brain. Anyway I am not a vegetable so that is always a good thing! Results of an Ann Arbor MRI 3 months later confirmed that they had indeed killed the remnant tumor's DNA and nothing has grown back in any MRI that I have had since then. Years from now there won't be a regrowth of that large tumor remnant, causing all that grief again and me possibly needing another operation, so I am most thankful for that! My brother Bob was able to stop by that day to check in on me. I appreciated that very much. None of the physical symptoms had taken effect yet and I thought I was home free. They showed up a few weeks later as I report in my journal entries.

Lake Michigan Shore

On our trips with Dave and his Ford Explorer in 2012 we made it to Lake Michigan, near Grand Rapids. I was not that stable at the time and I had my cane with me. Mom, who had open heart surgery a few years ago and is 80, still has a hard time walking and decided to stay in the car when we got to the park. She missed a fantastic view of Lake Michigan and the shoreline. Dave and I had to walk about a half mile to get to the shore. We offered to wheel Mom down there but she wanted to stay in the car so Dave and I walked to the shore. There was a nice gazebo there and I remember sand was everywhere. I remember it being very breezy and back then it was hard for me to keep my balance in the wind. Dave and I walked down to the shore through the lush park entrance. I was happy to see it and to be able to go there. Dave, as usual, had great patience with me as I walked around, mostly fighting the wind. It was a challenge on the shore as it seemed like I was fighting both high wind and deep sand dunes but I kept my balance. I wonder how I would do there today without a cane. I did not have the balance and control that I now have. Someday we may return to see how I do.

Midland Symphony

I used to travel to Chattanooga from Benton to attend symphony concerts. I also had opera season tickets a few times. I really like classical music and symphonies so naturally I was glad to hear that they had a symphony in Midland. It was a real opportunity for me to get some "real world" therapy and to enjoy some concerts. As it was a 40 mile drive to those concerts in Tennessee and they let out at about 10 pm, it was a long drive back home to Benton. It was usually on a Friday or Saturday night. I had to get back to go to work the next day. No weekend getaway for me back then. The symphonies in Midland would only be a few miles down the road. I naturally bought a season ticket. I could drive then (2012) so I took advantage of it. I used a cane at first. I remember snow blowing when I left one night (also around 10 pm) and slowly walked across the parking lot to the car. I really took my time leaving that night for safety. It was a wet and slushy snow. Several times later I went without a cane but I had to hold on to railings and walls for balance inside the building at first. I got better the more times I attended. For the symphony here (as well as in Chattanooga) I would "dude it up" or wear a sport coat (I used to wear a suit in Tennessee) and tie. Mom took some photos of me before I went out to the concerts. It was a pretty big deal for me and gave me a great feeling of independence. As mentioned, I would walk slowly across the parking lot and sometimes hug the walls inside for stability. The symphonies were great fun and therapy but to me they were always not quite loud enough. I realize now that my head was still muffled and felt like it was full of "cotton", probably by design as it shielded me from most of the tinnitus, which had just started to make itself known, but mostly in quiet times and mornings, fortunately. I never heard tinnitus at the concerts. I always thought that the acoustics in the symphony hall were not that good (compared to Chattanooga) but most likely it was my head and brain. I did not experience tinnitus fully until after the concert season ended in the spring of 2013. I always gained confidence in getting across busy parking lots to and from the symphony. Each time I would try to park farther away to test my walking abilities. I was quite unsteady then, much worse then now, but my driving has always been safe since the summer of 2012 when my vision improved. While sitting inside the auditorium, the stage would not be fully in focus. I could make it out and each musician but there was that constant gap between vision and the brain, the "brain lock" or delay that I have written about in my daily journal. I would usually wait until most people left the concert so that I could work my way out, holding on to seats, walls, railings, whatever was available to give me more support. My first time there I came in a bit late and wondered if I could get to my seat. I had good seats but they were towards the center of the auditorium and I had to go down one or two steps in elevation to get to my seat, a big deal back then. I just kept hoping that I would not fall into anyone's lap. After that time I would go early so that I could get to my seat without stepping over everyone. The last symphony was in April 2013 and I found a better place to park which was near the Dow Gardens next to the symphony hall. There was an easy exit there to the main highway, making it easier to avoid all the traffic jams when everyone left at the same time. The only problem was that it required that I walk a long sidewalk to the theater. That sidewalk was uneven, and I probably looked like I had one too many, but I managed to make it to the theater safely and to enjoy the show. I had learned to ignore most of the looks and stares by then.

SSDI Success

I was fortunate that the brain surgeries were later in life after I had made a career, ran a business, and could better handle a loss of both business and home. I was "forced" to retire, as mentioned, and I was fortunate that this was easier for me at my age than for a younger person. I will admit that retirement takes some mental adjustments but I am getting used to it now. Sometimes I feel a bit guilty when I see others still struggling to make a living, but then I think of all that I went through to get to this point. You could say that I did my time and now I must adjust and try to make the most of this new phase of life. Even though I lost it all, so to speak, I was able to get SSDI (Social Security Disability Insurance) on the first attempt back in 2012, most likely due to the severity of my surgery. I am very grateful for that. It is not a fortune but I can live off of it comfortably (it being my own money anyway) and not have to worry about employment anymore. I did lose my many debts as well as business, cabin, and home so I suppose you could say I had a default bankruptcy. I was dumb and paid some Tennessee bankruptcy lawyers in advance and then left the state. I guess I was being cautious and trying to do everything legally and because I really did not know what was around the corner. I tried to do the right thing but unfortunately there are unscrupulous people out there. It will all balance out in the end. I battled the IRS for months in 2012, particularly over business forms and taxes. Then again, it was amazing that I could even do this so soon after surgery. Finally the IRS made the decision that there is no more need for me to file business returns and that I am now just a "regular" citizen trying to get by on disability.

Michigan Fall Trips

As it is now 2013, I don't remember all of the details of these trips. One was in the fall of 2012. We took many pictures. Fall leaves and beautiful fall colors were everywhere. It was all so beautiful. We were in Dave's Ford Explorer at the time. It rode rough. I aggravated my bottom and felt it later. I had to use a circular air tube that Sandra got me for awhile, but part of that was my bum leg and bottom getting hot after sitting too long. It still does that but I can now sit longer and go without the tube. It used to really be tough to sit more than 5 minutes. My mall breaks after each lap were short by necessity because my bottom got so hot. The trip pictures show me with a walker on one trip. I used one at the Lumberman's Monument. On that trip Dave took us along the Au Sable River and the city of Tawas along Lake Huron. It was a fun trip with fantastic views. I was rapidly improving to use a cane, which may sound strange now, and I used one on a trip to Frankfort, the Sleeping Bear Dunes, Empire, and other areas where we used to vacation in the northwestern part of the state. We went to the pier in Frankfort where we went as kids years ago during family vacations. Mom took photos of Dave and I walking out to the lighthouse on the long pier. Mom sat on a bench watching us. I was getting better but still unstable so we only went halfway out to the lighthouse. We took some great photos from the pier. I was glad that I was brave enough to try the pier walk.

More Michigan "memories"...

Some of the following Michigan memories are about events that happened in 2013 as well as 2012. I begin speech therapy sessions at the Saginaw VA, I drove many more places, and did much more therapy in the "real world" that year...

Talking To Strangers

After the ordeal I have been through, I find that I seem to have a more outgoing personality than before. I guess I am less afraid of what others may think now. I am not as shy as before, probably because I have endured so much that it has given me a new perspective on life. I saw this when I had to talk with the Saginaw VA on the phone about speech therapy. I had just arrived in Michigan in 2011 and my talking was still difficult but I fortunately had the presence of mind to know what was going on around me. I was told that the only way I could get speech therapy back then was to check in as a patient at the VA hospital in Saginaw. I immediately barked on the phone, "No way!" am I checking into a hospital again. I had been down that road and I would not do that again. I wondered where did that come from? Was that me? I think the girl on the phone got the point, however. I first noticed this new side of me upon coming "alive" in the TN VA rehab. I had all I could do to keep this in me so that I could get out of the place. I noticed it when I arrived in Michigan and was talking with strangers more. As I discuss in my daily journal, it's sometimes as if the "throttle" has been removed or opened up a bit more. As my story is pretty remarkable, naturally I want to share it with others, including strangers. I find some people are interested, some not so. I am learning that it depends on whether they are busy or not. I am learning when to stop talking and not to overdue it or to interfere with others. At first I just kept talking. Now I realize not everyone has the time to listen, except maybe my speech pathologist, Anita, whose job it is to listen and evaluate. I sometimes am up early due to habit or tinnitus or both. I sometimes go to the Burger King near the Midland Mall before I walk and get a coffee and sometimes I talk with the "kids" working there. I now know that they are busy, especially with the morning rush hour with people on their way to work. I used to talk with the girl on the headset until I realized she is busy chatting to people driving through and taking new orders. Not everyone has the time luxury that I currently do. I was much more forward with the clerks at Walmart or Meijer (Meijer is a large local department store similar to Walmart with groceries and other comparable items) when I first got to Michigan. I would tell them what happened to me. They were polite and some enjoyed listening and were amazed, considering my great progress. Others would listen but they were busy. I began to learn when to "move along". As I wrote about in my journal, I did meet a nice young lady, a first grade teacher off for the summer. I met her going into the Barnes and Noble store in Saginaw on my gamma knife anniversary. I enjoy browsing the books there and sometimes I stop for a Starbucks coffee. Her sister also had two brain operations, but the gamma knife first and then the craniotomy. It was an interesting story and she patiently listened to mine, as best as I could get it out. Her sister is making progress but has some remaining mental problems. I bring the teacher to mind as I was forward enough to buy her a coffee, something I would be too shy to do in my former life. For more details of this encounter, see the daily journal. It was exactly on the date of the one year anniversary of my 2nd brain operation (gamma knife here in Michigan), July 25, 2013. I have stopped while walking to talk with some people lately in the mall. I have talked with the clerks at the optical shop. Lately I do sense a partial return to a quieter personality as I get more into "the world". I find I am sometimes hesitant to tell my tale as it is still difficult to talk. I am, however, doing what my speech pathologist recommends, talking more with strangers.

Right Leg

I was not aware of a right leg problem until I started to "thaw" out in Michigan. This problem was not know in Tennessee due to the surgery numbness. My tinnitus was a similar situation. In 2012, one day it became obvious to me that I had a bad pain in my right leg. It was very hard to sleep at first, the pain was so intense. Fortunately I endured and now in this year (2013) it is much better. I had always had a problem growing hair on the lower portion of my right leg and at first I thought that the pain was from a return of full circulation to that leg after the tumor was removed. It still could be a factor but as of this writing, I feel that it may be related to having the tumor "embolized" in a first surgery at Vanderbilt to reduce blood supply before the main operation. The embolization was a separate operation and I was put under anesthesia and I believe they fished a line or device up my right leg and into my brain tumor. I wonder now if my leg might have been damaged or that this is just a long healing process. The pain always gets better when I put my leg in a horizontal position and keep it warm, as in bed at night. If I sit in a recliner and lift the leg it also reduces the pain. Many times after a meal I will have to get up and sit on a recliner. I cannot sit around the table for long periods of time. This is in an effort to address the leg pain and not just rudeness on my part. The leg is continually numb and painful. Even today I must lift the right leg every lap at the malls onto a chair. I must do this at Mom's place, especially when eating at her table, and sort of self-circulate blood flow into the leg to make it more comfortable. It is a lingering symptom and one not well know by many. The good news, as I have mentioned and talk about in my daily journal, is that it slowly improves and compared to 2012 when it really bothered me, this year it is much better. My leg is much more comfortable in the cool pool water, as I noticed this summer.

Small Water Bottle

Occasionally saliva builds up in my mouth without me knowing it and it can choke me if it goes straight down my throat. This is something a "normal" brain could handle and probably does so without our knowledge. This problem occurred, or my awareness of it, early in 2013. It, like all of my symptoms, has not been as frequent or as severe lately. I carried a bottle of water with me from sometime in 2012 until the summer of 2013 just for such a problem. The water would be used to stop the coughing or choking spells that naturally followed. I no longer need to carry this bottle except on a long hike or somewhere without water. In 2013, I still get this on occasion, but I have much more control and will not panic if I swallow or spit it out. I have more swallow control because I try to be "in the moment" with my swallowing. I mention this often in my journal, as it has been a method to survive eating and swallowing problems. It has helped to save me from choking episodes. By this I mean that I have to pay attention to every swallow or bite. It does slow down my time at a meal, as I cannot talk and eat or drink at the same time like so many others can. I'm sure this will fade away in time.

VA Ann Arbor MRI Scans

Initially, as mentioned, I rode with my sister Sandra to the John Dingle VA in Detroit for my first Michigan MRI. She then went with me to Ann Arbor. My brother Dave went once to Ann Arbor for one of my MRI appointments. Now all the MRI and follow-up appointments are in Ann Arbor and I drive there myself, as I have previously mentioned. It is a bit over 100 miles one way. My next one, as I write this, is November 4th, 2013. I recovered well enough, as I have mentioned, to drive in the summer of 2012, so I have been to Ann Arbor on my own about four times now for the independence and therapy and it is easier for me to go early as I am usually up at that time anyway. At first I used a cane to walk from the car to my VA appointments in Ann Arbor but now I walk there without a cane. I remember one trip to Ann Arbor in the icy winter with much rain and snow on the roads. In recent visits, I have walked without a cane to the third floor for my MRI and then to an exterior room for my UM (University of Michigan) neurology follow-ups. Each time my abilities are better. My speech improvement helps me communicate better with the doctors. As of my last visit in July, the doctor said I looked healthy and fit. I certainly have more "presence" there. All recent MRI results have been good. They have been watching an area "of interest" but it has not shown any evidence of regrowth as did the remnant tumor they found back in 2012, which led to my second operation. Traffic always is busy around Ann Arbor but I am very much used to it by now. A couple of times I have used I-94 which is a major expressway between Detroit and Chicago. I have used M-52 on occasion and have stopped by the Owosso Public Library on my way back to Midland, still at the same building that I used to hang out on the weekends about 50 years ago. I noticed many computers hooked to the Internet. I wish I had that back then.

Saginaw VA Speech Therapy

After mentioning speech problems, Dr. Orringer (my current neurologist at UM, Ann Arbor) helped get me some additional speech therapy. I had a speech lab in Ann Arbor first and then the VA there set me up for regular sessions in Saginaw. I now see a speech pathologist at the Saginaw VA, my friend Anita Wierda. I currently meet with Anita once a month but it was more frequent a short time ago. I have made rapid progress in this area. The speech is still difficult for me but it does not seem to be as forced as before. It used to take a tremendous amount of energy to get the words out. It has been like that since the surgeries and into the middle of 2013. It feels like the words slowly come up almost into my throat, to where they are just inside my mouth before I can get them out. Now they "escape" much better but to me they are still very slurred and far from normal. Others say how much my speech has improved and I do seem to be much more aware when I am talking with Anita at each appointment. Everyone seems to understand me better. Early in our sessions she gave me cognition tests that were very simple. Now there was a time in Tennessee when they might have been difficult, but Anita had no way to know this and was just doing her job. For example, there were pictures of cats and dogs, then writings of the words, "cat" and "dog", and I would have to match the pictures to the words. It was very simple, of course, but she did not know that and I went along with her examination. I think she knows that my speech difficulty is a physical problem and certainly not a mental one at this stage. When I meet with Anita I have an urge to just let the stories come out, I have so many experiences. I tend to just sit there and blab my life history or at least the last two years of it. Anita is an excellent listener and I make her work easier. She always says I need to talk more so I do. She is probably the one person, besides myself of course, who knows most of these stories in my introduction before she reads them here. Each time she evaluates my progress. I have learned a bit of her history as well, as it makes for better conversation, and as I always tell her, having undergone these events has made me much more sensitive to life stories and I realize that each of us has so many interesting life experiences. I find I have much more interest in what others have experienced. I don't have to pretend to be interested. I am! When I go to the Saginaw VA I go down the expressways (US-10, I-75, and I-675) and that is no problem for me. Once this winter, I went there and came back during a nasty snowstorm. Again, I am always amazed and grateful that I still have my driving skills. I have used a cane when I was unstable at first in my visits. Now I am better and go without a cane. My skills continue to improve and I am able to walk up the hill to a temporary entrance there. They have the main entrance closed for construction. My vision and awareness, as everywhere, always seems to improve at each visit. Anita is seeing more and more of the real me slowly coming out. I am happy and grateful to be making regular progress.

Saginaw Fashion Square Mall

As I have speech appointments at the Saginaw VA, I am in the area of the mall in Saginaw at least once a month or every other month now. I often just go there anyway to walk the mall or shop or go to the large bookstore nearby. I get out of the VA around 9 am so I usually go walking at the Fashion Square Mall on Bay Road in Saginaw after my appointment. That mall is slightly larger than the Midland Mall and I will go there for variety sometimes. They have a nice large food court. I usually start my walk there. I have used a cane before but now I walk unassisted, however I am still slow. I no longer touch walls or stores for balance (except occasionally). I usually just stop in stride without too much loss of balance. For variety I have often headed over to that mall first, even without a speech appointment, as I have mentioned. I like to visit the large Barnes and Noble bookstore in Saginaw. I still rest after each mall lap to raise my leg for comfort. Many times, as in the local Midland Mall, I will play mp3s as I walk. They have almost the same stores and displays as the local mall here in Midland. I also wear a "brain" shirt now and then. I notice a few looks there as in the other mall. I usually only walk four laps or until I am tired so that I can shop or visit Starbucks at the Barnes and Noble and then browse the new books. There also is a large Michaels craft store near the bookstore. I have looked around that store now and then.

Saginaw Branch Library

I found a small branch library in Saginaw on Center Road (the Zauel Library). I went there a few times to work on this journal. I read some of the "Life of PI" book there (after I saw the movie in Midland). They were open early at 9 am, earlier than the Auburn Public [Branch] Library (10 am), so I went there to work on this book one morning. I parked across the library in a school parking lot. A young guy was shooting baskets. I walked down the road and over a wooden bridge to the library. I used a cane at the time. They were having a used book sale that Saturday to support the library. They were busy setting it up inside. I did not go as I have so many books now that I need to read. I resisted the urge to get new ones. The library was a nice place to work and I may go there again to write or read.

Saginaw Barnes and Noble

The Barnes and Noble Saginaw bookstore is larger than the Midland Mall store with more selection and it is more fun to browse. I enjoy having a Starbucks coffee there at their coffee shop inside the store. I then will browse the latest books. Every time I go there my vision improves. Now I can read covers with my long distance glasses on so I rarely take both pair in with me. I no longer use a cane in the store. I first raised up my body on the balls of my feet in that store (woohoo!). Again I include details in my journal. I bought two Seth (Jane Roberts) books there for my collection. Mine were getting worn out. I had bought my original ones in the 70s. They are my favorite books and have gotten me through some tough times. I have great therapy at this bookstore and it is enjoyable for me to visit. I have talked a bit about my brain operations to the coffee servers there. I often wear a "brain" shirt there and as always they get looks and sometimes help start conversations (one caught that teacher's eye on July 25th). I have had my favorite latte or mocha coffee there. One day I ate a cookie with the coffee. I have to sip slowly and use caution as the coffee is usually hot. I always see a few looks from the patrons and staff there, especially when I wear a "brain" shirt or have stability issues.

More Store Selection

Being over in Saginaw for speech therapy at the VA or to visit Barnes and Noble, I go to the Meijer and Walmart stores once in awhile. They are larger and have a bigger selection. I bought a pair of clip-on sunglasses at Walmart recently as the local store in Midland did not have my size. Meijer is across from the bookstore on Tittabawassee Road. Walmart is on Bay Road, north of the Fashion Square Mall. There is very busy traffic all around but I am quite used to that and fortunately have the same driving skills that I had before all of this happened.

Saginaw VA Neurologist

It took the VA system a long time but they finally set me up with a neurologist at the Saginaw VA. I finally got an appointment to see Dr. Janus. I did not even know that there was a "brain" person in Saginaw. Of course, that should have happened right away, but that's our government at work. I met with him and he talked with me about phasing out my medications. We both looked at my MRI scans and medical records in his office. He said normally a brain surgery patient is on seizure medication for six months after surgery and then it is phased out. I instinctively knew that I was on them for longer than I needed to be, as I wrote about in my journal, and he confirmed that. Dr. Orringer and Dr. Valdivia of UM, Ann Arbor, were and are still handling my case (or at least handled MRI scans and diagnosis). Dr. Janus was a bit of a comedian. The first words that he said to me stuck with me as not only funny but very deep. He said, "well are you crazy?" (very seriously). I said "I don't think so". Then he said "Would you know if you were?". I laughed out loud and we both cracked up. I knew that finally I might have been assigned someone decent. In our conversation, he said my records showed that I was "terminal". We both said that's probably why I had won SSDI on the first try. Again, we both laughed. Maybe that is also why my old creditors have not chased me down to Michigan. But again they just probably gave up due to the long time involved. I never knew if he was serious about my "terminal" status or was just clowning, but either way, obviously that status was wrong and we both had a good laugh over it. I found out later from my speech pathologist at the Saginaw VA that my neurologist was no longer working there. That was a real shame, as I liked him from the start. Maybe he had too much fun to be working at the VA or he found a better "gig". Hopefully, the latter.

Driving The Turnpike

I rode with Dave (in January 2013) to Cleveland, Ohio. He bought a Toyota Echo for his transport job and I drove his Ford Explorer back to Michigan following him. We took mostly the Ohio Turnpike on the way back. We took pit-stops in small towns off the main road. We stopped at a tow bar shop. I remember the heavy local traffic getting on and off the freeway. I remember it being late in the evening as we drove all over. As you can imagine, this gave me a great feeling of independence and a feeling that I would eventually be back to "normal".

Hacking Mom's Lawn

We had a warm period in the spring of 2013. I chipped around some golf balls on Mom's yard to see if I could. I had no problem but occasionally I had to lean on the clubs or stop for a rest. Dave set up a net and I aimed for it. I did pretty good and was happy to still have the skills to do that. I plan to try a local par-3 and driving range when I feel up to fully swinging a club. I would do that now but I am still unstable.

I see that problem when I swing a club (remote control) playing the Wii golf game on my TV in the living room. I have to grab a recliner now and then to regain my balance. I imagine myself there on a driving range or a golf course many a time so I am sure I will be able to do it again someday. I have always believed in the power of visualization. I have not played golf since Mom's yard but I frequently play it on my computer and once in awhile on the Wii, which burns up a lot of energy. I often play a video arcade golf game at the local Midland laundromat. Probably next year I will go to the par-3 course down the road from Mom and try it out. I hear they have a driving range also, so that will be a big breakthrough for me if I can manage it.

2013 Michigan Therapy Continues...

The following Michigan memories are of some recent events that occurred in 2013. Though most of my physical symptoms remain (as of this writing), they all seem to be slowly getting better. As I write this, next Monday, the 12th of August, 2013 will be the two year anniversary of the first brain operation in Vanderbilt. It's hard to believe that the time has gone by already. Dr. Sills, my chief neurosurgeon in Tennessee, says that this coming year (2014) should see a big turning point in my recovery. May his words ring true...

Tinnitus

Tinnitus, or the ringing in the ears and head, made itself known in late 2012 and early 2013. Fortunately it was quiet through the symphony season but it eventually got louder. It has probably always been there but the fact that I was so numb at the beginning blocked it from my awareness. Whether by design in surgery or just luck, it did not show in earnest until recently. My head felt like it was full of cotton before then and that helped to hide the sounds. Now that cotton seems to be fading, exposing the sounds. I certainly had enough to deal with before with my eyes, my walking, my leg pain, and my swallowing and speaking challenges so I am glad that this was not an issue back then.

Talk about taking things for granted. One of those "things" is the existence of silence. That is something I and almost everyone takes for granted. I miss it and do not have that opportunity right now. I miss being able to have a silent meditation, something I was able to do before the operations. I expect that I will have silence again eventually and I very much look forward to it. I purchased a hypnosis CD for the tinnitus. It talks you into visualizing a dial with the numbers 1-10 and to see your level of "unwanted sound" as one of those numbers. You then are suggested to see yourself reach for that dial and turn it slowly down to the number one when the noise is supposed to fade away. There is also the suggestion that your "awareness and perception" of the sounds will "fade away" and be gone "forever". I use it often on breaks or in the morning if I awake early and the noise gets too loud. I play it often in the car before I go walking. I find that it does help lower the sound level or at least lowers "my awareness" of it. Unfortunately, as of this writing, it has not totally "faded away" yet, but it is getting better. I know that there is no drug (as I have researched and asked my neurologists) that will "cure" tinnitus, but I broke down and bought the much advertised "Lipoflavonoid" product in a local store. This is essentially a vitamin supplement which won't hurt to take. It is expensive but I am willing to give it a try. One of the best ways I cope, and it has taken experience and a few incidents to show me this over these long months, is that, and it probably applies to other symptoms and to many things in life: it is the power of mental distraction. I have found that if I keep my mind or focus on other things, then I will not hear or think about the tinnitus as much. This was brought home one day when I spilled milk all over my Mom's kitchen floor bringing in some groceries. Fortunately I was getting better and could help her clean it up. But in that one moment of mental alertness to the milk spill, I did not hear head noises. I thought about this after and then the "light bulb" came on. I now play golf on the computer or Wii, I do puzzles, I swim, have a coffee in the mall, bookstore, or library, and even work on this book, all in an effort to distract my mind from the noises and I find that this almost always helps. Now there are times when the sound just naturally gets louder and that is usually in the afternoon and in the mornings when I am up early. I think it has to do with the quietness of the exterior environment so that I tend to hear my own head when it is quiet around me. The tinnitus sound is like a high tension line and a field of loud crickets all singing at once. On a rainy day or foggy morning, you may remember the buzzing of the electric systems and lines. It is similar to that sound and the crickets but much louder. Overall it has not gotten to be more than a 5 out of 10 in my mind but that can be loud enough. As I mentioned, the key seems to be in mental distraction. I find that as soon as I even think of the tinnitus, there it is. In fact, even at this time it is flaring up and seems very loud, mostly because I am writing and thinking about it.

Mental Distraction

As mentioned, some of the things that I do for mental distraction from tinnitus and other symptoms and because I enjoy them are: computer golf (Tiger Woods 2007), Wii golf (Tiger Woods 2010), puzzles, art, playing instruments, and of course playing on the computer, such as "surfing" the Internet or doing anything technical. I have much more balance and control now but at times I need to hang on to the recliner for support after I swing the remote control playing Wii golf. I do fairly well considering the circumstances. I think back to the time in Tennessee when I swung and spun around into a recliner. I do "puzzle therapy" for distraction. In 2012 and part of 2013 I worked on many puzzles. Many were 1000+ pieces and difficult even for a "normal" person. At last count I did about 40+ puzzles. I always take a photo of them when they are done and keep those in my scrapbook. As I talked about earlier, my mother helps me on occasion. If my occupational therapist back in Tennessee could see me now! I have come a long way from those ten piece puzzles that were so hard for my brain. Right now I am on a puzzle break while I work on this journal. I may resume doing puzzles again as they were fun and stimulating, and since I noticed I am not getting any younger, I may do them again for the mental stimulation. I know my Mom likes to help. I still have my art supplies that my brother and mother got me last Christmas. I may also do some of that "therapy" later on after this book is finished.

Bottle Returns

Michigan has a 10 cent bottle refund and has automatic recycling machines where you can return bottles for credit. Most stores that sell the bottles have these machines. I was aware of this in the 80s when I lived in Lansing, Michigan. I lived there for five years after my military service. I had a house and went to night school at Lansing Community College (LCC). Back then they had attendants and big bins at the recycle facilities. The people there would manually sort the bottles. Now it is all automated. I had not used these "new" machines before so I had to learn by doing. I did not know at first (due to vision limitations) that there was a separate machine for plastic and for glass bottles. At Walmart I had problems as those machines did not always recognize their own store brands. I switched to Meijer for bottle returns and have not had a problem since. Most returns are for beer as Dave and I (fortunately I can slowly sip beers again) drink quite a few towards the end of the day. There is a reason for that (besides the fun) which you will see in this introduction. Also Meijer has quite a large beer section. Like my brother Dave says, "so many beers, so little time".

In Their Own World

A big difference I have noticed since my operations is the explosion of mobile phones and handheld devices. They seem to be everywhere now and everyone, especially young people, have them. They are great tools but I have observed, and I notice everything much more now, that sometimes people seem to be lost in them. They are so busy using the devices to text, check email, or surf the Internet, that they are or they seem oblivious to the world around them. Now I texted also before all of this with my cell phone but I tried to stay connected to the world also. Here is an example of this. It happened while I was walking in the Midland Mall. I think it was a Saturday morning and the mall naturally draws in new people who are not regulars at that time. Those of us that walk the mall have a regular pattern of walking in a counter clockwise motion around the mall. This may be just habit but it keeps everyone from bumping into each other. I was near the Spencer's gift store and the Barnes and Noble bookstore when I looked up and noticed a young man, maybe in his 20s, buried in his cell phone, head down, and moving toward me quite fast. I was going counter clockwise as usual. He was headed towards me in the opposite direction. Usually those that use the phones will occasionally look up to get their bearings and to adjust to those around them. Not this guy. He was walking along fast and was lost, as I say, in his own world. I let him get very close, and then, and this is something I probably would not have done before the operations, I slammed my hands together in a clap, fast and loud, right in front of him as he was about to collide with me. I think I did it in self-defense partly but also in frustration that he had no clue to the world around him, or so it seemed. Maybe I was a bit jealous that he had all of his physical capabilities and seemed to take that for granted and I didn't, who knows? He was startled briefly and I yelled out, in my best slur, at the same time that I clapped hard, "Hey man! Wake up and watch where you're going!". I didn't swear at him. I just made a loud noise to get his attention. He mumbled something like, "Oh, sorry man ". At that point I really didn't care if he would fight me or what. I had no fear at that moment. It was fairly early before the mall opened at 10 am and there were local vendors setting up their booths for a craft show. One lady was nearby and she overheard and saw our confrontation. The young man kept walking and using his phone, I only disturbed his thought for a moment. I shook my head a bit in disbelief and the lady said to me, "Good for you! I'm glad you spoke up and got his attention". She said that's something we all should do. As I mentioned, I have less fear of any confrontation due to my experiences. I always think, what more can be done to me? My episode with the cell phone guy in the mall is just another of the many things I see daily that show me that most people are all wrapped up in their own world and in their own heads. I suppose I was back then as well. I am not necessarily saying that it's good or bad, it's just an observation that I see daily. It's not all young people either, as I see many older people early in the malls when I walk. They are into their own exercise plans, many with heads down, grinding out the laps, checking their times, and so on. I am in a unique position now and I bet that most people with any physical "disability" are in a similar position, in that as I improve, I can see what is happening in front of me much better than most. I have the "luxury" of time, no longer rushing to complete a load of laundry or make a delivery or pay a bill on time as so many still have to do. The great majority of people I meet, of course, have "perfect" brains, as I did before all of this happened. What I mean to say is that basic motor skills and brain functioning for most is a given (a no "brainer"). Most people can go to Starbucks, for example, buy a cup of coffee, carry it with them, drink it, even use their phone at the same time. Being that I can't quite handle multiple movements like that just yet, I see them and I think wow, do they even realize what they are doing? I know I took it for granted before. Again, to most people these are simple abilities, but to those of us just trying to get back to being able to do them again, they are quite complex.

Pierre Marquette

I followed the Pierre Marquette Trail by the Tittabawassee River, toward Clare from downtown Midland and discovered Emerson Park on a walk one day in 2013. I started by using a cane on the trail. I was quite unstable but it was a new area to walk and explore and it was a fun challenge. I ordered a hiking stick later that would look better than a cane and still give me some protection from dogs and animals. I walked to the park on the trail, then I would rest on a bench in the park, a total of about a mile to the bench. I had a backpack to carry books, writing items, even to carry the hiking stick which folds into sections. The bag contained its own water bottle. The backpack was a bit of an overkill but I looked like a hiker and not an invalid. I would walk around the Emerson Park sidewalk then back over the river on a walking bridge which also had a lane for cars. I would walk back toward the parking lot near the flea market area on another narrow sidewalk. I would walk to the car from the other side of the river (Tittabawassee) near the "skaters park", the Chippewassee Park, then back over the "Tridge" bridge into Midland again. It was about three miles in total. After I improved, I walked it without a stick or cane, both times carrying the stick and not using it. I stopped on the "Tridge" bridge on the way back one sunny day and just took it all in. I was at the center of the bridge facing downtown Midland. It was a gorgeous day and I soaked in the sun. I saw some girls on the center of the bridge that day with their cell phones out. They were texting and did not see me go by. I was even wearing one of my "brain" shirts but they, like so many others, were not that aware of the world they were in. I remember one nice Saturday looking down on the flea market there in the parking area from the bridge (coming back from my walk). As always I got a few looks when I wore a "brain" shirt but the majority of people are in their own world and do not pay that much attention to me. I wrote about this earlier. I saw a beautiful graffiti art mural under the overpass on the other side of the river on the way back. The park sidewalks and the trail have a slight slope at times. This was a bit tough for me at first but I rapidly adjusted to it. One day I took several photos of the walk and created a DVD photo tour of the whole trip so that Mom and Dave could see the walk and how beautiful it was. There were several nice homes on the trail, overlooking the river, high enough so as not to flood. There were many people jogging on the trail. There were several bicycles too. One day there were several school children out on a field trip on the trail and in the park. They came up from behind me and I let them go by. One day I wore my black beret on the hike. I later stopped going as it was getting hot in the summer and also it seemed to be a long way to drive for a walk. I later returned to the AC in the mall and it's flat floors. There was a lot of local flooding and ground water that I had to walk around on the hike. A few times there were people fishing or boating on the river. There were several portable toilets in the Emerson Park area. There were several ball fields and a nice volleyball area. There was a kid's playground and swing set areas at the parks (Emerson and Chippewassee). I remember a big power cable that was stretched across the river near the pedestrian walkway next to a small bridge. I could almost touch it. There was a nice big golf course on the right side as I walked back. The sidewalks narrowed on the way back to the "Tridge". They were challenging and great therapy. One Saturday morning there were several women's cancer awareness and support signs around the path. Apparently they were having a weekend run there later. We read in the local paper that a lady ran into a bear somewhere on that trail. I only found birds, rabbits, and small wildlife when I did that walk, thankfully.

"Waldo" Walk

Gas prices climbed to $4.27 a gallon in early summer of 2013 in Midland. They said there was a temporary distribution problem in the area but gas has always been higher in Midland than around the country so I suspect some price gouging was in effect too. I wondered why I drove 10 miles to the "Tridge" and Emerson Park to walk everyday so I decided to try a walk around the block from Mom's house. I measured the walk with her car's odometer. It was down Flajole to Patrick then south on Waldo to the McDonald's (past the little laundromat that I now use). I would take a break at McDonald's for a coffee or breakfast. That was about 2.5 miles there. I then headed to Midland Road (half was sidewalk) then back past the "Studio M" Plaza (they have a movie theater called "Studio M" there) and then past the local party store and storage place on Flajole. I would then walk past the railroad crossing then back to Mom's place. It was about 5 miles in total. I walk about 4 or more miles at the mall so this was not that much longer. I am used to walking, especially early in the morning, so I enjoyed this walk for awhile but then I ran into dogs. They were not chained up and their owners let them run free. A couple of dogs barked and charged at me but stopped short. I stood my ground and had my walking stick. The dogs and the heat, as it started to get hot about 11:00 am as I walked back over the US-10 overpass, made me stop doing the "Waldo" walk only after about two or three trips. Gas prices also started to drop so I decided to return to the Midland Mall where it is flat and they have the AC on during the summer. I have a rich history with the Midland Mall so I thought I might as well go back and recover there. As I say, I did use my walking stick that I ordered on Amazon for the "Waldo" walk. I also wore a black beret once and an older man in a truck stopped me on Patrick Road and asked me if I had "lost my sheep". I looked like a shepherd with the stick, beret, and backpack. He laughed and drove off. I was not quick enough to say "Ya, have you seen them?". I carried a backpack on that walk where I would store my stick when not using it at McDonald's. There was a sidewalk most of the way except at the beginning of Patrick and the last part of Midland Road, where I needed to walk on the road, but I would stop and step aside if cars came by. I stopped at the first bench on Patrick maybe a mile away from the start and read some of "Seth Speaks", a favorite book of mine by Jane Roberts. I then tried dictating into my little voice recorder (some of this journal) at the other bench on Patrick. I remember seeing an older man sitting outside his apartment. I waved and he waved back. This was just before I got to the Davenport University Library on Patrick. I turned south on Waldo and walked under Highway 10. There was a sidewalk under the overpass with long grass on each side. I walked past the laundromat and then would take my break at McDonald's. After the break I would reassemble the walking stick and head down to Midland Road. There was a nice sidewalk there until maybe the civic arena where they play hockey and teach skating. After there I had to cross the street and walk on the road against traffic. I came to the "Studio M" Plaza and the bowling alley there and took a break at a bench in the shade. There was a convention going on inside and they probably thought I was some bum going down the road. I resumed walking back over Highway 10, this time above the road. I remember looking down on the traffic rushing by. The walk was fun as I love to walk and it was usually a nice sunny day when I did it. But as mentioned, it got quite hot at the end of the walk so I went back to the mall for my walking therapy.

Less Shakin Goin On

My left hand had a tremble at times and the doctors said they expected that to occur because of the location of the large tumor and where it pressed up against my brain. I wrote about this when I spilled my coffee all over the BP station floor early that morning in Benton, Tennessee. It was one of the early signs of trouble. Most of the shaking went away in 2013 so that I could start to digitize this journal. I was finally able to type and control both hands. I could use the computer before but it was very slow and tedious, with many corrections. I used to be on Facebook and I would email people often but this was hard for me right after surgery. It is much easier using the computer now. I also got off Facebook last year because of seeing all my friends from Tennessee on it. That was very hard on me so I just stopped looking at their posts. I miss them all very much and it was hard for me to read about their lives and to know that I may never see them in this life again. One day I just decided to go away from Facebook totally. As many of you can imagine, that was a very difficult thing to do.

Hello Balance

In the early summer of 2013, just a few weeks ago as I type this, I made a great breakthrough. Balance and control, although there enough for me to walk, to drive, to do basic functions in 2012, started to really show up in 2013. It was a gradual change, nothing sudden or overnight. I saw it first when I got much better at going over curbs.

This is a bit silly to me now, and probably to my readers, but getting up and over a simple thing like a curb on a sidewalk was a major deal. My family remembers that I had to be helped many times at first to do this. Later I could do it alone and I did at my walks, but I was slow and deliberate. I probably looked very silly or ancient. I still need caution and can't "jump" over curbs but I do get over them much better. Now I can actually stop in mid-stride, something I could not do before, as hard as that is to imagine. This is very helpful if I start to lose my balance or tip. I just stop walking or moving and relax, stand there and rest. I then can go again when I am ready. I can even look at a mall window or display and no one would know that I am "resetting", so to speak. I found out that I can now stop and even back up to a small degree. As I mentioned, that first occurred one morning at Burger King. I can even stand on the balls of my feet and hold my balance. This I was able to do one day at the Barnes and Noble bookstore in Saginaw. It has all been a subtle change but it has allowed me to go swimming, to go to the stores with more confidence, to help my brother Dave hang blinds, all sorts of things that would have been nearly impossible for me just a few weeks ago.

Grave Sites

I took my mother to her parents and my grandparents' graves recently. It was Memorial Day, 2013. I placed a flower on my grandmother's grave. I put a small flag on my uncle's grave. I did not expect to be at my uncle's site and as there were several flags on my grandfather's site already, I saved this small flag for my Uncle Bob's grave. He, like my grandfather, was a veteran. I firmly believe that they are elsewhere doing other things but it was nice to visit and pay our respects. That was the first time I had been to either grave site. It was a sunny day and I went without a cane so I got some therapy in that day. I drove Mom over there to the sites in Owosso and near Lansing.

Mackinac Island Vacation

Dave drove his 4-door KIA and took Mom and I on a small vacation to Mackinac Island in 2013. It was very comfortable and it rode much smoother than his Ford Explorer. I rode in front and Mom rode in back. We talked about going to the island while swimming one day and the next thing you know we were there. We rented two cabins in St. Ignace just inside the UP (Upper Peninsula of Michigan). They were not busy at the cabins, despite it being the summer and a short rental notice. The property was for sale. The view was partly obstructed by a major highway but they were comfortable places to sleep. Dave and I shared one, Mom used the other one. We found a close-up area to view the Mackinac Bridge and went there late one night. Except for many bugs, we had great views of the bridge. Mom stayed in the car as she hates bugs. Dave and I got out and took quite a few photos. On the boat to the island the next day, we went under the Mackinac Bridge and the boat stopped so we could all get some great photos. Fantastic! The weather was ideal, sunny and in the 70s, light winds, and very low humidity. We did the tourist thing on the island. We walked around then took a carriage ride drawn by large horses. We visited the fort there. Going down the steep ramp from the fort to the town was a challenge as half way down we lost our railing at the fort. Dave escorted Mom across the park at the end of the fort while I held my own walking down the steep hill. I went without a cane as my balance and control were much better but I was still slow. We had raspberry shakes up on top of the fort overlooking the island and harbor. It was an unbelievable view and we took lots of photos. Kites were flying in the distance. We got some action shots of soldiers firing their weapons as in the 1800s at the fort on our way back to town. We bought fudge on the way back and some birthday cards for Sandra. It was a very full day. Before we went back to Midland the next day we went north to the Soo Locks in Suit St. Marie where we watched a large iron ore carrier go through the locks. We spent about two hours on the observation and viewing platform watching the ship go by.

Again we got some great photos. We talked Mom into climbing to this second floor observation deck and we all had a great view of the whole experience. We traveled along Whitefish Bay and Lake Superior toward the Tahquamenon Falls. On the way we stopped at the famous Whitefish Point Lighthouse. We got out for a break. Dave climbed to the top of the lighthouse for some photos while Mom and I sat on a bench in the back looking at Lake Superior and a large Canadian wind farm across the Lake. I remember being able to clearly see several white windmills and the distant rolling hills many miles away. When we stopped there was a lady dressed in 1920s clothing attending to some flowers on the lighthouse yard. She was in costume and she played a teacher for the visitors. She stopped us and was talking about the lighthouse and how her teaching wages were not as much as her male counterparts. Dave politely talked with her while we listened and then we moved along. I bring the story up as we later found out that Mom thought she was just a crazy lady who happened to be out there. That gave us all a good laugh. We later made it to the falls and ate at the pub there and drank some of their homemade beer. It used to be called Camp 33. We then took pictures of the falls. Mom and I both hiked about a half mile (no cane for me again) down a long path to see the falls. We both did pretty good but we needed frequent breaks. We went back to Midland over the Mackinac Bridge. On the way back we stopped at Trout Lake, a small town in the UP, and had some ice cream and ate it in their town park as it was warm and the ice cream started to melt. We drove back pretty tired from a full vacation and got back to Midland about 11:30 pm.

Well Bite My Lip

This symptom also made itself know in 2013. While eating, I would occasionally bite down on my lips or tongue, as if they were in the way. The brain was and still is learning to do the "simple" things once again. My brain is re-learning how to chew. This has improved but occasionally if I am not paying attention, I may bite down on my lips or the inside of the mouth. I use a napkin often and hold it near my mouth in order to try to catch this before it happens. Sometimes this works. If it does happen, as you can imagine, it is painful. It usually draws a bit of blood that would show up on the napkin that I use.

Mr. Gamma - Dr. Brian Copeland

Dr. Copeland was the head of the gamma knife clinic at the MidMichigan Medical Center in Midland, Michigan where I had my second brain operation. The method uses powerful gamma radiation. He also became chief neurologist there. He passed away in 2013. I learned of Dr. Copeland first by going online to his web site. The man had heavy credentials and was a gamma knife expert. I met him in person when Mom and I visited the gamma center for instructions on the procedure. Though a very busy man, he patiently took the time to answer my mother and my questions. As my Mom is hard of hearing, he patiently sat down with us to view my MRI scans and to explain the procedure in detail and to answer her specific questions. As we had two opinions about the operation at the time from within the clinic, he persuaded us to go ahead with the procedure, as he said if it was a member of his family, he would have it done. I immediately liked the man. He was smaller and more frail than I expected, but perhaps he was terminal at that point or his condition was taking a toll. Pretty classy if he was, as he never mentioned anything about it. He talked about the procedure but let other doctors and technicians do the actual operation. I heard about his passing from my Mom who read an article in the local paper. They never mentioned what disease he had. He was 64 when he passed away. He spend many years in La Jolla, California, a place where I also visited after he was there, while I was in the U.S. Navy. In respect for his knowledge and his help in my particular case, I attended his funeral here in Midland. It was well done and his close family members took turns telling the audience stories about him when they were all younger. I remember the one about how he built an entire dental lab out of Tinker Toys, complete with motorized drills and charged the neighbor kids for "dental" services. Very funny stuff. He was quite the character. They told us how when he got off the plane from California to Midland he wore a fake earring and tattoo that said "born to raise hell". He left them on just long enough to let the administrators of the hospital squirm a bit and then he took them off. He had quite a sense of humor. I was still unstable at the funeral so I waited until most people left then went out very carefully to the car. Funny, I expected to see more people like me or in a similar condition. Maybe I am more mobile than most who have been in my situation.

Beer And Tinnitus

Now this one is funny. I am just now learning to drink beer again. I have never been a big drinker but I like one or two now and then to relax at the end of the day, or at least I did in Tennessee. I could not handle a beer just a few short weeks ago due to a lack of swallowing control. I have learned to control swallows now and have healed to the point where I can now drink beer. My brother Dave also enjoys beer, even at meals. I have recently tried that and I admit that the beer does taste good with certain foods. It works out well as when we are using the patio or the pool, I am now able to join him in a beer or two or even three, but right now three is the limit for me when getting around, swimming, and so forth. I have noticed that the beer naturally relaxes me and helps to reduce the tinnitus levels which rise late in the afternoon and early evening. Many a time when we play dominoes or Scrabble at nights after supper, my head would be especially loud. It is not as bad after a few beers. It probably helps distracts me as I have mentioned before. To me I find this amusing as I enjoy being able to have beer again and it is very nice that it helps with the tinnitus. I enjoy having the control to swallow the beer and I think it is pretty cool that my Mom does not say anything about me or Dave having some around the house. So to me right now, and as funny as this may seem, beer is almost a medicine as much as an enjoyment. I told you my life is amusing and sometimes very funny.

Irish Pub

When I drove with Dave to Elkhart, Indiana (this is where his trucking/RV transport company is located) in 2013 we stopped by an Irish pub in Mt. Pleasant, called the "Green Spot". We each had a mug of Guinness beer and a patty melt with lots of onions. I held my own, sipping and swallowing slowly and carefully and as always controlling every bite and sip. Other than my usual vacant look and hard time walking, one would not know what I had gone through. I was not wearing a "brain" shirt that day. I enjoyed the bar and the food and drink were delicious and reasonably priced. I felt almost "normal" for a time. The funniest part was when we left. I, being still a bit unstable, staggered a little out of the bar. I thought that might have looked like I had one too many. If they only knew! I probably looked like I was over the limit. To me this was most ironic and a particularly funny moment, a great memory that I won't likely forget.

Mom's Pool

With the return of some of my control and balance, I got the confidence to try the pool for the first time in this second year of my recovery, 2013. I was curious if it would help with my constant right leg pain. I found out that it does cool off my leg. The first time in the pool I was extremely cautious and had the usual disorientation at the top of the pool. I had to get into the pool backwards due to instability and the brain not having fully recovered to height changes. The more times I get in, naturally the more confidence I have. As mentioned, the pool water eased the right leg pain (constant heat and numbness). I have good balance in the water and on rafts. I am able to sip beer slowly while in the pool. This helps with tinnitus and stress. I have been in several times now, but the weather and pool temperature have recently dropped (70 degree pool temperature right now in early August of 2013 and 60 degrees or less now in September). I help Dave lower and lift an umbrella on a stand into center of the pool. We sometimes use this in the middle of the pool as protection from the bright sun. I have gotten a good healthy tan from the swims and I have not turned any down yet. When I have a few beers, I use more than my usual caution getting in and out of the pool, especially as my leg is numb and exposed with just a swim suit on. I do not want to hurt my foot or leg with little clothing on. I may be slow but I do not take any chances when that "exposed".

Speech Recognition

In the summer of 2013 my speech made great improvements. To me it is still an effort to get the words out. In working on this journal I got speech-to-text on my computer to finally recognize my voice. It is at least 70% accurate now. This has sped up the digitizing of my journal. I tried this method right after I started this journal and my speech was just too slurred for the computer to make it out. My improvements and the advancements in this technology have shortened this project greatly. I really expected to be converting and working on the project all of next year.

Introduction Wrap Up...

So these have been my memories as best I can recall at this late date. I hope you have enjoyed reading them as much as I have enjoyed going back in time to get them down in writing. As I have said here and in my journals and to family and friends (and even strangers), I am amazed at how much of these memories that I can recall, given all that has happened to me. I truly am one fortunate individual and certainly have had a lot of help behind the scenes, a lot of prayers, a lot of concern, a lot of just good old positive vibrations and of course, love. These and fate have allowed me to still be in this world. You now know how close I came to "punching that ticket".

Maybe I have been allowed to recover enough to get these words to you, my reader, who can say? I know that most people have their own interesting life memories and history. Most would love to have the time to write a book or to recall their adventures while they are alive and to share these moments with others. I consider the situation I am in now to be a great opportunity to share with others some of my recent life moments. I think it would bother me if I recovered and did not share these experiences since I recall them so vividly and have the time now to write about them. On that note, and "without further ado", I present for your enjoyment my daily journal for the first seven and one half months of 2013.

Daily Journal   (12/31/12- 8/15/13)

CHAPTER 1   12/31/12 – 1/31/13

Mon. 12/31/2012 2:36 pm [living room]

[This journal entry is] A bit early but [it's] just a few notes to see if I can make the entries, **test** my writing ability (or printing, since that is easier to read and easier for me to produce). I am currently at my mother Doris's home sitting in the living room. I am recovering well from my [first] brain surgery (last August 12, 2011). [I also had the second one, the gamma in July, 2012] I can now see this journal and this room (both were a blur about 5 [7] months ago but I will probably [omit probably] write about that later). The VA cat scan in Murfreesboro, TN revealed an aggressive, large tumor but thankfully [it was] benign. It was putting severe pressure on my brain causing mobility issues, slurred speech, left side shakes, vomiting in the morning after trying some new BP medication, caused dry heaves and a cycle of vicious headaches that nearly brought me to my knees. This was in early 2011. I since have had the gamma knife radiation surgery here in Midland, Michigan [(July 2012)] because a piece of the tumor was <u>not</u> removed and began growing rapidly again in [the] summer of 2012. That [second brain] surgery went well and so far that tumor piece has not grown back. Luck again! So here I sit with much to be thankful for in 2011/2012 and optimistic that even better things are on the way. The writing goes well even though focus is still not 100%. As there is strain to control the pen and create this entry I will stop for today and try to make daily entries over the next year to document my progress. As they say, so much to tell, so little time. Until next time…

Tue. 1/1/2013 8:30 pm (bedroom)

Things are coming along well. I have a better sense of balance and control, especially noticeable when walking in the house. I am anxious to resume walking in the mall tomorrow morning. I will also be running some errands (washing t-shirts, mailing a letter to the IRS, going to the bank, etc.). As I write this I still have one eye fuzzy with my close vision glasses. Perhaps this will improve if I am able to wear progressive lenses again this spring. That would be great. The VA converted my progressives with a prism lens to help with my double vision which it has, but now I don't have the original glasses to try out. I will just have to remain patient. I do seem to be able to read the NY Times at the Dow Library without the eye weakening and/or the brain seeing the double image, especially the crease of the page. I will now read some more of the book Dave got me for Christmas, "A Canticle for Leibowitz". It is great and provides further vision therapy. Later on I will try playing on the notebook computer as I loaded [the] Udora [Ubuntu] O/S operating system and want to set it up.

<u>Wed. Jan. 2, 2013 (8:02 pm bedroom)</u>

[It was] A nice day of therapy and running errands. [I] Walked only 3 laps in the mall (2 miles) then off to Auburn to go to [the Chemical] [B]bank and make [a] deposit, deposit Mom's check, mail [a] letter and wash t-shirts--then to [the] Auburn [Branch] Library for about an hour to relax [and read newspapers and magazines]. I just [read] the Nepo journal story [Mark Nepo's yearly journal and reflection book purchased earlier at Barnes and Noble] for Jan 2nd about putting down what we carry before crossing a threshold or opening a door. Even though there is great improvement physically today (less leg pain, energy at [the Midland] Mall), I still am timid, maybe about making further progress. Am I afraid if I become more normal will I lose my sense of being different from others[?]. Is part of recent developments an ego issue? Do I need to drop fear in order to advance to the next levels? Do I need to not be afraid to try to be more like "normal" people and risk the lack of attention? Am I using it as a crutch of some sort? Just some random thoughts and I will see about making the next progress [one] that involves more "normal" behaviors. I do want to be "normal" don't I? Hmmm...

Thrs. Jan. 3, 2013 1:24 pm – (dinner table)

[I] Got back from walking, [and] running errands. Things continue to improve, especially vision and "brain lock" today. I still have many issues remaining and I now know that my earlier comments about needing to retain disability for some reason are not "mostly" true. I long for the day and I know it will come (It probably is that way for the me who is reading this journal now) when I can move my head around <u>and</u> walk [at] the same time without becoming dizzy or disoriented (as this writing, ha ha). Anyway it is teaching patience and great appreciation for the brain and for all it does and for all the "little" things like balance, walking, talking, etc.

Fri. Jan. 4, 2013 – living room 4:25 pm.

[I] Just got my "boot"-"heat" long socks [ordered a pair of compression socks to try to reduce the ongoing pain in my right leg and foot] from US Patriot/Amazon to try for my leg. Since "thawing out" last year around summer, I had a burning/numb sensation in my right leg -- a major difficulty for me but in the last few days that too is improving. It started with the whole leg on fire and painful. I have learned to deal with the pain patiently as in everything. I have a theory. I did try to mention it to my "nurse practitioner" [health care provider] at the Sag [Saginaw, Michigan] VA but I am not able to communicate well yet and she has an attitude [or seems to] with me. Anyway all my life I have had a numbness in the lower half of my right leg. Hair will not grow in that spot and I suppose I have always ignored it. I think maybe the large tumor had something to do with it and now that [it] has been removed, I think the leg is going back to normal blood flow/circulation and that is what I feel as pain. Just a theory, but perhaps correct as the pain is lessening and has gone from the entire leg to mostly the foot. For awhile last year it bothered my sleep, but now when it's covered up and horizontal the pain subsides. Also maybe these long boot socks will help. The [normal pain in the] leg and injuries in Dave's Explorer vehicle [on a hard, long ride it bruised my tail bone afterward] make it hard to sit at a table or chair for more than a few minutes. I use an inflatable tube seat Sandra [(my sister)] got me that helps. I look forward to this situation improving like everything else and allowing me more "normalcy".

Saturday Jan. 5, 2013 5:25 pm computer room

...as [omit as--I am at] Mom's place, [in] Michigan. Things continue to improve. The eyes are clearer and the head [is] more steady as I noticed when I drove to the ATM this morning (I now stay here on weekends and take a rest from walking the mall) [in other words I currently walk the mall Mon – Fri]. The close-up vision is still with the second pair of glasses. [I used to have one pair of progressive glasses prior to surgery for [both] long and close vision. Now my brain can't handle one pair and I am told that one pair cannot be made for my eyes and brain condition until further healing occurs.] The vision close-up tends to weaken and blur as it always has with two eyes open but I am thankful to be able to read and see. In time I look forward to normal vision. I am very anxious to see the VA optometrist Dr. Hrywnak (Veronica) in Feb[ruary]. Perhaps I will be ready for progressive lenses again. Close vision still requires me to switch glasses. I have been able to use "long vision" glasses to see the computer screen, [my Window 7 desktop in the computer office] to play Tiger Woods golf [on the computer,] but [I] can't read the screen unless I switch to reading or close vision glasses.

Sunday Jan. 6, 2013 8:00 pm bedroom

[I] Finished reading "Canticle for Leibowitz" (Miller) that Dave got me for Christmas. Good book, fiction, something I have not read much of. It had alternate realities of human madness with nuclear weapons and monks surviving to keep human knowledge. A good read but fortunately a future (now) that did not come to pass [at least in this world] (written in 1959 during those scary "duck and cover" days we [some of us] grew up in []). Hey little did I know I would be writing in a daily journal in 2013 after recovering from brain surgery [surgeries] (that continues...). I'm 62 now and of course lucky to be among the living (or privileged). Today I continue my steady improvement and we (Sandra, Mom, Dave, and I) went to [the] Ponderosa buffet for lunch. No [I am not using a] cane now but [I] still [am] working on "normal" behavior. I am sure it will come. I have to hang on to things, watch out for people, chew slowly (be in the moment) and [am] only hungry for one plate of food [at a sitting]. I [usually] have water to drink as coke [or pop as they call it here in Michigan] still chokes me. All and all I feel improvements--I can sit longer without my bottom and/or leg bothering me [as much]. My eyes are better. Things [are] still blurry at times but [there is] less double imaging while reading (especially in bed). There is also a reduction in the background ringing in my ears or at least I don't pay attention to it as much. Anyway [I] started reading E. Tolle's "Silence Speaks" to further help me block out noisy thoughts and worries.

Mon. Jan. 7, 2013 4:45 pm computer office

[My] Eyes [are] better. At [I visited the] Auburn laundry [Auburn Cleaners & Laundromat], washed sheets and bathrobes. [I had an] Accident with [the] sheets and [the] urinal so [it was a] good chance to get therapy and help out Mom too. [I] Worked on the puzzle that Aunt Betty got me for my Birthday, a rather difficult one. [My] Foot/leg [is] hot but even that seems better.

Tue., Wed. Jan. 8-9, 2013

[I went] With Dave driving to Cleveland, Ohio to buy his Toyota Echo for pulling/truck driving so no [journal] entries. [I drove his Ford Explorer back on the Ohio Turnpike following him as he drove his new Toyota Echo]

Thrs. Jan. 10, 2013 computer room 3:15 pm

[I am] Back in my "normal" routine. [I am] Noticing small improvements to energy [low energy and stamina after surgery], [and] speech. It is all so slow but going in the right direction. My book on art techniques came yesterday so I will start [reading] that now. I finished the puzzle Aunt Betty got me for my Birthday today while Mom played cards and Yahtzee in the living [dining] room [with Dave].

Friday Jan. 11, 2013 8:05 pm – bedroom

Today the [my] voice became easier to project, strong[er] and easier to understand and though to me it is projected "low" and strange[,] but [omit but] it seems to work better. [I am] So much better that I spoke to a lady at the IRS [on the phone] about my business return for 2011. I won't get back nearly as much but maybe a few hundred in the spring, enough to pay for some glasses. Sight, stamina, [and] vision continue to improve and in the morning while in bed I didn't seem to feel as much leg pain, though that returned during the day and is there now as I write this. Man[,] I feel the deepest hole in my neck now and [in the] back of [my] skull. They did a number on me, even with the latest technology.

Saturday Jan. 12, 2013 8:00 pm bedroom

Things continue to improve today. Vision [is] clearer so that I could make out the bottom lines (crawler) on the TV screen from the farthest lazy boy [recliner] chair, my usual one. Speech and stamina [are] greatly improving[,] with speech still difficult but understandable by others. [I am] Able to talk more during dinner meal[s]. The hot leg/foot continues to be a pain around 4 pm and after. Sometimes [it is] very intense but perhaps this is it's final gasp too. It always feels better when horizontal and covered with a blanket. Vision is good enough to write and do puzzles but as I write this the eyes tend to cross but the good new is that the page center or binding is where it should be and in the middle. [There is] No double imaging unless I read too much and then it appears. Also to note in this journal was when I went into the Auburn Food Center store to buy some lottery tickets, I walked across the lot with more confidence and not as much delay time needed standing near the car (if I don't take some time [at the car] I get dizzy or disoriented). The great rate of improvement lately leads me to one thought of importance, and that is that I hope I don't forget this struggle and what I have gone through to get back just to where I am "normal" like everyone else. I hope it stays with me forever so that I will appreciate the "little" things like walking, speaking, moving, seeing, and so on. I have a feeling that I took them for granted and that perhaps [I know that] this whole long and grueling episode has been a lesson for me.

Sunday Jan. 13, 2013 4:15 pm dining room

Steve is here and he and Dave are working on Steve's surfboard "harness" or carrier. Mom just left for Jo-Ann Fabrics to get a longer zipper to repair Steve's jacket. Sandra is home working. My leg hurts steadily as it always does but it seems more diffuse, hurting in the whole length of the leg again, a general aching. There is less concentrated pain in the foot area as there has been of late. I am hopeful this can clear up as it has been a real bother. I am upgrading the [desktop] computer [(from Windows XP to Windows 7)] and plan to back it up shortly. Vision [is] still blurred and not totally clear yet. I think soon it will be [clear] as it fades in and out properly. I am taking a break from the puzzle Betty got Mom [farm yard]. I think I am just getting burned out on all the puzzle therapy but I guess it's a good thing and helping my brain [to] recover.

Monday Jan. 14, 2013 7:20 pm bedroom

I am [have] covered over my leg now and it always feels better horizontal and covered. I wonder if anyone will ever know the pain I have endured in the leg/foot after I thawed out enough to notice it (May of last year, 2012). I have felt it very slowly improve over time to where it is now more of an ache than a pain in the leg. Today I resumed walking at the Midland Mall after taking the weekend off. I was more concerned about not falling or slipping on the icy pavement to the mall. We had an inch or two of snow overnight. It stopped snowing this morning but it was cold enough to cause it to ice all over. I cut my routine short at the mall in order to go see the movie

"Lincoln" at the Fashion Square Mall in Saginaw. We waited too long here in Midland to see it but it was still playing in Saginaw. I would invite Dave and Mom but Mom cannot hear well in a theater and Dave drove to Holland [Michigan] to get a tow bar for his Toyota Echo. He is now very busy with the final things necessary to do before he starts his trucking job. Perhaps in the future we can take a movie break but for now I did it for my own therapy and because I really wanted to see it. [It was] Very enjoyable but as [I] mentioned roads and drives were very icy so my mind was on making it safely. I learned more about focusing the mind as when I concentrated on safe passage I did not think about the leg pain and this [also] happens when I try walking. Always more to learn and this is a daily endurance. I sure hope it is all memory by the time this journal is read.

<u>Tues. Jan. 15, 2013 8:46 pm bedroom</u>

Well today is my friend Cathy's Birthday but I have not acknowledged this in card, email, etc. She did not for [do this for] me, neither did Shirley [my ex]. I think it is time to finally move on and I think that is a message from both of them. From this point on it is a new life for me, a "rebirth" you could say, as I am doing some amazing things on my own now [as I never know what is in the future, I perhaps am premature in writing this. PS: I later found out that Cathy did pass on a birthday greeting but it somehow did not get to me. Seems I was just showing some "thin skin" here as I ranted]. Today I saw the movie, "The Hobbit, An Unexpected Journey" (Part I of III), as [in the] Lord of The Rings series. It hardly seems possible that this [Lord of The Rings series] was released to theaters [in] 2001-2003, over ten years ago. Time flies as they say and so much has changed, especially in my life[,] of course. Anyway the movie was in 3D and quite enjoyable. My eyes and brain are now strong enough to use them [3D glasses] (thankfully!!). This was[is] the theater next to the Midland Mall, the Midland Cinemas, and the show started at 11:00 am. I rushed back to Mom's house but find [found] Mom and Dave had left to run errands. They returned about 6:00 pm. I had a sloppy joe and we played a game of dominoes. Eyes blur still in this journal but the entries I can see clearly. The handwriting is crappy as always!

<u>Wed. Jan. 16, 2013 4:25 pm living room</u>

Vision seem[s] strong today. [I am] Able to read TV "crawl" letters clearly now. They are not perfect but seem sharper. As I read what I write in this journal, the left eye is blurry but there is less double line, particularly the middle page separation. I still have to concentrate on the vision but it seems more stable. Unfortunately other symptoms are more noticeable now or maybe more intense. I still get the build up of saliva in my throat and this can choke me. I have had louder buzzing inside my head today. I particularly noticed it at Walmart and now as I write this. [It's] Hard to explain but [it seems] similar to an electric line that makes noise in the rain or early morning. But there still is no headache pain as I experienced before the operation. My right leg continues to be hot, mostly the lower foot region. I still think this is from better circulation in the leg after the tumor has been [was] removed. I have always had a cold/numb feeling there and unable to grow hair in that lower calf area. It is unlikely a nerve would remain pinched by now [this long]. I am hopeful this improves as it is most annoying. At least it is in the lower foot now and not in the entire leg as it was when my numbness began to wear off last May. Anyway some things improve daily, [and] some things are more slow. Patience is the key I suppose. I have noticed that as I concentrate on walking (not falling)[,] I don't notice the pains as much so that is hopeful. I can learn to control the mind, which is [makes the pain] tolerable, when pain occurs.

<u>Thursday Jan. 17, 2013 5:07 pm living room</u>

Eye focus [is] close but not exactly right. [The] Middle of [the] page takes awhile now to appear distorted (double image) but [it] does occur after reading a few pages probably due to strain. Light sensitivity to [in] both eyes remains a problem with much squinting during some sittings, especially under [at the] dining table and in restaurants with lower light domes [over the table]. The brain is still adjusting. Even though it is not that bright outside, I find it more comfortable to wear sunglasses in the snow as [I did] today. The ringing is still there fairly strong or I should say a constant high vibration or buzzing. I am sure this is brain trauma. Funny that it has taken this long to adjust [show up] but it may be from the gamma operation, I am not sure. I think often that I was fortunate that I was not aware of this during the first 5 or 6 months after the "first" brain surgery in TN. It would have driven me crazy – it would have been pain and loud buzzing [pain as in aches most likely as there has not been any pain since the steroids were used to shrink the tumor in the Vanderbilt ICU]. No wonder they gave me "happy pills" [anti-depression pills, which I stopped taking very shortly after arriving in Michigan] earlier. I bet they planned this delay in their procedure [delay in recovering from numbness] else no one would survive it. It's bad enough after over a year. It would be unthinkable if I felt it earlier [the tinnitus]. Now it's just an inconvenience that I try not to think about. I try to distract my mind. It is especially strong (the ear buzz) [tinnitus] in the evening when it's quiet and like now when I am making a journal entry. I did try some Ginkgo biloba (250 mg) this afternoon but this did not really help. But I will continue [taking it] as it is still good for the brain. I refilled my vitamin supplements today and laughed at how many there are. I just wanted to be sure my brain and body got the best nutrients and I knew early that I had outgrown the VA meds. I was off [most] all [of the prescribed VA meds] in 2012. I knew inside that it was time and I think the way the system works I would be on them indefinitely unless I made a move or someone [did] for me. I was correct per the neurologist at the VA. [In] most operations of [on] the brain, the patient is given seizure med [medication] for about 6 months then taken off [the medication]. I resumed [taking seizure medication] for awhile to make everyone happy but then <u>118 days</u> ago I woke up and said <u>no</u>. I am not taking any more of any [remove 'of any'] VA drugs, and I have had no problems since [then] and [I] am breaking my record daily now. I hope to write more about this when I can. Anyway meds are [removed?], [and] things are improving. The ringing is there and the leg bothers me often but I try to focus on the good things and all the improvements. I walk with more confidence and look forward [to] when this and other things are normal.

Friday Jan. 18, 2013 4:13 pm living room

Improvement continues in movement, [and] leg pains. I hear continuous high pitched sound in my head but it sure beats the constant headaches that were crippling to me. Given the choice I will live with the buzzing. I have a feeling now that [as] some things are better, [that] my mind now focuses on the buzzing. It will subside eventually. Vision is much better also with the brain/eyes [omit eyes] finally controlling [my] eyes so they don't bend in or lose focus so [too] soon. I still have high sensitivity to light so I wore my shades when out driving today. Leg pain is there but light. It is mostly the numbness feeling but [and] there is some residual pain (hot -- stinging) in the foot bottom area. I resumed my 6 trips around the mall with the new boot/shoes and this works out to be about 10,000 steps or 3 miles. Instead of my usual ending in the Dow Library, I stayed at Barnes and Noble and looked for a new book to read at night for me and my eyes. I picked up "Tapping the Source" about Charles Hanel's Master Key writings about [the] Law of Attraction and manifesting. [It] Should be a good read. Tomorrow starts the weekend and I will get some driving/walking downtime [in] and do other therapies like the puzzles, golf (WII and/or computer) and the art technique studying.

Sat. Jan. 19, 2013 [time and location not recorded]

The biggest thing noticeable today is the brain/eyes ability to lock into an image up close as this journal and my art instruction book. The pages "lock" as they are supposed to. There is not the immediate out of focus vision of the page where I see two images. This is great!, as I have endured about 8 months of this blurriness and brain distortion. I think things are coming around nicely. I have not written [in this journal yet] but one of the biggest advances was the return of balance/control a few weeks ago, possible[ly] late in 2012. While walking I had [now have] the ability to not tip over. Finally [I am] able to stand upright and not rely on objects, even able to step back slowly. Now this is not perfect yet, as I still am slow at the mall and occasionally grip a wall for support but with the brain better able to track and follow objects, I am confident that walking will improve. The right leg remains and [an] issue but it is much better, still really improves [is less painful] when horizontal and covered with a blanket as in bed. Swallowing, [and] speech are better but slow. [I am] Trying to eat grapes again and I always had a choke issue with them. Not so much now but I must still concentrate on each swallow. My big concern now is that I will forget the struggles I have had to return to "normal", thus I write in this journal as at the moment it is my only way to document things. Voice is still not working fully for any voice to speech [speech-to-text] recognition [software] and I make errors typing, especially emails. Without "spell-checker" I would not be able to use the computer to communicate. It is things like this I hope to remember so that I can document some of my experiences. Stay tuned as they say ... PS[:] The eyes are still locking but it requires concentration. Looking forward to my eye exam in Feb. as hopefully I can get some progressive glasses on order.

Sun. Jan. 20, 2013 3:22 pm living room

[I am] Taking a break from the puzzle Betty got Mom (farm scene with geese, cow, rooster). [It is] A very difficult puzzle but great brain exercise. I worked on that and played Tiger Woods golf on the computer, all fun and good training. Today my right leg has been hot all day, especially the foot. [It got] So bad I laid down and covered it for awhile midday. I am hopeful that this is not a permanent state as it is a real pain. This is one [symptom] only a few people know about. I thought it was getting better and it still may be and these are the final pains. It makes it hard to attend concerts or go to a baseball game as the leg gets uncomfortable unless lifted up. Again, by the time I or anyone [else] read[s] this, let's hope it is old history. The eyes are stronger but they still rapidly tire. I can see close-up clearer without the double image unless I try to read for too long a period. This also should improve in time. Next couple of days should be the coldest up here in some time – highs in the teens, lows in the sub 10's. But [remove But] a gradual warm up into the 20's later in the week is the prediction. Again as I have written before, this episode teaches patience, the healing is so very slow.

Mon., Jan. 21, 2013 2:30 pm living room

Although steps and balance has [have] not fully returned[,] I find more confidence in going down the center of an aisle or in a parking lot. I noticed that at K-Mart on my way back when I needed to stop for some index cards. The leg has been hot, [and] numb lately but in a less intense way[,] especially when doing a puzzle. When my mind is occupied then perhaps there is less focus on the leg pains. Vision still "wanders" and lacks full control. I can see OK and am grateful for that but [and] maybe soon I can get progressive lenses again, as the focus problems wear me down. [It] probably makes me tired at night due to the constant eye strain, there is strain in reading, eating, [and] anything that requires close-up work.

Tue. 1/22/13 3:23 pm living room

[It is] A very cold winter day with temp[erature]s single digit but a positive, hopeful day as far as therapy goes and I elaborate: My brain is beginning to lock on to objects much better, they are coming into clearer focus as well. The distortion in location and image [that] I have endured these past few months is lessening and I am truly optimistic that this will continue. It really is hard to explain but for the first time inside my head I have brief moments of "normalcy". I still am unsteady in walk, talking [is still] a problem, swallowing, leg, etc. but things are looking hopeful. As far as the leg is concerned, the pain is there but today it is different in feeling, less severe, sort of an ache and inner numbness, mostly still in the lower half of the right leg. Hopefully this is a sign of the end of this ordeal. I would love to take in a baseball game in the spring without needing to raise my leg horizontally for comfort. Voice continues to improve daily as well, still an effort to get words out, but this is better. That's a good thing as it looks like any [additional] VA therapy is not coming [this is before I obtained additional speech therapy]. Thankfully my body/brain will recover despite any lack of "official" therapy. Vision is sharper. There is a better lock when writing this journal. [It is] Still a bit blurry but the page margins remain fixed and just the letters fuzz up at times or maybe it's just my crappy penmanship. But overall the most striking advance is the brain's ability to start to see things as a "normal" person would. I noticed this while eating a McDonald's breakfast and scanning the food court [at the Midland Mall], of all things. I could grasp it all in correct perspective yet parts are still not in focus or "brain lock". One of the big observations I have made during my walks at the mall is that nearly everyone there is in their own worlds. They walk fast with their minds lost in their thoughts or carrying Starbucks [coffee] in their hands, or texting on their cell phones, while I struggle to regain simple things that I think people take for granted. I know I am sure that I did when I could do the same [as these people]. It took losing everything "normal" and slowly getting them back to bring me to simple appreciation. Again[,] as I have mentioned before, when I make total recovery (and I will!)[,] I hope I remember these experiences, these pains and struggles, and perhaps be able to pass them [the remembrance of them] on.

<u>Wed. Jan. 23, 2013 8:00 pm bedroom</u>

Things continue to improve but [do] so slowly. I expected more [improvement] at the [Midland] Mall when I took a McDonald's breakfast break but the "brain lock" did not seem there as [as good as] yesterday but I think it is just very slow. Walking still staggers [has me staggering] and there is the usual fear of falling on long stretches [mostly in the middle of the walking area]. There is the need to hold on occasionally for support [caneless walking]. [My] Eyes still have the persistent double vision on close-ups. The leg/foot still aches. I was hoping for more [improvements by now] but I refuse to be disappointed and will hope for better things tomorrow.

Jan. 24, 2013 Thursday 4:30 pm living room

[There has been] Improvement in stamina [today]; [my] eyes close [on their own but are] still blurry at times; [my] leg (foot) [is] hot but in [the] lower part of [the] leg. Patience I will continue to have. VA message on the phone; Mom got it first and grilled me about the 1 pm appointment in Ann Arbor [coming up]. [I told her] it's under control and not to worry. Dave has lots on his plate with trucking and is not a morning person [as I am] and it is time for me to make a point that I am well enough now to go to VA appts. [appointments for MRI scans in Ann Arbor]. Neither [Mom nor Dave] would probably let me [go to Ann Arbor on my own] without a fight so I feel this is the therapy I really need now and I plan to go [to Ann Arbor] early Monday [Jan 28th] (during my usual walk time) for the MRI and just leave contact info. for neurology [the MRI follow-up appointment originally set for 2 pm that day]. Also this is to show the power of good frequency/vibrations as I <u>know</u> there will not be further problems and if there should be they can contact me further. This whole "adventure" is something I need to prove to myself as well as it is now my life and time for me to regain control. The whole thing is somewhat mute [already proven] as I have already driven Dave's Explorer to Ohio via the turnpike (actually back) so I am quite capable to go to [of driving to] Ann Arbor for an MRI. Next time in April I may stay for the follow-up. We will see.

Jan. 25, 2013 Friday 4:00 pm living room.

[I] Skipped walking today as it was snowing and Mom needed to work and go to Walmart [the Oldsmobile is safer in snow]. I worked on the puzzle and played golf on the computer. My eyes appear pretty much the same. There are times when the eyes blur using close-up glasses but I am able to see and that's the main thing. Perhaps on [at my VA] eye appointment they [the doctor] will still have me wait for the brain to lock [heal]. The leg is tolerable today; [there is] some pain but [it] seems not as bad. The evening will tell as it [the leg pain] is usually stronger then. We will see how Monday goes with the VA [in Ann Arbor] but Dave is real busy. It [the weather] is going to warm up and my MRI is very early so I just may [will] take care of it [myself] for the therapy and ease of Dave's schedule. The eye appointment is the following Monday [Feb 4th at the Saginaw VA] and we will see [(ouch, bad pun)] what happens then.

[Saturday] Jan. 26, 2013 4:05 pm living room

I started back on mall walking on Saturdays also [again]. I will walk M-Sat from this point on. At the [Midland] mall there was the beginning of some general brain clarity looking around [the food court]. I still cannot [easily] divert my straight ahead look and concentration while walking lest I lose balance. Also I still need some [time] delay when rising, bending (any change in head elevation). [The] close-up eyes [glasses are] clearer, locking [occasionally as normal eyes do]. I still wonder about the left eye being fuzzy by itself [when I shut my right eye and use only my left eye with close-up glasses it is blurry...[later I am to find that the glasses had the wrong left eye lens/prescription per the VA]. I will ask the VA doctor about this in Feb. The [right] leg pain/heat seems concentrated in the foot base but I notice that the whole leg becomes hotter around 4 pm. I have to elevate it horizontally in a chair as always. I also notice [that] the head/ear ringing, which is always there, [is] more pronounced in the evening [or at quieter times]. Like all pains, it seems to be how the mind concentrates on it, whether it is prominent. But this is like [the] sound of telephone wires on a foggy morning, buzzing. I don't recall it earlier as perhaps it was the gamma [knife] treatment [in July, 2012] that was potent resulting in many of these recent symptoms, such as speaking, ear ringing, and so on. I has been 6 months since gamma now so let's hope it will go away, maybe by the time someone or myself reads this journal.

Sunday Jan. 27, 2013 5:02 pm living room

[The] foot [is] warm, vision [is] somewhat blurry, but [I] noticed that the brain is re-syncing. The ringing in the head, as usual, appears steady and loud about now, but still not the terrible headaches as before [surgeries] so I will patiently wait for this to clear also. Even though the vision occasionally blurs, the margins and pages are not drifting so [that] I see double images. That is a nice change of pace.

Monday Jan. 28, 2013 4:30 pm living room

[There is a] Snow/ice mix this morning. [I got] Up early out of anticipation [and] went to Ann Arbor for [my] MRI [appointment], no results known yet but [I] left [a] note at neurology to call or email. We will see. I felt compelled to go to test my abilities and independence. All went well. Looking forward to resuming normal mall walks tomorrow. I am currently playing a "white noise" mp3 on my player as I write this to try to mask the tinnitus I currently have. It just stopped so I will stop [playing] it for awhile. I will stop [taking] Ginkgo [biloba supplement, which is supposed to help with tinnitus; I resumed this later anyway] in [the] morning as that [the tinnitus] is new and probably a problem from the gamma [knife], but not sure. Hopefully it will go away soon as it is a living nightmare. The eyes are off focus here in the chair but the page is clear (binder). [I] think it is the left eye fuzziness. So the day was [a] non-stop rush to Ann Arbor and back (Dave and Mom did not know) so I was reading about stress and tinnitus so maybe that's the issue. I also want to back up [try?] some GABA 750 [a relaxant that I used to take in TN] and see if it would help in relaxing in the evening.

Tues. Jan. 29, 2013 5:30 pm living room

[My] Eyes [are] holding stable. Ear ringing [is] steady all day, more noticeable at night when quiet or I take time to notice it. Staying busy, doing things help[s] distract from it. [I had a] Blow out with Dave. Seems the VA talked to him by phone of [about] my MRI in Ann Arbor.

[I] Tried to argue my point that I felt compelled to go to test my healing. He is too into med[ical] doctors [in my opinion] and such so we left it a bit cold. Some day he may see my motivation as not against anyone but for <u>me</u>. Mom seems to follow so I will drop it now. There was no further tumor growth as I knew there would not be. Also they have set me up for speech therapy lab at [the] Sag[inaw] VA where I will have my eyes checked. Will wonders never cease?

<u>Wed. Jan. 30, 2013 2:30 am computer room</u>

Yes it's 2:30 am! I am going to try to write about the loud noises in my head now (tinnitus) and some of the recent events. Right now the high pitched buzzing or cricket sound is so loud I could not sleep and I am playing Mozart's Requiem Mass, one of my favorites, on my mp3 player. This does not drown out the sound but may occupy my mind and help prevent one from going insane(er)! This is the very first mp3 I used to play at Williams Township park [in Auburn] for walking. They say Mozart is good for your health; say, it can't hurt. I should play some Beethoven as he had hearing problems and I was born on his birthday [Dec. 16th], how ironic. Maybe I will try to find some [of his music] online to download. Say, luckily I go to bed around 8 pm still. I read for a bit. I read last night until about 9:15 pm. I woke up early this morning with the head set on so I think I got a few hours [of sleep] at least. This morning the noise is the loudest it's been, even in the evening at about 4 pm when it normally becomes loud. All I can do now is try to ignore it (and that seems to be the key), thinking about it as I woke up[,] it could still be worse, I could be losing all hearing or not to be able to hear at all. I always try to look on the positive side (I guess that is a big reason I am still recovering). Anyway here I am writing here and perhaps it will be me reading it someday when this is all past history...I am optimistic about the chance for speech therapy at the Sag. VA. My first appointment is at the speech lab on the 4th floor early Monday morning at 8:00 am. I think after walking in the mall today I will do a dry run there to check the mileage and times involved. I am also hopeful that the eyes will improve too. They are [improved enough] for me to see this journal and make entries. Anyway I will persevere and get some coffee and catch "Red Eye" [early morning TV show] at 3:00 am, a fun show, again to help keep my mind distracted. I will also grab some coffee after the show. I will likely hunt for Beethoven mp3s or golf or maybe both. Sleep right now does not look like an option. I will write more here later in the day.

1/30/13 4:45 am [computer room}

[I] watched "Red Eye" - [I] had coffee, cakes, [and I am] in the computer room now. [I] found [a] way to [the] Sag. VA via [I-]675, I-75, [and] US-10 via [using] Google Earth, [; I] ordered Mindful Mag[azine], [;] now [I am] ripping a Beethoven CD to mp3. Good news is that [the] tinnitus is about the same [and has not gotten louder]. As usual, [it is] just more noticeable in quiet times. I will continue to mentally distract my attention to [from] it. I am sure it is all due to the operation and/or gamma [knife] of recent [July 25, 2012] and will subside. I plan to walk today at [the] mall resuming with [the] cane for added safety until I am fully stable. After the walk around 10:30 or 11:00 [am,] I will do a dry run to the Sag. VA[,] 4th floor[,] to test times and abilities for Monday. That should be good for me and boost [my] confidence. Back to the CD ripping and more details to follow...

Jan. 30, 2013 Wed 5:15 pm living room

[I am] A bit tired from noise, lack of sleep, the day's activity and so on. I will continue a bit [more] now. The focus of the brain is just now returning,[;] I was able to turn my head more today while walking, the field of vision [is] more normal and my brain felt more "centered" as in my "former" life. As mentioned before, I did manage a trial run over to the Sag. VA. Here is how that happened. I went to the Midland Mall as usual and started to walk. I have resumed using the cane until full stability returns for confidence, safety, and I am not out to impress and I will use it until it is no longer necessary. Yes[,] I was [earlier] able to walk up to 3 miles without the cane but I was not stable getting around. I now hope to re-use it to gain in internal confidence which will mean eventually I will be stable enough [to go] without it. Until then it will be useful and I won't hide it. Anyway in the first mall lap I noticed my right ankle hurting and I can only think that maybe I should give it some rest. It could be the replacement boot/shoes [the hiking shoes Dave gave me worked well but I wore the soles off and then they smelled so I switched to some brown boot[-]like shoes I bought at Target], but either way I just stopped and decided that I would leave for the Saginaw VA earlier than planned. I made note of the time and mileage and had no problems getting there on US-10, I-75, I-675. I walked (with cane) to the 4th floor and made sure it was the right place for Monday morning. It is the same place I normally check in for routine exams (Gold Team). [I am] Walking with more confidence but the right ankle did hurt some. I chatted with a Vet on a hoveround, said hi to many people, more than I would have done before all this. I felt pretty confident and well[,] except the sore ankle as mentioned before. I left [the] Sag. VA and went down Weiss [Street] toward Bay Rd. and [to] the Barnes and Noble there. Why not check out the latest books[?]. On the way there I stopped[,] intending to use the restroom at the Fashion Square Mall and maybe check the food court out again. I then thought it would be nice to get a small lens kit/cleaner few [as] it has been a drizzly day with rain. I went to JC Penny's in the mall and was told optical was on the second floor. Well I rode the escalator up—this being the first time doing that since the operations. Once up there I had to get down and rode the escalator down—that was a bit more easy. I had the cane and orientation is still not 100% so I hung on for "life". I noticed [that] the big thing was the speed of the elevator—real fast [to me]. I almost did not take it [down], turning back and began to look for an elevator. I didn't find one so I better take the escalator I thought. I managed but to me it was like riding a thrill ride. Someday I will laugh at this memory. Even so it gave me lots of confidence so that should help in healing. I did not find a lens cleaning kit and ended up buying one at a nearby Meijer. I went to the bookstore and got another book on spirituality and a bargain [discounted] drawing book. I went to the Auburn [Branch] Library on the way back but some lady was there hacking and sick so [I] went back to Mom's. [Last night] I took a short nap with the mp3 player on as [and] the tinnitus got loud again early at [1:30 am?]. I drowsed [dozed] off and woke up at 3 am—again with continual "brain noise". I have been playing the mp3 player and reading and now the "brain noise" is better [I would later find out about the power of mental distraction]. It is there but muffled in the "tunnel" [or buried as my head is still mostly numb and feeling like cotton stuffed in there or as a tunnel] but again as I try to listen for it, it is louder. Now I will check for mail as it is getting darker [as I write]. More tomorrow...

Thurs. Jan. 31, 2013 4:30 pm living room

[I am] Taking a break from puzzles to make this journal entry. We lost our warm weather that I thought was spring.[:] From 50's to 20's and high winds, snow. Bitter weather. Dave sold his Explorer today and got some tow parts for his Toyota. He has an appointment tomorrow to have them installed. My eyes are locking now (as is my brain). Occasionally they are out of focus but more often than not I can lock into a page and there are occasions of excellent tracking. I can see how lousy my penmanship is yet it always was hard to read my writing. My thoughts outpaced [outpace] my script and always have. All this present mode thought and study [being in the moment], I will have to not rush thoughts and see if I can slow my mind down and my thoughts. I got my 1099 for the 401K distribution [I received a small 401K dissolution amount in the mail recently] so now I can do my taxes. They should be easier, no business returns and all [this year]. The internal head/ear noise gets louder a lot now. It is there as a constant buzz but also now [there] is a natural blockage of hearing that comes and goes so this acts to muffle out the louder noises. I woke up around 2 am again but I think that was from going to bed early and sleeping [at] about 9 ish [about 9 pm]. [This also is an old] Habit from my old job[. It] probably is a factor also. The leg pain/cold-numbness is there but not [as] severe. I am still favoring my right ankle. So [I] stayed off [of] it again. I went to Burger King [in the morning] for a [Cinnamon] roll and [a] milk then to Barnes and Noble at the Midland Mall where I browsed until about 9:30 am when I then went to the Dow Library. I had my usual coffee there. I have much more confidence getting around with a cane even though it is not as "cool" and ages me but who am I kidding? I right now I would rather be safe and confident getting around, especially in winter, than worry about appearances. Anyway [I am] thankful for a warm house, bedroom, and a meal on this bitter winter night!

CHAPTER 2   2/1/13 – 2/28/13

<u>Feb. 1, 2013 Friday 3:30 pm living room</u>

[It's] A new month, one filled with things new and those good promises, as they say. Today I slept in until my alarm rang at 7:00 am, [which is] very unusual for me[,] especially with the early morning walking. Dave as[is] up in the [taking a] shower. He and Mom have to drop off his little Toyota for [a] tow bar installation. They were going to the casino [in Standish] while they wait. They both enjoy this probably more than me so they deserve some fun. They have been through so much lately. My ankle on my right leg is still sore so I did not walk the mall for safety. I went to Meijer looking for a 0.1 mm pen as recommended by my art book for line drawings. Seems they only have 0.5 mm and 0.7 mm like I already bought at Walmart a few days ago. [I] Guess I will stick with them. The eyes are better today. "Lock" is good. The only problem, besides the occasional image drift, is the blurry left eye [bad prescription as mentioned previously]. It would be great if this clears up. I will mention this at my eye exam next week. I still may have to wait but if so I am inclined for [to get] a second opinion from an [another] eye doctor (commercial). At least they don't take 8 weeks [the time to get new glasses always given by the VA in Saginaw] and maybe I can get a pair of progressives to train my eyes too [or as a back-up pair]. So [Omit So] I went to Burger King [near the Midland Mall] for some breakfast after Meijer [and] then to Barnes and Noble at the Midland Mall. Things look much clearer in the store and I just stood around taking it in. I noticed more control of my head so that the brain tracks the image[s] and I don't get so dizzy moving the head. This is a more normal response and one "normal" people take for granted. Around 10 am I went to the Dow Library and had my usual cup of coffee in their cafeteria. They were breaking in a new girl [employee at the coffee shop] again. She was real cute and short. I noticed later after she left the counter that she was perhaps dwarfish [or a midget?] or at least very short. It's nice they hire folks with disabilities to work. Funny my saying this but I have a greater understand[ing] as I [currently] am one. But I am certain I will be "normal" again shortly and I really do not want to forget. After the library I stopped off at the movie center [Midland Cinemas] and took in ["]Les Mise'rables["], the musical/drama with Hugh Jackman, Russel Crowe, etc. Very nice! [I] Enjoyed being <u>able</u> to watch it and it worked out well as I doubt Mom or Dave would like it. It was similar to an opera almost like ["]The Phantom of The Opera["] but on a historical theme. [It was] Very enjoyable. I got back about 2:30 pm. Mom and Dave [were] still out as I expected. The head sounds [tinnitus] remain tolerable, enough to allow sleep and not getting up in the middle of the night. [It is] Still muffled and an "electrical" sound of a constant nature but [it's] not as loud and I am able to have to [omit have to] tune it out mostly. The right leg bothers me still, especially in a long movie, but there is relief when I lift it on my knee and/or massage it. I do notice that shoes/boots sometime aggravate it [where they touch the skin]. In the lazy boy [recliner] chair that I am sitting [in], it feels much better elevated (as at night). By the way, I should mention that at the movies there was a couple ahead in the theater and the man was using a walker. The lady asked if I wanted to pass by. I am using my cane and she did not see that (dark theater) and I said no and took the opportunity to speak to them about my surgeries and how I was just happy to be there and not in a [?]. I find myself more outgoing, speaking up more and trying to let my story get out. I am hopeful speech therapy will help that or just time!

<u>Sat. Feb. 2, 2013 living room 7:30pm (Ground Hog Day)</u>

Jim Putnam [a friend from school days in Flint, Michigan] just left. It is about 7:30 pm. [My] Eyes [are] good, still light sensitive and not quite in good focus, but closer each day. The [right] leg is [still] hot/numb. I tried to stay at the table longer after pizza [mall] but it's almost impossible due to the leg problems. I hope this clears soon, especially by spring training or Loon's baseball. I would like to see a game without the leg pain I had last year there [I had to elevate my right leg and it was in a constant pain]. I will try to visualize/manifest a more healthy body as the desire is there [more] each day.

Sun. Feb. 3, 2013 3:33 pm living room

In doing the puzzle today my mind wandered back to when Jim Putnam's dad, Richard used to take Dave, Jim, Rand [Jim's brother Randy], and me to HS football and pizza [which we stopped afterward for]. Yesterday Jim told us his dad died from a brain tumor that was cancerous, of all things. He had "eccentricities" back then and it seems all along he was probably battling the tumor. On a deeper level, I believe there are no accidents and [that] he brought this experience to him[self] to endure for deeper reasons. I feel I have done [had] this [similar experience, though benign] for reasons yet to be determined and for a deeper purpose. I won't [further] bore the reader with my own philosophy [,especially] as it would be hard now to write it all down anyway. [It is] Just that with Jim's dad [,] it makes me pause and think about it. Anyway here is how I am today as it's Sunday [and] I am normally resting from walking [on this day] and today is no exception. This is good as my ankle was sore and it seems better now that I am off of it. Tomorrow I have and [an] appointment at 8:00 [am] for a speech therapy review (lab) and then at 9:00 [am] my eye exam at the Sag[inaw] VA. I will make notes about this tomorrow. I will resume mall walking next if I am able, else I will just read and relax. Either way I note the daily and gradual improvement in things. I feel the brain is coming back. I seem to have more control, even though [it is] not "normal" yet. I write this with more control of my hand but the eyes wander in and out of focus and blur [are blurry]. [They are] Better daily, as mentioned before[,] but a ways to go yet. It will be real interesting what my eye doctor says tomorrow. I will mention also that I am OK to drive over there myself and to be sure [undergo] additional therapy as an out patient! Originally I was told [that] I needed to check-in as a [VA hospital] patient for [in order to get] speech therapy when I first arrived in Michigan 1 ½ years ago. "No way, Jose!", and fortunately I was able to tell them [that] on the phone. But [omit But] the eyes are able to [now] maintain the page image more clearly.

There is slight blurring but with concentration I am able to write and see the page much better. I am able to eat and swallow and seem to have better control but I must be "in the moment" and watch [be aware of] every swallow, and concentrate on them so as not to choke. The foot/leg [is] numb and needs occasional horizontal lifting to "cool" off. [It is] Better as well. I may have mentioned this earlier[,] but I am using the cane again for stability as I walk (outside the house), both [for] safety and less resistance to the condition of my body "as it is". I was pushing [my limits] and able to go without the cane but I was not confident and there were shaky times. There still are but I think I have grown less self-conscious about it and will use it until I <u>naturally</u> don't need it. I think it right now gives me more security and confidence to patiently wait until it is no longer necessary. It is more in tune with internal <u>acceptance</u> of the level I am <u>on</u> and not the level I <u>want to be.</u> I may write more about this later. So I will take advantage of any further therapy that comes my way but I think the brain will heal on it's own too. So far this seems to be the case and it is what I believe will happen so [most] likely it will!

<u>Monday Feb. 4, 2013 8:15 pm bedroom</u>

Today I had my first meeting with Anita, the speech therapist [pathologist] at the Sag[inaw] VA. I was chatty about what has recently happened to me but [it] looks like I will get some regular speech therapy there. [I] Also had a follow-up eye exam. The blur in the left eye was a mistake on their part [Saginaw VA optical had an incorrect left lens prescription], the eye doctor told me. They re-ordered 2 pair of glasses again. [There is] A slight change of less prisms in the long distance glasses and a corrected left lens in the close-up ones. I need to put up with those [the old pair] for another 8 eight weeks or so but the price is right! I didn't know if it was only my brain adjusting or the glasses. I guess [it was] a bit of both. I am not yet ready for progressives and I will see [bad pun] her in a year! I guess I am making progress and that's good. I drove there on the expressways – no problem [getting] there but [I had] some snow and slippery conditions coming back. I had my cane for stability and [I am] glad I did. I will try to resume some mall walking tomorrow if the ankle is OK. I will go slow and stop it early if necessary. [I am] Looking forward to that and I am now OK with using a cane until not necessary "naturally". Things continue their gradual, slow improvement. I seem overall to have more balance and muscle control and the brain is better at tracking head movements. [I am] Looking forward to better glasses to help me in reading and close-up work.

<u>Tues. Feb. 5, 2013 4:40 pm living room</u>

Hopefully the new VA glasses will help reduce the focus issue in the left eye. [I am] Looking forward to them[,] it just takes awhile there [time]. Since I seem to be able to handle puzzles and read a bit (fortunately)[,] I can't complain too much as I mentioned [before]. They [the VA] are working on replacements. The head noise [tinnitus] remains in the background with the back of the skull still numb[,] but not as much [as] earlier. Today's noticeable symptom has been the right leg [that is] still hot/numb but mostly the lower [leg] and foot area. Walking seems to aggravate it but the break [I take] around the mall[,] when I can put it horizontal on a chair[,] helps. It has been awhile since walking due to my sore ankle. [It] Does not seem to be an issue but I am gradually increasing the distances to be safe. In the mall I noticed the ability to move the head and look at stores [and] people, etc., while still moving. This still needs improving to be "normal" but I will take it. [It is] Really annoying to have to stop to look at my watch or to see others but I will not rush this and let it come naturally which I think it will. Today I only did 3 laps, half my usual [amount], then [I] went to the [Dow] Library to read. [I] Found [that the] Dow Library is open 9:30 am [I thought it was 10 am] M-F which is nice. After the walk and reading I came back and did some of the last puzzle [for now] (the sea dock). It is #34 and I will break [take a break] after it is done to work on art or writing for a change of pace. Dave continues to work on his car tow bar and this keeps him busy. Mom worked on her tax papers. I tried to get a 1040 Fed. [tax] form but they are not available yet at the library. I cannot do [1040] EZ this year as a [small] 401K was dissolved and I got a little money back but they took out taxes [after I asked them not to]. I will try to get those [taxes] back. We will see. As I write this, the focus in the mind is clearer, no double images but I can tell that [the] left eye is not right as it's blurry. I try to overlook it but once the new glasses arrive, this should clear up. Spaghetti is for supper. I continue to go to bed around 8 [pm] to read and rest and I get up [at] 4-5 [am] for walking. My job before made me a ["]morning["] person and the headaches [back then] caused me to go to bed early and of course the VA had us up everyday around 6 am at least [for breakfast] at 7 am.

Wed. Feb. 6, 2013 4:00 pm living room

[My right] Ankle [is] still somewhat lame and with a snowstorm predicted for [the] next day or so, [I] decided to stop walking short after 1½ laps of [the] mall. [I] Went to Barnes and Noble and got a calendar on sale that has landscapes to try to draw. [I got] back about 11 am and worked most of the day on [the] last puzzle for awhile. [I am] going to work [on] some other therapy for now[,] like drawing, computer, or something else. Today when spending long periods at the puzzle, I was not paying much attention to my right leg[,] so that is part of the key. It still gets hot when not horizontal and I keep hoping it improves like the brain. I'm sure it will in time. The left eye [still] blurs but vision elsewhere is clearer and locked. I'm sure [that] once the correct glasses arrive, [that] this will go away also. Speech [is] much clearer and logical, but [it is not] work[ing] as it should as it is still forced out from my throat. Anyway I will take a long weekend off from walking to test the ankle and stay away from the snow. I will finish the puzzle and move on to something else. Dave continues to install his tow bar in the garage. The mornings are [less than] 10 [degrees Fahrenheit] but rise in [temperature] to [from the] 20s to 30s [Fahrenheit]. No snow yet but [as I mentioned] they predict a small storm for tomorrow. With the glasses on order, I don't want to do too much new reading. I will finish the current book, ["]Impractical

Spirituality["], and hold off till [until] the new glasses [reading] any additional books.

<u>Thurs. Feb. 7, 2013 1:16 pm living room</u>

This is a bit early for my daily journal entry but I wanted to get some things down while fresh [in my mind]. I think my brain may have locked and the eyes as well, it's just [that] I cannot tell because of the incorrectness of my glasses (the loss of focus due to the wrong left eye prescription confirmed by the VA). Also [the incorrect lens causes] the inability sometimes to see the "crawler" clearly on the TV, [and] the lack of focus at the dinner table or [while] playing dominoes. I am really curious if these improve with the new specs [glasses]. I have a feeling [that] they will. In the meantime I am happy that these I wear will let me see to get by. I finished the "last" puzzle yesterday. I took a picture and documented it in the album. I tried a few pages of drawing and [it] looks fine. I will work through the drawing book. Who knows[,] maybe there [is even] an [art] class in the future. After some art, I played Wii golf and though I am out of practice and got beat by 12 strokes, I could see it [the screen clearly] and swing the club[s]. On drives I [sometimes] have to grip an arm [on a] chair after but I manage my balance [better] on other shots. I noticed [that] while doing art I did not notice or pay attention to my right leg but when [Wii] golfing it became hot on one side, so it's [partly] related to motion or my attention to it [or both]. Either way it's not a steady condition and likely will change or I will gain control over it. I am sitting with the leg horizontal in a lazy boy [recliner] as I write and the leg is better. I do notice a persistent ringing in the ears, again more when I pay attention [to it]. I did have a recent dream of hearing silence again [or not hearing the tinnitus]. Let's hope that comes true soon. Either way[,] as I have said before[,] the noise is a whole lot better then [than the] head pain as I had before. So the brain is locked and the eyes are on the mend. The art coordination and thought are there. Speech is still strained, balance needs more work and the head continues to buzz like a high tension wire. [It] makes life interesting, I suppose. We await some snow fall tonight with warnings posted and they are predicting 4-8 inches or more by morning. We will see. Either way, I am taking today and Friday off from walking and with this weekend off as well the right ankle should heal up well. That is all for now...

Friday 2/8/2013 8:10 pm bedroom

Rod Rust [my cousin] stopped in for a visit. He stayed until around 6 pm telling many stories. It was good to see him again [he was my last visitor down in Benton, TN before my surgeries]. He parked his [truck] rig at K-mart [he is a trucker working for the same company as Dave, just passing through] in Midland and Dave picked him up. [The] Light sensitivity of my eyes seems better [it has forced me to involuntarily squint under any light and during the daytime all during recovery] today. The overhead lights in the dining room still bother me but much less. I still have trouble focusing on people directly. I expect this to get better. [The] Eyes are strong but [I still have a] blurry left eye as you would expect with [my] faulty prescription. [The] Buzzing in [my] head [remains] constant and loud, but "tunnel' hearing block prevents it from coming through during the day [the hearing is excellent but [it] still feels like my head is full of cotton, that I am in a "tunnel", but I believe this has helped to keep the tinnitus under control]. At night when it's quiet, like now, is when it is [the] loudest...But I am learning to try to ignore it and to live "normally" as if there were no constant noise in my head. I sure hope this one [of my symptoms] goes away. I miss the silence, but again I am happy to not be in [headache] pain. Now it's a "mental" game to overcome these latest problems. It's tough writing this and not being able to always focus clearly on the writing. I have always had poor penmanship, but it's much worse now. The leg remains hot when not horizontal, worse again toward evening, perhaps again when [there is] more time to concentrate on it. Time will tell.

Sat. 2/9/2013 5:00 pm living room

Even though my left eye prescription is off and [that eye is] blurry, I will continue to make journal entries, but I have decided to stop all reading for now until the glasses arrive. I have already finished puzzling. I will replay the Harry Potter series [complete audio on CD I bought in 2012 for therapy when I could not see well enough to read]...then listen to other audio or music in the evenings to rest the eyes. I think it will be good for the brain and imagination as well. The Harry Potter series will be a repeat to the time last year when I was seeing double [from after surgery to May of 2012, as discussed in my introduction]. At least that is better [(lack of double vision)]. Also today the ringing in the ears seemed suppressed by the "tunnel" blockage to the ears. It's weird because I hear fine (music and tapes, etc.), but there is a constant electrical like noise in the background. I wrote about this earlier when it broke through a few days ago and was a real pain, noise in my head constantly as when I had the tumor before the operation but without any pain. I do still hear the noise, especially in "quiet" moments (which I really do not have yet). I will continue, hoping that one day it will be quiet. This morning in a dream or [a] half awake state I imagined that it (the noise) subsided or was more in the background and I just laid there enjoying the moment. I guess this was not yet the case. Someday (maybe as I read this journal) it will be so. The [right] leg continues it's heat/numbness problem, not as severe, more of an annoyance. I am grateful it is not up in the crotch area [my apologies to some of my readers]. That probably would drive me insane. Anyway we had lots of snow here as mentioned earlier and it should start melting Monday when it gets near 40 [degrees Fahrenheit]. I hope to walk again Monday, sore ankle permitting, but I will watch it and will just visit the library or see a movie or something if not able to walk. As also mentioned earlier, I am using the cane for stability in winter and [for] self-confidence. It seems to be helping. Eventually when balance returns (and/or after new glasses) I may ditch the cane again. We will see. The swallowing issue is still there so that I have to be "in the moment" for each swallow. [I must pay attention to each and every swallow or else I will choke and "in the moment" refers to the practice of mindfulness, which I have read about before my glasses problem]. I expelled coffee once when I was not paying attention [to every swallow]. Right now I need to [pay attention] ... on every swallow. Monday I am also depositing $100 in the [my] bank account so I can order a GSR (galvanic skin resistance monitor) that puts out an audio signal that you can [use to] try to control via biofeedback. I got the temp. sensor [earlier online] but this one seems more like the old one I used to have. I am working on meditation, [and] blood pressure control [relaxation techniques].

Sunday 2/10/2013 3:30 pm living room

I continue my slow recovery and I patiently await a corrected pair of glasses. In the meantime I endure these [this] close-up pair with the out of focus left eye. I am so used to [that] if these new ones correct it, it will seem like paradise. How much I took for granted before [the operations], like the ability to see! I am working back through the Harry Potter series on my mp3 player, burning a CD from [for] each book and listening at night, avoiding reading, as mentioned earlier. That series is a classic and once the glasses arrive, I will probably re-watch the movies also. This morning I awoke, and for a brief moment the buzzing [tinnitus] was subdued as if at a distance from me...a good sign. It returned loud this afternoon and I resorted to the white noise mp3 [I read where white noise sometimes helps with tinnitus so I downloaded a file online] and that helped to suppress it [momentarily]. Now it's doing it's evening routine in getting louder due to the quiet background. The [right] leg remains a problem but less intense. The ankle seems OK now and I will try it out in the morning again at the mall. It still gets hot if not horizontal or lifted. I recall it used to be the entire leg, as [and] now it is mostly in the foot area. Swallowing is improved as well as light sensitivity but I must remain "in the moment" while eating and drinking. I cannot do as others and converse easily while eating. This must appear rude but I do it as a matter of survival.

Mon. Feb. 11, 2013 3:05 pm living room

Last night I learned much more about my recovery and what is happening to my body at this time. I awoke around 12:30 am with extremely loud background buzzing (enough to wake me from sleep). It has happened like that just recently and I think I know why: This [It has been a] year and ½ since the first surgery of [and] a ½ year since the 2nd [gamma knife operation] (I really don't know which is responsible) [and it] has been a time when my body was so numb (from head to toe) that it [and it] served to block the ringing in my head that is always there. I am fortunate in that I did not hear those sounds early, which would mean that I would have had to deal with them all this time. The good news, if any, is that the body is thawing out, which would mean the muffled hearing, sometimes as if from inside a tunnel, may end. But it is this [muffled] hearing that served to block this buzzing earlier, or at least this is what I now believe. This could change. Anyway the background buzz/sound[,] always there, is really loud now. I have tried to ignore it or play white noise or audio mp3s. These help sometimes but the noise does not go away as it is internal. I can only hope that now that healing is advancing that this will mean that the sounds will fade in time. Anyone reading this who can sit in silence is very lucky and should not take that simple pleasure for granted. I look forward to the time when I can do the same, to simply sit in silence and contemplation. In the meantime I will offer little resistance and work in some acceptance of the condition but imagine/manifest a better condition for me. I suppose life is never dull and at least I am not in physical pain. [I have] Mental pain, yes, in ways hard to imagine, but I will remain positive and hope for the best. I will comment here when things proceed [improve] with this "new" condition.

Tues. Feb. 12, 2013 9:20 pm bedroom

The leg [problems] and all this "brain buzz" and how to deal or cope with it seems to be in the amount of attention given to it. When I first awoke I did not hear the sound most likely because my body and mind were in a detached/relaxed state, one of not concentrating on the sound. Throughout the day as I walked or watched a movie ("Silver Linings Playbook") or played Scrabble, I was not aware of the noise until I thought about it. It is always there now and loud but when I divert my attention[,] I do not pay [as much] attention to it. I got the GSR2 skin galvanometer today so maybe that will help in relaxation. Listening to Harry Potter again also distracts. In the meantime the eyes have locked onto pages despite the blurry left eye. I patiently await new glasses that should correct that. My right ankle remains sore so tomorrow I will just wash some shirts and go easy. I have some tax forms so I will look into that tomorrow. Now to try the GSR2!

Wednesday Feb. 13, 2013 5:02 pm living room

Dave is out running errands. Mom is with Rose[, her friend]. The house is quiet, unfortunately my head is not. However it has been better today until now. I [a]woke at 3:30 am and started working on my taxes [I was unable to sleep due to tinnitus] which I completed and mailed [at the Auburn Post Office before anyone woke up]. I stayed busy so my mind did not dwell on symptoms which, as mentioned, seems to be a big factor. Focus and "brain lock" [are] near normal and probably are better but because of my eye prescription errors I still don't have full focus. I am determined to make daily journal entries never the less [nevertheless], as it is my best way of expression for now. The voice gets better daily but I tire easily and it is a great effort to communicate. Typing on the computer is still very difficult as well as using speech-to-text [I got a headset and played with it a bit but the computer did not understand my slurred speech so I put if off for awhile]. I have a follow[-]up speech appointment at the Saginaw VA March 4 and I go to another evening symphony [bought a season subscription for therapy and because in a past life I attended symphonies in Chattanooga, TN] this Saturday night, Feb 16th. I really enjoy that even though ["]disabled["]. The last time in 2012 I went without a cane but was very unstable, especially in the parking lots so

I will use the cane for better support as I am now doing at the mall. I assume eventually this won't be needed but I will let it develop at it's own pace and [I] will take advantage of the cane in the meantime. The leg remains somewhat cold/numb and the bottom [of the foot] is uncomfortable for sitting for more than a few minutes as it has been for some time. Dave's Explorer and the trip we took "up north" to the [Mackinac] Bridge probably aggravated this but it was fun to get out and great therapy. Anyway I will try to ignore the buzzing sounds and keep my mind occupied. I can't read much now and [I] continue to listen to mp3s until new glasses are available. I am lucky that I can read/write fairly well with these [this] old pair as well as watch TV and movies.

Thurs. Feb. 14, 2013 (Valentine's Day--whoopee!)

I found my old eye patch [I got that at the VA in Tennessee to help me see during double vision right after surgery] just now and I am glad I did as patching my left eye does the trick [for the left eye focus problem] and let's me lock into close-up vision as "normal". It will make [help] me appreciate my new glasses when they get here and are correct. The page is locked, no blurring, yahoo! Go figure that it actually was an error in my close-up glasses and really wasn't [all] my brain. I will look on the good [bright] side: it will help all of this be even more interesting when I can recall it all. I fell deeply to sleep while listening to Harry Potter--Book 2, Disk 2. Dave was in the living [dining] room and it [my snoring] probably drove him nuts. I noticed he stepped out to run errands,[;] I probably would do the same. Anyway I awoke at 2 am to use my urinal and with the brain noise I could not return to sleep. I listened to tapes for awhile then got up around 3:15 am to have coffee and do my usual routine. The very early rise and the physical walking at the mall did me in and it all caught up with me this afternoon. Anyway it's nice to see this page clearly even if only [using] one eye again. The brain noise is tolerable. Perhaps it is partly blocked and/or I have been so busy [that] it's not the center of my attention. Either way it's a good thing [being able to hear] and I am grateful for it. I have to write this event down in my log. I need to remember that I am in my 60s and [that] these good looking girls [at the malls, coffee shops, etc] I see are much younger than me. Particularly there is a girl that works at the Cup and Chaucer coffee shop at the Dow Library who is very pretty and has a kind, friendly face [and a beautiful smile]. This is my second time seeing her and while still battling for "normalcy" she offers me a smile which is really appreciated. I will try to tell her this next time. Again, appropriate that it's Valentines and all, but as I said the age difference is pretty major so I best keep things in perspective. We will see. I guess it makes me feel good just to be noticed in my condition.

Fri. Feb. 15, 2013 4:04 pm living room

I have my old eye patch over my left eye as I write this and the view is crystal clear, all a good sign that new glasses (if correct) should be a great improvement and I should be able to read, write, do art, and so on without the need to block the bad eye. Today Mom's Olds[mobile] wouldn't start. Seems I had the interior light dimmer thumb wheel switch on high and it killed the battery overnight. Dave helped jump it and charge the battery. I went to the Midland Mall after that around 10 am. It was packed but I got my 3 miles in. Using the cane at this point gives me confidence and helps me to walk faster. I have already shown that I can walk without it but [I] will accept that I still need it for stability and confidence. I will use it for the first time tomorrow night at the symphony. In last year's concerts I did not use it but felt unsteady crossing the busy parking lot or walking the halls. I always had to hold on to the walls or railings [inside]. As I have mentioned before[,] using it for awhile should make getting around easier. The [right] leg may be on it's final phase. [It is] Not as hot as before but now it gets numb with the new walking boots. The foot gets warm to where I need to still use a chair at breaks (each mall lap) to ease the discomfort. I still can only sit for 5-10 minutes without bottom discomfort. I am hoping that by spring it will be much better so that I can watch a ball game (Loons) better than last year when it got real hot after a bit. My stability is greatly improved (like my vision) to where I can carefully move my head when in motion. It's not 100% but it is improving daily now. It should make tomorrow's concert more fun. I will just have to adjust to all the looks. I get plenty at the mall, but from what I have gone through, some stares are nothing. So everything is better but still all must be handled carefully, from walking, seeing, swallowing, and so on. I do have great freedom when taking the car out in the morning, considering in all likelihood I would have been sent to the VA nursing home in TN unless the family intervened.

Sat. Feb. 16, 2013 noon computer room

[I am] Writing this early as I have a resumption of symphony concerts tonight and [I am] going to the mall with Dave to check out pontoons [first]. Using the [eye] patch helps me [to] see up close. [My right] Foot is a bother a bit [still] . [I am] Listening to Eckhart Tolle's "The Power of Now" which I loaded into [my] mp3 player. I think using the cane again is smart for safety and allows me some "acceptance" of the present moment, as Eckhart would say. I still will walk and exercise but will use the cane for confidence and support as I have written about before. Then with my mind less on striving to go without the cane, I expect there will be gradual, steady healing so that I may not need the cane [eventually]. I will only do this when the stability is better and the device is not needed. I won't rush this as I think I was doing previously. I intend to use it [the cane] tonight at the concert for the first time. Making it across parking lots will be a lot easier. I intend to park at the Dow Library if possible so I can leave turning right and heading behind the concert hall/library and going down Sugnet [street]. This way I should be able to avoid the [heavy] traffic coming out at 10 pm I think. Back to [In] previous concerts that I enjoyed but thought they were just not loud enough or the acoustics were poor, when I think now it was just my brain situation and hearing as in a tunnel sometimes, which I now know has blocked the loud buzz [tinnitus] from the operation, so I won't complain!

Sunday Feb. 17, 2013 4:30 pm living room

[I am still] using [the eye] patch over [my] left eye and [then] the old close-up glasses to write in this journal and to see clearly and it is working well. I will make my daily comments on my condition and some of the happenings here. I went to the 5th of 6 [Midland Symphony] concerts last night at the Dow [Center for the Arts]. It was snowing off and on. I took the cane with me and it helped. I parked at the [Dow] Library and only had to cross the road [St. Andrews], challenging enough in the snow but easier than the parking lot without a cane[,] which I did last time. Up and down the stairs [is] still difficult due to pressure [and elevation] changes but thing[s] are much better. And now I know why it was slightly not as loud to me as the concerts in Chattanooga. My hearing is still tunnel like or subdued and now that I know that this is a great thing![,] as it masks off some of the background tinnitus[,] which is always there. Right now I am avoiding reading until my eyes have the right glasses[,] so I am listening to Eckhart Tolle's "The Power of Now" [as mentioned yesterday] on [my] mp3 player. It's hitting home on my current use of the cane. I have been using the "present moment" as a problem and something to be avoided or used as a stepping stone (pun) to me. [It is the] Next level of improvement instead of seeing it as a "life situation" and accepting it [a fine balance on this is walked (ouch, another pun) between recovery and acceptance, I see now in retrospect] and enjoying the [present] moment. [I now see that we should do all that we can to rectify the situation, and then, if it is to be, we need to live and deal with it]. I will continue to improve but at this stage I will work harder to be "in the moment" and to enjoy my mobility with the cane and not care how it looks. I have been looking in advance to a time when no cane would be needed and in fact for several weeks this was so [before the gamma radiation treatments which knocked me back some] [(]at the park and mall where I was able to go without it but [I may have] got[ten] ahead of myself exactly [omit exactly] by looking ahead and not being "in the moment"[)]. I look forward to allowing healing to occur more naturally at this point. I think this will eventually be the case but in the meantime I will use the cane and be more confident and enjoy the moment more, struggling less. If for some reason I continue to need the cane for support then so be it. I will be thankful for the advancement I do have and as I thought about last night at the concert, I will be thankful that I can do such events and not be stuck in a [wheel]chair or at a nursing home. Anyway [the Tolle mp3[s] is [are] very timely and I will apply what I learn.

<u>Mon. Feb. 18, 2013 4:15 pm computer room</u>

[This has been] An especially "noisy brain" day; it all started early at 1:30 am when I awoke to pee [use the urinal] and the buzzing was loud then. [I] Listened to mp3s [hypnosis, meditation] a bit but [there was] really no choice but to get up. It is loud again as I write. I can only hope that it is a sign of more healing to come. I did something on impulse today. Cathy [Lewis, my very close friend] sent me an email of her and a bird [cockatiel named Buddy]. I said hi and told her of the highlights here. [I have received] no answer [further reply] yet. I know logically that I should not contact her to lead her on because our time together is most likely over for this lifetime, though one never knows. She was [is] a great friend and more and I felt she deserved a note on the latest so sue me! Anyway [I am] back in the walk routine at the mall. [I] Did my 6 laps (3 miles) and had a free cup of coffee at the [Dow] Library [you buy 5 coffees and they punch your card for a free one]. [I am] Better and confident with the cane but [my right] leg [is] still hot. I think the shoe [new boot like shoes from Target] does [do] not help. Maybe I will look for another tennis-like shoe [as Dave gave me] as the weather gets warmer but [omit but]. The [right] leg is warm (or the foot) even without the shoe [being on] here in the computer room.

<u>Tues. Feb. 19, 2013 3:15 pm living room</u>

[I am] Still using my eye patch on my left eye with my close-up glasses. [I] awoke again today feeling the buzz [hearing the tinnitus] further away [from my perception] or reduced but it was early and this may have been in the state between sleep and awake or even dreaming. The buzz is still there now and pretty consistent, like the noise of many electric tension lines all going at once or as they crackle and hum in fog or rain. This is a constant high pitched whine all day and night long, loud [and] persistent[,] but when my mind is occupied on something else like walking or something taking full attention[,] then my mind does not notice it as much. [It] Seems to be loudest in the afternoon [and during sleep] when things begin to quiet down. Today I got some GABA 750 [pills] to take (GNC). They relax the body. There are some reports that they calm tinnitus (but others that say nothing you can take will do that). Like anything, it's all mental and what you believe to work probably will work. Anyway I will take some at bedtime, as it is a relaxant [I used to take these before surgery and they did indeed relax the mind, or I believed that they did], and also calms [and] reduces seizures [as a result], etc. We will see if it helps me to sleep [get] through the tinnitus, get a bit more sleep, and so on. I was [am] curious how it affected [affects the] pain in my [right] leg and [as well as] tinnitus, so I took one about 1:30 pm. So far the calming is there [as I remembered] but the ringing is there too. It will probably take time for this to heal as it is from my head either being opened or zapped. I think it's always been there, except things are "thawing" out so I can [now] feel my hair and hear the ringing. Anyway enough talk about it as it [seems to] only make it louder. I noticed in the library today that even though my glasses are not correct[,] the brain and glasses [vision] continue to improve. With [my] long distance glasses [on,] I could make out titles of books on the shelves much clearer. In the library coffee shop[.] I did not have coordination and swallowing issues with the coffee as usual. I also seemed to be more aware of surroundings. Also Mom and Dave brought home some fish sandwiches and milkshakes from Rally's. I had an easier time eating them (without forks). The light from outside still seems bright and causes me to squint still. The [right] leg at the moment is tolerable, propped up horizontally in this chair [my usual recliner] so overall there is improvement. I seem better able to get over curbs, walk in the parking lot, etc....all with more confidence, particularly with the cane. Now if time and this GABA help with the tinnitus we will really be making progress!

Wed. Feb. 20, 2013 3:40 pm living room

Again this morning as I awoke it seemed [that] the head noises had subsided but they were there in [after] waking. Most of the day, fortunately, they were suppressed and not as loud as they sometimes can be. Just now[,] as in every day at this time as the TV is off and it is quiet, the noises make themselves known. Overall today I had good control of my body in walking the mall. I was able to look at store signs and windows and other walkers as I walked (people across from me). I had not been able to move my head for fear of losing balance. I think using the cane now helps that but it is also the brain's improvement to a more natural stage. I did get a wake up call that things are not perfect yet as[omit as]. When I had my daily coffee about 10:30 am at the Dow Library [the "Cup and Chaucer" coffee shop,] I had a moment of inattention or daydream and as I sipped the coffee it caught me off guard and I blew coffee all over the table. This happens when I take my mind off my swallowing only for a moment, an important lesson for me to pay attention while my brain/body works to be "normal". The right leg is somewhat numb, most of it in the right foot as usual but this seems less than usual of late, perhaps a mental thing as when I pay attention to the noises [tinnitus] inside my head, I don't notice the leg pains as much. I am learning that what you think about or concentrate upon seems to be that which you most notice. A lot of this is just common sense but something that has always been a struggle, so to say. I am happy that I now see this page clearly and there is absolutely no focus drift however I am still mostly [only] using my right eye [using the eye patch] as I await corrected glasses from the VA. Speech continues it's slow recovery perhaps related to the noises/hearing blocks [stuffed, cotton feeling inside my head] that make it hard[er] for me to hear my own voice. I still have to force out the words [when I speak.] I have a VA follow-up [speech therapy appointment] March 4th but by the time they get me on some regular [speech therapy] sessions I may not need them. Unlike some other opinions[,] I know that this [speech] will come back in time [even without regular therapy]. All functions are doing this [coming back to normal] slowly so I see no reason for speech not to follow. Time will tell. Of all the senses, speech can be [seems] slow. I am just very grateful that general balance and sight are OK now. I will add a comment on my right leg[:] Although it feels better[,] I still have the odd sensation of burning and/or I am restless [and] uncomfortable after sitting or being in one position for a moment. This has gotten better so that I eat at the table or play games there for a longer period without having to get up and relieve the pain or annoyance. As I write this my bottom right side is painful so I will end this and walk around for a bit.

Thurs. Feb. 21, 2013 3:08 pm living room

It is probably too early to tell whether the GABA is helping with the ringing[,] but the noise does not seem as loud or as bothersome today. Perhaps it's very appearance of late is a sign of it fading on it's own. Either way I will continue the GABA 750 at night to relax and help with sleep. This morning I awoke early at 2:30 am due to needing to use the urinal [bottle] and then when awake I hear the noise which prevents sleep. I took a shower after listening a bit to the Guided Meditation [Ether and Jerry Hicks "Into the Vortex"] tapes [mp3s] (financial and physical). Dave was up so I went and laid back down to give him his space. I could not sleep so I listened to some of the final chapters of Peter Pan [Librivox recording] on mp3. I left the alarm set for 6 am to walk. Well I fell asleep during some of it or nodded as I did not remember [having listened to] these chapters when awake. In fact I replayed them later in the day. I had a good walk in the mall and library, I used the cane in the mall for walking but in the library I tried to avoid it at the coffee shop and in the newspaper and magazine room. I will probably continue that until I am totally confident to go without it at the mall. That may not be until I get new glasses as I think they may have a positive effect. When I read the papers or magazines [at the library] I use the patch over the left eye and the close-up glasses [to read with] as I have already mentioned. This makes the view very stable and I no longer have the double vision where one image is fuzzy and in the background angling down behind the main image. I have struggled long weeks with this [double, blurry image when reading] and I always assumed it was all my brain adjusting to seeing again but now I find part of the problem was the VA getting the left eye prescription wrong in my close-up glasses. This all should be greatly improved soon. The [right] leg remains odd with pain and/or heat in the lower foot, especially when walking. I put it horizontal in lazy boys [recliners] as always and it is less bothersome. It was very tough to handle a few weeks ago but it too is on the mend. People just don't realize that "little" things like eyesight and proper limb circulation are so special to me and there is such an appreciation for what I have. I hope [that] by the time this journal is read or transcribed that these will be memories but I also hope that I never forget them and the struggles I had to endure then. It is still cold and wintry up here with a forecast for 1-2 inches of snow tomorrow. I am looking forward to spring and perhaps [to] resuming walking in the park. Swallowing of the coffee today [was] much better, however I made an effort to be mindful or pay attention to each sip. I also had a cookie there [at the Dow Library coffee shop] which was very good. Again[,] the head buzzing was mostly suppressed. It's there now in it's usual afternoon increase in volume[,] but when put out of mind it is better. Sandra [my sister] and Steve [my brother in law] are expected here tonight for supper. Steve will tow Dave's car to test it out late. I will likely try to retire to the bedroom my usual time to unwind and [to] get my rest (8 pm).

<u>Friday Feb. 22, 2013 3:45 pm living room couch</u>

Again when I awoke early (2:30 am) there was a period of no buzz sound but it came back shortly to keep me awake. I took a GABA with my regular supplements [before sleeping] but it only made me tired. As usual the sound eventually died down or I just got distracted from it. But since I was tired even with coffee I laid back down about 5:30 am but could not sleep due to the buzz. I may have gotten some [a] little rest as I had headphones on listening to music and that or audio books usually puts me to sleep. During the walk I was concentrating on balance and sights around me [so much] that I did not notice the sound as much. I was [up] early so I left for a Burger King coffee around 7:00 am. We got a brief snowstorm about 7:30 am and it kept coming [down] so I left the mall about 10:00 am after only about 5 laps (2.5 miles). I skipped the library today because of the weather. Side streets were messy only because of not being plowed. As I write this a local truck and [with] plow is digging out the driveway and Dave is going shopping and running errands. He is doing last minute things for his orientation at the trucking company in Indiana next week. This afternoon as I was listening to mp3s (Walden) the noise in the head increased to where I had to stop and play music and/or white noise loud to drown it out. That helped some, but even now as I write this, it is back but then it always seems to be audible this time of day. The [right] leg is hotter than normal as well so I played computer golf while white noise played on my mp3 player and I alternated my foot from the ledge near the computer to make it feel better. Horizontal position helps for a few moments. Thankfully when horizontal in bed and covered the leg feels best and I can manage to get some sleep. [I am] Still only averaging 4-5 hours as when I wake up to urinate, I hear the noise and I just have to get up. Oh the life! Hey at least there is no more headache and vomiting over and over [again]. Everything can always be worse but this is pretty hard to bear sometimes. I will try to distract my sound [tinnitus] with TV or something later. Anyway the snow has stopped and the prediction is for a bit warmer temp[eratures] so hopefully spring won't be too far along. All for now...

Sat. Feb. 23, 2013 6 pm computer room

[My] Eye patch [is still] on [my] left eye [when reading]. Mom is putting on supper leftovers. Dave is working on his car for his trip to Indiana tomorrow. I fell asleep again [this afternoon] listening to mp3s but it did help on forgetting about the buzzing which is strong now as I write. It always is more noticeable in the evening. I keep busy listening to mp3s and playing golf on the computer just to fight back against the sound and to keep my mind busy. The leg again today is a bother but always feels better covered and horizontal. It again is in the lower foot mostly now. I am grateful that it is not in my crotch [which I have mentioned], ha ha. That would be a true nightmare. As they say, things can always be worse. I am listening to ["]Sidhartha["] by Herman Hesse in mp3, a great book [that I read years ago]. Looks like I will replay [the] last four chapters because I think I fell asleep again listening in my bedroom. Supper is almost ready so I will end this for now.

Sunday Feb. 24, 2013 4:30 pm living room

[I] Spent most of this day until now listening to audio (mp3s) of "The Power of Now " by Eckhart Tolle. Dave is getting ready for his trip. Mom continues to work and stay busy. Still I cannot do much [to help them] but try to survive and get better. I am going to try to stay more in the moment at the mall when I walk. Perhaps I will stop wearing the "brain" shirts [my shirts mentioning brain surgery that I wear now and then at the mall or in the park] as they connect me to the past and I suppose I need to be in the "now" and listen to my body to see what it is saying to me [later on in discussing this with my speech pathologist, Anita, she said I should wear them and be proud of what I went through, so I have continued to wear them. As I have always said, they keep people from staring too much]. Today the foot still annoys me unless it is horizontal. I do think it improves slowly with time. Now it is that time of the day when tinnitus really kicks in. Even with nightly GABA I still wake up early. Some of that is habit, but once I hear the buzzing in the morning it is very difficult to go back to bed. I just listen to audio or go get coffee and play on the computer. I have been exploring the free "public domain" books on the Librivox [web]site and there is quite a collection of classics, even some spiritual and poetry [which I enjoy]. Until I get new glasses, this is the way to go, giving my eyes some rest [while I listen and not read]. Maybe even after the eyes are better I will listen to mp3s for the fun and convenience. Anyway progress is slow and steady. The swallowing gets better. Coordination and balance is [still] tough, but [so] I will be cautious. I am in a low point on physical biorhythms [I check these usually daily] [so] if there is anything to that I will be super cautious tomorrow during my walk but I [usually] am anyway.

Monday Feb 25, 2013

It was a very tough start today. Dave called Mom about 12:30 am from Indiana saying that he made it OK (3½ hour trip). For some reason that call I heard and it woke me up. I think having to take a leak at that time was also a factor and so I may have been already awake. Anyway the tinnitus, always there[,] was especially strong. I suspect the "thawing out" of my head is allowing it to be [more] noticeable now. I can only hope it is a sign that it too will vanish. I would love to enjoy peace and quiet or silence again. I could not sleep due to the loud head noise so I got up at about 1:30 am after listening to mp3s for about an hour or so. I had two doughnuts, a bagel, 1½ cups [of] coffee[,] surfed the [television] channels, watched some adult cartoons ["Adult Swim",] and news about the Oscars and the Daytona 500 race. I then got so tired about 2:30 am [that] I laid down but could not sleep. I got up again for more coffee (not too smart, I suppose) and then [I eventually] laid down again and I was able to get in an hour or two of rest. This shows me that if the body is tired enough it will sleep or try to rest even if having severe noises inside. So I was up about 7:30 am and dressed and made it to the [Midland] Mall. I felt OK as in total I probably got 3-5 hrs. [hours of] sleep, usually enough for me. Walking went well. I did the first two laps ([about] 1 mile) without my usual break. I did laps 3 and 4 the same way but I was in no hurry on each walk [lap], stopping to look at windows and things, enjoying the ability to turn the head better. Vision is as good as these [older] glasses allow. [I] Had a close call at the Dow Library where I had coffee and read the NY Times. My close-up glasses fell out of their case [on the way into the library]. Fortunately[, they] did not break but hit cement ground and [which] caused a slight scratch. I can still use them while shutting my left eye [or using a patch]. Thankfully they are OK but [and] a new pair should get here in a few weeks. I just hooked up the [automobile] battery charger that Mom found in the garage. The Jeep [my Jeep Cherokee Laredo that has been parked at my Mom's house] did not start and fortunately it looks like I got to it before it [the battery] was too discharged [I had to buy a new battery in 2012 after this happened]. It is 5:00 pm now and I will check it at 7:00 pm or so. It is at 25% [charged] already so maybe I can [further] test [charge] it tonight. Dave is in Indiana for trucking physicals, indoctrination and is trying to get a trip or more [setup] after. Mom is cleaning out the garage after going to the doctor. I hauled out some trash to the curb. I can't quite bend over and pick up things easily [without getting my brain dizzy] but I am fortunate that I can hook up a car battery charger and take trash to the curb. Say I just noticed that while doing that I was not focused on the ear ringing. That, so far, seems the best method to alleviate it, distract the focus of attention. I picked up some JVC earbuds (earphones) at Walmart today and the sound is terrific. Dave recommended them. They are great and may further help me deal with the ear noises. Speaking of Dave, as it's after 5 pm, [so] I will check my email in case he sent something and tell him about the buds [earbuds].

<u>Tues. Feb. 26, 2013 5:00 pm living room</u>

[Its been] A very interesting day. Others looking from the outside would say how boring[,] but I am writing about what is going on inside, however words may never fully explain. I was reading in my daily journal books ["365 Ways to Live The Law of Attraction", [by]

Mira Lester and "The Book of Awakening" by Mark Nepo. These I try to read daily before I make my own journal entries], before writing this, about not rushing things and about how we usually go through life so fast that we fill up the resume but usually experience so little [and that is] so true. By circumstances I am now in a position to experience so much that I never could [before]. There is much [physically] wrong and I tend to write about that as it is most immediate to [for] me to recover as well as document my remaining life for someone to read, if not [only] myself. I hope it is not boring to others including my "future [or probable] self" but it is the [a] form of therapy and right now [it] is about the only way [that] I can communicate. Anyway enough words on this for now [and] back to the daily log. This day was significant to me and I hope it's a sign of good things to come. I have hardly heard the head noise today and you cannot imagine the relief. I was up very early again (1:00 am) out of habit and also sort of just enjoying the quieter state of mind moment. If I really listen [hard] it is still there but it either is suppressed and/or healing so [much] that my attention is not fixed upon it. Oh how great that is. As I say it's early to tell and I will know more in the days to come but it is a hopeful sign. I had coffee, doughnuts, cookies (I was hungrier than usual) and went [and watched TV] until about 4:30 am then I put on my Peter Pan movie [one of my favorite ones]. I watched it as I have before [many times], even with the current long distance glasses [that I was told are slightly incorrect for my brain now]. They still work good enough for that, fortunately. I went outside to check on the Jeep at 7:00 am when the sun was coming up. It charged fine overnight. I learned that I must press the brake [in order] to shift [as I struggled a bit with the shifter]. I let it charge and put away the long electric cord [back] into the [tool] shed. [There is] Still much snow and ice on the drive[way]. Using the cane I was very cautious [when walking on it]. It gave me a great deal of confidence doing that and naturally I did not focus on any noises [at the time]. I left for my mall walk after [that]. I only did 3 laps as the right ankle was sore again and there is supposed to be a snowstorm coming even though nothing yet.

As I write about it[,] it is windy and feels cold. I fed the wild birds outside later (Dave is in Indiana waiting out the snow one more night). Again I maneuvered in deep snow left in [on] the ground using my cane. The drive[way] is all clear for now but they are predicting 4-8 inches [in the] next 2 days. We will see. Either way I will stop walking tomorrow and just listen to "The Power of Now" mp3s or something. I don't want to read or do puzzles yet until the glasses get here as I need the left eye covered. It is nice [that the eye patch] takes care of the eye drift I had before. There [That] is a memory that I am happy has changed. I wonder if it will ever be told how I had to endure bad vision for nearly a year. Maybe someday I will be able to document that. Today thanks to the brain being quiet[,] my mind focused on the bad right leg. Always something right? Well that thing is so slow to heal, those words I read about things going to [at] their own speed sure applies, but come on it's been a year[,] as I remember needing to prop the leg up at a Loons game [minor league baseball here in Midland] last spring. [I] May need to do that again but less so. [It's] Hard to believe I was there last year and getting around [I used a cane then]. I am much more aware and "present" this year. Perhaps I will have more enjoyment. Well I could "yack" on but I will continue next time.

<u>Wed. Feb. 27, 2013 1:30 am living room</u>

I will write this early as well as [make some more notes at] my usual time. I write while playing my Mozart Requiem Mass in my ears with my mp3 player. It is 1:30 am. I awoke at 1 am unfortunately with a return of severe tinnitus. I am going to write down some thoughts this morning, try my GSR device and just [try to] relax. Diversion will be next, if I can distract my mind. The good news is that it is not [now] snowing and only a couple of inches [is] on the ground, which is light up here. We will see if we get more today but so far not so bad. I awoke from having a dream that I was a veteran with others (new to the VA?) and in an auditorium. I saw nurses coming. They had cigarettes to dispense. I found that to be the case after I went from my auditorium chair and went down to see them. I was forceful and demanded the cigs[cigarettes] so that I could distribute them to the "rehab" ward. I later explained to the vets [veterans] with me that you had to be forceful and "in their face" to get things done. I felt I had nothing to lose (some of my feelings now after having survived this ordeal). I then awoke to the loud tinnitus which I am now enduring. The dream may be saying to me to use the same spirit of determination and endurance. This I plan to do (what choice is there?). Anyway I can be of the mind that the ringing is a relatively new symptom as well as the rapid stability and vision recovering and therefore a sign that things may be changing to the good so that after I endure this the ringing may go away. In the meantime I will try to do things as "normal" to distract myself from it and catch brief naps if possible. Either way I will document here as best I can.

Wed. 2/27/13 3:15 pm living room (Part II)

I return to comment on this eventful day. The buzzing is slowly returning to mind but it died down a few hours after I awoke and distracted my mind. I got involved in checking fuses with Mom [in the basement], putting some money in the bank for Dave, and thus I think that helped [me] to forget or just get distracted from the sounds unless there is a regular pattern to them. I am about to check for mail and start the Jeep. We only got about two inches of snow but much of that has melted. The temperature was greater than 32 degrees all day. They do expect it to be colder this weekend so I will need to watch for ice. Mom works to "babysit" tomorrow and I will resume walking and therapy, weather depending. So far this year there has been much more snow and cold. We are all looking forward to spring.

[Thurs.] Feb. 28, 2013 1:00 pm living room

Mom is sitting, Dave [is] in Georgia or nearby at [on] his truck[ing] job. I just watched "The Way", a $5 DVD I got at Walmart today [Martin Sheen and Emilio Estevez]. I walked about 3½ laps [at the Midland Mall] as I am just getting back into it and also I wanted to get back in case Mom had any van trouble (she has no spare [tire]). I woke up at 2:30 am instead of 1:00 am [as yesterday]. But [omit] I crashed [went to bed] around 8:30 pm the night before so I got some sleep. The buzzing, while still there, seems under control and was not as loud as it has been upon waking. [I] Got a new coffee pot at Walmart for $9 instead of trying to wash out the old one. [I] Did the mall walk as mentioned [earlier] then [I] headed back, [as] this afternoon Tom, [and] Emily will take us to the annual pancake supper by the Rotary club [of Midland. Tom actually took us]. I remember going to my first one last year. I had [was using] the cane then and [was] laid up. I'm more aware now with balance mostly back and I can handle curbs and general walking [much] better. I suffered and am suffering a setback probably from the gamma [knife] procedure. As well as [omit] my head [is] finally beginning to ["]thaw["] out. Speaking is tough and the ringing gets loud at times. The [right] leg still is a pain, but it too seems better by being localized. Eating and swallowing are slow when [and] I must [continue] to pay careful attention to each bite and I can't yet handle carbonated drinks. I am going to wear a brain surgery T-shirt to give gawkers something to look at. It should be fun to go again.

CHAPTER 3   3/1/13 – 3/31/13

Friday March 1, 2013 4 pm living room

Again this morning the electrical buzz inside my brain is there but not as loud as it has been before, especially in the morning as I awake. I could say it's the GABA working but I believe it's the gradual healing of the brain and perhaps the numbness has not completely revealed it to me. As I write this it grows louder as it always does in the afternoon. Again and again it appears to subside if the mind is occupied doing other things. It is a real "bitch" to someone like me who likes silence and meditation. Of course when at the VA I did not do this [meditate] due to being tired and out of it. I may have here in Michigan earlier[,] I don't recall[,] but now that I am very alert and aware inside I cannot yet get to a quiet state with my mind as it currently is. Like everything related to this, it may change and subside. Now it is a matter of endurance and gratitude when I awake and the sound is still "masked". Today I felt good and alert at the mall with better head control, still needing to be careful when I turn my head and walk at the same time. I stopped early after two laps to take care of some laundry and also because the leg (right) became sore so why aggravate it by pushing. I am not going to do that now. I did some laundry at the Auburn [Cleaners &] Laundromat to help Mom out and also for therapy. I did some banking, mailed a letter, and bought some doughnuts. Now that the weekend is here I will stick to the plan of resting for a couple of days. I have a speech therapy meeting on Monday morning at the Saginaw VA. Speech is rapidly improving but still forced. I am using the recorder to record and play back the speech daily. It's cold here until next Wed[nesday] and the driveway is a mess with lots of ice. [It's] So bad that I drove the car to get the mail. Why chance any accident[?] So now I rest and avoid reading with these bad glasses. I will watch TV or listen to mp3 tapes.

Sat. March 2, 2013 3:15 pm living room

Tom, Emily, and perhaps Ben are to be here for a spaghetti supper. Dave is in Indiana, headed for Aunt Betty's in Morris. He is driving back to his trucking company to pick up another vehicle. He may be here late tonight and stay for a couple of days. I have my speech therapy app[ointment] early Monday at the Saginaw VA. Today the buzzing is steady but within control. [It is] Loud now in the afternoon but was controllable earlier and not [as] extremely loud as before. I went to the store and back in Auburn earlier for Mom. I have been busy driving, salting the steps, and so on. Wow, what a pretty girl cashier at the Auburn Food Center [there I go again]. I talked to her about my operations. She was friendly but quite young. I must remember that I am an "old man" but it's still fun to look and no harm to talk. She could be a daughter [or granddaughter], lol. She was probably in [her] 20s and attached so back to reality as they say. I have probably had my time with relationships and now is the time for recovery and self-analysis but who can predict the future[?] Always [it is] unpredictable [and fluid]. I feel pretty good today--good balance and awareness. The [right] leg is a bit warm, hotter toward the foot [area]. I first thought it might be related to heat from improved circulation after all these years but I wonder as it hurts above the knee also. Even if it was the result of how I was positioned in surgery, you would think that [it] would heal by now. I will keep going to [on] walks and treating it normally[,] hoping it will keep improving. It sure is taking it's time. It is still better at night when in bed, covered and horizontal so I think circulation plays a part. I suppose we will play dominoes or Scrabble tonight. I am no card player as the people who live up here are[,] so I will pass on that. Even so it [my vision] is a bit blurry with these [current] glasses and any close-up work so [like] cards would be difficult. Maybe when I get a new pair of [glasses] but I still doubt it as I just don't care for cards that much. Guess I better get well and head back home to the South?

Sun. Mar. 3, 2013 5:00 pm living room

The buzz noise is louder today but I managed to mentally not pay much attention to it so that helped a lot. I also listened to Harry Potter stories on mp3 (Chamber of Secrets) and that helped. I also play computer golf. The leg has been a bother today with [it] feeling hot below the knee to the point to where I needed to put it horizontal in the computer room or on a lazy boy [recliner] chair for relief. [It's] Probably because of the lack of focus on the buzz. The mind has more time to pay attention to the leg. [It's] Just an idea. Anyway the leg is cool/hot/numb [cool to the touch but feels hot] and I have been pampering it today. Vision is good with the patch that I now use to write this journal or to use the notebook [computer]. Speech [is] still a problem to get ideas and words [across] to another person. Tomorrow morning is my second speech therapy meeting in Saginaw. [I] May visit with Betty and Jerry and Dave but working on [???] now as ... Dave is here now for a couple of days and has to deliver that RV ... [to Birch Run near Flint]. I will write about how that turns out tomorrow.

Monday March 4, 2013 8:20 pm bedroom

[I] Just got back from a trip to Betty and Jerry's. Pat was there as well as Kathy. We had some pizza. That was interesting and the entire day helped keep my mind off my symptoms, especially the buzzing and right leg. I started the day driving over to the Saginaw VA for an exam by the speech therapist [pathologist] there. She is nice and ran some cognition and speech tests on me. Now they are very easy (the cognition tests). The speech remains an issue but [so] I have a follow-up appointment next Monday morning. Hopefully with these and practice, the voice will return to normalcy. The leg seemed less bothersome today. It was left down (not horizontal) much of the day and it felt OK, with no real urge to lift it up. Swallowing remains a caution to me with the need to be very careful. I am back to write this in bed, surf the computer, and so on so that I may tire and get some sleep before I possibly might be awake [wake] ...[scrambled writing here] ...GABA pill is kicking in [as well as the long full day of activity] to help me sleep. More later...

Tues. March 5, 2013 2:40 pm living room

[There are] Some interesting developments perhaps: [I was] Up at about 2:30 am due to urination and loud ringing or buzzing which is normal [at this time in the morning]. Luckily I slept [went to bed at] 8:30-9:00 pm first. As I ate doughnuts, drank coffee, the usual [morning] routine[,] the ringing suppressed some (or I didn't pay attention to it or both). It is like a noisy electrical device or high tension wire or [and] a field of loud crickets, all surrounded by a cotton blanket or gauze so [that] the sound is muffled at times (thankfully). When I quiet my mind to listen it is always there now. As I have mentioned before I will try to continue the walking, the normal daily routine in hopes it stays muffled and begins to subside. When I drove to the Dow Library after walking I thought I heard it change sound briefly and that gave [me] a thought that something was changing but it is still the same as I write this. The leg is similar today. It is much more comfortable. [There is] Less ache and heat it seems. I have noticed the right foot getting hotter as a boot and walking is used [are combined?] [shoe to skin contact causing the heat?]. I will keep walking, however, as I think this outweighs a little foot heat. I still rest it [my right leg] up on a chair at the end of each lap and that makes it less painful. The walk was good today. I felt more aware and able to see around me. Again I am hopeful [that] the new glasses will make this even better. I think we are at the tail end of winter. Mom's drive[way] is icy but they are predicting 40s for late week/weekend so all [ice] should melt. [The] Main roads are all clear. When walking I seem to have much more control. Each curb [I cross] is not that difficult for me to go up and down. There [still] is disorientation on any change of direction [of my head] or [change of] altitude but I predict [that] it won't be long before I won't need the cane. Dave is making last minute arrangements to get his third RV delivery [set up]. This time [he] goes back to Elkhart, Indiana [his RV transport company headquarters] then up to Duluth, Minnesota. He then will try for a trip to Alberta, Canada or out West somewhere. He may leave tonight but I predict more likely in the morning. There is some snow going through Indiana now but Duluth looks clear.

Wed. March 6, 2013 7 pm living room

[I] Just finished listening to the Harry Potter mp3 (2nd year – Chamber of Secrets) again as I am avoiding reading or puzzles until [the] new glasses are ready. [It was] Very enjoyable and [it] brings back memories. Mom is out taking Rose shopping and to see her Aunt as it was her [Rose's] birthday recently. I'm OK enough for her to do this [she no longer has to be here to take care of me]. Ice is melting now as [it is] the first day above 32 [degrees F] and they expect a week (or more?) like this. I think spring is finally here but one never knows up here. Dave is driving to Duluth, Minnesota now on a run [RV delivery]. I walked briefly at the mall but left early to get Mom her car and to wash it and to check fluids. [The] Awareness improves in walking. [The] Buzzing seems less intense and the [right] leg feels less hot though it does heat up some when I walk and in the evenings. I will continue to play the Guided Meditation tapes ([Esther] Hicks) on physical improvement ["in the Vortex"] and that will help [helps]. I may check out Argo, the movie that won the Oscar this year [I never did]. They have an early morning showing at 11:00 am at the local theater. [It's] good therapy and [a] good reward. The awareness [and] improvement is [are] really enjoyable [now] as I maneuver over curbs and in snow so much better. I am using the cane until stability fully returns and [I get] new glasses also. I have been able to get sleep [recently], some even after I awake to the loud buzzing. I am able to relax and even catch some [sleep] before I walk [early in the morning]. All is improving and it is just fantastic!

Thursday March 7, 2013 3:10 pm living room

[The] Ice and snow on the ground [is] beginning to really melt now as temp[eratures are] in the mid 30s and [with] sunny [skies]. I awoke at

2:30 am and the buzzing was loud enough to keep me awake. I listened to the Guided Meditation [mp3s] for awhile but the sound was intense so I got up. I drank coffee, had doughnuts, and watched the usual [TV] channels, then I watched the second movie in the Harry Potter series again, as I recently finished listening to the mp3s [of] The Chamber of Secrets (movie 2). That killed time and distracted me from the noise which seemed to resume it's normal muffled [sound] and reduction around 7:30–8:30 am, walk time. [The] Walk was good. I did several stretches [laps] at first with the cane lifted [off the ground] and then a man with a cane came over and asked where I got the ice tip for the [my] cane [collapsible sharp tip at the end of the cane to grip ice and snow in bad weather] [I bought that on Amazon online earlier]. I talked (or tried to) briefly [with him] and [then] resumed [my walk] using the cane for each lap [as he was using one]. I never saw the man again. He said he had a deteriorating spinal condition so you never know what a person's story is. Thankfully [for me it] looks like I will [fully] recover eventually though it has taken months now. I bought some melatonin pills to take to see if they help me sleep more at night. So [omit So] I will add them [to the many pills and supplements I take now] and see what happens. I had a free cup of coffee at the [Dow] Library after [walking], [I] read the [NY] Times and then headed back [to my mother's house]. The [right] leg seems better, less hot but [and] the socks are thinner also and perhaps that helps. Either way when I walk it is more painful, causing me to rest each .5 mile (once around). I refilled the bird feeder Dave made [he made one up close to the main dining room window with a string loop you can use to lower it down for a refill] and sprinkled more [ice] salt [on the porch, walks, and driveway]. By the end of the weekend all should be melted. I am [still] listening to Harry Potter mp3s, The Prisoner of Azkaban, my favorite. I should get [an] Elkhart Tolle CD delivered soon so I will burn that to my [mp3] player. I am basically avoiding reading [as previously mentioned] until [the] new glasses arrive. The buzzing, while loud and steady, seems to not be [as] noticeable, if I distract my mind elsewhere [as I have mentioned].

Friday March 8, 2013 1:45 pm living room

[There have been] Some interesting developments since making any [further] journal entries. In the mail yesterday I received my near vision [close-up] glasses rushed from the VA. I think because my original [VA] ones were wrong (left eye not focusing), they rushed these and mailed them. I had to work with the frames to get them to feel right but I think they will be fine, they work great despite both lenses looking like a "Coke bottle", that is just thick. There is some adjustment [to come] as the eyes still see some background on occasion and some blur. This time it's probably me and my brain as [because] when I use each eye separately they are fine. I think it is the eyes locking and when I use it [them] for a period of time and in writing this, it's better. Anyway it will be nice to read again and perhaps my new long distance glasses will also be in the mail soon. Those are only slightly different, I am told, to account for the changes in my brain from [since] my last eye exam. Today walking is improved with better balance but I only went 4 laps and went to the library early as my throat seemed a bit sore like the start of a cold. Right now it is fine so maybe I won't get anything. Sandra, Steve, and their kids are expected over this afternoon for sloppy joes and games. I hear the person [mail truck] so I will go out shortly [and check the mail]. Perhaps my other glasses are there. The snow continues to melt (and ice on the front porch also). I will add [sprinkle] more salt and feed the [wild] birds some seed and enjoy this first sign of spring. [My right] leg is hot but perhaps better as [there is] less pain at [during my] walk breaks – a good sign indeed.

[My] Last comments [for today] (4:00 pm)[:]

I just left Chemical [B]bank in Auburn. I received my 940/941 refund from [the] IRS (about $800). I went to deposit it into my checking account and the lady there [manager] gave me some grief as the check was made out to "Caylorco, Inc" [and not to me personally since it was to the business]. I did my best to explain [that] I was the president [former] and they finally cashed it. I went to the ATM later and took [it] out. The maximum [amount of cash available per day is] $500. Tomorrow morning I will take out $300 [to get the full amount of the deposit]. She said "well, if it returns then you are "responsible". It shouldn't be a problem as the IRS should honor their own checks but I don't trust them or banks so I'm taking out the money upfront. Now to relax and try to forget how messed up the govt [government] and society can be, ha ha. Also the brain buzz has been well suppressed today after about the first hour up (about 2:30 am). Perhaps because I have been so busy or [it's] just the body suppressing, but either way, no complaint here!

Saturday March 9, 2013 3:45 pm living room

[The] New close [-up] vision glasses are clear individually (in each lens) but together with both eyes open words don't quite line up at all times [one line of text is at an angle, causing a blur in reading]. I can still read and I suspect it is my brain re-training and that when the two images align, the full image will finally be clear and sharp. Until then I will give it some time yet. The electrical wire, buzzing head noise is consistent and especially loud today but again I am able to not pay attention to it at all times so that I can ignore it. It did wake me at about 2:30 am again so I have been up since then. This is one reason to continue to go to bed early so that I get a few hours sleep before it gets too loud. I take the GABA 750 and melatonin to help in sleep[ing]. Some early rising may be habit from my "former" life as I had to do that to get my laundry done for the nursing home before regular customers arrived at the laundry [as mentioned in the introduction]. The [right] leg remains hot, even after it is lifted horizontally in a chair, but I was able to endure a regular seat at the [dinner] table last night to play dominoes with Sandra's family. I still went to bed about 8:00 pm. I have been listening to Harry Potter – Prisoner of Azkaban mp3s and ripping this afternoon. I also had some raspberry wine to sip and [help me] relax. I will now take a TV break for awhile.

Sunday March 10, 2013 9:00 am living room

[This is] An early entry as an unusual event happened when I awoke [this morning]. I was up about 5 am. We set our clocks ahead for Daylight Savings [Time] the night before. I got some sleep and upon awaking I again did not hear the buzz. I didn't know if I was dreaming but I seemed awake, but I could not hear the buzz. Maybe it is changing. However as I got up to get coffee unfortunately [it] returned and is quite loud as I write this. I remain optimistic that this really did occur and was not "in my mind" and that it may portend good things to come. Mom just got up for church with Sandra so I will continue this later on.

3 :00 pm [3/10/13]

Some further comments[:] When switching glasses there is some adjustment [time] but the new ones seem to get better the longer I wear them. I continually need to adjust the frames but now they are pretty close. The occasional mismatch [overlap of text lines occurs]: the left eye [image] is now clear alone, [and] so is the right, but when using two eyes the image does not always align exactly right, which leaves a bit of double image with [when] reading sentences but this seems to also improve with time which makes me think that this will improve as the brain "trains" to lock both images more quickly. I just finished watching the third movie in the Harry Potter series after having listened to the mp3: The Prisoner of Azkaban. This has to be my favorite, the one where Hermione and Harry go back in time to save Buckbeak and Sirius Black and where Harry thinks he sees his Dad [rescue him] but it is really [him seeing himself] coming back in time. [It is a] Great piece to read and watch. So the glasses look like they will work ([, the] new [close-up] vision ones received first by [in the] mail). I look forward [to receiving] the long [distance] vision pair soon, as they are slightly different [than my current pair] to better match changes in my brain, according to the OD [optometrist] at the VA [Dr. Hrywnak]. My electrical buzz has been strong today after I did not hear it upon waking for awhile, which I commented about [earlier]. The [mental] distractions help and I will need to continue these (either mp3, golf on the computer, reading, or TV). I have my speech therapy meeting tomorrow morning and I need to get Mom a new toaster [that does bagels] so that will keep me busy. I may try to walk some at the Fashion Square Mall [in Saginaw] after the [speech therapy] meeting.

Monday March 11, 2013 5:00 am living room

[This is a] Short note to write about some changes to the buzzing this morning. Woke [I awoke] at 2:00 am to pee [urinate] and the buzz was not there [again]. I was in a dream where I owned a mall and we were in an unused area and I noticed the quiet [then]. In reality it remained buzz free for about 5 min[utes] until after I sat up and used the urinal [bottle]. It returned or I was aware of it then but it was not as loud as lately. Right now as I make coffee it is back but again seems not as loud, all hopeful signs that this is changing and may be more controllable.

11:15 am [3/11/13]

The app[ointment for speech therapy] at the VA [in Saginaw] was canceled—Anita Wierda did not make it in—I bet she forgot to set her alarm clock to Daylight Savings time. Any[way] it was rescheduled for next Monday. I did get to read a brochure in the waiting room on tinnitus, and just like online, just mental adjustment [is all] the person can make [do to relieve it]. If [you] take drugs [for it] mostly they are sedatives, [or] sleep agents, which probably explains why mine dies out in early morning lately. Could it be the melatonin? Anyway they also mentioned stress and that relaxation techniques might help. I will retry that biofeedback device [GSR] and some meditation, although that is tough in a noisy head. Anyway when busy in the store or walking with a cane, I do not pay attention to the ringing all that much. I notice it, as now, when it is quiet (TV is off, Mom is checking emails [using her computer], [and the] birds are quiet). I wrote this earlier than usual as it follows what is happening to me now and [it] is still fresh in my mind. I am continuing to adjust to the close-up glasses so [I] may try to do some more reading. As the focus is better I may try drawing and/or using the art supplies [Dave and Mom got me some for last Christmas]. Also of note [is] the [right] leg, while still a bother, at times is better in that I seem to be able to sit longer without putting it horizontal to relieve pain. The entire leg and especially the "seat" gets a bit hot still and occasionally I need to get up and move around. This probably helps with the circulation. As I choke up [on] some coffee I am reminded to write a bit about my swallowing issue. I am better able to control it now. This really improved after I seemed to regain a lot of my balance, with the ability, although to you [dear] reader, it may sound as trivial, to walk a step or two backwards and to still [be able to] keep my balance. Something I used to take for granted [like balance and swallowing] was a "big deal" [to me] to [be able to] re-gain again. So the swallowing I can now mostly control if I pay attention to each swallow and live "in the moment". I have found [that] many a time if I daydream or try to talk with food in my mouth, I will choke. It's like my body is forcing [me to develop] new habits. Sure it probably seems a bit anti-social to those without this condition but I am currently happy to make it through a meal without an episode. Occasionally, "spit", for lack of a better word [or saliva], will build up in my mouth. If I don't swallow [,spit,] or keep that down, it can surprise me and go right down my throat when I don't expect it. This causes me to choke. This is not often, fortunately, and has not yet happened during sleep.

3:20 pm [3/11/13]

I have spent the rest of the day reading, [watching] TV, [listening to] mp3s, anything to occupy the [my] mind and that really helps [me suppress] the tinnitus. I have not thought about it and only hear it as background static, so to speak. Mom is going to make me some eggs and sausage for supper which sounds great. I take care of breakfast and lunch for myself but let her do supper as [so] she feels [a] part of things. I am phasing out [in the doing of] my own laundry now, using a hamper [in my bedroom] and playing "laundry" customer (not owner) to [at] the local laundromat in Auburn [Auburn Cleaners & Laundromat]. I see they do dry cleaning. That is what probably keeps them surviving. Anyway it's fun and a flashback to the [my] former life and also works as great therapy. I am thankful that I am able to do that and especially thankful for the ability to get around and drive each day. That gives me a great feeling of independence and also it helps me walk daily and improve in many areas.

<u>Tuesday March 12, 2013 4:00 pm living room</u>

I have finally adjusted the frames of my near vision glasses that arrived by mail so that they feel OK and don't slip. There is a bit of line bend and bleed when reading [misalignment of images] but that may well be my brain continuing to adjust. I will probably continue to tweak [the frames] a bit and that may remove [help with] it [the misalignment] I wrote about. This [as I wrote about earlier], how that each eye image is OK independently [when I close the opposite eye] but that they don't always align the two images up exactly, thus causing a little focus and reading problem. I don't seem to see this [as much] in this journal. I still have a cold and sniffles but have not mentioned it to Mom as she is too old to get one [should avoid one at her age] and I don't want to influence her as I am now certain [that nearly] all disease is started in the mind. That much I have learned [in my readings and study and experience]. Dave is somewhere in Montana driving. Mom is reading the paper. My birds [two cockatiels] are chirping, as they got excited seeing me recently outside. [I am] getting mail and filling up the songbird feeder [that] Dave made. I went walking and [then] to the Dow Library again today. The noise [tinnitus] was tolerable, not nearly as loud as before, thankfully. I hear it now [as I write] naturally that it is quiet in the house. The leg [is] hot as usual but most feeling [heat is] in [the] foot area. It's a pain and I hope this goes away on it's own but it has been a year now, still if I have to live with it, it beats losing a leg I suppose. I am hopeful I can try out golf this year at the local par-3 [golf course] down the road. I will try the driving range first, then chip the ball around as in the front yard [I was able to chip the golf ball in Mom's front yard during a warm snap in 2013] and hopefully I can give that a go [note: maybe next year for a driving range as stability never quite got that good in 2013]. It's a bit colder today and most of the rain/melting has been absorbed by the yard. I am anxious to resume walking/training at the local park [Williams Township in Auburn – something I do when it is warm enough to be outside] as there are less people there [than in the mall]. Changes continue in the right direction but they are slow and steady. I have much to be thankful for and will continue to record my events and reflections as best as I can.

<u>Wed. March 13, 2013 2:30 pm living room</u>

Today the [right] leg feels better (or is less noticed) as the buzz noise is extreme now. It was fairly loud upon awaking at 3:00 am and has been steady [loud] all day. Now it is extremely loud. I have done normal routines like walking. I did my laundry. Anytime I do something that distracts, it is helpful to get the sounds out of my immediate attention. Right now I have CNN on and I have it where [and there is breaking news that] the Catholics have selected a new pope (white smoke was observed). They have not presented [him] to the public yet [as I write this]. I will try to read or play my mp3s to drown out this loud noise [tinnitus]. I can only hope to surrender to it [accept it] and hope it [the increasing loudness] is a sign that the body and this sound will change for the better.

<u>Thursday March 14, 2013 3:15 pm living room</u>

I awoke at 5:00 am. I listened to the Guided Meditation tapes for awhile. [It] Seems that the inner brain noise was weak or not there [or my awareness of it was missing] again. It was nice not to wake at 2:00 am or earlier. After I got up I was aware of the noise again. [I was] watching news, having coffee and doughnuts as usual. I ignored the noise [as] best I could. In walking I only did 4 laps as I had my old "combat" boots on [boots I used to wear at my laundry job] and when I returned to the food court there were jackets left at my table so I left to [for] the Dow Library early, about 9:30 am. There I read the [NY] Times, fighting some blur in the new glasses (some overlap or inaccuracy in aligning both images as I have written about earlier). I did not have coffee there but came back early and had it at Mom's. As I write this the eyes adjust to the new glasses but there is a lag time [noticeable when switching between the two pair]. I have been listening to Harry Potter's "The Goblet of Fire" (book 4) [on] mp3s. I missed his outsmarting the dragon (task 1) in the Triwizard Tournament so I must have slept through that part [again]. He is currently under water breathing [using gilleyweed] and rescuing Ron, Hermione, Flo's sister, and so on. I have read the book and [have] seen the movies before surgery, then [after surgery] I listened to the [CD/]mp3 version [read by Jim Dale] here in Midland while I could not see [well with both eyes] and was recovering. Then I watched the [Harry Potter] movies I [had] ordered [on Amazon] and will watch them again. I no longer have the books as Cathy loaned them to me in Benton. Fortunately I returned them to her before the surgery. My foot/right leg is a bit hot/numb but it was not so bad this morning [while walking] in the old shoes. [The] worst thing is that it got hot after 3 or 4 laps [in the mall]. Either way I lifted up my leg in a [mall] chair after every lap[,] in the food court. I will try these shoes [again] tomorrow as they may be better for walking than the replacement pair I bought at Target. I was using Dave's shoes [he gave me a pair of hiking shoes that were not his size and they lasted several months until they fell apart] he gave me and they felt fine but became very smelly and I could not make them not smell after awhile with sprays and powders so I got rid of them [Mom and I had glued the soles and they lasted a bit longer] at a dumpster [public trash can] at the Dow Library. They were that bad. I enjoyed them but they just became too sour to use. Well, Mom is working in the garage and [on] a lot of "chores". She just won't sit still, even at 80. I have given up trying to change her[,] that is her ["]thing["] I suppose. [It is] Time for me to go check the mail. I am looking for a possible tax refund on the taxes they took from a 401K distribution and my other pair of glasses [to be in the mail]. After that I may read or use the computer.

Friday March 15, 2013 12:30 pm living room

Mom took off to the store. Dave is out west and headed back. There is a couple of inches of snow possible here late today or tonight. This is a day of change in some of my abilities so I am writing in this journal earlier than usual. At the mall I only did 3 laps but the last two without using the cane. I did have it with me in case [I needed it]. [On the] second lap I carried the cane fully extended [lifted up]. [I did] The last lap with it folded. I will probably use it to and from the car if the weather is poor but at the [Dow] Library I only carried it as I walked to the library through the [parking] lot. I was there at 9:30 am early and took a coffee break as usual but left my coat and cane in the quiet [(]newspaper/magazine[)] room and walked to the coffee shop [without a cane]. [This is] Sort of a big deal as I do it now with more confidence. I am also priming for spring which is around the corner and I would like to switch back to the park [for my morning walks] without the cane if possible. I will need to use a tennis or walking shoe out there but I look forward to a place that is less crowded and more [omit more] outside.

Sunday March 16, 2013 3:15 pm living room

Snow is outside--about 1-2 inches. Soon it will be spring. I went for the mail just now and found my long distance lenses [glasses] mailed to me. Also [there was] a letter [from the IRS] saying [that] they adjusted my [personal] taxes and will refund me about $931 soon. A nice surprise indeed. I still am awaiting any report/refund on my [personal] 2012 taxes so we will see. I am adjusting to the new [long distance] glasses (for TV, driving, etc.). They were adjusted for changes to my brain according to the OD at the VA [Dr. Hrywnak]. Already I see [the] crawler better on the TV and the remote [control] buttons so they probably will be fine. It will take a bit of adjustment time but I am very happy to get them. I will just "have" to watch TV today, ha ha. Not much else [new to report] except the eyes and good news in the mail. Dave is in Minnesota and probably will be back tomorrow or [the] next day before heading to Texas.

Sunday March 17, 2013 (St. Patrick's Day) 3:30 pm living room

Dave came back this morning from BC, Canada, a long grind. He is out washing his car, running errands for his next trip to Texas. I was listening to Harry Potter read by Jim Dale again and got to see [saw] that disk 9 of "The Order of the Phoenix" is warped and won't rip [into mp3 format]. Luckily I have heard it before and I was doing it mainly as I was waiting for new glasses. Well as I wrote about [earlier], they have arrived and I am breaking them in so I will just finish watching the H.P. movies and skip [listening to the] mp3s. Perhaps sometime in the future I may buy the books and read them again. As I write in this log I am aware of the burning in my right foot/leg which usually gets intense this time of day. I patiently await improvements there. The buzz in my head remains steady but I have learned to ignore it mostly or don't pay attention to it. Perhaps this is the secret to the leg too. Both pair of glasses seem better, especially the reading glasses. The long distance pair helps me to see the numbers on the remote control plainly and I see the crawler on the TV screen bottom however there is some blur noticed under some letters, especially white on black, I will not rush to judgment as I still think my brain is still changing. Mainly now I am tweaking the frames to make them comfortable and being very careful not to snap them. I think I will still use the clip-on sunglasses for the long distance pair but I adjusted them so as hopefully not to rub as much and thus scratch. I am sure there will be some wear but I think I can use them before the follow-up [eye doctor appointment] next year. I look forward to this [coming] year and feel [that] the eyes, the buzz, and the [right] leg/foot will all improve. [I would] Love to go to a [baseball] game or movie without favoring my legs, eyes, etc. I wrote previously that I will try to go without the cane more and more as the weather improves, but likely will still use it to get to and back from the car, especially when snow is on the ground as now and when going to the VA in Saginaw for speech therapy, which I do tomorrow morning.

Monday March 18, 2013 5:15 pm living room

[I am] Still adjusting to [the] new pair of glasses but they will come around. At least I can still see and I will take that. [It's] hard to imagine what life would be like not [being] able to read, write, drive, and so on. Although my brain has not yet "locked" into normalcy yet, things could have been much worse. I hope this journal does not come across as whining or complaining as I only mean it as a record of recovery and to reflect what I can't express any other way yet. Today was busy--I had my speech therapy with Anita this morning. [I am] basically improving but [and she says] ["]keep up the good work["]. [I am] Still forcing [out] words and running out of gas [energy] but better each time [I visit with her]. Recording my voice helps me hear what it sounds like to others. I [may have already] mentioned the xaphoon [cross between a clarinet and saxophone that] Dave got me [for Christmas]. She [Anita, my speech pathologist] says [that] it is good for my breathing, strength, etc. I also got a replacement pedometer [to measure walking distances] from Amazon today. My original locked up. Before [with the old pedometer] I did around 10,000 steps which was about 3 miles. We [I] will try this [new] one tomorrow. It clips on my belt. [I have been] following the news today (financial) where in order to impose European debt reduction, that Cyprus, the island nation, "suggested" or put forth the idea of taxing insured bank deposits! Needless to say, this caused a run on the banks there, exhausting all ATMs. People [are] waiting in lines to get their money out of banks. They may not do it but they started a panic. Time will tell if this will spread. Anyway [it] makes for interesting news. I bought a book and a tape today at Barnes and Noble in Saginaw, [and] walked a bit at the Fashion Square Mall there. The tape is about mindfulness. [I am] anxious to see if it will aid in healing. Sounds [Tinnitus] today [were/was] suppressed enough to function. Dave left early for his trip to Texas. He was gone when I got up around 5 am. [I am] about ready to have a bowl of chili and wind this day down. I will go back to the walking tomorrow and see how this new meter works.

<u>Tues. March 19, 2013 4:50 pm living room</u>

[I] used the new belt clip pedometer. It measures the mall (6 laps) as 3.8 miles [closer to 4.8 miles now as I type this in June, 2013], a bit more than the 3 miles the other device says. I will test the calibration at the mall tomorrow [I did have to adjust for longer strides now]. Anyway it's easy to use. I walk better [now, I am] more aware[,] but still unsteady and with the new snow (about 1-2 inches) and icy patches (come on spring!) I am still using the cane but [I] can go several steps without it but still [I am] not comfortable or stable without it. Those [recent] times without it, I wonder if I did not use [it because of some vanity] but [I] was unstable and my ego told me not to [use a cane?] or is this recent unsteadiness just a relapse.[?] I don't want to use it unless necessary but I don't want to take chances either. When the weather is better we will see, but I would rather stay with it until <u>very</u> confident without it. This morning I awoke at 2:00 am and laid back down until about 4:30 am even with the noise. It was there but not extreme so I was able to grab more sleep (yahoo!). Right now the hearing is good but the head [remains] blocked as if having a head cold. Whether that is still numbness from the operation or the body's self-defense mechanism it's good that I don't hear the full force of the head sound. I usually feel the [right] leg hotter. Today it was a bit uncomfortable but either a bit less annoying or improving some. Maybe I did not pay that much attention to it as I was listening to my ["]Mindfulness for Beginners["] mp3 [by Jon Kabat-Zinn]. As the tapes [CDs] say and as I am learning[,] you [can] direct the mind's attention. Now I am wondering if paying symptoms any attention only magnifies them. But I do like writing in this journal while things improve, as it is one of the easiest ways for me to yet [omit yet] communicate these things.

Wed. March 20, 2013 3:45 pm living room

[It's the] Official first day of spring this morning. You wouldn't know it [by looking] outside. [It is] Quite different than last year at this time when it was in the 70s. Now it's in the 20s or less with snow on the ground, ice in patches on the roads. It will all end eventually but it just seems slow this year. This has been a tough one [day] to endure. I awoke at 2:00 am to use the urinal and the noise was strong and steady. [It was] Too much [noise] to sleep [further] and I had my 5 hours or so in from retiring early[,] thankfully. I had coffee, doughnuts, and watched the 5th movie of the Harry Potter series, "The Order of The Phoenix", to distract my mind from the noise. It helped but today the sound has been very steady. I got back early today and watched another Harry Potter movie, 'The Half Blood Prince" and again during the movie, my mind is occupied and I don't pay attention to the noise. As in all afternoons about this time, the sounds are louder and steady, so I will try to stay busy, dope myself with GABA and melatonin [in the evening] and try to get more sleep. I will try to finish the H.P. [Harry Potter] movies (again) in the next couple of days. Mom is downstairs doing laundry. I have started doing my own [laundry] now at the local laundromat [Auburn Cleaners & Laundromat] for the therapy and for the old role reversal [being a customer instead of an owner]. I enjoy that and it should help her [Mom] out. Dave is in Texas probably by now and will drop [off] his RV and head back, probably [he] will get back here sometime this weekend. At the mall in the second lap I got a "coffee" [acidic] stomach, most likely due to more than two cups drank this morning. I will avoid that [next time]. I left [the walk] early, did some Walmart shopping for Mom. I did get to check the calibration of the pedometer [at the mall] and I ["]tweaked["] it a bit. It was 22 inches per step and now it is [had to be adjusted to] 23 inches per step. I will check it tomorrow. I like it as it clips on to the belt, very convenient. [It is] Time to clip my nails, check the mail, check the computer [for email], maybe play golf [on the computer] to distract [my mind], the usual routine.

Thursday March 21, 2013 3:30 pm living room

[It has been] Another noisy, loud [tinnitus] day, [I was] up at 3:00 am. [I] watched ["]Red Eye["] [a TV talk/comedy show that is on at 3:00 am] then [I] watched my DVD of Harry Potter movie #7 (Deathly Hallows, pt. 1). [The] Noise died [down] somewhat when 7:00 am arrived. [I] Took a shower (still using a sit down chair for safety as [I am] still unstable), [and] shaved. [I] left to [do my usual morning] walk, [with] high alertness and presence, enough to realize [that] my older shoes (boots [that I used to use] from [my] laundry days) were a bit loose and [when] walking around the mall [it] felt like walking on ice [even more than usual]. Even though the drive and road patches are icy I will avoid these and try tomorrow with tennis shoes [in the mall]. After walking I will do some laundry again at the local laundromat. Mom has a cold and I need the therapy. I watched the last H. [Harry] Potter movie this afternoon. I thought of drawing some but I could not find a small card table and did not feel that motivated with my head buzzing. The right leg [is] a bit warm as it gets [that way] in the afternoon but on the whole [it's] tolerable. [I am] Still lifting it up at breaks and in the morning at Burger King [near the Midland Mall] (I started early about 7:30 am so [I] went over there for some milk and two cinnamon buns). As mentioned [earlier] it is still below 20 in the morning and maybe 25 now. Some spring! But soon all this will be memory. Today Mom went to her doctor (assistant or provider) for her sinus/cold [symptoms]. Then she went to Walmart for meds [medicine]. She was going to her first bazaar [of 2013] in Bay City Saturday morning with Sandra but decided to skip it. [It] Turns out [that] Sandra does not feel that good either so both may skip it. As I recall last year they did not make much money there. So I plan on the usual routine this afternoon. [I will have] Some supper then [watch] TV and maybe some ice cream or cookies. I still turn in about 8 pm to read, wind down and try to sleep by 9 pm in case I awake early in the morning. This way I get 4-6 hours [of sleep [which seems to be] enough.

Friday March 22, 2013 4:00 pm living room

[My] Eyes continue to adjust to new glasses, head has continuous, steady buzzing, right leg [is] always hot, prickly, swallowing remains something I must pay attention to [on each swallow,] as I have written about before, but I am patiently optimistic [that] all will become normal or at least more tolerable in [the] next few weeks. [I] Switched [my] shoes to [the] blue/gray strap shut [Velcro like] sneakers which helped me finish my full 6 laps at the [Midland] Mall. I then caught up with laundry in Auburn [Auburn Cleaners & Laundromat]. About this time in the afternoon the head really gets loud and the foot aches a lot. I must work at distracting the mind so that I may make it to bed where I can take pills to help sleep. Funny, [I] never thought that would be necessary for me [taking pills to sleep].

Saturday March 23, 2013 3:30 pm living room

[There has been] Progress today but so slow. I went to the mall on this weekend morning. Mom was sleeping, Dave delivering to Canada... I awoke very early, 12:30 am but, even though my brain was noisy, I managed to go back to sleep and woke up about 6 am. That's good! I had coffee, doughnuts, watched TV (not much on), then left to walk at the mall. I managed [to complete] all six laps, feeling better, more stable but still needing [using] a cane. After walking till 10 am I went to the pet store [Sultan]. I got some bird [cage] paper and [digestive] gravel. They did not have small perch [sandpaper] covers that help [trim] the bird's nails. I came back about 11:30 am. Mom was taking a shower [bath], so I did a semi-clean [all but the paper in the bottom of the cage] of the bird cage, as I can do this now. I also filled up the outdoor [wild] bird feeders. Again I have a bit more stability [so] I did not use a cane with the feeders. Today the noise [tinnitus] is with me [constantly]. It was very loud upon awakening but thankfully has remained suppressed most of the day, or I am just not paying attention. I have been reading a book about letting things pass through you, so to speak. It is about not letting things internalize in you so that they don't have to be dealt with later. Perhaps there is something to be said for that with the head noise. [My] Continuing to ignore it or to "let it pass" may be a good approach. Like all these symptoms I suspect it will reduce also [in time]. My leg is slightly better as well as [is] swallow control. Also speech is slowly getting back as well. I have Monday morning therapy with Anita soon and it all seems better each time [I visit]. I have been recording the voice each day, playing or blowing long notes on the xaphoon Dave got me. I seem to have better stamina daily. Even at the mall today I had better energy as [I] seemed to handle corners better [without losing balance as I changed direction around those corners] and to not need as many breaks. I did two laps with only a restroom stop, for example. Usually I need a 5 minute break each lap [now mainly to lift my leg for comfort]. Our ice continues to melt but it is still [only] in the mid 30s but [with] occasional snow. There is now a clear path for me to get the mail [thanks to Sandra]. I use the cane for that chore. I am expecting one or two more weeks at the mall and then hopefully by mid April I can resume walking the local park [Williams Township] where there is more privacy and outdoor enjoyment.

Sunday March 24, 2013

A PS on yesterday's entry: I did try to use the art supplies that Dave and Mom got me [for Christmas]. I set up a small card table in the living room. I worked a bit on a landscape (a winter scene) but right now I have little motivation for it. This probably will change and may be related to my adjustment to these new close-up glasses.

Sunday [regular] notes: 11:00 am living room

Dave came in about midnight last night. He is [now] playing cards with Mom. I am writing this early to record a change in the head buzzing. I was waking in a dream state I think and I heard the buzz but it was much lower and seemed to [be to on] my right and at a distance. I think I dreamed or imagined the location [and] change of the buzz but I must report that it does seem not as loud[,] or more muffled. I am happy that it is staying suppressed no matter what the reason. I am hopeful that this is an indication of a change for the better and a gradual improvement [reduction] of the noise. While Dave watches[d] his usual morning MSNBC and had coffee I played golf on the computer. I did well until I landed in a weed patch and had to forfeit the hole. This happened twice. I dropped from 4th to 80th! ... but I did finish 70th. Currently [I am in] a normal tournament [and] I am tied for 1st after the first round. Either way it's good fun, [and] good therapy. I watch a little MSNBC in the mornings [mostly Morning Joe] but I just can't watch as much as Dave. I give him his morning space that way. I did get up earlier at 5 am for my morning coffee, doughnuts, pills [vitamins and supplements], and a banana. As I mentioned, the sound [tinnitus] was well suppressed and I enjoyed that. I even went back [to bed], laid down until about 8 am and was able to listen to some mp3 music. Now as I write this about 11:00 am the noise is there but muffled and not as loud as it has been. I go to speech therapy tomorrow morning with improved speech as well as control. Anita has me down for 4 [additional] weekly appointments. If I continue to improve at this rate she may reduce or eliminate further appointments. We will see. The weather today is [in the] mid 30s and cloudy. There are traces of snow and ice around but in the next week they are predicting [temperatures in the] 40s. So I doubt much [snow and ice] will be left in a week. It's about time. I am ready for warmer weather and for going back to the park for my daily walking.

[12 noon]

I will put down a few notes on another change I noticed today. I am reading using my new close-up glasses. At first and over the last couple of days both eye images are clear but not 100% aligned. In reading a page this causes some blurriness as you can imagine. I think I wrote about this earlier. Any[way,] today, just now, those two images seem[ed] to align so that I can take in the whole page [without blurred lines on top of each other]. Now this is great and a sign of improvement to come. There is stress upon the eyes [and/or] brain and I have to stop, close my eyes and let the soreness [strain] pass but it's nice to be able to see these two images align. I will make a comment about the long range [distance] glasses. I may have [said this] before but [I] don't remember. At the mall they seem fine and I can read signs and see well. I do notice a slight blur under some letters and that is because I see a second image misaligned [with the first]. This is not as it was before with my reading glasses when they were the wrong prescription and I <u>always</u> saw a second image off at an angle [about 30 degrees and angled up]. I think this was partly my brain adjusting as I have always had this problem as my brain was retraining. I am hopeful this blurred image clears. Sometimes I think it is my eyes adjusting to morning blur but it may have to do with my brain adjustments and may clear up. Most other things [images] remain clear, most letters, signs, and so forth. I see it mostly with the crawler on the [bottom of the] TV and certain letters [certain font sizes and background colors]. [Also when I watch from a distance such as from my favorite recliner, it sometimes clears when I go closer to the object being viewed] I will monitor this as they can make errors at the VA. I want to give my brain a few weeks to adjust to the glasses as I am [I have with the] close-up glasses. I will go back to reading and keep an "eye" on the situation.

[5 pm]

Some final comments on this day: I read from "The Untethered Soul" [a new book I bought], played golf on the computer, would have ordered WRTH book (World Radio and Television Handbook) but I don't have $19 in my [bank] account. I will wait till payday or maybe deposit some [money] early as I would like the book. I have setup the shortwave radio [my old Grundig Satellit 500 Millennium] and I think it will help distract thoughts in the evening [from the loud tinnitus]. The edition [of the WRTH book I still have] is 2001, slightly outdated. I may deposit some money on Monday, then order it Monday afternoon [online]. Anyway the [right] leg [is] a bit warm/numb but other things like eyes and speech get better. The head noise remains under control but always a bit louder [at] this time of day.

Monday March 25, 2013 3:00 pm living room

Today I "thought" I had my regular Monday morning VA speech therapy appointment [so I drove to the Saginaw VA as always]. I did not realize it had been switched to Wednesday mornings instead (for at least 4 weeks starting this Wednesday morning). Oh well, I am a morning person now anyway (today was about 1:30 am [when I awoke] but fortunately I was able to get a bit more rest until about 4:15 am). I just left [for] the VA [without checking the appointment date] and [then] headed for the Fashion Square Mall [in Saginaw] where I do my walking on [speech] appointment days. I did four laps before I began to feel chafing so I stopped. I then stopped by the Barnes and Noble bookstore on Tittabawassee Road. It is a bit larger than the one at the Midland Mall and I have shopped there several times now. I found the science section and I was surprised that they had 1 [a] copy of WRTH (World Radio and Television Handbook) for 2013. I did not have enough cash with me (too close to pay day) but [so] I was going to deposit some cash later so I could order WRTH online. I could not find a price on the store copy so I drove to the [Chemical] [B]bank in Auburn (about 15 miles away), made the deposit to cover my debit card and drove back to the bookstore. Kind of out of the way but I really would like a copy of WRTH for my recent shortwave radio listening. I came back and asked for a price check and she [the clerk] said $35.00. That was way too much. I know Barnes and Noble could use the cash but I can get it online for $19 plus shipping so I said I would wait and no thanks. I came back [to Mom's] and ordered it online with an antenna booster [for weak shortwave signals] and some other stuff all for $8 shipping. Sorry Barnes and Noble but it is hard to beat that price. They [Amazon] said I may even get it later this week which would be great. Dave is here for Easter break and has decided to take one more RV to Minneapolis from Indiana before Easter this Sunday. Sandra, Steve, and Heather have invited us over and Dave will try to make it too. Anyway it was a busy morning ...[??] It went fast and when I was walking in a new area and driving to the bank my mind was not on the buzzing or other pains. It was on balance and that helps my attention to stay off the noise. It was not as loud when I awoke and remains blocked off. I do hear it more in the afternoon now as I write this and it's quiet [around me]. I have mentioned this before. Anyway looks like Dave may leave early tomorrow morning for Indiana. He likes to pick up the RV before anyone is there during regular work hours to slow him down. I plan to resume walking at the mall, visiting the [Dow] Library[,] most likely, then buying some items at Walmart for Mom on the way back. I have not switched to the park yet as it remains around 25 to 30 degrees in the morning. [This is] not quite decent outdoor walking weather yet. Now they project 40s the next few days (high) so soon the lows will be warmer too. I am ready. It's been a long cold winter. The latest prediction for the spring here is wetter then normal so if it rains I will likely return to the mall to walk.

Tuesday March 26 2013

[5:30 am]

A morning note while I wait for the coffee and vision to kick in and improve things. Some comments about last night: I went to play golf on the computer before supper and moved the frame on my long distance glasses and snap the left frame broke. Damn! I had my old pair and I managed to get that frame attached. I think I have the right lens back [in my new glasses as they got mixed up]. I hope it's a lesson for me to stop the tweaking. I can live with how it is now and I have no more backup glasses. Anyway these seem to be the right lenses because I see the crawler on [the bottom of the] TV and the slight blur [as before]. I can live with them. I don't see the VA optical department until next Feb.[(2014)] so hopefully these last and by then I can handle progressive lenses. I could buy a spare set if I wanted to but as my eyes and brain are adjusting to the post-surgery world, I would like to hold off until the next optical meeting [appointment]. This "temporary" fix appears solid and lets me fold the glasses. It is a wire through the frame holes as I could not align the original screw back. Dave says that is intentional in those types of frames. Dave left early this morning for Indiana and will deliver an RV to near Minnesota before Easter so he should be back here at the end of the week. I will now take the birds out [of their cage] for their morning break and [then] resume my mall walk and library [visit] and so on. Last night was stressful [due to fixing glasses] and I finally got to bed by 8:30 pm. I went to sleep about 9 pm but woke at 1:30 am to rather loud head noise. I listened to Guided Meditation mp3s for a bit and just lay there enduring it and apparently got a bit more sleep as I woke up about 4:15 am. Dave had left earlier for his trip.

[2:30 pm] living room

I got my usual mall walk in today. Balance [is] getting there but [there] still [is] some wobbling and unbalance so I will stick with the cane until I get full confidence back again. I really expect that to happen someday. It's close and better daily despite thawing out and hearing head noises. I think even the leg will get better in time. I should mention [that] it gets warm around the foot area about on the 4th lap (near 2 miles) but I think that would be expected. I notice I need to keep it warm by wearing slippers or socks [in the evenings]. I cover it up in bed and I wear socks to ease the nightly pains in it. It will be nearly a year now since I became aware of it. I remember going to a couple of Loons [minor league] baseball games last spring and needing to lift my right leg horizontally for relief. I hope there is less of that this year. I know I did not hear the head noises then as I was too numb ["]up there["]. It all should prove interesting.

Wednesday March 27, 2013 4:45 pm. living room

[It's been] A very busy and unusual day from the start. Mom is out shopping for Easter and [for] other things with the Olds[mobile]. She is doing this now to mail some bills, beat the crowds in the next few days and with the Olds[mobile] as it has a spare tire, unlike the van, and is

[more] reliable. I will recap this day as I sit in the purple [burgundy] lazy boy chair [recliner]. I will note my head noise seems less now or more muffled and blocked. That's good! It may be because the day was so busy [and] there was not much time to notice it. I awoke at 12:30 am to take a leak and my head was good enough for me the lay back down until about 5:30 am. When I got up it seemed cooler. [It was] not bad but around 65 degrees inside. I raised the temperature on the thermostat and heat did not kick in. I first thought of fuses, then the pilot light being out. I made it downstairs, looked at the fuse box paperwork and found no reference to the heater. I had my speech therapy appointment today at the [Saginaw] VA so that rushed me. I looked inside the furnace to try to find the pilot light [but] no luck. It is [a] gas and electric furnace so I did not want to mess with it and blow myself up. I got Mom up about 6:30 am and she called Consumers [Energy Company]. I left for the VA at 7 am. I had my appointment with Anita, [and] she agreed that I am making steady improvement. I came right back after to check on the furnace and Mom said she was told Consumers could not make it out until Thursday. They told her to call someone else to get quicker action. She did and got a repair truck from Midland. They found a blown fuse (bottom row) and replaced it. All seems okay now. We will see for sure as the temperature drops in the morning. If I was not rushed to make my appointment perhaps I would have checked all [the] fuses but best to have experts check it out. They said they would send a bill so that was nice. After some coffee and cookies and roll [after I got back from the VA] I went to the Midland Mall about 11:30 am to 1:30 pm to get my 6 laps in. I then stopped to Walmart on the way back to get some half and half [for my coffee] and miscellaneous items. Things are really getting better there [at the store] as I can make things out fine and get around. There is still slight disorientation but no [head] pain as before and I hold on to the cart for stability and no one really pays much attention. I still have the "blank" look so I'm sure they can tell [that something happened] if they were to watch me closely. In the mail I got my IRS refund/adjustment for $930 which is nice and payday is next

Wednesday, so you can see it was a nice, however busy, day.

Thursday March 28, 2013 3:45 pm living room

[I] Woke up 2 – 3 times early to urinate but laid back down because [the] head noise was absent or subdued. It has been that way all day giving me hope that it is changing for the better. Naturally I can hear it now as it's afternoon and also I write about it. Dave is headed back and will be in shortly from the UP [Upper Peninsula]. Mom is back from getting stuff for tacos. I was busy walking at the mall, but I did stay up[,] when I awoke at 2:30 am[,] in order to catch [the] "Red Eye" [TV] show[,] which I enjoy. I later took a shower, played some golf [on the computer], eventually made it out to the mall to walk as usual at 8 am. I was done early, maintained a fast pace for me, had good balance and control, able to turn my head more and more confident[ly]. I went to the Auburn [Chemical B]bank after to deposit my refund/adjustment check from the IRS. I took out $500 [from the ATM] and came back early. Mom was sitting for the elderly lady[,] using the van. I got back in case she had auto problems. I started one of the puzzles she brought me after taking a break from it for a couple of months. My right leg/foot is [was] warm but seemed tolerable today, however the foot gets warm after a few miles of walking. All and all, thanks to the head noise suppression/improvements, not a bad day at all. It is sunny now and in the upper 40's outside, birds are eating seed, real nice to see.

Friday March 29, 2013 noon living room

[This is an] Early entry to be sure [that] I remember some events of this morning. I went to the Midland Mall as usual. Before that I woke up at 1 am, noise in my head [was] not there or reduced so [I went] back to sleep until 6 am. Dave came back from Minnesota last night about 6 pm. I saw him in the morning briefly at 6 am. At the mall I felt a bit better: stability and balance. I went partly without using the cane for several steps but ended up using it for the remaining laps for safety and because I am still not normal enough to do without it. I went to

Target after the walk to get some super glue to try to glue on my glasses (long view) the nose pads I bought a few days ago. The last glue or adhesive did not work so I will try super glue one more time (overnight tonight). After the mall, I headed for the Dow Library but they were closed for Good Friday. I went over to the "Tridge" park in downtown Midland since it was only 10:30 am and nearly 40 degrees and sunny. I walked around the park and to the Riverside assisted living condos [Retirement Center] and sat down for a bit at an outside bench and just enjoyed the sun and warmer weather for a bit. Before that I walked in front of the "H" hotel and some Chinese young tourists were [just] leaving. I walked through them and said hi. As I walked down the sidewalk further I heard them following me and giggling (because I kept walking and they were trying to catch up). I stopped and they said they could use help with their map. They were not sure where they were. Their English was good and I told them I was just a visitor too but I would [try to] help. I had to remove my long distance glasses to see their map [by holding one lens close to my face, I can read close images in the one lens] and [I] helped them find their way to the [nature] park across the "Tridge" [bridge]. They headed over the bridge and I walked over to the Riverside condos [Retirement Center]. On the way over to the condos in my head I briefly heard a tone similar to a high pitch hearing frequency test. It was distinct and occurred only for a moment. After my head felt like it does when you pop your nose after a flight. It popped then I heard the tone. What I think occurred was as things continue to ["] thaw["], perhaps the head briefly thawed enough for the full brain to expose its ringing sound to me. If so, fortunately it closed shortly and only lasted a few seconds. I thought it was interesting to note in my daily journal.

[3 pm]

[And now for] Some final words for this day. I got my Amazon order [shortwave antenna booster] except for the WRTH book [which is coming separately]. I will try the products tonight after 8 pm. I go to bed [at] that time but usually read or listen to radio or mp3s until about 9 pm. I go that early for a number of reasons: my leg usually is more painful at that time and when I cover it with two blankets, lay it horizontal in the bed and wear a sock, the pain greatly subsides so that I can sleep. I detect a very slow but steady improvement in this but it's like [how] a lot of symptoms expose themselves. [It was] last May 2012 when I think my brain began to thaw from the original operation. I could not see clearly with both eyes before that time. I could not feel my hair or sense that my hair was being touched. My head and hair were very numb and because of the suppression of sound and pain, this is [was] just fine. [I am] Glad those surgeons know what they are doing. [I am] Sure no one wants to wait over a year for improvements but with the brain it seems necessary. Anyway the last part of this day has shown me the great <u>daily</u> improvement in short (close-up) vision. The two images (one for each eye) are now both aligning so that there is no or very little misalignment or overlap. Close vision is very sharp and sharper each day. I just resumed doing puzzles and reading now that I see the full page clearly: Talk about being happy about "small" things. This is a great joy to someone who reads a lot like me! It has been a long haul, almost a year. [It has been] This [last] May since I stopped the eye patch and forced the [two] eyes to slowly fix themselves. [I've come a long way] From being fuzzy and out of focus to seeing sharpness come, to fighting with an incorrect prescription (causing me to see a second image at an angle). I thought all along it was my brain, but not all of it. It was human error at the VA or their lab and I have previously written about this. My eyes now (and/or brain) seems to be able to align both right and left eye images so that text is clear with the new close-up glasses. My long distance ones also are good but I need to try again to glue the nose pads on them as they need slight tweaking upward of the glasses. I don't want to stress them too much and cause a breakage as before so I will try "Krazy Glue" overnight. Last time [when] I tried to glue the nose pads on, they came loose. On the long distance glasses, on [viewing] some letters and words (I see it mostly on a TV crawler), I still see an[other] image of the words/letters underneath. I see most things clearly but that does show up now and then. This could be my brain still returning, re-adjusting and it will clear up shortly. The brain/mind is better daily at this, which means my balance and control get better each day. It is still shaky to where I use the cane which I have mentioned before. Well I could probably go on which is a further sign of improvement but that is enough for this day. I will mention that I have resumed walking and being out 6 days a week now (Mon-Sat) as I have improved greatly and I think this will help speed healing and not to mention I enjoy the feeling of improvement, the independence it gives me, and the nice spring weather!

Saturday March 30, 2013 2:30 pm living room

[I have been] Fussing around with the loop antenna but stopped to fill out this journal. I need to test the loop antenna at night when shortwave is stronger. Today my mind [attention] moved to my leg as the noise in my head is well suppressed today. I have noticed how the mind changes attention to the strongest symptoms. The mall [walk] went well, [I] got my 6 laps in but forgot my pedometer. I went to the Dow Library which was open today to read the newspaper and some magazines. As it was only 11 am I went over to the "Tridge" park. I just rested in the car in the sun enjoying the moment and the quiet in my head. I came back around noon. Dave was out to the bank, getting a haircut, [and] running errands before his trip. I had a pork chop sandwich [for lunch] and ended up messing with the antenna a bit as I mentioned. It hangs in the window, runs behind the bed. [I am] Not sure [that it is] the best input to use on the Satellit 800 as there are a few [different inputs]. I will try different ones and see what is the best. [It] May take a few evenings to get the best hookup. As mentioned[,] today is very warm (at least compared to the winter this year). They say there will be a final blast of cold Monday and Tuesday but after that things should head to spring.

Sunday March 31, 2013 7:30 am bedroom

[I was] Early up as usual. Dave and Mom are sleeping. It is Easter

Sunday today. I went to bed at 8 pm as usual, [and] read until 8:30 or 9 pm. I awoke at 2:30 am to urinate. The brain buzz was fairly strong [then] and steady. I ignored it and laid back down and awoke at about 6am. I had coffee and a roll. Dave fixed the sink leak last night by installing a new sink [faucet]. Pressure is low as always but it works and there are no leaks. I shaved, flossed, took a shower around 7:00 am. We go to Steve and Sandra's for dinner about 1 pm today. Amy and James[, her boyfriend, are] headed back probably to Ohio or New York. Heather eventually [will be moving] to Colorado. Good for her. I played a bit of computer (Tiger Woods) golf. I'm in the PGA now-- sometimes I do great, other times, so so. I am looking to try real golf soon, perhaps this year. There is a par-3 course down the road past Wheeler [road]. I may check it out when I no longer need the cane. I have decided not to rush it and will continue to use the cane for stability until it's not necessary. This may be a few more weeks. Yesterday I did walk the mall. I have returned to a six day schedule [as mentioned previously]. For several feet I was able to walk just holding the cane. There still is instability so I finished the last few laps using the cane. The brain is much better at locking on to the surroundings. There is the steady brain buzz or hum but I tried to ignore it and to me it seems to be not as intense. It is always there but I am optimistic it will fade. The [right] leg is also a _slow_ improvement. I would rather it be a bit numb/painful than to have to walk on one leg. It's all relative so I continue to work with what I have. The weather this morning is in the 40s and some light rain passed through earlier. Temperatures in the 50s are predicted for today but they expect winter's last gasp on Monday and Tuesday when it will drop into the 30's and 20's. Wednesday it should resume the warmup towards spring. Already Mom is thinking about her pool sand filter and how it needs a blade. I think this year I can be of more help with that. I expect I may even be able to mow. With Dave around he may do that. Well time to update my walking log for yesterday which I forgot to do.

CHAPTER 4   4/1/13 – 4/30/13

<u>Monday April 1, 2013 2:40 pm living room</u>

I awoke at 10:30 pm and found my headphones on [last night]. I fell asleep listening to mp3s I guess. I had to take a leak. The head sound [was] there but not bad enough to stop me laying back down and awaking at about 3:30 am. I tried to sleep after that but the head noise was too intense and I got up, took a leak, combed my hair[,] and sat down in the computer room to plug in my mp3 player [for charging]. Dave came by the hallway and I was startled as I thought he had left earlier as before but he was just heading out the door at 4:30 am. He gave me an envelope to mail and I saw him off and had some coffee and cake. I let the birds out for a break around 5 am and they did their usual thing. Christy was on edge looking for the dog [as she still does sometimes] who has been gone months now. I put them back [in their cage] about 6 am, played some [computer] golf, got dressed and filled up the bird feeders [outside], mailed Dave's letter at the Midland post office and headed to the mall. The noise subsided some, blocked as usual [at] that time and all I heard mostly was muffled buzz. I walked 3 laps, [it] felt good, [I] used the cane but then the mall administrator tested the sirens and they stayed on several minutes. [They were] Very loud so I left. I already get enough buzz inside [my head], thank you. I went to Walmart and picked up some D batteries for my SW [shortwave] radio, a card for Tom's Birthday and then a new glasses [lens] cloth at the optical store on the way out. I went to the Dow Library and read the [New York] Times as usual and a few magazines and then headed back. Even though I have a free coffee [coming to me at the Cup and Chaucer coffee shop in the library] I did not feel like one today. [I got] Back about 11 am. Mom was up cleaning. I had a couple of leftover pizza slices [for lunch]. [I still am] Cautious with [my] swallowing. It seemed to be easier to eat [today]. I also spilled my small water bottle [that I carry for choking emergencies] in my pocket [at the library]. I think I will now be OK without it and [I] won't need it anymore. I have enough swallow control now and can watch for any saliva build up. While in the library, I roamed around some shelves and noticed [that] the new glasses and brain improvements allow me to see the books [book covers] more clearly. Things are not as fuzzy using the long distance glasses. I noticed that it was easier to see the dominoes at Sandra's also yesterday. I have been doing some of the puzzle [today]. Both glasses are now good enough so that I don't have to tweak the frames further and risk breaking them. They should now last until next February's [eye] appointment [at the Saginaw VA] with just minor scratching. I also note that the right foot/leg, although a continuing problem, seemed a bit better today. [I had] Long periods at the puzzle and sitting at the library with both feet on the ground [for a longer time] was possible. Today's most noticeable difference was the clear vision and louder head noise.

Tuesday April 2, 2013 2:45 pm living room

I awoke at 3 am to urinate and the head buzz was steady and strong. I laid back down but got up at 4:00 am due to the noise. I had been dreaming of when I worked as an electrician (Navy or Wyeth [Labs]?) and I was trying to visit the boss's office way on the upper floor [of a high rise building, by elevator]. I was not sure what room. I awoke and it took awhile for my eyes to adjust. With the long distance glasses I see pretty clear[ly] except the TV crawler and some words have a blur and double word images underneath them. I don't seem to see this reading small words, signs, etc. at the mall so it seems early morning related and something in the TV. I am not worried to much about it. My head/brain coordination is very close now but still [there is] enough delay to throw me off and causing stability not to be totally cane-free. I use the cane for support around the mall and outside as the brain tends to move or bounce [my bobble head feeling] when walking but things are much clearer now. I had my coffee, snacks[,] then took a shower. I played some [computer] golf, took out the trash, then headed to Walmart. The noise became suppressed as it always seems to when I go to walk. I got some doughnuts and cookies and some lotion there [at Walmart]. It was still early so I went to Burger King for a breakfast and left about 7:50 am and waited to walk. I parked further away from the [mall] door because it's just so much easier for me to walk with a cane now. I do not have [nearly as many] problems on curbs now and there is virtually no snow on the ground now. The morning was [in the] mid 20s but warmed up to [the] mid 40s later. After walking 6 laps, I went to the [Dow] Library, had my free cup of coffee and read a bit. I was back around noon for a sandwich. I later worked on the puzzle and now this journal entry. The leg seems a bit better too, still a bit numb, but I noticed I did not have to favor it as much. Speech sounds better and the voice seems closer to "the surface", [that is] not as hard for me to project it out. I hear it well. Tomorrow morning I have my weekly VA speech therapy. Every time it [the speech] gets better a lot on it's own. I have to be patient now as it won't be long and the brain/head will "lock" as normal and I suspect that when it does, walking will be much better. Now I will check for mail and wind it down this afternoon.

Wed. April 3, 2013 3:15 pm living room

I had my weekly speech therapy today at the Saginaw VA. I make it easy for Anita. She just sat there listening [and of course evaluating] as I spilled my guts once again. I guess because I can talk better each time, I talk more there than anywhere [else]. Like Mom said, she can't hear me that well and Dave is too busy talking himself (her words, but funny). Ya, he's busy getting his job going. Anyway I noticed a few improvements while walking. First, my buzzing was loud this morning as I awoke but was well buried [in] time. I got to the VA. Hard to say [but] it just got muffled or going [went] away. Either way a real joy not to have to deal with it. [My] Eyes [are] clearer. That disturbance or double image under some words may be my brain, as true "lock" or synchronization is not quite there yet. It is very close and the slight gap in images may show in these certain words. All other images are quite clear, I can happily say. My right leg seems better. I lifted it up while walking but held it down for [a] longer time. It did not seem to be much [of] a bother. After the VA appointment I walked one time [lap] at the Fashion Square Mall [in Saginaw] but the foot got hot and I stopped. I had to get some stuff for Mom so I stopped to the Meijer, bought them, got some money from the [Chemical B]bank [in Auburn] and headed back. All in all, more control, better images, voice [still seems] strange. I am thinking [that] part of the leg issue is sensitivity to touch as when I walk it gets hot at [in] the foot area. As I sit in this chair writing, where the leg contacts the chair is where there is more sting. I am glad it will get better as all of my symptoms will. I looked at the Lipoflavonoid supplement supposed to help tinnitus but they want 30 dollars for an 11 day supply [where] you take [it] 3 times a day [which I mentioned earlier]. Hmm, serious sleep[?]. Maybe I will do further research on it or other things that might help. As usual it gets louder in the afternoon and middle of the night[,] but as I have written about[,] it is a matter of focus in how my mind deals with it: attention direction.

Thursday April 4, 2013 3:00 pm living room

[I] Awoke at 12:30 am after going to bed about 8 pm and starting to sleep about 9 pm. It [the tinnitus] was extremely buzzy. [It's] Very loud. I suppose that's a sign of further thawing out. I was so tired and that was too early to get up [so] I just laid back down until 3:15 am. [I am] Not sure if I got any [additional] sleep but I stayed [up] due to the noise and watched "Red Eye". I stayed up with coffee, [played computer] golf, [and] took a shower. [There are] improvements in coordination, [and] morning focus seemed clearer. The big change was the noise being quite loud. Yesterday it flared up also and I went online to look at Lipoflavonoid, a much advertised product for tinnitus [which I mentioned earlier]. I was at Meijer yesterday and looked at it. [As mentioned before], it was mostly supplements and was priced at $30 for a 10 [or 11] day supply. Online I ran across "bioflavonoids" and the reviews were good (they could have been planted) so I ordered some. They [it] should be here next week. I have nothing to lose but a bit of money. Right now it is loud and has been steady all day. I have carried on trying to ignore it. I walked, went to the library, the usual routine. Today it's been sunny and has really warmed up. For next Monday and Tuesday the lows are in the 40's. Almost park weather. [It] Won't be long now. [I will] Probably use the mall one or two more weeks. Since I get up so early, it remains pretty cold out for any walking. At the mall, my head and brain are very close to synchronization. Not quite[,] so I still use a cane[,] but I walk a few steps then use it and am becoming more confident sometimes not using it [the cane at all]. All [of] these [activities help to distract me from the head noise or tinnitus]. I sure hope that will subside soon!

<u>Friday April 5, 2013 3:00 pm living room</u>

[As] spring blooms all around us here and the temperatures rise, I sense changes in my recovery of late. Not only am I coming back to "normal" control of the body as in balance, stability, and so on, but I am slowly getting my voice back. It is very slow. As with these changes and the eventual thawing out of my head and body there is the one troublesome symptom I am now aware of and of which I have previously written. It is the constant and disturbing buzz and ringing inside my head. Granted, compared to what I had to endure before with the constant and increasing headaches, the vomiting, the loss of motor functions and so forth[,] I hate to complain. I have had no head pain ever since [being at the] Vanderbilt ICU when they put me on steroids to shrink the tumor. Now is the constant noise which was probably always there but hidden or blocked. I woke up at 2:00 am (2:11 am exactly) and this time [I] could not get back to sleep. I had coffee and watched "Red Eye" and knew at least I probably got 5 hours of sleep due to early bedtimes I still am on. That has helped me survive. I downloaded an mp3 book on self-hypnotism or something like that or auto suggestion [which] may help. I also ordered another supplement with good reviews for tinnitus. I will try starting tonight to relax and plant some suggestions of a good [night's] sleep and reduced ringing. I know it will take awhile but maybe with the supplements also it may reduce the ringing. It has been loud all day but not loud enough to stop me from doing my daily activities and when I do them and <u>concentrate</u> on them the attention to the ringing subsides. As I have written, one thing I know is that it's all in the attention, and if I can distract my mind, the ringing drops off or least my awareness of it. So I did walk for 4 laps but [I] cut it short to wash the car, check tires, and do laundry in Auburn. [It's] More therapy and [I used] no cane inside the laundry but still [I was a bit] unstable there but [I am] better each time. So I remain optimistic in general recovery (also note my [right] leg did not require as much lifting up) and [I am] more confident outside to check the Jeep, get the mail and so on. I got some doughnuts, ice cream, and some Coors Lite [beer at the store]. I can take [drink] beer but like everything I can't swallow it straight down the throat. I have to wait for just the right moment and swallow sips at an angle. All liquids and solids have been like that for some time but this too continues to improve. If I do choke, I seem better able to recover from it. The choke is usually small and quick.

<u>Sat. April 6, 2013 11:30 am living room</u>

Dave is driving back from Canada via the UP [of Michigan] and should be back any minute. Tom, [and] Emily [are] coming over [at] 5:30 [pm] to celebrate Tom's Birthday early. [I] Got him a card and some money. I went to bed at 8 pm as usual but did not start reading until about 9 pm. I was looking for something that apparently I lost or threw out in the trash. I got to sleep probably around 10 pm. The noise was strong but I was tired. I awoke this morning [at] 5:30 am, which is unusually late for me. That's good. The noise in my head seems suppressed or weakened. Good news there. I had coffee, some doughnuts, and a banana and went to the mall for my walk, as I am now resuming Saturdays. [I] Felt good, [the] brain is very close to full "lock" of images in both eyes, or so it seems. It's a slow process and I have to patiently wait for improvements. I went online and ordered a self-hypnosis CD for tinnitus from Amazon. What have I got to lose[?] I will try it as I sleep and wind down in the evenings. [It] Should be here in a week or so. My antenna connector for the SW radio is coming too so I look forward to that. I hung the antenna in the window and need this RNC connector to attach the antenna to the SW radio. I have the WRTH handbook and another guide to SW listening. It's an old hobby I have not enjoyed in years. So the noise remains tolerable and hopefully the CD and supplements, one of them or all should reduce it further. I am eating a banana and apple for lunch, taking my supplements, and will do some of the puzzle for therapy until guests arrive. It is the blue shark puzzle that Mom picked up recently.

Sunday April 7, 2013 10:00am living room

Emily came over for Tom's Birthday dinner and we played a couple of games of dominoes. My vision continues to improve and a real good thing is that my head noise now and last night has been well suppressed. That has made a big difference and makes it easier to do things. I played some computer golf this morning and worked on the puzzle (blue shark) a bit. I stayed up late last night and had much more energy but I did notice a tendency to slur words, especially after 8 pm, my usual sleep/wind down time. I probably got to sleep around 10 pm and slept undisturbed until 5: 30 am; that is late for me and I did not awake in the middle of the night to urinate or because of head noise. Next week I should receive the self-hypnosis CD and supplements and that should help further. It would be great if the head buzz stays suppressed until then. If I listen carefully, I can hear it as it remains very steady but lately upon waking I don't hear it, a further sign that relaxation as in a sleep state seems to reduce the sound (or maybe I just am too sleepy upon waking to be aware of it). Dave is back. He was here for the dinner but went to Steve's for awhile to get his oil changed on the Toyota. He is headed back for [to pick up] another Mercedes RV to deliver to Canada later this afternoon. I see on the Loon's schedule [local minor league baseball team] that they only have one 3 pm Wednesday game this year, a bit of a surprise. That game is this Wednesday. I have the VA appointment that morning but if things work out I may try to catch that game. I will report more on this as it gets closer in time [note: I never did make it to the game due to leg pains].

Monday April 8, 2013 2:30 pm living room [(Tom's Birthday)]

[We] celebrated [Tom's Birthday] here earlier (last Saturday). [I] Went to bed [at the] usual time at 8 pm, [I] read for a bit, started sleep about 9 pm. [I] Woke up every 2 hours or so to urinate[:] 11 pm, 1 am, 3 am. Weird. I feel a bit tired and was so at the mall walk today. I left early and got some items at Walmart--an adapter plug for Mom's piano, some coffee and mouthwash. I then stopped into [at] Burger King and told a new girl there what happened to me as I still have the slur and use a cane. She seemed interested but was busy taking morning orders. I had a milk and egg sausage sandwich and fries [potato patty]. I then did my usual 6 laps at the mall, stopped by Barnes and Noble [and] browsed[,] then got back about 10:45 am. The adapter worked and now Mom can use her headphones with the piano. I ordered some 3 1/2 half inch disks for it also online. [I was] Surprised [that] they still sell them. My head sounds have been well suppressed today, thankfully. Now I notice [that] the right leg/foot [is] still hot (after all these months). That is a bit disappointing but it's better than when I first discovered it last May. I took a printout [picture] of the shark puzzle. Dave called and said his company is sending him to California on short notice while they fix an RV he was going to take to Canada. He will do that right after this CA [California] trip so we probably won't see him for a few days. He sure has his share of adventure. I played some computer golf but have not started a new puzzle yet. I ordered a new book online of piano chords, [and] scales and I may take a stab at it. What a hoot if I end up learning to play. Hey, why not while I am here? Rain is coming down good here. They expect it through Wednesday and then cold this Friday and weekend. Typical Michigan [weather]. [I am] Looking forward to walking in the park but [it's] too cold in [the] mornings still. I may have to wait for a few more weeks. Well, [I will] probably listen to mp3s now until mail call. [It's] A lot different routine then what I used to do! [in Tennessee]

Tuesday April 9, 2013 4:30 pm living room

I got a long period of sleep for a change last night. [There have been] No real [significant] changes [today]. [I] went to bed at 8 pm. [I] played on [the notebook] computer until [the] "sleep" pills made me tired and [I] slept [until] about 7 am but did not wake to urinate until 4:30 am. Wow for me that is sleeping in and probably what I needed. The head buzz, although there and steady, seemed well suppressed today. No complaints here. I hear well but the head feels like cotton still and [it is] still partially numb which holds down the head noise. I walked at the mall but only did a bit over 3 laps because I then [omit then] went to the movies and saw "OZ, the Great and Powerful" in 3D at the Midland Cinema. They had an early showing from 10:40 am to 1 pm. It was raining when I got out [of the movie] and it is still raining now. There is some ground flooding and hopefully it will stop soon before any problems. Dave is out west somewhere on his way to California by way of Arizona to see some old friends. I got my bioflavonoids and another pill to try to help [with] tinnitus. [It is] hard to tell on a day like this when it is not so bad. It [There] is the usual increase in volume around this time each day. I will just try it for a bit and see if it helps. Also, as mentioned before, I have the self-hypnosis CD on tinnitus coming later this week to test out. I will try that for a while too. Lately the whole situation has been tolerable enough so [that] my attention has shifted to my right leg/foot. I had to hold it [my leg] up and down in the theater for comfort. I also noticed a high amount of disorientation to the point of almost falling down at the theater after sitting for 2 hours. I was careful and smart enough to use the handrail and to stand for a moment [but I started moving too fast to exit the theater]. This [dizziness] occurred maybe a minute or so after rising. [It is] something to watch for the next time. The weather is supposed to get colder in the next few days but still [a] rain/snow/ice mix. Fortunately my VA appointment is tomorrow morning so it probably won't be too bad. I disassembled the shark puzzle and started a small 500 piece one for Mom to [also] work on when she wants. I think she enjoys doing it. It does not look too difficult compared to the larger ones.

Wednesday April 10, 2013 5 pm living room

I received the hypnosis CD on tinnitus today in the mail. I burned it to mp3 and tried it out in my room just now. It is very relaxing. I think it helped tone down the usual head noise that normally gets louder now [in the afternoon]. With the pills and this self-hypnosis exercise [mp3] I am encouraged that this noise will dissipate, or at least my awareness of it. I am glad I tested it because it suggests waking up (with suggestion of the speaker) after[,] so I will read some then use the tape [mp3], maybe read more or whatever then sleep. Tomorrow the piano scales book and diskettes should get here so I will take a crack at that.[:] Distraction and a test to see if I can learn a "new trick". On the tape [mp3], of course, it did not remove the sounds yet [or my awareness of them] but I feel with it's use over time and natural healing, the sounds will dissipate. Silence will be most appreciated and honored! Today I went for my speech appointment at the VA with Anita. She is a good sport and listened to me "rattle" on [again, as usual]. [My] Speech is better but still slurry. I babble on and she does happen [seems] to understand what I say. Each day I hear my voice in the recorder and it gets better. Like all things, [there are] slow improvement in time.

Thursday April 11, 2013 3:00 pm living room

Despite using the [self-]hypnosis CD (download [and burned] to [my] mp3 player) yesterday and today, it's been a noisy day in my head. It's not been a steady loud noise but [it's been] breaking through, [a] throughout the day kind of noise (as the tape [mp3] uses [says], it's like a 3-4 on the scale of 10). I'm glad it's not louder but I awoke hearing it, [and] it bled through [mail break--piano scale book and 3 ½ inch diskettes arrived] during coffee and doughnuts and even at the mall while I had mp3 music on. I did confirm that it can be "squelched" when the mind is distracted. I got Mom some groceries and spilled milk (the cheap sacks broke) all over the kitchen. I spilled it twice but I was good enough [physically] to help mop it up but in the middle of that concentrated action I did not hear sounds because my attention was elsewhere, more proof as suspected [and mentioned before] [that] the redirection of the mind can help "ignore" the tinnitus. With me starting the piano lesson[s] and getting better [physically] to do other things, I hope that the distractions will help me get through this. I am also thinking that as the perception, balance, brain "lock", and all get better that the head may be exposing the sounds more and that maybe this is a sign of more healing to come, particularly in tinnitus. [I am] Just thinking out loud in this journal and I will comment more about this later. I will continue to use the CD/mp3 on tinnitus and take the special supplements and see how they help. Today [I have] even better control of head, balance, [and] walking. [In the mall, in my] First lap I tried some steps without the cane, which I can do, but [I am] still not stable enough to do completely without it. I notice an increase in strength. I did two laps without a break and this is over a mile. I am looking forward to walking in the park but mornings are still too cold [as I have mentioned] so I will continue [walking] at the mall. Every day there are smaller [small] improvements that I hope I will not take for granted.

<u>Friday April 12, 2013 2:45 pm living room</u>

It was a tough night but I managed to get some sleep. I was not sure I would. I went to bed around 8 pm as usual and played my tinnitus [hypnosis] mp3. It is only about 30 minutes in length. I planned to read after as it brings you out of sleep. Well not this time. I fell asleep with it playing and woke up about 10:45 pm. To make matters worse the ringing was loud then. Because I needed sleep for my [walking] exercises and because my niece Heather may stop by, I got up[,] had two melatonin pills and slowly drank a beer. It worked [to make me sleepy] as I lay back down about 12:30 am and awoke at 7:00 am, having gotten some much needed rest. I was able to walk the mall this morning then shop at Walmart for Mom. The head noise was there but manageable. I have played the tape [hypnosis mp3] this afternoon as the noise is [as] loud as it has been lately. It comes and goes as I direct my attention to it. I got a book called "The Undefeated Mind" (at Barnes and Noble), so after I check the mail I will start that book. I played on the piano yesterday but [I] am taking a break because Heather will be here and I need a break anyway. She told me she had a complete series of The Big Bang Theory, a [very popular and funny] TV program. When she heard [that] I watch that show, she wants to watch some with me. She is always nice to me and we get along [very] well. I will go get mail and carry on in the day and in this journal tomorrow, Saturday.

Saturday April 13, 2013 4:00 pm living room

I just played my tinnitus mp3 a couple of times. I fell asleep twice to it due to the voice and its relaxation [effect]. Dave emailed from out in the desert in Las Vegas: a very long trip he has taken. He is headed here to take care of some medical appointments. My tinnitus is under control and I hope it is decreasing either naturally and/or because of the tape. As long as it goes away I will be happy. The long winter lingers on here with wind and flurries today. [It is predicted to be] Up into the low 40s but in the 30s earlier. [It is] Still too cold for using the park, so back to the mall I went this morning. I wore one of my brain surgery t-shirts because the mall is usually busy on Saturdays. There were vendors out as well and I might as well be proud of my history and show off the shirt. If just one person notices then gets some hope and realizes maybe they don't have it so bad or maybe they can be inspired to not give up then it's worth it. I know I am lucky to be here wearing it. I went to the Dow Library for a bit [after my walk] and read from my book, "The Undefeated Mind", which I am really enjoying. I finished a small "beach" puzzle, dabbled with the piano a bit, and will now read some of my "Mindful" magazine that arrived today and some more of the book. I was able to eat two hot dogs for lunch which is unusual for me now, but I am stuffed at the moment. All else continues on track. The leg improves, the sound I am dealing with, and

I am alive!

Sunday April 14, 2013 4:30 pm living room

I am watching the Masters golf tournament. It is on in the background as I write this. I just got up from playing the tinnitus [hypnosis] mp3 in the bedroom but fell asleep doing so. The head buzz returned a bit and is it's usual afternoon loudness. I will get by until bedtime and [play it] again. Sandra and Mom took us out to [the local] Ponderosa [buffet] for lunch. I was able to eat better but [I] still [am] unsteady so I used the cane to get from the car to the restaurant. I used no cane inside but had to hold on to the buffet area to remain steady. Anyway [I] worked a bit on the small puzzle of Dalmatian dogs and now [I am] writing some in this journal. I will now relax and watch golf and log more in this tomorrow.

April 15, 2013 1100 am living room

[I am] Back from my morning therapy/exercise early to make a few notes on a breakthrough morning. I awoke at 12:30 am, the buzz was steady but I laid back down to [until] 3:30 am. I did not know the exact time (in fact I thought it was late) so I played the tinnitus hypnosis mp3 and stayed awake this time. It helps suppress the sounds a bit so I got up around 4:00 am to get coffee, watch the news, the usual morning routine. The noise got better as it usually does about 2 hours after waking. I took a shower and headed out about 7:00 am. I played some computer golf before leaving. Since I was early I went to Burger King near the mall for a small coffee which I slowly sipped until about 7:40 am. Not on purpose but I noticed that while waiting for the coffee I was not relying on the cane I had with me. I was able to keep balance and even step back [for the first time since the surgeries] (balance, though not fully returned is much better of late). Anyway that inspired me to test a bit more and at the mall my first lap was completely caneless (I carried the cane with me but never needed to use it or to hold on to anything). I took my usual break at the food court [to lift my leg] but was happy to be able to do a lap without cane use. I noticed several looks from other walkers, as they are used to seeing me with the cane but my balance was not so hot so I decided to reuse [use] the cane. Also the winter weather was [is] a factor with lots of snow and ice late in the season. Now it is only rain and a flurry or so but [and] the ground is very clear at the mall. Anyway I made a second non-cane lap and on the third I decided not to stretch my "luck" so I left for the car (no cane--I had left it inside the car the second lap) after stopping by Barnes and Noble for a bit. I can see now sharply with the new long distance glasses enough to read the cover of books and magazines. I still need to use the close-up glasses to read but even that gets better with less and less lines out of focus. Like my brain-head combination, it's almost as before [the operations] but not quite. [It is] Very, very close, however, thankfully! So I [then] went to the Dow Library. I was going to stop and try the Irish Barber Shop near downtown [Midland] but they're closed on Monday. I could use a trim before the last symphony concert this Saturday night. So [it] looks like I will go without a cane at the mall both inside and to and from it, weather cooperating. Perhaps I won't need it at the park. [It's] too early to tell just yet. Balance, however better, is still a problem and I have to stop and touch something to get steady at times. However, the whole cane transition is good for my confidence and should keep me from being dependent on the cane. I may use it to [at] the concert, at least in and out of the parking lot as it is so crowded. Now it's 11:30 am so I will grab a salad. Dave is headed back from Colorado so is still traveling. Mom is taking a bath.

5:30 pm. living room

I will make one final entry for the day to report an advancement with tinnitus. I was watching the close of Wall Street on CNBC when the tinnitus got very loud, maybe a 5 out of 10, the loudest ever. I played [the] tinnitus [hypnosis] mp3 right away and I am happy to report that it suppressed it (or it just suppressed on its own) but I think it really helped and that would be great as the only other thing I found to help is mental distraction. Also at the same time they were running bulletins about two explosions at the finish line in the Boston Marathon. Crazy world. I will monitor the tinnitus and my drama with it later in this journal.

Tuesday April 16, 2013 4:00 pm. living room

I managed to get some sleep despite waking at about 11 pm (I fell asleep again [listening] to the tinnitus [hypnosis] mp3) and 12:30 am. I awoke about 5:30 am and got up for coffee and rolls. [I] Watched the news, sports, CNBC then played some [computer] golf. I took out the trash bags and left for the mall about 7:30 [am]. Temps [Temperature is] about 40 [degrees outside]. [I was] feeling pretty good. I walked about 4 laps (about 2 ½ miles) with no cane, but taking several breaks along the way and a 5 to 10 min[ute] break after each lap. [My] Eyes [are] better, [with] balance continuing to improve. After walking[,] I went to the Irish Barber Shop in downtown Midland, met a barber named Mike, a young guy, and told him some of my history. I needed a trim for the Saturday final symphony [of the 2012-2013 season]. I went in without the cane and did OK. I went to the Dow Library after and had a coffee and cookie. [I am] Eating and drinking very carefully and slowly,[;] it went well. I then read some more of my book, ["]Undefeated Mind["] and browsed a New Yorker magazine, mainly the cartoons. The sun is out today, high in the 60s, which is great. Trees [are] still bare. They expect colder nights, [and] mornings this weekend but hopefully [in] the next few weeks it will warm up and the park will bloom so that I can shift out there to walk. I think I will continue to try to go without the cane to force my balance to get better. I worked on the Dalmatian puzzle, filled my vitamins rack [container], [and] used the tinnitus mp3 again. The buzz is there as usual but suppressed. I hope to keep it that way! Mom did some grocery shopping in Auburn and is back now doing things in the kitchen. The birds were acting up as usual but are now quiet. Tomorrow I have the final scheduled speech therapy session at the Saginaw VA. Dave is near Indiana coming back from California and is planning on delivering another RV before heading back here.

Wednesday April 17, 2013 5:00 pm living room

Mom is making some food in the kitchen. I just did some of the Dalmatian puzzle. I listened earlier to [my] meditation/hypnosis mp3 and that helped with the tinnitus. I fell asleep last night listening to the tinnitus mp3 and unfortunately awoke at 11:00 pm (after about 2 hours sleep) and I just could not get back to sleep. I knew my VA speech therapy was today so maybe I kept thinking about that. I tried a beer and melatonin but no success. I heard the train at midnight as I was surfing the TV [notebook computer] so I got up at about 6 am and got a shower and had my appointment. Perhaps I did manage to get some rest as the appointment went well. I blabbed to Anita as usual. She patiently listened as always and set me up to see her every 2 weeks now as I have progressed. I also came to the VA with no cane and did OK. I left it in the car and carefully walked up the hill to the building 22 entrance (the main entrance is under construction still). After the speech meeting I walked a couple of miles (2 laps) at the Fashion Square Mall on my way back using no cane. [I was] Unsteady and it felt like ice skating without knowing how! I survived and it seemed like the last lap was a bit more stable than the first. I stopped by [the] Barnes and Noble bookstore on Tittabawassee Road (this time I used the back entrance and stop light [which avoids a left turn onto that very busy highway without a light]. I am able to see the books on the shelf and use my long distance lenses as a magnifier to briefly read covers. I still use the close-up glasses to read or to write in this journal. I headed back about noon, had a salad, took my [lunch] vitamins and did my normal afternoon of therapy at the piano and puzzle. At the VA the right leg felt slightly better as I did not have to lift it horizontally as often it seems. Also the reception room TV seemed clearer which is nice. There still is some blur under certain words, but mostly at a distance. I look forward to more walking at the Midland Mall without a cane. I expect to be there a few more weeks as it is still cold in the morning. Mom tells me Dave may come back late tonight for a much needed rest. He also has some medical lab work to get done. So that's it for now. Hopefully I can get more sleep in [tonight] and have a "quiet" mall walk in the morning.

Thursday April 18, 2013 12:38 pm living room

[I am] Now using no cane at the mall, both to and from the mall. [I was] Shaky at first but [I have] more confidence each time. Today was especially solid. My head seems less "bobble" headed, that is my brain is more locked into movement or can just handle it better [at times the brain will "bobble" as the dolls do and as you can imagine that is very annoying and makes it hard to walk. The brain feels like it follows every step, up and down. The vision then follows the brain and I just have to stop walking]. [I am] better around corners, [with] less fear but I stay close to walls. I imagine that will improve also as I get more practice. It has been raining all day and there is a tornado watch here and I almost did not go [walking] but I wanted to see my improvement and once inside [the mall] of course it is all dry. So I did a full 6 laps as if with a cane. [I am] Still hesitant and requiring full concentration and not much head turning. I also expect that to improve. It is all [very, very] gradual. I had a coffee at about 7:30 [am] at the Burger King near the mall which I occasionally do but this time it was nice to walk in without a cane. It was raining too and the help had just mopped too. [I am] much better at getting around and seeing hazards. I still do occasional "goofy" things like spilling the milk in the [Mom's] kitchen. This [following story] perhaps I shouldn't report but I want to keep this honest (to a point) and it is funny in hindsight. I took a shower in the morning before walking and thought I would try some of Mom's baby powder in [on] my privates, so to speak, to prevent chafing as I walk. As I am blind as a bat, as they say, without my glasses, I reached for the blue bottle in Mom's cupboard above the toilet. I sprinkled some on, resumed toweling off and immediately felt pain down there. I got it off with my towel and before I left to walk I wrote about it to Dave so he could avoid the same thing. I just thought it was a cheap powder that I reacted to. I got back today and found out that the powder is medicated foot powder, ha ha. Of all things, no wonder it stung.

Anyway lesson definitely learned on that one and I will be using the glasses before I reach again.

[5 pm]

[These are] Just some more comments on the day. I just listened to the mp3 on tinnitus to help block any additional sounds. It relaxes me and seems to help. It is [The tinnitus is] there as usual and stronger in evenings. This may help me sleep through it in the evenings when it gets the loudest. I noticed the leg is slightly better also each day. I seem to have to favor it less and less. That is really great news as it has lingered on about a year now. It was last May that I began to thaw out enough to notice the little "surprise" symptoms. I have been using the regular chair without the inner tube [to sit on] and it is helpful. Also I am able to work on the puzzles for longer periods of time [without getting up due to a hot bottom and leg].

Friday April 19, 2013 4:00 pm living room

[I] Woke up around 4:15 am and probably [was] asleep by 10 pm so [I got] about 6 hours [of sleep], [which is] good enough [for me]. The buzz [was] there upon waking. I played my tinnitus and meditation mp3[s] in bed for about an hour and got up around 5:30 am. [I ate the] Usual coffee and rolls and a banana. [I] Took a shower, played some [computer] golf and went to the mall about 7:30 am. [I] Walked better today without a cane, handling corners well (or better than before)! A couple of times I had to merge out in the center of the mall walking area. [There was] Much less fear when I had to do that. After walking I did my laundry at the Auburn [Cleaners & Laundromat] for therapy and to help Mom. I played on their golf [arcade] game a bit and then in [at] pinball and my left hand responded much better [with less shaking]. [I was] More steady. Of all things, I stuck one of the balls in the game and had to tell the owner about it. Pretty ironic to be on the other end of that but in a way I am glad not to have the hassle of repairing the games as before. After laundry Dave treated us to a Ponderous [buffet] lunch as he had to fast for some lab tests [earlier] today [and was hungry]. It has been cold and very windy out today. Winter lingers on but I would bet that next week it will warm up. The grass is already green due to all the rain of late. After we got back from the buffet, I worked on the puzzle and we saw a brief period of hail and snow. Weird weather. The noise in my head remains there but suppressed (thankfully). It usually is loud in the afternoon about now but now it is okay. I may not have to use the hypnosis tape but I may at bedtime [anyway] and try to stay awake this time.

Saturday April 20, 2013 12:45 pm living room

[I] Got back from a good therapy session at the mall and library. [I have] More balance daily now, real progress. [I am] Better it seems if I look beyond my current limitations, using caution, of course. I walked without [a] cane for about 6 laps in the mall which is about 4 miles. I take a 5 to 10 min[ute] break every 0.7 miles or one lap. I see the older folks keep on walking [after each lap] but I have my own pace and that still requires me to take a break. That also helps with the leg pains as I lift my right leg [up on a chair] during the break. It now averages about 20 to 30 minutes a lap but I am in no hurry and I am still being safe. I think to myself that it feels like skating on ice only without skates[,] like walking on ice I should say. I need to keep my attention on what I am doing as if it were ice. I know this seems odd or silly to someone "normal" reading this, but this is my current reality. Thankfully it improves daily. I am writing this earlier than usual as I attend the last symphony event tonight. I will write more about this tomorrow. I will do the usual puzzle and game therapy this afternoon until it's time [to leave for the symphony]. I always enjoy these outings and they give me good therapy out in the real world.

Sunday April 21, 2013 11:15 am living room

Dave is talking to Rod Rust on the phone. He will head out later to Indiana (Dave) to pick up a motor home and take it to Washington State. He plans to fly back and perhaps pick up another. Mom and Sandra are at church. I just finished the Dalmatian puzzle and took a picture of it for the record. I thought I would update the journal [now]. I am thinking about transcribing this journal into a computer, in other words digitizing it for the record. I may look into that using the notebook computer later after Dave heads out. My left hand and coordination are good enough now to try this. Last night I went to the final symphony concert at the Dow. It [My stability] was better but [I am] still shaky walking in and focusing on the stage. I did leave with everyone else but hung around the hall until I got an opening to walk outside. I did not use the cane and handled the open parking lot okay but walking on the sidewalk was dicy as it was not all that even and it was dark out. Now soon this will not be an issue (a no-brainier, ha ha) but for now I must use caution in simple things. The concert was great with ["]Time for 3["], a three person string quartet with orchestra background. [It] was great. I really enjoyed it. I parked next to the Dow Gardens entrance to avoid a parking lot jam (we had flooding and excess rain lately and one of the [back] exits was road-blocked). Then I walked down a long sidewalk to the theater. I used no cane but I had to go slow and cautious. This will get better in time.

Monday April 22, 2013 4:30 pm living room

Dave left early this morning for his trip to Indiana and off to Everett, Washington. I went to bed my usual early time of 8 pm [last night] to get some sleep as I never know when I will awake and if I will be able to resume sleep due to the tinnitus. That hypnosis tape [mp3] for dealing with tinnitus seems to help suppress it and relax me so I use it often. I just played it this afternoon. I also got to the mall early and since it was a sunny morning I played it in the car as I waited. I think distraction is still a big factor in just ignoring it. I get very distracted as I struggle to walk the mall. I did well with no cane again but it is still a struggle. I only completed almost 5 laps due to some slipperiness I noticed. I first thought someone spilled something, but looks like the soles of my tennis shoes have been smoothed off in my walk so I picked up another pair of shoes at the mall. They have an excellent tread, a good price at $19[,] and I just slip into them. They are a half size larger than my usual size 9 but I picked up a Dr. Scholls insert and that helps. Mom also recommended a thicker sock which I will also try. I noticed some slipping at the heel but I will see how they do in a full walk. If they are too big and sloppy I may look for others. I tested them at Walmart on their smooth floors and they had good traction. I always thought walking in the mall was like skating on ice with only shoes, so maybe besides my brain condition[,] I was fighting smooth soled shoes. I will see and report further here. The right leg, still warm, seems better in one position each day for longer periods of time. I noticed this while doing the puzzle and listening to the mp3 tapes. I did read at the library and did some puzzle this afternoon. Tomorrow after walking I may catch a movie Tom recommended, "42" about Jackie Robinson. He said it was good and I notice it is playing in the morning at 10:40 [am] at the local cinema. Sounds fun and is more good therapy.

Tuesday April 23, 2013 4:45 pm living room

It's been a "buzzy" day with the tinnitus on the noisy side ever since about 3:00 am. I stayed on the [notebook] computer too late, so it was probably 10:30 to 11 pm when I went to bed [sleep]. I awoke at 3:00 am to the noise and I listened to the mp3 tape on hypnosis which did not help that much so I got up and had coffee and doughnuts, played some [computer] golf, flossed, shaved, took a shower, took out the trash, made it to the mall and listening to the mp3 [hypnosis] tape again [in the car]. I walked about [only] four laps due to new shoes so after that I picked up Mom's prescription [at Walmart] and some ice cream and went back to Mom's place. I had a salad for lunch and found Mom had dropped off her van for brake work at Midas and got a lift back home. We picked it up in the afternoon and all is OK now except the back driver tail light/blinker is not working. She says she will have Dave look at it when he gets back. I played the [tinnitus] mp3 one more time. As mentioned it has been a steady noisy day. Perhaps that is a sign of more healing going on. I worked on the puzzle some and soon will have supper, go to bed and start the cycle all over again.

Wednesday April 24, 2013 4:00 pm living room

The noise in the head continues quite strong today. I heard it while up at 11 pm, 1 am, 3 am. I listened to the [hypnosis] mp3 and that helped. I think I got a little sleep as I dreamed of the IRS and I had sent some payment in with a new IRS number and I awoke thinking it was real and that I should check my tax/SSN number. I got up about 4:30 am and did my usual [routine]. I walked a full 6 laps in the mall with the new shoes. They felt comfortable. Stability is still not a hundred percent but continues to improve daily. As I mentioned [the] noise in the head seems strong of late. Perhaps this is a sign that healing is closer if I can stand the noise. What choice is there? After the mall I saw the movie "42". Pretty good. [It was] About the first black [major league] baseball player, Jackie Robinson in the Brooklyn Dodgers. I enjoyed it and got back about 1:30 pm. Mom had been called to sit for that lady again. She also made a bank deposit for Dave. He is on his way to Washington State still. I test started the Jeep and it is OK. That is a strong battery in it now. The leg sometimes is better, but like the hearing, it acts up about this time of day. I may try to play the mp3 meditation tapes before bed to help. If I wait until bed, I have been falling asleep while listening. Then I wake up too early. Tonight, being tired, I may sleep well.

Thursday April 25, 2013 2:30 pm

Mom should be back from sitting for that older lady any moment. Noise in the head is mostly suppressed now. [Mom just got back. I decided to check out the movie ["]Life of Pi["] down the street tonight at Studio M [theater] . It's still on and may not be 3D as the original. The theater is cheap for sound and all but I want to see that show and it has long gone from the main theaters. Anyway yes, I played my tinnitus [hypnosis] mp3 and others and I am relaxed so [I] will check the show out later. As for my day, I walked 6 laps at the mall (around 4 miles) and with better control. However it still requires full concentration and is not automatic yet as before [surgeries]. I came back around 10:30 am, had a coffee, played some computer golf, played on the piano, played the mp3 player. The leg slowly improves as well. Last night I tried the SW radio antenna after my connector arrived. That was fun. I think keeping the mental distractions going will distract from ailments as well.

Friday April 26, 2013 3:30 pm living room

[It's been a] Pretty routine day. Pretty much the usual therapy routine reported here many times. The one exception today is the weather. It is nice and sunny now and should remain [that way] with lows in the 40's for awhile instead of the 30s when I awake. This may allow me to switch to an outdoor setting for the summer. The mall has been crowded lately and I just may check out the local Auburn [Williams Township] Park tomorrow morning and see if it is time. I was going to wait another week and I still may but I think I will test it first. The cane I may drag along to fend off any creatures and possibly to use on occasion but I want to avoid this if I can as I am doing better without it. Recovery of balance and stability is, so far, not an instant thing but a very gradual thing. It tries the patience but I know each day improves so I hang in there.

Saturday April 27, 2013 2:30 pm living room

The vision and brain are locking well together. There is disorientation when I change positions still, mostly elevation changes. I notice this greatly when sitting and rising to walk; when I watch a movie I have to be very careful walking after [sitting] due to the long period in one position. I see this walking where I have to still use extreme caution when the head seems to bobble or I round corners which required a movement of the head/brain. For the record I am again using the cane as I thought hard about this yesterday. Yes I can go without the cane in walking or getting the mail, even visiting the VA[,] but normal stability is not there yet and why take a chance too soon[?]. I expect that things will get back to normal but as I have gone through before, it's an ego battle in a way as a part of me thinks I don't need a cane and canes are for "older" people. I got to thinking about the instability and the arrival of spring weather and an eventual shift outside. In a park I would feel safer with a stick or cane with me for animals and as [omit as] it helps my current instability. I have decided to make it easier on me [myself] and use the cane here [on] out until things improve. You watch, now that I have dropped back a bit, so to speak, improvement will come faster. This is usually the way when you stop trying so hard. Not that I will stop trying but that I will kick it down a notch and see how things go. I will not worry about what others see or say. Sounds good in theory at least. I guess Dave is picking up another RV and delivering it to Minnesota so I will make it to the VA in Ann Arbor for my scheduled MRI this Monday [on my own again]. I plan to use M-52 through Owosso, Perry, and take this shortcut to avoid construction currently going on (and detours) at I-75 near Saginaw. The sun is out and today [it] is near 70 and they expect [the] same conditions Monday. As I have plenty of time to get there[,] maybe I will stop by the Owosso Public Library for a nostalgic visit [I used to hang out there for hours as a kid]. We will see. Either way it's amazing to me that I am able to do this and save Dave some time. I look at it as the most excellent combination of therapy possible--independence, driving, walking, cognition and so on.

[5:00 pm]

[I am making a] Second entry about the park. About 3 pm I went down to the Williams Township Park, the Auburn Park as I call it. It's in the 70s, sunny, and I caught up with puzzles, journal entry [entries] and [the] piano. I tested the length [of a park lap] in [with] the new pedometer. It came out about 0.7 miles, almost the same as one lap around the mall (using all the store corners). I think now if it is 50 or over in the morning, I will use the park, else go to the mall. [It] Sounds like a plan to keep me motivated and hopefully I will be able to use the park mostly until October or so as last year. Today [it] seemed people were there using it because it's Saturday (remember that old song by Chicago?) and people are off work and it's the first real day of decent spring weather. Better late than never. People were walking, using the playground [and] picnic area and [playing] soccer and baseball. I stopped and watched the [a] soccer [game] for a bit and thought back to the day when it was all so easy. I think they were high school kids but big ones or maybe I just shrank. Stability is not where I wished it was but perhaps by fall [it will be]. I had to resort to the cane throughout the walk. I did 3 laps around the outside of the park in total, stopping to rest after each lap, and to watch soccer half way (far end of the park). It felt nice to be back there. Even though walking is about the same, cognition, vision, balance, are much improved and the head noise has been suppressed to about a 2 out of 10 today. [It is] Real nice and something to be grateful for. Now Sunday I will take some time off. Mom is sitting, Sandra is supposed to come over [tomorrow] for lunch and bring me a fish sandwich. Monday I go to Ann Arbor and will resume this journal then with the details.

<u>Sunday April 28, 2013 3:30 pm. living room</u>

Sandra just left. She stopped by for lunch and brought me a fish sandwich. I worked on the puzzle a bit today. Earlier I played the tinnitus [hypnosis] mp3 to help silence the sounds. They have not been too bad today, maybe 3 out of 10. Now it's bit stronger. Perhaps [it is] from the stress of the puzzle or maybe I need a refresh of the mp3. I will do this at bedtime. Tomorrow I take my trip to Ann Arbor via M-52, Owosso, [and] Perry. I may stop at the library [in Owosso] if they are open for old times sakes[, as I have mentioned]. It should be a nice pleasant drive with most likely good news. My vibrations will be good so I expect good results. I will take a reading break then catch the latest golf tournament [on TV]. It's been in the 70's mostly with some sun. They expect that same pattern through Wednesday so [it] should be a good travel day tomorrow. I will report more about it tomorrow. Also of note: A day or so ago I ordered a lap desk for the notebook computer. I intend to start transcribing this journal to digital format for posterity or whatever before I get too along in it. It may take several days but I think it will be worthwhile. Also I ordered [some] smaller

["]one-a-day["] vitamins for ease of swallowing so I will phase out some of the many supplements I take for this smaller pill.

Monday April 29, 2013 7:30 pm living room

[I am] Writing this while a Tiger baseball game is on TV. We had a late supper, Mom and I. Dave is on his way back from Minnesota. I drove to Ann Arbor on this warm, foggy morning via M-52 and it took about 4 hours. I was in no hurry. In Owosso, the little public library is open 10[am]-9 pm Mondays. I was there [at] 8:30 am so I kept going. The MRI went so-so. The past tumor that started to regrow [that led to the gamma knife operation] is still dead and not a threat. The [omit 'The'] Dr. Orringer [the neurologist in Ann Arbor] saw a small "something" and wants a 3 month MRI to follow-up on it [he wants to observe it in the next routine MRI to look for any growth]. This will be late July sometime [actually July 8th]. I will try not to dwell on it and go about my summer therapy in the park now and hope for the best. Perhaps like Mom said, it is just scar tissue. Either way I am told it is small. I told the doctor about my tinnitus but he had little reaction. He seemed impressed that my speech had improved. He checked that I could touch his finger with mine from each hand. He did not talk too much [he never does], but wrote [typed] a lot on the [his] computer. I was hoping of course for a full clear MRI but will have to wait longer now. I got little sleep last night so [I] will retire shortly. The noise is getting louder so I will play the [hypnosis] mp3. Tomorrow (Tuesday) I may walk in the local park if [it is] warm and not raining.

Tuesday April 30, 2013 3:30 pm living room

I sit in the tan lazy boy [recliner] chair after having worked on the puzzle of the fruit baskets. This is one of the more difficult puzzles I have done and I have done about 40 now. I suppose that it is excellent therapy. [Mom just wanted me to look at a video of Brooklyn, Josh and Sarah's girl, saying "Dada"--very cute. Mom loves Facebook. I got off it about a year ago as it was too difficult still seeing friends from Tennessee on it.] Right now my head noise is suppressed and the leg improves. The noise has been well in the background today. This morning the temp[erature] was 50 something so I headed for the Auburn [Williams Township] Park again. I got two leisurely laps in with good breaks (2 per lap). On one break I played the Hicks physical "in the Vortex" mp3 meditation, which I have played on and off during recovery. I will try to play it and other tapes [mp3s] more often in order to keep a good attitude/frequency about the newly discovered "blob" [or whatever it is] in my head. [I] Hope it's just dead skin but no matter what it turns out to be I am going to live each day positively and do the things I like to do. Into the third lap it started to drizzle so I stopped the walk and in the interest of doing "fun" therapy I went to the Saginaw Barnes and Noble store on Tittabawassee Road. [It is] Amazing that I can do this! I stopped and had a Starbucks coffee at the store and browsed with no big deadline which is nice. I kept my mind off the new MRI results and looked for a new book or CD to start reading. I picked up a CD to rip [to my mp3 player] about relaxation, something I can use as my BP [blood pressure reading] was still high yesterday. I may play this at night and/or morning, perhaps even on park walks, we will see, but it can't hurt. So I headed back after [visiting] Barnes and Noble as it was raining quite hard [preventing further walking in the park]. I was going to resume walking had it cleared up. I messed with Mom's projection [ceiling] clock as it still wants to mix up AM/PM [times]. It looks broken and I will visit Walmart in Saginaw tomorrow when I go to the VA for speech therapy as they [are supposed to] carry one that perhaps will program better than Mom's existing one. Speech continues to improve and now it [my appointment] is every two weeks, which I probably mentioned before. I enjoy going there and talking with Anita, my [speech] pathologist. I make her job easy as I basically go there and tell stories and blab, which she says I should do. So I will perhaps walk at the Fashion Square Mall on Bay Road in Saginaw after the VA [meeting] which I usually do. Either way I intend to enjoy the day and to keep a positive attitude.

CHAPTER 5   5/1/13 – 5/31/13

Wed. May 1, 2013 3:00 pm living room

Dave made it in from the UP [(Michigan)] late last night. I had a VA speech appointment at 9:00 am [today] so I left early to try to find the Saginaw Walmart on Bay Road which was supposed to have a projection alarm clock for Mom. Hers does not program well and changes AM/PM [times] randomly. Neither Walmart or [nor] Meijer had the clock so this Friday, payday, I will order it though Walmart.com to deliver to the Midland Walmart where I will get a receipt so I can get a return if necessary. Things are more fluent, "brain lock" [is] better, focus [is] better, [the right] leg [is] slightly better[,] and [the] brain buzz [is] subdued so I had better speech this morning at the VA. I meet every two weeks [now] and I just talk and she [Anita] listens and evaluates. I have made it easy for her and most of the healing has just been natural as I knew it would. Nevertheless, it's good to get her feedback. Like the neurosurgeon in Ann Arbor Monday [Dr. Orringer], she said my speech is much improved, [with] more energy, [and it is more] more lucid. After the VA I went to Walmart and Meijer to check out the clocks (there was not enough time before the therapy meeting). I then stopped by McDonald's for a quarter pounder, fries, and milk before walking in the [Williams Township] Park [at Auburn on my way back]. I did two leisurely laps with the cane for stability. I took the cane to the VA as well for safety. It was warm today in the 80's by noon when I walked[,] with lots of sunshine. Tomorrow I will remember to take my hat with me for shade. I stopped at 2 laps as I noticed my [new] pedometer was set for km [kilometers] not miles. I got back about 1:30 pm and talked with Dave some about speech and the MRI appointment. He was paying some insurance bills. I finished the hard "fruit basket" 1000 piece puzzle and since there are no more [puzzles] here, I have decided to take a "puzzle break" for awhile to catch up on some reading or other therapy.

Thursday May 2, 2013 1:00 pm living room

[I am] back from my morning walk. I got the lap desk from Amazon today so I will try that shortly. I walked 5 laps in the park with 1-2 breaks each lap. I took a long break at the end of each lap to play the meditation/hypnosis tapes [mp3s]. I did not rush and could have done more laps now that my energy is stronger but the [park] mowers were running so I decided to head to Barnes and Noble [in Saginaw]. I did sort of a repeat of before [yesterday, being in Saginaw again]. I had a small mocha coffee at Starbucks there and just browsed for awhile. I bought the fiction book (something which I rarely read), ["]The Life of Pi["], as I saw the movie down the street [Studio M] and now I would like to read the book. Sort of the reverse but I enjoyed the movie [and I wanted more information on the ending from the author's viewpoint]. I will now attempt to read three books at a time, in sections daily of course. Talk about distractions. As I have mentioned I think mental distraction and "spoiling" oneself are the real secrets to enduring tinnitus, these remaining symptoms, and the new MRI results. Distraction really works as [during] most of the park walk I did not hear the buzz as I was concentrating on my balance (I use the cane as I have mentioned, however I hit it on the grass at the sidewalk edge to reduce the physical blow to the arm) [which I noticed after I started to "thaw"]. During the coffee break and browsing at Barnes and Noble I did not notice my buzzing either, but to be fair I did play the hypnosis tape [mp3] on tinnitus during the park walk. Dave is here and was playing on the piano. He is now looking at Mom's yard and is going to get some grass seed/fertilizer for the yard at a local hardware Mom recommended. I will now try out the lap desk in an effort to start digitizing these journal entries and possibly to write about the things that have happened to me these past months [I actually did begin to digitize this book on May 2, 2013, [my niece Emily's Birthday as I mentioned earlier].

Friday May 3, 2013 6:20 pm living room

[I had] Another morning at the [Auburn] park. I continue to use my cane but I let it pound the grass and not always the sidewalk. I remember the stiff arm I developed after using the cane in the park last year. I only did 4 laps as I wanted to do some laundry and also my SanDisk mp3 player died in [while I was] walking. I ordered a replacement, [and it will be] here sometime next week. I also jammed up (or the machine died) a big washer at the laundry [in Auburn] (go figure) but I managed to do my wash. I may try Mom's machines next time or a different laundry. How embarrassing. I also ordered another projection clock for Mom online as her's is dying. I worked on a my [the] digitizing of my daily journal and an introduction. It's [The introduction is] an overview of events that led up to my surgery[ies] and recovery. Time for a beer break...to be continued.

Saturday May 4, 2013 6:05 pm living room

[It's been] Quite a day physically for me. I have noticed quite an increase in strength and endurance. I had a good night's sleep. I had some beer with Dave last night and I think that relaxes me and helps me to sleep better. [The beer helps] So much so that I think I will look for some local beer to keep on hand to help with sleep. [The] Head noise is well suppressed today, despite not having a working mp3 player and [not] being able to play the hypnosis/tinnitus tape. I went to the [Williams Township] Park in Auburn about 7:30 [am] after stopping for some cash at the bank ATM [this morning]. I did 6 laps in the park, or about 4.2 miles. I only needed short breaks in between. My energy was very good but I am still relying on the cane. I was done around 10 am, kind of early to return so I went to the Auburn Burger King for a coffee and stayed there until about 10:30 am. I got my "second wind" and decided to walk some more at the Fashion Square Mall in Saginaw. I would have gone back to the park but the place was getting busy with "soccer moms" and families, it being Saturday. So I decided to go over to the mall [in Saginaw]. I am glad I did as they are displaying art works from local high schools. It was fun to look at them. I have more control of my balance to where it is near normal, [but] there is still some disorientation when moving fast or getting up or down and so on but control is much easier and I am confident at the mall with the cane. I do better from the parking lot to the food court also and am able to climb up the curb more easily. I used to have to stop and study each movement before attempting it. Some of the time walking in the mall I did not use the cane and lifted it frequently but then I thought I'm not out to impress anyone there and the pretty girl[s there] can be my grandchildren so to heck with it, so to speak, I went back to using the cane. It's still safer and I need it [now] for stability. So [omit So] I was up to about 6 [additional] miles by the end of the mall walk and went back and Dave was talking [to me] about Mother's Day and what to get Mom. I finally went with him over to Home Depot where I helped him pick out a couple of barrels that work as planters. He said Mom has mentioned them to him before. So now I will get her a card as well. Dave is leaving tomorrow for New York to deliver another RV (by way of Indiana of course). He is going to try to stop by Niagara Falls if he can while he is there and is going to try to be back here by Mother's Day next weekend.

<u>Sunday May 5, 2013 4:30 pm living room</u>

When I awoke around 5 am (a good sleep again) I heard the head noise but I am learning to ignore it or look past it. When making coffee I noticed the pot [coffee container was] pretty empty. I made a cup and had doughnuts then I made a list and drove over to Walmart. I had my black brain surgery t-shirt on and got a few looks inside Walmart. I got the coffee and a few other items then got back before Mom and Dave woke up (about 7:00 am). Being conditioned to early hours is part of the reason I get up [so] early. Also I hit the sack around 9 or 10 [pm] after reading. At the VA they always got us up around 5:30 to 6 am. Before that [the night nurse woke me around 3 am] to get [give me] my stomach shots, several [all] at one time. Dave watched MSNBC while I played computer golf. He then took a shower.

He will be leaving later than planned for NY. It has been a beautiful day in the 70s with the doors open. Tree buds [are] blooming everywhere. We are now starting spring. I plan to continue [walking] in the park for as long as the weather holds. It will be interesting to see how the walking develops now that physical energy has increased greatly. I typed a few more entries of [in] this journal today [into digital format]. Then I took a "break" and started one of the puzzles Rose gave me. [It] Does not look too bad and [it] is a nice break when the journal entries get too tedious. Mom is cleaning her room (what else?), Dave is working in the yard, the birds are squawking[,] both mine and wild birds outside. I will probably enter some more into the computer [and] then wind it down.

<u>Monday May 6, 2013 3:45 pm living room</u>

I write this while I load and charge my new 8G Sansa Clip mp3 player. The original I found worked all last year but finally locked on me or went totally flat (black screen of death). Maybe this will last a long time. I am loading lots of things on it. Of primary use is my hypnosis and meditation tapes but I like to listen to music too. This is [has a] 8G base and has a slot (micro SD) to expand [it] even more—cool. [I am] Looking forward to trying it tomorrow [during my walk]. Also Mom's projection replacement clock is here but I need a lithium battery which I will get tomorrow. It's 60 to 70 degrees out [and] sunny. Dave is headed to NY now and Mom is playing with the rain water in the pool. I started the ["]fairy["] puzzle Rose got me and [I will] do it for awhile and then take a break. I also am working on transcribing my journal. The right leg remains hot, the buzz is [still] in the head but both are much better and tolerable. The noise, fortunately, while the mp3 was dead, remained buried or my mind is [was] able to not think about it. Walking in the park, I only did 4 laps (only, ha ha) as I needed to contact [the] Ann Arbor VA to try to get [my next] two meetings (MRI and follow-up) on one day for ease of travel and because they [the VA] now will not pay for [my] gas [even though I am] on disability (I make too much, in their eyes).

Tuesday May 7, 2013 2:40 pm. living room

[It's been] A hectic morning and day so far. I have been busy from the start. I woke up at 11 pm, 2 am, then 6:00 am. I fell asleep listening to the tinnitus hypnosis tape [mp3] after I loaded the new mp3 player with all my songs and meditations. The 2 am [wake up] was to urinate and 6 am was when I arose after playing the hypnosis mp3 and three meditation mp3s so I guess it [I] was up around 5 am. It gets lighter earlier now and of course it's still light now at 8 pm when I crash. I went to the [Williams Township] Park [in Auburn] and walked 4 laps slowly and with several breaks to play meditations. I cashed in a $5 winning Lotto 47 ticket into [at the] Marathon [gas station] in Auburn. I then bought 3 more quick pick [lotto tickets] then headed for Walmart in Midland to shop for some things for Mom. When back I helped Mom set up some umbrellas [outside]. I set up her new Memorex [ceiling] projection clock, filled up my vitamin container and before entering some more of the journal transcription I stopped to enter my daily log in this journal. Dave is headed for Niagara and may be back late tonight.

Wednesday May 8, 2013 5:15 pm living room

[It's been] Another day that seemed to go fast. [I was] Up about 5 [am] to listen to meditation/hypnosis mp3s until about 6:15 am. [I was] Up a few times in the middle of the night as usual to urinate, but [I am] still taking the easy way and using a urinal bottle. No nurses can hide it from me this time. I walked the Auburn [Williams Township] Park for 6 laps taking long breaks for hypnosis and meditation tapes. I was there from 7:30 [am] to about 11 am. [It] Started to warm up. Dave came in late last night from Niagara Falls. He took some photos. We chatted briefly but today everyone had things to do. I did not type any journal entries today. I needed a break. I burned some more CDs to my mp3 player and finished the "fairy" puzzle from Rose and started the New York skyline puzzle, the long, horizontal one. This also is from Rose. Tomorrow I probably will type some more journal entries. Tonight

Dave is going to grill some hot dogs again and we'll probably have some beers. I will probably sleep better. I also took a shower when I got back from my walk as I really needed one. I had worn the same clothes for 3 days. I will now take an evening break and enter more here tomorrow.

Thursday May 9, 2013 4:25 pm living room

I have been doing the New York skyline puzzle Rose got me and digitizing my journal. [I have been going] Back and forth [between the two] this afternoon as Dave drives my lawn tractor around. I got up about 6:00 am. [I] Got up a few times to use the urinal as usual [during the night]. [The] Noise in the background is persistent but [I am] ignoring [it as] best I can and catching some sleep in between [before finally] getting up. [I] Walked [in] the park [this] morning (around 8:00 am) as usual but only did 3 laps as my shoes were getting too lose. I listened to meditation and hypnosis tapes on breaks and the ["]Seth Audio["] tapes on the walks. I burned these in yesterday. I figured they might inspire me to change [my] reality for the "better". It's a nice spring day in the 70s. A cold [cool] down will be here Friday and into the weekend. Dave bought me his ladies man t-shirt [from the popular "Duck Dynasty" show on TV] which I will wear on a walk when it's warm. [My right] leg is warm but tolerable. Speech [is] slowly better. I noticed that vision and brain "lock" [are] almost complete [or normal now]. All I feel now is that I am [always] drugged or drunk, with eyes drooping, [a] goofy feeling you could say. So it's not exactly full[y] normal yet but very close. Walking improves. I walk more stable and confident but as I mentioned my shoes I really liked [like] (a good tread, slip-ons) but they are [size] 9 ½ so I found the same style at Walmart and in size 9 so I spent $19 [and bought them]. They feel good as I wear them to the pet store and to K-Mart. I will know more tomorrow as I walk in them. So I am down to droopy eyes and [my] brain tiring a lot still, but we will get there. Of this I am certain. Dave is supposed to grill some pork chops outside so we will probably have some more of his Canadian beer which is tasty. I am okay if I still pay attention to each swallow and let it in on an "angle" and not straight down the throat. If I forget I pay for it in a nasty cough[ing] spell. As I have read about[,] it certainly keeps you "in the moment ".

Friday May 10, 2013

I woke normally around 6 am to a rainy, cool morning. I was going to the mall to walk but I had trouble with the garage remote and by the time I got around to it, it was nearly 8:30 am so I just drove to the Dow Library and waited in the [parking] lot until 9:30 am for them to open. I played some ELO [Electric Light Orchestra] music on my mp3 player ([their"]Zoom["] album), happy that my hearing allowed this. I spent time there writing [transcribing] some more of my [this] daily journal into [digital] text [using the notebook computer]. I got a lot done so I may do that tomorrow as well as it is supposed to be cold in the morning. The writing/typing is tediously slow but so is my recovery. It may take me a year to do it [actually it took about 6 months, thanks to advancements I talk about later] but it will be worth it and of itself, it is a valid therapy and helps keep me not paying attention to my tinnitus sounds. That stuff is always around. I sure hope it goes away soon. [I] Came back to work on the computer (notebook) or the digital work and the puzzle. Back and forth, good therapy!

Saturday May 11, 2013 3:45 pm living room

[It's been a] Cloudy, cool day but I still made it to the park and walked 3 laps until it got too cold. I played the Seth [Jane Roberts/Rick Stack] audio tapes. I went to Dollar General [in Auburn] for a Mother's Day card and then to the [Auburn Branch] Library to read a few chapters of ["]Life of Pi["]. I mentioned this before but I enjoyed the movie and now I want to read the book to see what they left out [in the movie]. It had a cool ending and I'm sure the book will tell more. I came back [later]. Mom went on a garage sale with Sandra [my sister] and Amy [my niece, Sandra's daughter]. They dropped Mom off [back home] about 1:30 pm and Dave and I went to Lowe's to get some flowers [and planting barrels] for Mother's Day, which is tomorrow. [I] Got back to make entries in this journal. Dave took off just now to the casino in Mount Pleasant to kill some time as Bob and Marsha [my brother and sister-in-law] are coming over late for pizza and they don't get along well [Dave and Bob and Marsha]. I stay out of it as it's their business but it's a shame. My [right] leg is getting warm but it was not too bad at Lowe's. When I am out with the cane walking it is not an issue.

Sunday May 12, 2013 8:15 pm bedroom

I sit here in bed after Mom, Dave and I played 2 Scrabble games. Steve, Sandra, Heather [my niece, Steve and Sandra's daughter], Amy, and Tom [my brother] were here for Mother's Day. We took Mom out to [the Midland] Ponderosa buffet after she went to church. I paid for everyone because I can afford it more than anyone there [being that I am retired and now on disability] and because I wanted to do it. It was fun but now that I write this I think we are all tired out. Mom went to her room to read the Sunday papers and to enjoy the rest of her day. Dave is watching TV. I retired early as is my habit to write in this journal, to read, and rest up for the resumption of walking and a [an upcoming] week of therapy. It is supposed to get too cold for the park so I think I will go to the Fashion Square Mall if up early enough as I don't really want to be at the Midland Mall again until I can go without the cane. It's [The Midland Mall is] too small, everyone knows everyone else so the mall in Saginaw is larger and I feel more anonymous [there]. Maybe I'm just being paranoid. Anyway after some walking I may find a library there to do some more of my digitizing of this journal and my introduction. It is supposed to warm up they say later in the week. I marvel as I write this as [to] how much my eyes have improved. They are now as normal as can be unless [back when] I only had one pair of glasses. I feel a bit of [eye] strain but perhaps that is from the Scrabble too. It's just a real joy to see again, to not see double vision, page margins fuzzy and moving and all [of] those things I have previously written about. I have truly come a long way and I will try to use this to stay in a positive mood to use for further improvements and VA scans.

<u>Monday May 13, 2013 3:20 pm living room</u>

[I] Woke up a few times in the middle of the night to use the plastic urinal. [It's] very handy as always. [I] awoke at 6:15 am after playing [my] hypnosis mp3 for tinnitus and listening to the two Hicks [Vortex] meditation mp3s, abundance and physical. It was cold this morning, about 29 degrees, too cold for the park so I went to the Fashion Square Mall and walked 4 times around the mall. I noticed better stability and much more energy but I am using the cane still for the unstable steps I still sometimes make. I found a local branch library on Center Road [the Zauel Library in Saginaw] that I used after walking for awhile. I read some more chapters of ["]Life of Pi["]. While driving around Saginaw on this cool but sunny morning I [reflected on how I] was thankful to have survived surgeries, to be retired (never thought I would see the day) and [to be] able to drive[,] which is very liberating for me. I was grateful Mom has allowed me to drive the car in the mornings. It has made a big difference in my recovery. I headed back after reading and had some biscuits and sausage Mom had just made for breakfast. After lunch I typed some more of the daily journal into digital format. I am up to January 30 now. It is going to be a long project but hopefully worthwhile. I will take a break now and talk to my birds then watch some TV and wind down. My stomach is a bit sour with all the sausage and then munching on candy, probably not the best thing, but it does show that my appetite is improving.

<u>Tues. May 14, 2013 2:33 pm living room</u>

Dave and Mom are fixing the pool. I can't do much to help yet. Mom is headed to get another part from the pool place on Midland Road. I just played some computer golf. Dave is leaving late for 2 trips to [Western] Michigan from Indiana and then to South Carolina. He will have a busy time. Today I did not walk. It was cool and [there were] raindrops when I left. I decided to work on my journal digitizing. I am editing files now. I went to the Library in Saginaw that I stopped by yesterday, the Zauel Library on Center Road. I would have stayed at [the] Auburn [Branch Library] but they did not open until 10 am. [The] Dow [Library] opens at 9:30 am. Zauel is [open at] 9 am on Tues[day] so that worked[,] even though it was further away. I worked until about 10[:]30 [am] then took a break and drove to [some] downtown [Saginaw] parks near the rivers [I had seen them on a library wall map]. I was down on Gratiot Road (US-46). It was once again good to be independent and be able to drive and to now read and write better. It makes a big difference to me, particular being a former and/or present [day] nerd. I came back about 12:30 [pm] and Dave and Mom we're leaving to get pool supplies. I will now finish the day working on some more journal work.

Wed. May 15, 2013 4:40 pm

Dave is delivering 2 RVs from Indiana to Western Michigan, near Grand Rapids, then he will make a delivery to Myrtle Beach, SC on another long ordeal. He cleaned Mom's pool and planted some grass, set up Mom's plants, etc. before he left. Mom is now outside doing things, adding pool chemicals, watering grass, etc. It stays light out until after 9 [pm] now. She is taking Rose to garage sales in Auburn tomorrow so [she] will be busy all day. She certainly has lots of energy. Speaking of which, mine continues to increase now. I went to another speech appointment with Anita at the Saginaw VA today. Again I drove down I-10, I-75, [and] I-675. [I am] Thankful I am able to do this. She [Anita] says she cannotice [notices] the improvements. So I [will] see her again May 29th. On the way back I walked [the] Fashion Square Mall 3 times then bought some GABA 750 [that I use for evening relaxation] at [the] GNC [store there] and some melatonin/Valerian root sleep combo [supplement at Meijer] to help me relax and sleep through any tinnitus. Lately it's been under control but about this time in the afternoon it seems to fight for attention. I am nearly normal [in most] functions now but I do [still] have trouble swallowing, walking, the [right] leg [is still] slightly hot/numb, tinnitus, all the usual fun I often write about. I [try to] direct my mind now to other things, such as golf games, digitizing this journal, writing an introduction, and so on and these help distract my mind from all the remaining symptoms. Tomorrow I will shift my walk to the "Tridge" area in Midland [a famous triple bridge where three rivers meet downtown] so I can then go to the Dow Library at 9:30 am to work on this journal, [and] after Mom has some items at Walmart for me to get. I would use [the Branch Library at] Auburn but the library there opens at 10 am so that extra time at Dow helps, plus it's close to stores, etc. Around noon or so I will head back for some lunch as I usually do.

Thursday May 16, 2013 4:00 pm living room

This morning I switch[ed] attitude and location for my walks. It was a great, sunny spring morning. I had to get some items for Mom at Walmart and I wanted to walk outside so I needed a place in Midland [near shopping]. I picked the "Tridge" area as the [recent] flood there at the rivers is nowhere to be seen [also I used to walk there with Sandra]. I got there early at about 7:00 am. Mom was up and ready to pick up Rose [her friend] for the annual Auburn garage sales. I walked around the ["Tridge"] park, more in control, more of a sense of balance[,] although far from normal and still needing the cane for [additional] balance. I then walked over the "Tridge" bridge. I remember doing that for the first time last year and it was just barely [possible for me]. I still held on to the rails most of the trip [this time] however at the center I released and enjoyed the view of a totally clear [blue] sky and the sun bright[ly shining] over [downtown] Midland and shining in my face. I loved it and had a moment of reflection and gratitude for being able to be here [to be alive] and for enjoying the physical sensations. I walked slowly down the "Tridge" [bridge] with [on the "skater's park" side of the bridge] and sat at the picnic [Chippewassee Park pavilion] area. I then walked back over the "Tridge" [bridge toward the Midland side]. There were several young people on bikes. There were two cute girls in the center of the bridge. I was wearing my "I had brain surgery, what's your excuse?" [dark blue] shirt that Bob [my brother, and his wife Marsha] gave me [last

Christmas]. I thought they would see that and say hi or at least acknowledgment my existence but no way [they never looked up]. Instead they were both lost in their "smart" phones, probably checking text messages. I walked on. After all [I thought,] I am 62 anyway and my time for [as a] "yoot" [youth] is gone now. On my way back to the parking lot and down the "Tridge" [bridge] I cut a piece of my skin (probably where a sliver briefly was)--my left hand where I was gripping the bridge [too tightly] to keep my balance. No sliver [it turned out], just some missing skin, only about a 16th of an inch or less. No big deal. However it was only 8 am or so and instead of waiting at the library parking lot [for them to open], I went back [to Mom's] and put some hydrogen peroxide and antiseptic on the wound. It felt better. I met Mom there still waiting on Rose. It was 8:30 am. I left [went] back to the [Dow] Library, where I spent about an hour editing my intro[duction] to this journal. I then stopped for a "slow" coffee at their cafeteria. I noticed the back of the books near the coke vending machine. They looked clearer [sharper] than the last time I was there a few days ago. That, I thought, shows steady progress. I still needed to lift the right leg to help with circulation but it too is better. Lately I have a new "possible" theory on why it [the leg still] hurts. I recall a first surgery to drain blood from my [original brain] tumor. I was under [anesthesia] and a doctor [Dr. Singer] fished a line up my leg and into my tumor [to drain blood from it], or at least I think he did. That may explain the pain if he went into the right leg. I would have to check the record to be sure but perhaps a nerve got disturbed or something. The good news is that it slowly improves as do all my symptoms. [In] The month of May 2013, I finally feel that things are returning [to "near" normal].

Friday May 17, 2013 3:00 pm living room

This is a day of a new sense of adventure. It is the start of an experience that should distract my mind and thoughts from pains and "bad" futures to the "joy of the moment", to the excitement of new things. What is it you may ask? Well to the average reader, it may not sound that exciting, but to me now in my condition it is, and it is already distracting me from the tinnitus and from the leg pains. As I have written I went back to the "Tridge" (three bridges that intersect in downtown Midland) area to walk, as it's close to shopping, the library, and so on. I am expanding and trying out new areas [for walking] near the "Tridge". This morning I walked down the Pierre Marquette Trail (it goes to Clare from Midland, some 30 miles away in its entirety) from Midland to near the Emerson Park and across the [Tittabawassee] River back to the skater area. In total it is only a [3] mile [walk]. I came back to the "Tridge" bridge from the opposite side from Midland—from the Chippewassee Park, or the "skater's park" as I like to call it. It was fun. It was a cool morning around 7:00 am. [There was] hardly anyone around. [It was] all a nice trail. I had no idea there was a park (Emerson) at the end. Tomorrow I will go to the park, do a lap around its path [sidewalk] then head back. On Google Earth the park loop looks like a mile. I will gradually work up the distance [I do now at the mall] by looping the park, then going back. Anyway with all the nice sidewalks and paths, it will be fun to explore. Though shaky with cane, even after a year and a half[,] I did not pay attention to head sounds, leg pains, and so on [while there] and that's great. This should help me get coordination as well as train my mind to look beyond symptoms. I was going to see the new Star Trek movie with those young actors today while Mom sits [for the older lady], but I spilled my [small] water bottle that I take on walks inside my [pants] pocket at the [Dow] Library making a wet mess all over my pants. I just headed for Mom's place and worked on this journal. Mom should be back shortly but she decided to go to Kohl's [the department store] and use a coupon she got. Dave is headed for South Carolina and should be back next week sometime. [I am] Really looking forward to my walks now. Also of note, I bought a [new] notebook/laptop carry bag at Walmart this morning so I can go to the [Dow] Library after walking and carry my books and computer [in the bag].

May 18, 2013 Sat. 4:35 pm living room

Betty and Jerry [my Aunt and her ex-husband] just left. They went out for a drive [they live in Morris] and did not tell Mom first to avoid her [Mom] planning a big meal. We played "Spoiler" dominoes [on the patio]. Jerry is getting around but it is extremely difficult for him [he had a stroke and uses a cane and must have constant help]. They needed to get back for his regular shots. Mom said [after they left that] I was lucky and could have reached a point where no further recovery would be possible. I was fortunate and though I have my share of symptoms which I have labored upon in this journal, everything is a matter of perspective and I could have stayed where Jerry is now [I was almost there at one time as mentioned in my introduction to this journal]. We all have a different path to take or a "cross to bear" for those religious readers. [I will say how much I admire how tough Jerry is to endure this. I have some idea but no one can really know what it is like except him]. It does make me stop and reflect that when we think things are bad, they might not be as bad as we think. For the record I made it to Emerson Park this morning. What a great place to walk and I will be there again. [It is] Quiet, lots of rest spots and ["]Porta Potties[" or portable toilets]!! Perfect. The whole route was about 3 miles but the path in places slopes, and is bumpy which is good for me, not to mention the "Tridge" and the challenge in crossing that big bridge. I created a DVD of several photos I took on the walk. Mom saw it. I will show it to Dave when he returns from South Carolina.

Sunday May 19, 2013 4:15 pm [Mom's] patio

Today is Heather's Birthday and she and her family will drop by for some cake and ice cream around 7 pm. It's hot now, in the upper 80s. I helped Mom vacuum the pool bottom and water the grass. I did this without a cane [very] carefully. It felt good. The tinnitus is acting up as I write this. I took a shower and am relaxing on the porch. I played the hypnosis tape on tinnitus and as always when I distract myself it is better. [I did] No walking today, made lots of [digital] entries for the month of February in the journal and drank coffee. Dave is driving back from South Carolina today. I will resume my walking tomorrow at the "Tridge"/Emerson Park which is fun. We [I] will walk some stretches with the cane [lifted] up just because I can. It's nice and cool and quiet in the morning and I enjoy it. After [walking] I will go to the Dow Library to work in [on] the journal. My [right] leg is hot now so I will go play some computer golf to distract [my mind] and to be able to lift it [my right leg] horizontally.

Mon. May 20, 2013 2 pm living room

I went to bed late and probably started sleep[ing] after 10 pm. Sandra, Heather, [and] Amy stopped by for coke ["pop" as they call it in Michigan] and ice cream to celebrate Heather's Birthday. We got her [Heather] a card and I played the Birthday song on the electronic piano [that used to be Heather's]. It's hot outside as I write this, mid 80s and storms on the way. They are expecting mid 60s toward the weekend. Dave is driving back from near Detroit. Mom is outside working on things. My tinnitus kept me up early and has been loud and steady despite the hypnosis tape, or perhaps it would be worse without it. I hope it's a sign of a correction in the condition. I only hope I can bear it in the meantime. I continue to use distraction when I can. I took my usual 7:00 am walk at the "Tridge"/Emerson Park. [I] Got back just as a few drops [of rain] fell. I typed a little [of this book] at the Dow Library. I then bought Mom some items at Walmart and some junk food, naturally. While I was waking up [and checking the computer], I got an email from Cathy [Lewis, my friend in Tennessee] about the death of her brother. Tough for her. I wrote back to her. Perhaps she will send another [email]. A part of me still misses her greatly and I doubt that will ever change. One thing I have learned from this ordeal is to not try and predict the future. So who knows where I will be coming [ending] up. Right now it's recovery one day at a time. That's all I can do and the chips will fall as they will. So I am typing some more into the journal now, trying to tolerate this heat for a few more days. Mom has no [central] AC but we do have [individual] AC units in the bedrooms [thanks to Bob and Marsha]. [We] May have to use it [them] tonight unless it cools off some. I will mention a couple of other events for the day. Dave is back from Mount Clemens (at about 4 pm). Today I did not use my cane at the Dow Library. [I was] Slow and steady but [it was] nice to not need it. I went to the coffee place [shop] without it as well.

Tuesday May 21, 2013 10 :30 am Dow Library

I will write an early entry to report some changes in my walking and morning routine. We had rain when I woke up at 6[:]30 [am] and [I] remember using the urinal around midnight but [I was] just too tired to get up, tinnitus or not. By the way, that [tinnitus] went back to being blocked[,] or at least my "perception of it" as the hypnosis tape [mp3] says[,] is much less. Anyway I decided to walk as the rain stopped around 7[:]30 [am]. Dave and Mom were sleeping and the birds were yapping as always. I got to the "Tridge" about 8 am. [It was a] Beautiful morning, in [the] 60s, rain puddles everywhere[,] but blue skies breaking through. I did my walk but [and] noticed more control after awhile, even with all the puddles around, which I was able to avoid. I did well. [I did] Well enough to lift my cane on occasion, which felt great. At the park on the other side of Midland, the Chippewassee I think [omit I think], inside I lifted my cane on the way up the ramp to the "Tridge" bridge and I walked completely up and over the entire bridge [back to Midland] just carrying my cane. It was a real breakthrough so I thought I would mention it here. We will see how it develops. I will try more and more to go without the cane and we will see but I know enough now not to rush things. I then went to the Dow Library where I worked on the [digital] journal some and now made this [written] entry. I will [now] take a coffee break. As I mentioned I do not use the cane at [the] Dow [Library] now.

Wed. May 22, 2013 3:35 pm living room

I am writing this as I play Cyndi Lauper's "Time After Time" [on my mp3 player in the Dow Library parking lot], a great song and it helps me masks noises, which by the way are well controlled or as I thought about it, it's as if the T[t]iger has been put back in his cage (sorry I have been reading ["]The Life of Pi["] recently). Also I am going to listen to more mp3s as I write so I hope it [the writing] is logical. A bit of the activity for today[:] We are getting lots of rain but no storms so it's helping with the grass and pool. [It] Rained so much [that] I decided to do some laundry this morning first. ["]Totally Clean["], the small laundry near Mom [in Midland on Waldo] is nice and clean. I stopped in there and did my laundry. [The] Machines ran great. [I] Told one of the customers [there] about my history. The cute girl attending overheard. It's a small laundry, a small town, and these customers looked like ["]regulars["] and of course people are curious about who is the new guy in town. I did not use the cane. I also went to the Midland Mall [after] and walked 4 laps without a cane. It's not a 100% yet but I am now able to do this. I will try this on the "Tridge" walk to see how stable I am but I will [continue to] carry the cane for animal protection. I went to Walmart and Meijer [in Midland] then came back to work more in [on] my journal [project]. Dave was cleaning the pool inside it in the rain. He, like Mom, does like to keep busy. I laugh but I do it [stay busy] also just in my new ways that now involve therapy. Now that I think about it[,] I am proud of myself staying with it, walking every morning, overcoming great odds and many pains. I guess there's something to be said for good genes.

Thurs. May 23, 2013 2:30 pm living room

I think I am in "in-between" land, that is I am now to where I was before the gamma knife [operation], going without the cane for walking. I went to the Midland Mall again as it was steady rain this morning. I did not even take the cane with me. I did my usual 6 laps around [the mall] which is about 4 miles plus (with new strides [longer] and [a] new pedometer). Balance and control are so good now that I was able to do this caneless. I am anxious to try this out at [the] "Tridge"/Emerson [park]. I should be able to do this tomorrow.

Now I was just online on Amazon looking at animal/dog sprays, whistles, other repellents for walking. However at the last minute I ordered a collapsing walking stick as used in hiking. It looks like it all fits in a bag or could even be used in a backpack. I probably don't need it but I wanted a stick or something just in case of animals. Now I probably will never encounter one but if this works and I only have to use it for defense, then cool. Perhaps I can put it in a backpack too. I would just like to walk without a cane/stick but [I] did want to have one just in case of animals. I still took [take] my "leg" break (ouch) at [the end of] each lap and I will do that at the "Tridge"/Emerson Park also but it would give me further confidence to do the walk mostly without cane support. I[t] will take a week or so for the hike[ing] stick to get here. I think it was $26, not too bad. So [there is now] great balance and control in walking, especially around corners. The young man who I have seen at the mall [probably 40 something] before stopped me and offered his congrats in not using a cane. I got lots of looks also so I know people there pay attention. My right leg still is an issue but it continues to not hurt as it once did. I will now work more on my digitizing of this journal.

Friday May 24, 2013

I have had a few dreams [that I have recalled] but this [one last night] was pretty intense and gross. I will touch the highlights and skip the gore but be warned[,] any squeamish readers. This probably came from [my] surgery, [and] thoughts of the brain, and who knows what else. Some redneck [my apologies,] or stupid guy[,] was tormenting me verbally or something so that I had to kill him with my laser (gamma knife?). I did so right in his head, but he would not die, so I was (and sorry for this) cutting his head open and pulling out parts ... anyway you get the picture. [It was] So vivid [that] I woke up. I had been up every few hours [anyway] to urinate then. I was thirsty so I drank some water that I have at the bed side for pills, and then the cycle repeated. With the plastic urinal I am spoiled not to have to get up [to use the bathroom]. I tried [omit tried] listening [listened] to my hypnosis mp3 for tinnitus about 3:15 am. I finished and listened to some of the Hicks meditation tapes then got up around 4:15 am. I had coffee, rolls, watched TV, listened to the hypnosis tapes again as the tinnitus was constant. That helped. I took a shower, dressed, and headed to the Burger King near the Midland Mall. There is flooding downtown near the "Tridge" and rivers so I will walk at the mall for a week or so. I am still waiting for my Amazon hiking stick to guard against animals on my ["Tridge"] walk. I am back to no cane at the mall now and doing the full 6 laps. I still take the 5-10 min[ute] break between laps, mainly for resting my leg and comforting it. So [as mentioned before] things are nearly back to where [they were before I had the] gamma knife op[eration], using no cane, however I have better balance control, awareness, vision and less leg pain. All and all, pretty good--lots to be thankful for.

Saturday May 25, 2013 9:30 pm bedroom

Mom, Dave, and I finished a game of "Spoiler" dominoes. Mom won and was tired, Dave was coughing. I was ready for a break. Dave grilled some bratwurst and sauerkraut, [and it was] very tasty. I was late to enter this [into this journal]. It's been a fast, busy day: a day of progress. [I had] Great control inside Barnes and Noble in Saginaw where I had a latte coffee after walking in the Midland Mall a couple of laps. My mp3 player locked up [again] so I bought [a new] one at Walmart. However, I was able to get it [my old player] to come back alive [by holding the power button on for several seconds] so I will take the replacement [player] back next week. It's late and I am in bed making it hard to write. I felt in good control mostly today. There is still some unsteadiness but it's better. [The right] Leg is hot/numb but not that bad. Tomorrow Mom and I go to Bob and Marsha for a party for Heather moving to Colorado and Emily going to the UK. [The party] Should be fun. I will note [that] the tinnitus is better and under control. [It's a] Bit noisy now that it is quiet [outside]. I may look for hypnosis download[s] for visualizing good MRI results or a clean brain. We will see.

Sunday May 26, 2013 7:30 am living room

[I] Got back tired from a visit to Bob's [and Marsha's] for Emily (going to the UK to live and marry) and Heather [going to Colorado to live]. [I] Went to bed to read, [and] unwind around 8 pm. [The] Tinnitus [is] loud lately and [especially] this morning as I awoke and [now, as I] write this. Dave [is] in Port Huron most likely and is going to try to deliver to Canada an RV today. It is the US Memorial Day [holiday tomorrow] but not in Canada. Mom and I are headed to Grandpa and Grandma [Rust's] grave site today, then to Betty's [and Jerry's] to drop off some picture frames. It's [in the] mid 40s now but [it is expected] to be sunny and in [the] 60-70 degree [range later today]. I will resume walking, probably still [at] the mall. [I am still] Waiting for [the] flood waters to go down and my hiking stick [to arrive] before I resume [my] park walks. As I probably mentioned, I am going without a cane now. It is still dicey, especially down to Bob's basement and outside but I did pretty good. I drove Mom over there [to Bob and Marsha's place] and I will be driving her to the graves Wednesday. I have an 8 am speech appointment at the Sag[inaw] VA. One more [appointment is likely] after this. My speech gets better daily but [it] is still a bit hard to deliver and there is [still] slurring. This most likely will fade away as every other symptom [has].

Monday May 27, 2013 3:30 pm living room (Memorial Day)

Mom and I visited Grandpa and Grandma Rust's and Bob Rust's [my uncle's] grave sites. I had never been there. Flags were put at [on] the graves since Grandpa and Bob were veterans. I planted a small one at Bob's and some flowers at Grandma's. It was a clear, cool, sunny day with not much traffic until afternoon. We went down M-52 mostly. Mom bought me some gas at Oakley and some lunch at [the] Burger King in Perry. We had a shake on the way back in St. Charles. I walked all day with no cane. We stopped at Betty and Jerry's briefly to drop off two puzzles and frames. Betty was busy taking care of Jerry. [We are] Back now after [and I was] printing some copies of a grandkids and Doris photo for Mom. My tinnitus has been active since morning but distraction at the graves helped. I am charging my Jeep battery as it would not start this afternoon. Dave is headed back from Canada and was planning on another delivery to the same place tomorrow morning.

Tuesday May 28, 2013 3:45 pm living room

Urination seems more frequent now. I notice[d] this at the mall, at the graves yesterday with Mom, here at Mom's and especially through[out] the night. [It] Seems every two-three hours I am using the urinal. What a change [from the hospital]. It really does not have me concerned as it was not that long ago in the hospital I could not go at all and they forced it out of me. Now it comes quickly and frequently and is likely an older male thing but [again] I'm not concerned. Maybe I'll get some saw palmetto. I was taking it for a while and phased it out as I ran out. I don't remember if it helped or not but I will experiment [with it again]. With the nightly urination of course there is the tinnitus [that] I wake to. I am sometimes able to sleep despite the sounds if I am tired enough. Sometimes I need to get up. It was later suppressed [today], whether naturally or by me playing the hypnosis tape, who knows. Now it's loud as it's afternoon. I got some rum and coconut liqueur, Malibu[,] to try to allow more sleep. The beers I have with Dave help too. He is in Canada for a delivery. He was here last night and we [Dave] cooked or re-cooked some food. Today was cool, thunder and rainy. It's clear now and they expect warmer [temperatures] tomorrow. I did 4 Midland Mall caneless laps. [It] Felt good. I stopped to shop at Walmart [afterwards]. [I] Returned a [my replacement] mp3 player and [later] made a [bank] deposit, [I] basically ran errands. I entered some more journal entries into digital files on my notebook computer. I will now sip my Malibu [drink] and wind the day down.

Wed[.] May 29, 2013 12:45 am

Today I went to the Saginaw VA for another speech therapy

appointment. Right now it[']s developed to where I just tell Anita, my pathologist, what is new and some more about my symptom improvements. I throw in some stores about my experiences at the VA in Tenn[essee]. She says I am improving and I am. The [My] voice felt deep within at first and I really had to force the words out. It's not so difficult now but [and] since I don't hear my own voice 100% [of the time,] due to the numbness and "tunnel" hearing that hides tinnitus. It is close to normal now. We both talked about how fortunate I was to still be able to remember events back then. After the meeting I got to the Fashion Square Mall about 9:30 [am] and walked a full 6 laps without the cane for the first time [first time doing that many laps there]. Balance is much better with the ability to stop suddenly and make motion changes. Stability is, like speech, not 100% but close. I have less fear of going into the center of the aisle to avoid people, where there are no sides to touch. I noticed this at the Midland Mall recently as well, a sure sign of improvement. I got back about noon and will work on my journal [transcription] and read some more later. Dave is probably headed back here from Canada. He and Rod [my cousin] are looking for some RVs to take to the West Coast [starting] this weekend. We had some storms roll through very early [this] morning. It rained all night off and on. At 2 am a crack of lightning hit nearby. I thought the [my] birds would freak but not a peep from them, so to speak. A train then came by about 2:30 am, but even with all that [noise] I managed to get a bit more sleep till about 6:00 am.

Thursday May 30, 2013 4:15 pm. living room

Thunder is in the air; it is very humid, [with] some rain showers, about mid to upper 80s or 70s during [the] rain. Dave is headed back, [and] should be here shortly unless delayed. I had a good caneless walk again this morning. I did my usual 6 laps there [at the mall] with a short break [after each lap] to lift the still hot [right] leg. Tinnitus [is] still around but [I am] not thinking too much about it. Amazon said they shipped my hiking stick and a new relaxation-anti-anxiety CD I ordered. I continue to get better, [and] to have more confidence walking, going down the center of aisles just because I can. I got a bottle of pina colada mix to go with the rum and coconut alcoholic drink. I tried it straight but it is too strong as it is (Malibu is the name). Mixed in with the pina colada it is tolerable but I need to still watch each swallow, but this is also getting better. I came back early to start the Jeep, take care of the extension cords [by putting them] into the shed, fill the song bird feeder and other feeder[s] and give the outside birds some fresh water. They are almost as spoiled as my own cockatiels.

Friday May 31, 2013 1:45 pm living room

I was up quite early so I will write about today's events a bit early while they are still fresh. I awoke at 3:00 am. I went to bed about 9 [pm] and probably was asleep by 9[:]30 [pm] so I probably got 5 ½ hours sleep which is enough for me. When I awoke at 3:00 am I had to urinate. After [that] the tinnitus was continuous [and loud] so I played the tinnitus hypnosis tape [and] that helped some. I also played the 3 Guided Meditation tapes by Esther Hicks. I then got up at 4:30 am. I felt wide awake, so I got my coffee, a couple of doughnuts, watched the usual [TV] channels, [and] let the birds out about 5:00 am. Smokey was awake and raring to go. He flew to the couch and walked around. I put them in the cage about 5:30 am. I took a shower then played computer golf on and off. I left the house early at 6:30 am intending to go to Burger King near the mall[,] which I have done before[,] but I was not that hungry and didn't feel like [having a] coffee. Instead I parked near the BK [Burger King], actually near a stop sign quite away from the [my] usual mall parking place. It was [a] nice sunny morning with nice breezes. It was still muggy from storms in the area. I played the tinnitus tape again to get me to 7:30 am. I then drove to my usual [parking] spot [at the mall] and played the financial and physical Guided Meditation tapes [mp3s] again. Then it was 8:00 am and time to walk the mall. I'm still not using a cane but on lap 3, I noticed a bit of instability and my brain and head [were] bobbing more than usual [my occasional "bobble head" feeling]. Normally your brain can account [adjust] from [to] walking but more at this stage [it] seems locked to my skull and bounces on every step [as I have talked about before]. I thought about stopping short after only 4 laps but I realized I had my mp3 player with me, so I played some Enigma [a great group that I enjoy]. My walking improved and I finished my full 6 laps or about 4 miles. After the walk I went to the Dow Library. There I read some of a new book I re-started (since I read it years ago) "Beyond The Winning Streak" by Linda Dahl, based on the Seth teachings [(Jane Roberts)]. I then had a free cup of coffee and a cookie at the coffee shop [Cup and Chaucer]. I was wearing the fairy t-shirt, [a shirt with a fairy on the front, a shirt I saw daily at the Flying Tiger import shop in the Midland Mall and really liked] maybe a bit "gutsy" of me [it's more a girl's shirt I think] but after what I have experienced lately, no big deal I say, I just like it so I will wear it [now and then]. [My opinion is that] If you don't like it, don't look! I was slow and deliberate with the snack and all went well. Images [are] very clear but still not 100% "locked" as normal. I went back to the "quiet room" where the magazines and newspapers are and I listened to the first [??] tapes [mp3] (into [up to] ch[apter] 2) of the ["]The Power of Now["] by Eckhart Tolle. I know I have heard it many a time and have read the book but I played it again. At about 12:30 pm I played some of the Plum Village ["]gong["] meditation tapes [by the Vietnamese Zen monk Thich Nhat Hanh]. I left for Mom's about 12:45 pm and got back at 1 pm. Dave was going to take a shower, Mom was outside doing some things. I guess she cleaned the pool. No stopping her! I had a piece of homemade pizza that we had last night. Dave is [now] taking a shower then will head out for [to run] some errands. He and Rod (my cousin) are teaming up to take two RVs to California over the next week [as I have mentioned], to save expense on the way back. I hope my hiking stick gets here so I can go back to the "Tridge"/Emerson Park. It should be okay to walk now that the rain has let up (it was flooded out this week).

CHAPTER 6   6/1/13 – 6/30/13

<u>Saturday June 1, 2013 5:48 pm living room</u>

I just finished some more journal digitizing. Dave is out cleaning his car, running errands, [and] getting ready to drive to Indiana, meet Rod Rust and take 2 RVs to California. He will cook some chicken on the grill later. I got up about 3:00 am to urinate, but I got a solid 5 hours or so of sleep. I am still walking the mall without a cane and feeling better. Today in the mail was my walking [hiking] stick I ordered so I am anxious to use it back at [the] "Tridge" or [and] park. [As it is] Sunday tomorrow I will take the day off [as I usually do]. I have a lot of laundry built up and some errands to run Monday so I probably will not walk until Tuesday. Everyday things improve with the brain's focus or "lock" as I like to call it. [It is a] Very hard subject to explain, without going through it [again in greater detail], which I would not wish on anyone [more than they have already endured], but perception is slowly focusing, or the two eyes are beginning to respond like they used to before the operations. That is very encouraging. I still have suffering as in my very hot foot/right leg last night. It was the hottest it's been in a while but once covered [in bed] it was tolerable. I have been playing Eckhart Tolle's "The Power of Now" [mp3] again at the mall and library and with it's emphasis on being in the moment and the now, I may concentrate on that again to redirect the [my] mind from these problems. I was just online trying to order a [Midland] symphony subscription [as I did last year] but apparently my SSDI [Social Security Disability Insurance payment that I receive monthly] has not been processed yet. That actually gives me time to re-think about it [the symphony]. I may pass [on getting a season ticket] this time due to the weather and also they have a [Frank] Sinatra show this time and I'm not really into that. I see that there is a Saginaw Symphony so if I get the bug who knows [I may go there]. I will hold off [buying a subscription] for now.

Sunday June 2, 2013 3:17 pm living room

I woke up around 3:15 am and the tinnitus was loud, maybe a 5 out of 10. I played the hypnosis tape a couple of times. I was up after the first time but I saw [that] Dave had not left early as he [had] planned (to join Rod Rust) so I played the mp3 a second time [in bed]. Playing the tape seemed to help once I was up [as the sounds died down]. Dave was delayed [in leaving] because Rod got behind in his work. I made coffee, talked with Mom who eventually went to church with Sandra. I went to Walmart to get some items for Mom and a backpack for my "Tridge"/Emerson Park walk (which I plan to resume tomorrow). I will use my walking stick and backpack for the first time so it should be fun. Dave left after 10 am. I got back from Walmart and worked on this journal (digitizing) while listening to [Dr.] Wayne Dyer's TV show on PBS [a "new age" spiritual speaker talking about manifesting]. It is time for a break and to wind down for this night.

Monday June 3, 2013 6:00 pm living room

Today was another change in therapy day. I have made the switch "officially" from the Midland Mall to the "Tridge"/Emerson Park (I will use T/E for short). It was [in the] upper 30s to low 40s first thing this morning so I stopped at the laundromat on Waldo Street in Midland to do my laundry ["Totally Clean"]. A different attendant was there and two other customers so she was talking with them. I pretty much had privacy and kept to my business at the other end. I did not converse this time with [the] people there. I did play about three golf games on a golf [video arcade game] while I waited. It's all fun and gave me a chance to wait out the cold morning. I went to T/E after, got there about 8:30 am and it [the weather] was much better, probably 40-50s. By the time I finished the walk it was near 70 and sunny. It is about a 2 hour leisurely walk. I am now using my walking (hiking) stick and backpack. Tomorrow I will use the [my black] fedora [beret] hat so I will be the "whole package" [look like a hiker], won't look [that] disabled at first (there is that ego thing again). I noticed today it is fun [hiking with a stick] and gives me confidence to have it and it also will help if any animals cross my path. I noticed it [is] a little tougher [walking here than at the mall] as [and] I seem dependent on the stick. Now the mall was [is] perfectly flat too. I will slowly phase out the stick as I grow more steady but it will give me confidence in [during] the walk. It sure is great to be able to do this and on my own time, literally being able to stop and "smell the flowers". I have noticed a louder tinnitus all day [today] but when doing laundry, walking, and so on I do not notice the noise [as much]. It almost seems it appears when I bring my attention to it. I listened to Eckhart Tolle's "The Power of Now" [mp3] again. It's fun to work back through [my] books and music while I walk. So after the laundry and the walk it was around 10:30 am. I went to Meijer to get a new [plastic] urinal [bottle as mine was getting dirty] and some odds and ends. Again, simple things like shopping and pushing a cart, being aware of shoppers, and so on is a treat now. The more I do things to show my independence the faster I think I will heal!

Tuesday June 4, 2013 3:20 pm living room

I went to bed [at] the usual time (around 8 pm) due to the tinnitus and the fact that I never know when I will awake to urinate and then not be able to go back to sleep [due to the tinnitus]. Lately I just ignore it all and sleep anyway. That is close to the answer and it has taken me sometime to see it: just ignore it. Ignore the sounds, play the hypnosis and meditation tapes [mp3s] and then accept [things as they are]. There has [have] been small, daily improvements, which I have written about in this journal. I won't rehash that now but just go on to new changes and updates for this day. I woke up at 3 am, I slept from 10[:]30 pm till 3:00 am. I got up around 5:15 am after resting some more, had my morning routine. I let the birds out, gave them food and water and headed for the "Tridge". As the tinnitus was loud this morning, I played the hypnosis mp3 at the park from 7[:]30 am to 8[:]00 am and then walked the T/E path with my backpack and hiking stick. Today I wore the black fedora [beret] hat. I found myself [able] to walk a bit more without relying on the stick. I walked 2-3 steps then used the stick [by touching the ground], then repeated this. There was still lots of ground water [from recent rain] and a sloping path [mostly the trail] so I used the stick quite a bit, but felt less self-conscious than if I had used a cane. Back over [at] the "Tridge" bridge, I just held [lifted up] the hiking stick and walked up the ramp and over the bridge [on the way back] with no assistance. I will continue to force myself to walk more and use the stick less as I notice a dependence on it. There still is a lack of stability but things in that area are much better. I particularly notice this when helping to clean the pool and water the new grass this afternoon. Besides this I am working on editing my journal introduction. I will resume some of that before Mom is ready with supper.

Wed. June 5, 2013

[I was] up early as tinnitus [was] loud, then fell back for [some more] rest during or after [listening to my] hypnosis mp3, I don't remember [which]. [I] Did my morning routine, headed for [my] "Tridge"/E walk (3rd time). [I] felt unsteady but [I] did lift [my] cane [hiking stick] every few steps. The thing that stood out was [that] the Pierre Marquette Trail is slightly sloped at the edges. To me in my current state, this seems highly pitched and keeps me off balance, [making it] difficult to walk, [perhaps because] I am used to the mall being so flat. This will change and I will look back in amusement [at] how I could possibly think [that] the "trail" was hard to walk. I did stop at the [a] bench inside Emerson Park to jot down ideas and topics [for my writings]. After I got back today I tried out the [Google] Chrome browser ["]Dictation["] site [a speech-to-text website]. It translated my [currently] slurred speech quite well, surprisingly so actually. I had to do some editing [as always in speech-to-text] but not as much as I thought. I will try more tomorrow. It does not work on the Linux notebook--I get "network error". I am tired, it's late and I will stop this early. [Note: For those not familiar with speech-to-text: it is software or a website that will translate your speech into a digital file format.

The speaker then has to edit that file extensively for errors in translation, but once done there is a digital or computer file created from the spoken word. This method, although difficult, greatly speeds up the process of creating a digital file by typing every word. Early in the morning in 2013 I read my complete journal using a microphone into this dictation website on my Window 7 computer and saved the many digital files. I then spent hours editing these files on my notebook and later laptop computers, mostly in the Dow Library, for errors. I did this many times to come up with the digital version of this journal which I then formed into a printable book format, the one that you are now reading. This took about five months in total. Due to advancements in my speech and in speech-to-text programs, the time was much less than I expected. I think it also helped being a nerd and knowing about such methods, how to format files, how to generate table of contents and indexes, and so on. I am still amazed that I retain these abilities after the surgeries.]

Thursday June 6, 2013 1:10 pm living room

[I] Got some sleep last night! [I was] tired [and] went to bed [at] 8 pm, sleeping [at] around 9 pm. [I] woke up at 5:30 am, straight through—nice! With more rest, a good listen to Tolle, I accomplished quite a bit at the "Tridge"/Emerson Park. I went several feet (as in hundreds!) without relying on the hiking stick. Yesterday the trail seemed so slanted to me. Today I nearly walked it all without support. I noticed that when I get unstable, I now just stop and I am able to stand with good balance. After all there really is no rush. So I felt good at this progress and [at hearing] Tolle's [words] of not seeing ourselves as victim and [that is] not perpetuating bad health by seeing yourself as a victim. I will begin to apply [this]. I will drop wearing the brain shirts now as they tend to label me as I have always thought. I will not tell strangers my story as much, I will make an effort to appear more normal, to "blend" more [As of this writing I still wear the "brain" shirts and I notice that I may be "thinking" too much about these things]. I think, as in today, I will see a lessening of pain, tinnitus, leg heat, vision problems, and all that stuff. Perhaps even here I will not stress things that are still not right, but mention more of daily events and [things that reflect] positive progress. After [my] walk I went to the Dow Library and read some. I also listened to [in the] Chippewassee Park [to] some Guided Meditation mp3s. I then went inside the Midland Cinemas. I was going to see the new Star Trek "rip off" but it was 2D only and I wanted to check it out in 3D version. I will have to try that later.

Friday June 7, 2013 12:05 pm

Mom is sitting [for the older lady]. Dave is on his way to California with Rod. I had a breakthrough at the "Tridge"/Emerson Park area. I awoke at 1[:]30 [am] to use the urinal but I manged to go back to sleep until around 3[:]45 am despite the buzzing noise (tinnitus). I did my [morning] routine, let the birds out, took a shower (still on the [shower handicap] chair for safety), then headed to T/E. I played the tinnitus hypnotic mp3 until about 8:30 am. I received "The Essence" CD (Deva Premal) [that I ordered on Amazon] and I played it during the walk. Among the chants and meditations is the famous Gayatri Mantra. I played it several times during the walk as it is [reported] to help with healing, brain problems and so on. Now here's the great news[:] I walked the entire distance [from the "Tridge", up the trail, around the Emerson Park, and back over the bridge from the Chippewassee Park side] without touching my hiking stick to the ground, including grassy areas off the path. Not a big deal to those that can walk, but in my current state of weak stability, it was a big deal! I continue to improve rapidly and could see a breakthrough [to full recovery] any day now. Things are that close [It is painfully slow, as I write about, and as I edit this on August 30, 2013, I still am struggling to be stable in walking] now! I am going to work in [with] the notebook computer now [on this journal] then [I] will go see the new Star Trek movie in 3D. I went in and bought a ticket yesterday morning but in walking to the theater it dawned on me that the movie was 2D only. They gave me a refund, which was nice, and I will try again this afternoon.

Saturday June 8, 2013 5:15 pm living room

I played the "secret" meditation tape [I ordered recently] by Kelly [Howell] last night. I did fall asleep with it on but that's what it is supposed to do [allow]. I seem to recall playing it during the night as I awoke enough to play it again. [I got] up around 5 am or so and after the [morning] routine I went to the "Tridge"/Emerson Park. I walked it again with minimal hiking stick use. I filled up the car on the way. It cost $60 at [$]4.29/gallon. Crazy! I am thinking of walking from Mom's house to the mall where [the] Studio M [theater is located] or even past that to Waldo. I may phase the longer walk in later. This will save some gas, get my walking in (I really don't care where I go), [and] give me a new area to explore. It will reduce wear on the Olds[mobile] [my mother's car she has allowed me to use every day for recovery] also. I will try this on Monday. I worked on the journal (digitizing) this afternoon. Now Mom is going to make some supper so I will wind it down now.

Sunday June 9, 2013 4:15 pm living room

[There are] Big changes, at least in Dave's adventures, [and] job. Dave got back (earlier than I expected) and came in while I was deep into upgrading my notebook [computer]. Well that did not work so I will pass on it for now and keep Ubuntu 12.04 [my current notebook operating system] on it. I was trying to install [the] "Precise Puppy Linux" [operating system] in order to try the dictation feature in [the] Chrome [browser] again [on the notebook]. It just is not worth it [the effort] now. Maybe at another time if I hook up the DVD player to the notebook [it has no DVD writer] but what a pain. I may just use dictation on the Windows 7 machine and transfer it to the notebook like before. Anyway I backed up the Windows 7 machine and Mom's Vista [computer], both hadn't been done since [last] January [I back up entire images of the machines]. The big news with Dave is that he had a run-in with Rod on the road and Rod hit a deer and smashed the front out of Dave's car. He [Dave] always has the luck. At least no one was injured but it puts him out of trucking for the time being. [I am] Not sure what he will do now but [maybe] try to find another job. It's a real mess. He is talking to Mom outside[,] we will see. I can't let it bother me [too much] as I am on the way to recovery come "hell or high water" as they say. Gas is so high here[,] now ($4.29 [a gallon])[,] that I have decided to try walking around the block while Mom and Dave sleep. I will shoot for Flajole to Patrick to Waldo then back Midland Road. All in all it is 5 miles or about what I am doing at the mall. I will take breaks when I can and I plan on a long break at McDonald's on Waldo near the ["Totally Clean"] laundromat (that I go to now). I will likely have a coffee there. I am walking with the hiking stick now and backpack (if needed) so it should be a good test. I don't know what Dave will do but I must continue to progress no matter what. I think he would want me to do that.

Mon. June 10, 2013 12:30 pm living room

[It's] Rainy this morning so I went to the Fashion Square Mall [in Saginaw] to walk [inside]. I did not want to go to the Midland Mall yet until I get better at walking [without a cane]. I also wanted to check out the latest books at Barnes and Noble in Saginaw. I did 6 laps at the mall [there] without a cane and then had a coffee and cookie at Barnes and Noble, then [I] browsed the books. I did not buy a book. I bought some doughnuts and milk on the way back at the Auburn Food Center and they had the new Sam Adams Porch Rocker beer so I got some for Dave and I [to try] later on. He is working on Mom's new curtains in the living room so I entered this [journal entry] and will hang loose [as the curtains, ha ha]. I may enter more later.

Tues. June 11, 2013 5:45 pm living room

Today I tried the "Waldo" walk for the first time. I walked over to Patrick, then south on Waldo to McDonald's for a coffee then past the car wash and back to Flajole [where my Mom lives] via Midland Road. It was a real workout but I did it. I tried to walk just holding the stick

[up] for a good portion of the trip. It took about 4 hours but I was not in a rush. I will resume it [the "Waldo" walk] Thursday as I have my speech therapy [appointment] at the Saginaw VA in the morning at 8[:]00 am. I drive myself [there, as I have mentioned].

Wed. June 12, 2013 4:40 pm computer room

Dave has been working in the living room on the blinds. Mom is outside raking. I was looking for ideas on speech-to-text plans and entered some [more] in my [written] journal. I am now at the [dining] table with my right leg up and that still helps. Today started at 1[:]30 am with the loudest yet tinnitus. It is strong as I make this entry. I played the hypnosis mp3 3 times and that knocked it down. I then played the sleep [Kelly meditation] mp3. I knew I had a speech therapy meeting this morning so I knew I needed a bit more rest. Luckily that came, despite the loud sounds in my head. After my morning routine (I left the birds in the cage as they freaked yesterday morning when they were in the living room and saw the [new curtain] box on the floor and the curtains down. It was too much for their little brains to handle. Christy flew into the dining room and I found her walking under the dining table. Smokey flew up to his favorite "safe" spot on top of the entertainment center. So today they stayed inside and I left for the VA about 6[:]30 [am]. It was real foggy and muggy out (near 80 today). I got there [at the VA] about 7:10 am, so I played the tinnitus hypnosis tape one more time. When talking with Anita I have [had] no notice of tinnitus or not as much, proving once again that the mind can be tricked into not noticing it. I am sipping on a strawberry beer daiquiri that may relax me also [but it does not taste that good]. I find that [the alcohol] helps [to "wind" me down]. I may look into the relaxation tapes and biofeedback device also and test them out. Anyway speech therapy went well, more improvements [that] I [have] talked about [before]. While in the waiting room [at the VA] I could almost read magazines if held out about an arm's length away (with long distance glasses) so that tells me they [my eyes] continue to get sharper. I don't need to take both pair of glasses into the Barnes and Noble bookstore, which I visited on my way back and had a latte [coffee]. There I did notice how everything looked sharp with my long distance glasses. After a coffee and browsing (I did not buy anything as I may start to read again my Seth books, my very favorite books.), I went to Walmart on Bay Road in Saginaw after [visiting] the bookstore and got some snacks and more Killian beer (Dave and I like that [brand]). I headed back [this] afternoon and have been working in the computer room until coming out now. As mentioned, Dave is running errands and the birds are squeaking and watching me as I write. I will resume my walk tomorrow, going for "Waldo #2", so to speak. [As mentioned,] My walk [is] down Patrick to Waldo [and] back to Midland Road. It's about a 5 mile walk. I take a break for a coffee (or sometime a breakfast) at McDonald's on Waldo near the ["Totally Clean"] coin laundry, the very laundromat that I have been using of late. I want to comment on a good thing, too often it's a complaining like loud head noise or a hot leg, but it's my balance. That [improvement in balance] has really helped during my walks, the mall, the bookstore, everywhere. When I am tired, [and] disoriented, I can now just stop and start with good balance, something that is new with me. I am sure that people reading this might say or think, yeah, what's the big deal[?] But to me it's just another small thing that has returned to me and something I, like everyone, took [takes] for granted.

Thursday June 13, 2013 12:50 pm dining room table

I got back from "Waldo" walk #2. Dave is working on the living room blinds, painting now. Mom is with Rose. I took a shower and feel better now. It started [starts] to get hot around 11[:]00 am now, just as I get to the overpass over Highway 10 near the RV park on Midland Road. I left about 7[:]30 am, [and got] back about 12[:]30 [pm]. This time I stopped at the first bench [on the walk] and read the intro[duction] to "Seth Speaks", Seth's first book which I just started to reread. [At] The second bench opposite [the] Davenport Library [on Patrick], I read into the recorder some of this journal. I will play with digitizing from this recording and see how it works. I use the dictation site and the Chrome browser when the microphone does not lock up, [and] it translates even my speech pretty well. I have transcribed the first 3 months of this diary. I will proof it later. Today the swallowing [is] a bit better this morning. Walking [is] pretty good, several miles of the "Waldo" walk were just walking with the hiking stick just carried [not used]. Today several dogs were out, unchained and barking, a couple on Flajole at the start came at me but backed off. I will have to be careful of them. Mom told me this morning about the death of Dr. Copeland [chief neurologist in charge of the Midland gamma knife clinic] (in the paper). He was patient with me and Mom [taking the time to explain the gamma procedure to my Mom, who is hard of hearing] when I met him at Midland Hospital [MidMichigan Medical Center]. I may stop by [attend] the [memorial] service this Saturday in Midland. I feel I should do something. We will see. Dave and I will probably go out for Chinese later for supper [as Mom may be late]. I may enter more [in this journal] after that or just go on to the next day.

Friday June 14, 2013 4[:]00 pm living room

Today I decided to go back to the Midland Mall and to drop [the] "Waldo" [walk] for now. I ran into some dogs yesterday and it is getting hot [with the] summer sun [up] by 11[:]00 am now. The mall is flat, air conditioned, and forces [allows] me to go without [a] cane or hiking stick. I did my usual 6 laps, I went to the Dow Library for reading of [to read] chapter 1 of "Seth Speaks". I also had a small coffee at the coffee shop there. I was the only customer there at 10:30 am. I left near noon. Summer is on the way. We are humid and in the upper 70s now. I did enjoy going back there at the mall. I am not 100% [normal] yet but pretty close to it. Perhaps by fall it will be okay again. Dave put in the front door, or laid it in place for further adjustments. The birds like the bigger view. I will now wind it down and watch some TV. We are headed out later to the Ponderosa buffet for supper.

[8:20 pm]

A short follow-up note for this day: Mom, Dave, and I just got back from [a] Ponderosa supper buffet. For a Friday night, it was pretty empty. [The] Food was great. I don't yet eat more [as much as "normal" people do at a buffet] than one plate plus dessert. I just don't have the appetite yet. Who knows[,] I may never have [it] as I really didn't eat that much when I lived alone. Mom and Dave will probably play cards [later]. Due to the late hour for me and my tinnitus [being] loud, I headed for bed and covered my hot leg as usual. I am writing this and will read and/or work on the computer for a bit until tired and ready for sleep.

Saturday June 15, 2013 8[:]45 pm bedroom

Dave just cooked us some hot dogs and we tried some strawberry pie and ice cream. I am stuffed on just a bit. The 3 Killian's [beer] filled me up, no doubt. It is pleasant outside. We spent a few hours on the patio just chatting. I attended [Dr.] Brian Copeland's funeral service in town. I did not know him [that] well but I came to show respect for his life, knowledge and the help he had [provided] in giving me the gamma knife treatment. The relatives [of Dr. Copeland] told stories of his life, mostly funny ones. I had a good time [even though it was a funeral]. I had to sit [down at the end of the service] when we left [started to leave] due to the large crowd [all leaving at once and because of my current lack of full stability]. Earlier I did my 6 laps at the Midland Mall with eyes and recognition much better. I will now read some and/or play on the [notebook] computer until time to crash.

Sunday June 16, 2013

Ah, the miracle of the brain when is starts to come back to life! Words are hardy able [available] to express it [how I feel]. I hope to point the "reader" at least to [how] my brain [should function] and how it is slowly coming back. Sure this journal is a tedious read and I have noted [noticed] much repetition and for that I do apologize. I start today['s] entry this way just to note the leap in development (or return to functionality) that I am now experiencing. Sure there is [are] still leg pains and they have been constant over the last year, sure I still have tinnitus to deal with, stability is not [fully] there [yet,] but my awareness and precious balance and "brain lock", that I often write about, are coming back, everyday. I see it at the mall now as I again go without the cane, even if slowly. I see it as I speak into my voice recorder to help transcribe this journal. I just printed out dozens of pages [of the digital version of some of this journal] just now and [I] will [again] go to the Dow Library to edit them. I have transcribed through April 15 so far. Even I am impressed but it gives you an idea of my progress. I stopped working on the intro[duction] [to this journal] and will resume once this journal is [the daily entries are] caught up. Today was quite productive and this week with the editing, I expect more advancements.

Monday June 17, 2013 4:40 pm living room

I awoke once at about 2[:]30 [am] to use the urinal. I probably got to sleep about 9[:]30 pm. I finally got up about 5:45 am. After my morning routine, which included letting the birds out for awhile, I took a shower and headed for the mall about 7:20 am. I played the Vortex financial meditation [mp3] (about 15 minutes) while I waited in the mall parking lot. In the mall I only did 3 laps for a couple of reasons. 1) I am editing the journal entries now. I have finished file #7 (through April 15th) and I thought I would work on the tedious job of checking for errors and mistakes in the library after walking. 2) I did not feel all that stable in walking today so I thought I would just go to the library early and edit. 3) I had to get some items at Walmart for Mom. So all in all I quit early, and went to the library. There I edited for an hour then I had a coffee at the [Cup and Chaucer] coffee shop. I seemed more in control of my coffee and cookie. I ended up done and at Mom's about noon. I ate a hot dog [for lunch]. My head noise (tinnitus) has been acting up a bit[,] [but] no more than usual. I played the hypnosis mp3 at the Dow Library [parking lot] at about 9[:]00 am while I waited for them to open. That always helps some. Now it's the afternoon and I am aware of tinnitus more. I have been editing further today in the living room and [I] updated the files. I am done with journal_01, journal_02, the first two files. I will try to continue the work, even though it is tedious [as mentioned before] and [sometimes] boring, but it is necessary work.

Tuesday June 18, 2013

[10:40 am] computer room

I am back early in case Dave finds a vehicle online and needs to drive there [to pick it up]. He had to turn in his Toyota Echo due to his cousin Rod smashing it up with a deer on his last trip to California. He got good money on it but State Farm picked it up yesterday. He cashed his check for it and is now looking to buy another. I also want to report more advancements and improvements in my recovery while they are freshly in mind. I went for my 6 laps at the Midland Mall this morning. It took about 2 hours and I am averaging about 2[+] miles an hour, not in a big hurry and still cautious. I am [still] without [a] cane and the brain almost feels normal now. There [It] is just a bit off now, which is still [likely] messing with my walking and stability. But it is very close now and I expect that any day I will return to the state I was before the operations. I am going to continue now to work on my journal while Dave surfs [the Internet on his phone], shops, and has breakfast. Mom is doing her checkbook after I got some money out at the bank for her.

[4:22 pm] living room

I worked on file #3 (journal_03 - Feb[ruary] 1-15)--editing it on the patio this afternoon. I walked my 6 laps then came back early in case Dave needed to pick up a car. Looks like he may travel to get one. I spent a nice sunny spring afternoon out on the patio, as I mentioned, editing this journal (digital version). Things are getting clearer at the mall, and everywhere for that matter. The brain is nearly OK again. The slight[ly] off part is still giving me difficulty with all my symptoms, including walking, but this is very good now. I sure hope the leg improves as much as it is now the most painful of all the symptoms, but yet again I mention that it has gotten much better than when it was first noticed last May.

Wed. June 19, 2013 4 pm living room

A couple of urinations in the middle of the night, then [I got] up around 6[:]00 am. I went to bed [the] usual time of 8 [pm] and [fell] asleep by 10[:]30 [pm], a bit later than usual. Things are really close now [to where they were before the operations]. I can tell during [the] morning walk as I have less fear of falling and better balance and control. I am walking again caneless and in the middle of the walking areas [mall and store aisles]. I almost feel I can take off as before [the operations] but I will have a bit more to wait [for] on that. It is sunny in the mornings now and comfortably in the 80s. The temperature is slowly climbing and it has stopped raining and none is expected until the weekend. We have had some hit and miss storms. Mom and Dave are at a country music concert outside in Freeland. Mom really liked it and Dave is being nice to take her [there]. I edited another file in this journal today and continue to make progress. I will get a bit to eat now, watch some TV, [and] then read later [on].

Thursday June 20, 2013 6 pm living room

Again [it's been] a day of progress. The mall walking went well but I took my time, enjoyed it and only walked 4 laps. At the Dow Library I read chapter 4 of "Seth Speaks". I was back a bit after noon. Dave, Mom, and I used the pool [It was my first time in]. That was interesting. It did seem to reduce the pain in my right leg. I had to be very cautious going up the ladder due to elevation changes. Dave and I had a couple of beers. I got some sun and that's good. I wore shades as it was pretty bright.

Friday June 21, 2013 4[:]00 pm living room

I kept to my usual routine. I listened to the tinnitus mp3 in the middle of the night (and I fell asleep) and also in the mall parking lot from 7:30 am to 8 am. The soun d has been about [in the] 3-4 [out of 10] range most of the day but as always, when I am busy it's not so bad. After walking my full 6 laps, I went to the Dow Library, read a chapter and a half of "Seth Speaks" then had a cup of coffee. Things [are] getting better. I speak more with the help [at the coffee shop] there. After the library (around 11:30 am) I went to Walmart but had trouble returning their <u>own</u> beer, Batch 19 [in the bottle return machine], so I went to Meijer and their bottle return took the Batch 19 [bottles] and also the Sam Adam's "Porch Rocker" [bottles], which they carry. They have a wide variety of beer, liquor, and wine [there] so I may try them [Meijer] now. They always have [more] registers open [compared to Walmart]. I felt alert there and even went around with no cart at times [I often use a cart to steady my walking]. Things are improving rapidly now. I got back about 12:30 pm. Dave was working on a plan to get an RV to [deliver to] California, so he could check out a VW Golf [vehicle] out there in Stockton, CA. He is doing that and I told him I could drive the Olds[mobile] back from Indiana and we may do that this weekend. I will write more on this later in the journal. I [later] worked on [the] digitizing of this journal. I have done the first 6 files now through mid March. I will continue more when I can.

<u>Saturday June 22, 2013 10 pm living room</u>

It's hot outside and in. It's in the 90s and sunny. Mom and Dave are outside. Mom is in the basement at this time cleaning her crafts. I am likely taking [riding with] Dave to Elkhart, Indiana tomorrow [his trucking company location] and he will then drive an RV to California. While there [in California] he is going car shopping. He has his eye on one in Stockton that I mentioned. We will likely stay in a motel and then I will drive back Monday. It will be a long haul but I am up to it [230 miles or so]. I don't really think Dave and Mom believe [are sure] that [I can drive that far] as physically (outside the car) I still have [stability] issues but they rapidly get better [Actually they believe I can drive now that I have driven to Cleveland, Ohio on the turnpike,

Saginaw, and even to Ann Arbor for my MRI appointments]. I walked 6 laps at the local mall, then read some at the Dow Library. This afternoon I edited another file of this journal (06). I have one more file to go [at this date] (07) and then back to the [any] further files to digitize. As it's late now and it takes a couple of hard hours to edit a file, I will take a break for now. I probably will create new files more next week. Brain synchronization or "locking" as I have called it is very close. The closer it gets the better my walking. I think the walking is directly proportional to brain "lock" improvements. Now that it's Sunday [tomorrow,] I will break from walks and I will be helping Dave get to Indiana (most likely). I will update this journal of [about] that adventure [later].

Sun. June 23, 2013

[7:30 am]

I am on the porch [patio] and it is a nice pleasant summer morning, probably in the 60s-70s. It is expected to rise to near 90 degrees again here [today]. Dave and Mom are sleeping. Mom will likely get up soon for church with Sandra. I thought I would work on this journal (editing) while the weather is nice and make an early entry before Dave and I go to Elkhart, Indiana later this afternoon. I woke up around 6:00 am. I remember hearing Mom go to bed after talking with Dave (loud enough to wake me) and that was about 11[:]30 pm. The tinnitus was quite loud this morning when I awoke. I played the self-hypnosis mp3 for tinnitus and gave it a rating of 6 out of 10. That, as always, seemed to help but again it naturally dies down in [the] mornings when my attention is elsewhere on coffee, birds, and so on. Other symptoms are fine and always improving. If a positive attitude helps recovery, then it is certain that I will recover, because I sure have one. I have been fortunate in that and it has helped to get me this far. This long drive there and back to Indiana will be a real test. I know that I will not have a problem with it and that the Olds[mobile] is quite reliable. I will just check the oil and tire pressure on the way back. I will now resume my editing and I will write more about my adventures later.

Monday June 24, 2013

No entry today. [I am] On [a] trip to/back from Elkhart, Indiana with Dave. I will make comments Tuesday.

Tuesday June 25, 2013 1:00 pm living room

I am writing this early to make a few updates for our trip to Indiana and also what I have done so far this day. Dave and I left for Elkhart, Indiana Sunday afternoon around 5 pm. It was a smooth trip. We stopped at an Irish pub in Mount Pleasant near the casino ["The Green Spot"]. Dave had been there before. We had a glass of Guinness and a patty melt smothered in onions. It was delicious. I did well with a [the] meal [and drink] but I was very careful on each swallow, still out of necessity. We got into Elkhart around midnight and finally to bed around 1 am Sunday [Monday]. We slept well at a nearby Holiday Inn Express until about 8[:]00 am. We ate breakfast there of some eggs, bacon, biscuits and sausage. I immediately noticed a greater "brain lock" in vision, particularly at the continental breakfast room. I did not use the cane, walked fairly well, but coordination of vision, brain, and basic functions is still slow so I had to carefully maneuver and pour coffee and so on as I usually do. I was able to walk and carry the [a] cup of coffee (it had a lid) back to the room. [It was] a big deal to me in this [physical] state but probably silly to someone reading this. Dave left for California with his Mercedes diesel RV about noon and I headed back, mostly up route 66 [in Michigan] through Ionia, Sheridan, and Stanton, [and] our old vacation area of [near] Holland Lake. The whole trip was 234 miles and I drove with no problems. [I am] pretty lucky with the driving skills coming back since last summer. When I got back I was really knocked out and fell asleep on the recliner. I went to bed a little past 8 pm and had to put on the room AC. It was near 90 degrees. Today, Tuesday, I mostly took care of some put off errands. I went to the Midland laundromat off Waldo and did my laundry. I had much greater control and balance to where I could walk around the laundromat much easier. I got a haircut at the Irish Barber Shop [in] downtown Midland after the laundry. Again I noticed better vision, control, [and] balance. Michael the [a] barber did [trimmed] my hair, same guy as last time. I went over to Meijer and picked up some items after [the haircut]. I wore my black (one of the two) "brain [surgery]" shirt and got a few looks. [It is] Much easier to get around thanks to the brain almost in synch. [I] Got back around 11 am, put things away, took a shower, and I am now catching up with my journal work. The right leg seems a bit better. The tinnitus is strong but only when I direct my thoughts to it. I notice swallowing is getting easier too, still I must watch the swallows and collect the food and liquid first [in my mouth and] then swallow only when [I am mentally] ready. I will now work on digitizing this journal [again] and get back in the usual routine.

Wed. June 26, 2013 7[:]20 pm living room

It is very hot as I write this. I just finished working on digitizing more of this journal. Earlier Mom and I took a swim. I have been in it [the pool] a couple of times and at first it was scary but I am getting better. Sometimes the right leg feels better under water and I don't seem to notice it while floating on a raft. I also didn't notice any tinnitus. It is near 90 or [the] upper 80s but [and] Mom's place retains heat so looks like another night of [using] the small AC unit. [Our] Thanks [go] to Bob and Marsha for putting that [AC unit] in last year. What a life safer. Mom sits tomorrow so I will probably work out on the patio on this journal. I did my full walk at the mall and got a compliment from the lady that uses a cane there on how I have been making rapid process and she is right. It's an exciting time as brain recovery is nearly there. I see the small improvements daily and I am very grateful.

Thursday June 27, 2013 4:45 pm living room

[It is] hot [and] muggy still. We got a brief thundershower and rain that watered the lawn and filled the pool up. We could not swim so Mom prepared some strawberries that she bought at Walmart. I worked on typing these journal entries. I am up to April 28. The computer somewhat understands my voice so that I just have to edit the files, a big enough job. I am getting my speech therapy in [when I dictate into the computer] and that's good. Dave is out west looking for new wheels. It is brutally hot there. [I am] Not sure when he will be back. I did my usual 6 laps at the mall. [It is] Slow but steady and everyday I see glimpses of normal functioning. The day will come soon. I am relaxing with a Killian beer which [as] I have more swallowing control. That is today's big advance. The [right] leg is better but warm now that it's afternoon. All in all I can't complain too much. As I always say, things could have been much worse.

Friday June 28, 2013 3:36 pm living room

[It is a] Rainy, thundery day. Pat [Patrick, my nephew,] is here helping Mom get her mower ready and cleaning off [out] the roof gutters in between rain and thunder. I was finishing up [the] journal_08 file today (April 16-April 30). I am slowly catching up with this project. Fortunately speech recognition is OK enough to pick up about 70% of my voice. So I dictate to the large [Windows 7] computer, this journal, then I correct it on the notebook computer. It is still a long process but I see myself catching up soon. I will then resume work on my introduction, a brief overview of the events I went through. Today I walked 6 laps [again] without [a] cane. All things like balance, stability, and so on are near normal. I am not there yet but each day brings new advancements.

Saturday June 29, 2013

I took a leak just before going to sleep around 9[:]30 pm. That helped as I slept till 4[:]30 am or about 6 hours. I played the tinnitus and Vortex tapes [mp3s] then got up about 5:45 am. I had a coffee and two old glazed doughnuts. I walked 6 caneless laps at the Midland Mall. Balance and control are improving but I noticed some bobble head motion and that is when the brain <u>tracks</u> the head movement up and down [with each step] and does not adjust to it [it goes up and down not] as a normal person [person's brain] would. That makes walking a bit tougher as you can imagine and it felt like walking on ice. Due to the great improvements and the confidence [of late], I kept going. I headed back [after walking] because Sandra was coming over to swim but it was cooler today (70s) and a few sprinkles so Sandra decided against it. Dave is out in California in record heat looking for a car. I work[ed] hard on journal_09 (May 1-15), I have a lot of editing to do but the speech-to-text feature on the large computer is speeding up the process. Before heading back today I stopped at Meijer for some things and picked up a [pool] chair float. It might be good for me as it has neck support, something Moms raft[s] do not have. Again, I will have to wait for clearer, warmer weather to test it out. Tomorrow I take a break from walking. I will work on this journal (digitizing) and then maybe help Mom in her yard. We will see.

Sunday June 30, 2013 3:45 pm living room

Today I took my usual Sunday break from walking. The sun is starting to shine as I write this. We have had cooler, rainy weather of late. We have not been able to swim but the nights are much easier to sleep. Mom is playing on Facebook. We are not going to work on the grass and droppings from the roof gutters that Pat knocked down until Tuesday. Mom works tomorrow and by Tuesday it should be clear and dry. I will try to help her as I can. I was able to clean out the bird cage again and to vacuum behind it also. I still need to be careful as all the motion is still disorienting. I worked very hard on [the] journal_09 file (May 1-15) of this journal. Soon I will be back to finishing my introduction to this journal. I did some editing on the patio. After this daily entry I think I will sip on a beer as the tinnitus has been strong today and that may take the edge off. I have done enough work for one day.

CHAPTER 7   7/1/13 – 7/31/13

<u>Monday July 1, 2013 5[:]00 pm living room</u>

Well it[']s a new month. This month is Sandra's Birthday and my one year gamma [knife operation (brain surgery #2)] appointment [omit appointment] (July 25th). How time flies when you are having fun. I had a couple of dreams [last night] to write down today. I am trying to recall dreams and [by] giving myself nightly suggestions to recall dreams. So far it seems to be working. Last night I fell asleep playing the tinnitus hypnosis tape. [I woke up and] It was 11[:]30 pm and [I had a] noisy head. Normally [this is] a problem, but I seem better able to ignore the sounds, especially when tired. I remember getting more rest until about 4:30 am, when I finally got up. I did not let the birds out as I wanted to use the speech-to-text ("dictation" in the Chrome browser) feature to record the input for [file] journal_10 (the last weeks of May). I am catching up now and it's hard to believe my progress. Soon I will be back to finishing my introduction. So [omit So] I read the files [into the dictation program] then headed to the Midland Mall. I only walked 3 laps as I needed to get some shopping in for Mom at Gordon Food Service [(for the 4th of July party at her place)] and Walmart. I tried the [using] Commerce Road behind Home Depot to get back to Diamond Road. This avoids a dangerous left turn [out of Walmart] and no [eliminates the] need to go out to Monroe [a further shortcut but way north of the mall area]. Control was very good again at the mall, but the brain is too closely following every walking movement, thus causing the phenomena I like to call "bobble" head. So [omit So] I was happy to leave at only 3 laps and go shop. Around the shops, things are much clearer, almost OK again. This afternoon I got back early and worked in [on] this journal. I also helped Mom carry out some limbs and trash that got stuck in the gutters. Pat [Patrick] pulled them out recently [as I wrote about] and we [I] just hauled them to the curb. These are things that I certainly would not be able to do just a few short weeks ago. My progress is breathtaking [to me at least] sometimes! PS.[:] Dave is driving back [from the west coast] and is in Nevada now.

Tues. July 2, 2013

[10:44 am]

This is an early entry as I came back early to work on this journal [book project] and I want to get the mornings activities down while they are fresh. I remember getting up a couple of times to urinate. I had 2 beers before bed to unwind after my progress on this journal. I finally awoke at 3[:]30 am, listened to my hypnosis tape [twice] ([tinnitus level:] 5/10 and then 3/10). I then listening to [my] prosperity [(in the) Vortex mp3s) twice and then [my] physical ([in the] Vortex) once. Both [All] are meditation tapes [mp3s]. I got up a little after 5 am. I had coffee, [and] a roll with white frosting. I let the birds out around 5[:]30 am. Smokey flew up to the entertainment center. Christy was a bit on edge, more than usual, but she ended [up] walking on the floor. As I was early, I flossed, took a shower and played a round of computer golf. I walked at the mall a full 6 laps. I remain in good control, but not exactly fast or real steady yet. I was able to rub my nose while walking [two independent movements at the same time], something I could not do before. I went straight back to Mom's to work on the journal [book]. Dave was [still] in Nevada where there is [a] real heat [wave] last time he checked in.

[6:15 pm]

I just took a 2 beer break on the patio. Dave would be proud, ha ha. Really, I needed to wind down from my editing session (this journal [book project]--May 16-31). I am making great progress and [but now] I needed to relax. The weather is ideal, a little cool for swimming[,] but nice for relaxing. Dave emailed from Nebraska and continues to make progress back. We all have a path to follow and we do our best [as he does now]. Mom is preparing spaghetti. I will make my editing changes to [the latest] file (journal_10) when I am clearer in the head, ha ha!

Wed. July 3, 2013 5:05 pm patio

I am having a Killian's [beer] to relax. I worked in [on] the journal [book] some but most of this afternoon I cleaned the pool and emptied some grass for Mom into an open field. I also worked on her computer to get rid of [remove] temporary files to speed it up. It's near [the] mid 70s and sunny but the pool went down to 68 [degrees]. It's cool. Tomorrow Steve, Sandra and Amy [not Amy, who is at a wedding in Tennessee] are stopping by [for the 4th of July]. We will see who is brave enough to swim. The pool is quite clear. Dave is on his way back. I will be surprised if he gets here for the party but who knows. Tomorrow I will skip the walk and work on this journal [book until people arrive] then we [will] have the July 4th party later on. One day at a time, the famous saying goes. Oh one more thing: This morning as I woke up about 5[:]15 am (I played mp3's for an hour again). I did not hear the electric tension line sound in my head [as much as usual]. I heard some cricket sounds but I really thought the worst of the tinnitus sound was gone. Later in the morning while I walked and did my routine I heard the normal sounds. Well, one day it just may stay away. I have found that not only does the nightly beer relax me, [and] help me to sleep, but it seems to dampen the tinnitus as well. Go figure!

Thursday July 4th, 2013 [4th of July]

[7:30 am]

Mom is sleeping. Dave is still driving this way. Just a few notes before anyone arrives. [As mentioned,] We are having a little cookout and maybe a swim [here] if it warms up. They expect 80s but the pool is [in the] upper 60s [as I mentioned]. [The pool is] Clear but cold. As I always say, we will see. I have been suggesting [to myself] that I recall [my] dreams of late. It seems to be working. In between getting up to urinate I managed [to get] some sleep and [more] dreams [that I recalled]. I wrote down what I could but the interesting thing about this [last] dream was the thoughts of running, [and] walking normally again. Also Cathy Lewis [my close friend in Tennessee] and Shirley [my ex-wife] was [were] in it. Now that I think about it I am not sure which one [was in the dream, or maybe a "blend" of both]. Funny, but like most dreams when recorded, we try to make them fit into a logical [this world] pattern but they are [usually] far from it. They seem to just be emotions/events/what have you all mixed up [to our logical mind]. I am just writing them down [as they come to me] as best I can remember at that early hour. Right now before anyone arrives I will get some more work done on this journal [book], so here I go... [Dave did make it for the party. I am amazed that he did so many miles in such a short time]

Friday July 5, 2013

Even though [it's] a holiday [weekend] I went to the mall to get my 6 laps in [this morning]. Needless to say, [there were] not many people there but [just] a few ["regulars"]. I had much more control and I seem to have more everyday [now]. I have had the tinnitus strong [loud] all day but have managed to stay "busy". I have worked on the journal at the library and at Mom's. Mom and Dave went out to buy a new weed whipper. I blew up some rafts, we [Mom, Dave, and I] [later] swam in the pool until about 6 pm, had supper and then I finished entering this [written] journal entry. Everyone's tired [after the swim and full day] but I guess we will play some "Spoiler" dominoes before bed.

Saturday July 6, 2013 5:30 pm living room

I just took a shower and dressed after Mom, Dave, and I had a pool break. We were in there [the pool] about 2 hours. It has been calm and in the mid 80s, perfect weather for a [the] pool. I was working on this journal [book project] this afternoon. Mom was washing, Dave was mowing and wanted to take a beer break. Thankfully I have enough [swallow] control now to drink beers. It was hot on the patio so we all decided to swim. Earlier today I got up at my usual time. I did hear the neighbors shooting some fireworks off [late last night] but I was tired and managed to get some sleep anyway. The tinnitus was loud in the morning as usual. I played the hypnosis mp3 and that helped as usual. I went to the mall after getting out some more cash from the [Chemical B]bank ATM and walked 6 laps from about 8 am to 10 am. I went to the Dow Library afterwards and digitized [edited] a few more days in this journal. When I got back about 1 pm (I had to run some errands [and buy some things] at Meijer), Dave was out doing some banking. Mom was [baby] sitting. I took care of things [and] then worked in [on] the journal [book] until the beer/swim break.

Sunday July 7th, 2013 4:00 pm living room

[As always on a Sunday, I took] off today from walking. I spent most of the day working on the month of June in this journal [book] which amazes me. When I catch up, as I have mentioned, I will go back to writing [finishing] the introduction. It has been muggy today. Dave has been working in the yard. Mom is working on her financial papers. I just printed out the June files (number 11 and 12) and will now edit them. I did 11 earlier this morning but I will read it again. Dave and I watched [a funny movie] (I mostly listened as it is too hard to switch glasses from TV (long distance) to journal (close-up)). It [the movie] was pretty funny. You have to get away from the serious (as on MSNBC) sometime[s]. OK[,] back to editing and I will continue this tomorrow.

Monday July 8, 2013 6:30 pm living room

I write this totally drained of almost all energy. It has been a very busy day. I did not get too much sleep, probably restless over my Ann Arbor MRI and follow-up [appointments]. I went to both today, leaving the house around 6[:]00 am. I was up at 4:30 am. It's over a hundred miles [one way] as [and] I went down M-52 through Owosso, [and] Perry. I [then] hit [took] US-94 to Ann Arbor. I got turned around, going by the UM stadium, but I turned back, found Huron [Street] and ended up at the VA grounds around 9[:]30 am. I played the Gayatri Mantra [for healing and to calm my nerves about the MRI] a couple of times

[(Deva Premal)] waiting on the third floor [next to the MRI office] and got into the MRI about 10 am. My follow-up neurology appointment was at noon. I [found] I had to get re-qualified for them [neurology] to see me since they did not have my annual [VA] financial information [on record]. I came back [to neurology] then waited about an hour. Finally about 1 pm I met with Dr. Valdivia who said the results were good and [there was] no growth since my last MRI in April. My follow-up MRI will now be in Nov[ember] (4 months from now) instead of October. So [omit So] that was great news but I am too tired to let it sink in but I'm sure it will tomorrow. I am even too tired for a beer and had to decline the offer from Dave. He is back from also going to Ann Arbor to get a new trunk door from a junk [salvage] yard there [for his KIA that he bought in California]. I can't wait for 8 pm [my usual time to read or sleep] as I will definitely crash then and try to catch up with my sleep. I plan to do my laundry and maybe go to the Fashion Square Mall and/or the Barnes and Noble bookstore in Saginaw [tomorrow] for a celebration [of my good MRI results] coffee.

Tues. July 9, 2013 9 pm

Dave, Mom and I just had a late supper of pizza and salad. Mom bought [the pizza and] Dave picked it up [at the local party store]. It was great but as it's [it got] late so I had to take a pass on [evening] games. We swam earlier, had beers and I am ready to call it quits for this day. I started the day doing laundry at the little laundromat on Waldo ["Totally Clean"] that I have used before. I think this is the third trip there. [I am] Better and better each time. I came close to telling the owner [or manager who was there that morning] my tale, but speech is still slow and slurred so I will wait a bit more. It's going to be great when speech is normal again. I took a pass on the mall [walk]. At 9[:]30 [am] I headed to the Dow Library and worked on the journal [this book], editing the last couple of months. I [will] start "finishing" my introduction soon. Then we will see what we have made. I worked on it after getting back from Meijer. I picked up some more beer and a few items. Dave attached his trunk [door. He picked up a new trunk door at a salvage yard, his original was dented and leaking] and registered his KIA, which he got in California. After the journal [book] work we swam and had our beer. We reserved cabins in the UP so that Dave, Mom and I could go up there this Thursday and Friday [and Saturday]. We are also including a trip over to Mackinac Island. It's been a few years [since we have been there (40 for me)] and Mom wanted to go again. We all deserve a little vacation and [it] looks like we will get one. I will break this off for now as I am writing [this] in bed and that is not that comfortable.

Wed. July 10, 2013

[12:30 pm living room]

I had to put [some] money back into my checking account at the [Chemical B]bank so I would have some for our trip tomorrow to Mackinac Island. I left at 7:00 am to [head to] the Fashion Square Mall in Saginaw. I walked 3 laps or about 2.5 miles. I wore my [one of my] black "brain" shirt[s]. I went to Barnes and Noble there after and had my MRI celebration coffee, a mocha. I enjoyed that, [and] I looked around and books were even more sharper than before. I browsed them after the coffee break. I even lifted my body on the balls of my feet while I looked (because I now could!). I left a bit after 10 am and went to the [Chemical B]bank in Auburn [and] put money into my account. I stopped at the [Branch] Library [in Auburn] after and worked a bit on my introduction to this journal [book] but stopped shortly. I was just not into it. I think now with the trip [to Mackinac] tomorrow and a few days off I will stop the work until Sunday or next week and make it a real vacation break. I had a slice of pizza for lunch then charged my batteries for the digital camera. I then made a packing list for tomorrow. Maybe I will clean the bird cage while Mom and Dave are out working on the yard.

[8:15 pm bedroom]

Dave and I took a late swim after supper. Mom already took a bath [so did not join us]. "Wanda, the Whale", the automatic pool skimmer or bottom cleaner worked [was working] and [we] noticed that the hose swiveled around [and did not kink up and it caught our attention]. It started getting cooler (a cold front came in). The weather for our trip tomorrow should be ideal. I am in the bed winding down a fun day. Tomorrow should be fun [also], bringing lots of positive things [and a well deserved break].

Thursday July 11, 2013

[written from [Dave and my] St. Ignace cabin 7 am 7/13]

We (Mom, Dave, and I) left for our trip to Mackinac Island/St. Ignace today. We got underway [you can tell I've been in the Navy] about 10 am in Dave's new (2005) KIA he bought in CA[California]. It's white, drives well and is quite comfortable. We went out west 10 [Hwy 10] to US-127 north. We stopped at the rest area that had [has] all the brochures of things to do and see in Michigan. I did not take a stick or cane on this trip. I walked better (not perfect yet by any means) but I believe I used a cane last time at that [rest area] location [I did last fall]. We headed up to the Mackinac Bridge and got to our cabin[s]. The place [motel and cabins] was for sale and not that busy, surprisingly for a summer. Due to the late notice I expected $100/night at least [for each of the two cabins] but it was only about $230 for two cabins for two nights. They are not the best [they were right on a main highway and the view to Lake Michigan was mostly blocked] but they are a comfortable place to sleep. We were [stayed] up later than I am used to and we ended up finding a [viewing] spot very close to the [Mackinac] Bridge. There were lots of bugs around but it was fun to see the bridge lit up at night. We got a few photos [Mom stayed in the car] and [we] finally hit the sack around 10[:]30 pm.

Friday July 12, 2013

[We were] Up for our trip fairly early, 7[:]30 am. We got [took] a boat over to Mackinac Island that went under the Mackinac Bridge first so we got lots of photos. Dave and I rode up on top. [It was] Great fun. Mom stayed down in the enclosed part of the boat. We got over to the island about 10 am. To Dave it was crowded but to me it seemed less than a normal summer crowd. We did the tourist thing. I wore my brain t[-]shirt I got from Sarah and Josh. One of the bicycle rental boys [people] commented on it [they are paid to drum up business that way] and I told him a bit about it. I got a few looks as I wore it. Both Mom [she had open heart surgery a few years ago and is 80 years old] and I did pretty good getting around. We took frequent breaks. She treated us to a carriage ride [and] we had a raspberry shake[s] on top of the fort there taking in the awesome views of the grounds and marina. It was a chamber of commerce day, sunny in the upper 70s[,] low humidity, low winds. It was just ideal conditions. Walking down the [steep] fort ramp back to town was challenging but we both [Mom and I] did it and ended up walking across the park grounds. I felt pretty good just being able to walk almost like everyone [else]. Both Mom and I (and perhaps Dave) felt tired at the end of the trip around 6 pm. We stopped and bought some fudge, naturally, and got Sandra some also and some birthday cards (her Birthday is this Sunday, July 14). All in all[,] a memorable day we had. Again we stayed up late and went to BC Pizza in St. Ignace for pizza and beer [about 9:30 pm]. The beer, as always, helps with my tinnitus. It all tasted good and I was careful and could eat and drink like everyone else except more slowly. One memorable moment there: we moved inside [we were out on a deck by a bay] [and we moved inside] because Mom was [getting] cold and some guy [at a big party on the patio] took our picture of beer, thinking we abandoned it I guess. Dave got it back after probably telling him off. The nerve of some people I guess. Anyway we hit the sack around 11 pm and we are now up at 7 am taking showers and getting ready for the rest of our trip. I will report on that later on.

<u>Saturday July 13, 2013</u>

<u>written 7/14/13 on the patio Sunday morning 8:01 am</u>

We made it back to Midland late last night about 11[:]30 pm. It was a full last day of our 3-day "UP" vacation. Dave and I shared a small cabin in St. Ignace and Mom had another one as I wrote about previously. [The last morning at the cabins] Dave and I awoke again early around 7[:]00 am as the sun broke through. Mom was already dressed and packing up. We left the cabins around 8[:]30 am and went to McDonald's in St. Ignace for coffee and breakfast. We traveled north to the Soo Locks [Sault Ste. Marie] and just happened to get there as a large freighter headed for Canada passed through the locks. I don't recall seeing that before. The next boat scheduled was around 3 pm. It was 10[:]30 am when we got there so it was great timing. The weather [was] still almost perfect, 70-80s with blue skies and sunshine. We stayed and watched the freighter which came from Lake Superior (it had iron ore [to deliver]) and lowered down in the locks to get to the level of Lake Huron and left. It was a slow process but we were there to see it up close and [we] got lots of photos. We talked Mom into walking to a viewing platform right over the locks and [we] saw the whole thing. Mom did well with several breaks. I also did well with improved brain "lock" and stability. As always lately, I go without a cane. We checked out a gift shop across the locks. Dave got a beer opener (of course) and a crushed penny souvenir for Sandra's Birthday which is today [as I write this]. We left Sault Ste. Marie about 12[:]30 pm and headed for Tahquamenon Falls via the shoreline of Lake Superior, [and] Whitefish Bay. We stopped at [the] Whitefish Bay Lighthouse and walked around. Dave climbed the lighthouse while Mom and I waited downstairs. As [it is] a national park, there was an older lady in character as a teacher in the 1920s. She was in the garden tending [to] the flowers. She asked us to tell the lighthouse keeper [that] she was there, while in character [Later we found out Mom just thought she was some crazy woman as she was talking about unfair wages]. We had great views of Whitefish Bay and a large

Canadian wind farm across the bay. [These were] All great photo ops [opportunities]. We continued traveling along the coast to the falls and stopped to see the [Lake Superior] beach a couple of times. As it was the weekend, there were quite a few people out enjoying the beach and weather. We got to the falls about 3[:]30-4 pm. We stopped at the restaurant/pub (Camp 33 [replica]/Tahquamenon Falls Pub) where Dave and I had a white fish sandwich (of course) and some of their local brewed beer (of course again). Mom had a barbecue beef sandwich. I wore [one of] my dark blue "I had brain surgery, what's your excuse?" [brain] t-shirts and got a few looks. After our late lunch we talked Mom into walking the .4-.5 mile hike down [over] to the Upper Falls viewing area. Several visitors were around. Mom had park benches and hand rails to use in her walk [and I used them as well]. She did well with frequent breaks. I held my own, not 100% steady yet but OK. We slowly walked to the falls and then took many photos. I think it was good for Mom [and me]. She did have a close call back at the pub after we left. We were outside and there was a gift shop area [on a wooden deck]. She had flip flops [thongs] on. Dave was walking ahead and I was behind [Mom]. One of her thongs got caught on the floor [in the floor cracks] and she stumbled forward too fast for me to respond and reach her. Dave did not see her do this. Luckily she held her balance and found a pole ahead and made it there [stumbling forward very fast]. I tried to grab on to her but couldn't reach her [in time]. Luckily it turned out OK, but it could have been bad. After the falls we got back to St. Ignace, filled the car [with gas] and headed across the Mackinac Bridge for Midland. I think we crossed the bridge around 8 pm. We did stop earlier in a small town called Trout Lake in the UP and had an ice cream break. Dave had a double [dip] large scoop cone and we had to use a park so he could eat it and not spill it in his car. His car is a stick shift or manual transmission which would have been a disaster. Mom waited in the car while Dave and I sat on a park bench and worked on our ice cream. It was kind of weird to be in a park on a Saturday night in a small town named Trout Lake [in the UP], eating ice cream [especially since I was recently loading dirty laundry into machines in Tennessee]. I am reminded of our raspberry shakes high up at the fort on Mackinac Island last Friday. That was a great moment and I previously mentioned that in Friday's [journal] entry. So the birds (mine) were OK, a bit startled I think to see us get back late. Smokey [my gray male bird] was chirping, Christy [my yellow female bird] was covered and sleeping. I got up this Sunday morning (7/14) to let them out, feed the wild birds [outside], and to catch up in this journal [book] on the cool porch [patio] (so far as they expect near 90 today--good pool weather). More later...

Sunday July 14, 2013 [Sandra's Birthday]

[9 pm bedroom]

Sandra and Steve came over to swim [today] and have bratwurst, salad, [and] chips for Sandra's Birthday. Dave and I got her cards, [and] some Mackinac Island fudge. Mom got her some money and a card and washcloths and towels that she [Mom] made. After the swim Sandra and Steve left about 6[:]30 pm. We swam some more then played a game of "Spoiler" dominoes. I have my speech therapy appointment tomorrow morning. Dave needs to drop off his car for repairs and take Mom to work. I will probably stop and/or walk tomorrow over in Saginaw [at the mall there]. The temperature is getting warmer, near or at 90 degrees Fahrenheit but that makes for great swimming weather. It was a nice day but swimming tires you [out] and the extra sun also contributes.

Monday July 15, 2013 patio

[noon]

I went to see Anita for my now monthly speech appointment [this morning]. I had some rest as I had "hit and miss" sleep most of the night. Again it was very humid and hot so I turned on the room AC unit [during sleep]. That, as always, makes a big difference. I generally just talked the hour away [as I always do] (8[:]00 am to 9[:]00 am) at the VA with Anita listening and observing my progress. I told her about the latest clear MRI (July 8) and how I stopped at the Owosso Public Library on the way back. I also told her [of] the rapid advancements I have made in digitizing this journal using the computer power of speech-to-text. The hour, as always, went fast. I decided to skip my usual walk at the Fashion Square Mall due to the heat taking away my motivation. I instead went over to Michaels (the craft store) and browsed. I was looking for a picture frame for the souvenir carriage ride photo I bought on Mackinac Island. Also I was looking for something that could be used with my long distance glasses shades to reduce lens scratches [it's missing a tube protector]. I think heat shrink will be the best so I may check at Radio Shack or online for some of that [I just replaced the sunglasses later]. After Michaels I left the Olds[mobile] in the Michaels parking lot and walked over to Barnes and Noble. There I had a small mocha coffee. After [that] I browsed the latest books. As I am still reading "Seth Speaks", I did not buy anything new. I did notice that they have that book [a more modern printing] and Seth's "The Nature of Human Personality [Personal Reality]". Being my two most favorite books I almost bought them (my own are getting pretty worn). I may yet get them but I wanted to see if there might be an audio version of them out there. I enjoy using the mp3 player to listen to audio books. It was still only 11[:]00 am so I went back to Michaels to look around some more. They have so much to see and AC too. It was nice to walk to my VA appointment [again] and in the parking lot at Michaels as well as inside the store. All of these tasks would be much more difficult just a few short weeks ago. Anita today asked me how I was feeling and I do feel good and optimistic about my future recovery. I know that is the best attitude to have right now. I left Michaels for Mom's [place] about 11[:]15 am. I checked my ATM balance in Auburn then got back around noon. I spoke with Dave who is [was] watering the front grass and working on hanging the dining room blinds. I am now making these notes on the patio in hot climate and little wind. I am sure we will go swimming later.

Tuesday July 16, 2013 8:15 pm bedroom

I had a pretty good night's sleep thanks to the pool, some beer, playing dominoes, reading, and so on. I did awake to a pretty loud buzz [not the good kind from beer] and there is some now as well. This morning [it] was about 5 out of 10 or so. Tonight it's about a 4. I played the hypnosis mp3 for tinnitus this morning before getting up and it always seems to help. This morning I wore a [one of my] white "brain" t-shirts ("What's your excuse" type). I went to Meijer first to return bottles and get my [two] birds some seed. I got to the Midland Mall later than usual, about 8[:]30 am, but I only walked two laps. I wanted to go to the Dow Library as soon as I could to work on this journal [book]. I was there [at the library] when they opened up at 9:30 am. It was sunny out but already getting muggy and hot. I worked until about 10:45 am editing July 1-15 (file 13). I then took a coffee break and had a chocolate chip cookie. My coffee was free. I worked more on my file [after] and then left about noon. I stopped by Walgreens because my pedometer has been missing. I got a new one and broke down and bought some Lipoflavonoid that has been advertised to help with tinnitus. We will see, but as it is mostly supplements of B vitamins, it can't hurt to try it. I will take it three times a day as they direct and then write about the results [only mental distraction and self-hypnosis seem to help so far]. I have only taken 1 so far and I will be patient. Dave worked to change my plastic nose pads on my long distance glasses [to silicon] because he said the original plastic kind may be the reason they slip and that I should not try to glue [temporary, sticky] nose pads onto them. He gave me his pair from his computer glasses. I will try to get my close-up glasses changed out [silicon nose pads installed] tomorrow at the mall and pick him up another set of silicon pads. Later on we went for a swim as it is [was] still very hot, in the 90s. Dave made his favorite mixed drinks, gin and tonic, with Schwepps tonic, Bombay Sapphire [gin], lime, and ice. We enjoyed a couple [of them] in the pool at our "floating bar" [a raft that holds drinks] under an umbrella in the center of the pool. Some life! I actually held my own, swallowing, like anything else, quite slowly. We had leftover bratwurst from Sandra's Birthday dinner [on the grill] and it tasted great. Mom made strawberry shortcake but I just can't eat as much as her and Dave [so I passed on that], and I think that is more my eating habits for years and not all related to swallowing problems. After supper it was already after 8 pm and I wanted to get caught up in this journal so I took a rain check on any games. It's too hot now to read (I have my room AC unit running as hard as it can but it's only at 82 and I am trying to get it [the room temperature] down to 76 or so for comfort. It will eventually make it down there as it did last night. I want to mention a bit more on my trip to Walgreens on the way back from the Dow Library [yesterday]. They have some good prices on some things, including a new pedometer. Theirs was $20 and not $60 as in Target or Meijer. I talked with a nice lady and her coworker in the perfume section where they checked me [my items] out. As I had my [a] "brain" shirt on I ended up telling them (as best I can) a bit about my operations. They both seemed very interested. The older lady [said she] knew Mom and let me use her [Mom's] name for a small discount (only 20 cents this time). I may stop in there sometime again as they were both nice and polite. Now I will surf the [Internet on the notebook] computer while the room cools down. They say storms will be here Thursday with cooler (mid 70s) temperatures this weekend. I don't mind that at all. More details to follow...

<u>Wed. July 17, 2013 6 pm living room</u>

I woke up about 4:30 am. I went to bed "early" at 8 pm [last night] to update the journal for the day, surf the [Internet on the] computer, then crash about 11:00 pm, a bit late for me but I was not that sleepy, so I eventually got a few hours of sleep. I did not recall dreams, but my head was rather noisy, again about 5 out of 10. It [the tinnitus] has been steady all day but, as always, I have manged to divert my attention from it. I played the hypnosis therapy tape [mp3] twice and I got it down in a range of 3 out of 10. I did a few morning errands after coffee, banana, and a doughnut. I emptied the coffee grounds into the compost [bin outside that Dave built], took in the trash containers, gathered my stuff and headed to the mall about 7:10 am. As this was a bit early I thought about going to Burger King for a coffee or snack but decided to play the tinnitus [hypnosis] tape [mp3] one more time [in the car]. I did then I walked 5 laps before I stopped to the eye glass shop [Traverse Vision in the Midland Mall] and had my plastic nose pads swapped for some silicon pads that Dave had mentioned for better grip and less slip. These were my close-up glasses I use for reading. I also got Dave a pair as he had loaned me one pair for my long distance glasses yesterday. I went to the Dow Library after and edited file 13 (July 1-15). This is currently the last journal file. They have a nice working AC in the library with working desks [desks to write on]. I had my journal and notebook computer, as I always do. I did not have a coffee break today. I came back around noon. I had Dave swap my (actually his) larger silicon nose pads in my long distance glasses for the newer small ones. I don't care [which ones I use] and it's only fair that he get back his originals. The house was roasting. It was 90 degrees and above. I did some computer work [on this book] and finally when Mom got back from some shopping, we had a swim. With the heat so bad here lately, it's been [going swimming is] a nightly habit. Just now as [just before?] I write this, we are out [swimming] due [close] to supper time and [with] some light rain and thunder outside. Dave and I sipped on his tonic and Bombay [gin] drinks under our floating bar and umbrella in the center of the pool. Life is so tough! Soon now we will have some chicken and other things then probably play a game, then call it another day.

<u>Thursday July 18, 2013</u>

[noon - living room]

It is very muggy and [it is] warming rapidly today. They expect lower to mid 90s. Dave got his KIA back from the shop and is working on hooking up his tow bar and will probably stop early when Mom gets here. She is out shopping and may pick up some pool rafts. Again we will all probably swim just to survive the afternoon. The good news is they expect this heat wave to be gone this week and temps [temperatures] to return to [the] more normal 80s for July. I would rather it not be too hot. We can swim in the 80s. Today I was planning to walk the usual [laps at the] Midland Mall but got diverted to Walmart, then [to] Meijer looking for a replacement pair of clip-on sunglasses for my long distance glasses. My old pair were scratched up pretty good [and a rubber piece was missing]. Neither store had the right pair so I drove out to the Walmart in Saginaw where I found the correct pair (#57), so it was [worth] the drive. It is way too hot to walk [at the mall] anyway. I went over to the Barnes and Noble and had a latte coffee. [I see] Sharper images again and I briefly chatted with a male [coffee] server there about my operations. I intended to buy both Seth [(Jane Roberts)] books [that I have talked about] but passed again. I still probably will play more with mp3s and PDFs first, as I have [both] full books in those formats. I drove back to Auburn around 10 am and wrote a page and a half further in my introduction to this journal [book]. I think the coffee helped and I may do that again (have a cup before writing). Dave is blowing up some rafts Mom bought. One is a [another] floating bar complete with ice [and drink] holder. She is now back so soon we will test them out.

Friday July 19, 2013 9:30 pm bedroom

Mom, Dave, and I just got back from the "Green Spot", an Irish tavern in Mt. Pleasant (the same one Dave and [I] stopped at on the way to Elkhart, Indiana awhile ago[)]. I should note that we also went out to Miller Road in Flint last night to a late supper. We ate at the Golden Corral, like the one in Cleveland, Tennessee. That was the closest one [to us]. That and the Irish pub were hashed out in the pool. We had [have] been in the pool everyday during this terrible heat wave. They say it will break eventually but it is still muggy and near 85 degrees. We had a sudden thunderstorm about 2:30 pm and had to scramble out of the pool as we experienced thunder, lightening and high winds briefly. It took out the power here for at least a couple of hours. This brought on the idea of eating out somewhere with [that still had] power and using the cool AC of Dave's car. We also needed that [AC] last night as it was real sticky. I had a corned beef sandwich [at the pub], Dave a Reuben [sandwich], [and] Mom a BLT. Dave and I had a Guinness, [and] Mom a pop [as sodas are called here in Michigan]. I walked only 4 laps at the mall [this morning] and headed over to the Dow [Library] to work on my introduction to this journal [book]. It is finally progressing [I took a long break at page 5 to edit more journal entries]. I record [using a microphone] to the [on my Windows 7 desktop] computer in the morning, transfer [the] file to [the] notebook computer, take it to the library and with a hard copy printout, I edit the new additions. Tomorrow it is Saturday so I will write some [more] out on the patio [in the cool morning]. I am going [later] with Mom and Sandra to garage sales, of all things. Dave will likely work on his car. It's late [as I write this], so I will surf [the Internet on my notebook computer] some, relax, and drift off to sleep.

Sat. July 20, 2013 6:47 pm living room

I did not walk today at the mall but instead went on garage sale visits with Sandra and Mom. Dave stayed [at Mom's] to work on his car and the dining room blinds. He is now fixing some chicken fajitas for him and I and some cube steak for Mom [she does not eat chicken]. The day went [by] fast. I did not find much I wanted [at the sales] (or needed) but I bought a small birthday party megaphone [hearing aid tube] and used it in Mom's van [I was sitting in the back talking into the "megaphone" towards Mom]. That was funny [and we all had some laughs] but it actually helped Mom hear me. We got back around 2 pm. Tom [my brother] stopped by shortly as he got back from his trip to California and found out about the storms that went through our area [he wanted to check that we were all right]. Apparently near him it was much worse with more power outages. He was lucky and nothing struck his property. Before the yard sales this morning, I was up early and used the patio to edit more of my [this] journal [book] introduction. It was much cooler with the storm[s] having gone through, maybe in the 70s with less humidity. I will try to do that tomorrow as well [write on the patio in the cool morning]. I will mention that Smokey Joe, my bird, is back to begging and performing in his cage around supper time as usual. The last day or so he has had a sore foot. I[t] didn't look broken as he was getting around some. Today it looks finally healed and that is a real relief. I suspect he could have snagged his nails in [on] some of the material we use to cover him and Christy up at night. His nails are long now. I use sandpaper perch covers to help keep both [the] bird's nails trimmed. It usually helps and I put a new set on today, as the existing ones look pretty chewed up and worn. They may also have been spooked by a shadow or noise at night. I does not take much to do it. I am so thankful that he [Smokey] looks OK now. Dave just cooked us up some fajitas using the leftover chicken I mentioned before. I am stuffed now. After the [this] long day I am ready to wind it down. Mom and Dave may want to play a game [after supper as we often do]. I will make a mention [now] on my great improvement today. At the yard sales I got in and out of the van and to the sales pretty good for [using] no cane. Before supper Dave and I drove to Auburn (the Food Center) and got some items for supper. Again I walked inside the store without a cane and in good control. [I am] Still shaky [as in not fully "back" yet] but better and my eyesight and brain behavior are now about right. I still always have the tinnitus but, as mentioned here, [I] can mostly control it by controlling my mental attention.

Sunday July 21, 2013

[1:36 pm] patio

I am out on the patio. It's a beautiful day, sunny, blue skies. The front must have gone through, as there is lower humidity. It [is] in the upper 70s most likely, close to 80. It's much better than the 90 degree heat wave we have had for a few days. I am on the patio [as mentioned before]. I just finished cleaning the pool which I am glad that I can contribute [by doing this]. [Doing] Other chores are [is] pushing it right now but things are improving. Mom is on the computer. Dave is working on painting and spackling the dining room window. After he does that he will probably work on his car. Earlier I found a website/online program that converts YouTube videos to mp3s. I found some "Seth Speaks" postings [videos] and I converted the files and loaded them to my mp3 player (who could have guessed? ha ha). I have been playing them and they sound good. I believe it is mostly excerpts from the book (probably in order to avoid legal matters). I think [that] now after [the] August [government] "pay day" I will purchase the full [both] books either at Barnes and Noble in Saginaw or online. I have the earlier ones [books] from the 70s that I read while in college and the Navy but they are getting worn. I started reading [my old copy of] "Seth Speaks" at night but I now think its time to "upgrade" my collection. So as I am here biding time until we grill or swim I thought I would add some [comments] about my health. Lately I have just added what I have done that day and not that much about health issues. Maybe that's a relief to someone reading this, but for the record I will add the latest. As I write this, I still need to lift my right leg on a stool now and then. It is still a bit numb and hot. Compared to last year, as I have mentioned, at least it's more comfortable. It still gets quite hot in the afternoon, but like the tinnitus, it too seems better if not thought about or dwelt upon. I have been using the pool a lot lately. The first time was a bit scary for me. It was quite disorienting and I had to hang on [carefully] as I stood on [walked up] the ramp area [stairs]. I had to back into the pool (sorry no barrel flips quite yet). This has improved to where I can enter better and climb better but I still need a firm grip while standing and climbing, and still kneel down to enter the pool backwards. As for my right leg, being constantly numb, it is much more comfortable underwater. I must use extreme caution [while walking barefoot and drinking], as since I don't feel much in the leg, it would be easy to hurt myself there [in my foot/leg], such as a stubbed toe, and so forth. The funny and probably [the] most excellent therapy I usually indulge in is having a couple of beers or 3 in the evening in the pool. While it tires me out, it is fun and relaxes me. I know that it helps lower the tinnitus [volume] to a level where I can sleep better. I must use great caution and sip [when sipping] the beer, swallowing only when I am mentally ready. I still cannot drink any liquid or eat any food directly down the center of my throat as in my former life. I suspect this will get better in time [as it has so far]. So I swim and carefully sip beer. That to me is funny and I wonder what those nurses at the VA would say to that. If I do choke, and I sometimes do, I am much better able to recover and clear my throat, something I was unable to do [had difficulty in doing just] a few weeks ago, as silly as that seems to me now and to you my reader. Speaking of readers, earlier this morning when it was cool out, I used the patio to further edit my introduction to this journal [book]. I have digitized [nearly seven months] of entries through July 15 [as I write this] which I still find unbelievable. I likely will do [journal entries] through August [15] before publishing [or printing the journal/book] as that is [around] my two year anniversary [August 12th] of the first and most major brain surgery. To give you an idea [of the difficulty of this project], 6 months of journal entries is about 180 days, add July of 15 days and we are talking about digitizing 195 days and that is a very big deal to anyone who has done this or knows computers. I can speak with some authority on this as in my earlier days[,] as my friends know, I made my living with technology and PCs. It would be an unbelievable[ly difficult] task for a "normal" person who could have his or her speech interpreted by a computer. Of course, as I think I have mentioned, speech-to-text has improved greatly [in recent years]. In reality I thought I would be working on this task [book] well into next year. As my whole life has been pretty unpredictable, so has been this task [book project,] but I am thankful to be able to do it [and to now have the time to do it]. As I am writing a lot here I will let this be today's entry. If anything "earth shaking" occurs this afternoon I will mention it tomorrow. On the tinnitus, this is constantly there and more so when I try to listen to [for] it. All I can do and, as mentioned, have discovered, is to try to ignore it as best I can. I play the hypnosis mp3 occasionally, but mostly I play computer golf, swim, drink (ha ha), anything to distract the brain and/or senses. I still hear high tension wires or lines or [and loud] crickets [which is as close as I can come to describing the sounds in my head] and it can be loud when I try to listen as I mentioned [earlier]. It reminds me of when I went into Walmart in Tennessee and heard all that head noise. Now I don't have the pain or headaches (not since getting powerful steroids at the Vanderbilt ICU, thankfully), but the sound is there, but not usually as loud [as back then before surgeries]. Speaking of Walmart, I woke up today and noticed we were close to running out of coffee and half and half. I made a Walmart run [early]. I assume I have mentioned this but [and] I am sure the reader can infer that I am driving Mom's Olds[mobile] all around town, the store, and yes I guess I have discussed my outings to Ann Arbor, Cleveland, Ohio, Indiana [and so on]. It still amazes me [that I can drive] but as soon as my double vision cleared last May, [and] June of 2012, I was able to drive again. That, fortunately, was a skill I never lost and only had to wait until my vision was safe enough [to allow it]. And thank the powers that be, I had the sense to know when I could drive. What if I didn't? Well, that's some other reality I suppose. But yes, I have been driving quite a long time now and I am always very grateful at the sense of independence it gives me. You can stop right now as you are reading this and imagine what life would be like if you could not drive or get around, or you were stuck in a wheelchair or walker or [had to use a] cane and could not physically get around. If you can imagine just a part of that life, then you will know how happy I was [and am] to still have that [driving] skill and to have my Mom allow [let] me use her car for errands, therapy, and so on. It's truly been something amazing! So bottom line, I still have symptoms but vision sharpens daily, [and] the brain is locking into images. I never had a cognition problem [except probably right after the first surgery]. Even from my VA days, thankfully, I was aware and mentally alert [soon after the first operation]. It has [most] always been a physical condition for me though from first impression upon meeting and or listening to my speech you might think otherwise. The rapid improvements bode well and reflect back to my chief neurosurgeon, Dr. Sills's, prediction of full recovery after about 2 years. He's been pretty damn accurate so far, if you will forgive my "French".

Monday July 22, 2013 5 pm living room

This morning I did not walk [at the mall] but caught up with my laundry. I went to the "Totally Clean" [laundromat] on Waldo. Every time I go there it's [my vision is] clearer and clearer. I have better control of my walking, though it is still difficult to maneuver. I played some games of [their video] arcade golf (naturally!), had some of their coffee and was done about 9:15 am. I turn in [recycled] some bottles and cans at Meijer and bought some [wild] bird suet. I looked for pool rafts and ship models [I told Mom I might try to build one sometime] but [I] did not find any [that I liked. I will now wait until after this book is done before I do other therapy]. After Meijer I went to the Dow Library where I worked on listing on paper what I wrote about in my introduction [the beginning of my "memory" pages]. I will try to organize my thoughts that way so further work will make more sense and maybe go faster. I came back about noon. Dave was working on his KIA, Mom was out running errands. I worked on file 14 of the journal and edited it some on the notebook computer in the living room. Dave came in and wants [wanted] a pool/beer break. As beer helps reduce my tinnitus and the pool water cools my constant hot right leg, it sounds [sounded] like a plan.

Tuesday July 23, 2013 3:30 pm living room

Mom is down [in] the basement doing some laundry. Dave got back from Mount Pleasant earlier (about 1:30 pm) (he was getting a prescription from CVS Pharmacy there). He is now back to working on his KIA and tow bar. I am on the [my favorite] recliner taking a short break from editing this journal [book] to enter today's [written journal] notes. It is much cooler outside now, [though] for my taste it is quite pleasant. We have been able to sleep with the windows open. It is expected to be this way for another 6 days through [next]

Monday. Today was pretty much the usual routine. After getting to bed around 9 pm, I listened to mp3s, read some, fell asleep with headphones on and pillows propped up (no wonder I have had a neck ache lately). I woke up a couple of times as usual to use the urinal bottle (it's less disorienting than stumbling down the hall to the bathroom. I am used to using it as a convenience). I listened to the tinnitus [hypnosis] mp3 and [that] knocked down the head noise a bit as I usually need to do. [I got] Up at 6 am, had coffee, a roll and a banana. I let the birds out for a break. Before heading to the mall, I took out the trash as it's a Tuesday [trash day here, one of Mom's favorite days...just kidding Mom]. At the mall I found [discovered] I did not have my pedometer with me [during my walk]. It clips on the belt, similar to the last one, but easily drops off. I found it under the car after my walk. I only did 3 laps (up until 9[:]00 am) as I wanted to work more on this book at the Dow Library. I did that, then left for Meijer where I tried [bought] some new brands of beer. In Meijer and earlier in Target, as well as in the mall, I noticed an even further adjustment of my brain to "the world". My clear [clearer] field of vision seems to expand and I am more aware of the entire store or mall area [in front of me]. This is extremely hard to convey to others. This is almost one of those times when there are no correct words. All I know is that the daily improvements in everything have been painfully slow. I wish sometimes [often] that I would awake and there would be rapid progress, leaping back to normalcy, so to say, but I only see tiny improvements daily, however they are improvements so I am grateful. As I have said before, this whole experience certainly teaches great patience. Can the reader imagine a "distorted" world for [over] 2 years? It's been that long. I'm sure the extra [second brain] operation with gamma radiation has taken its toll, probably extending [delaying] recovery time. All I can do is to hang in there and hope that someday it's all a distant memory.

<u>Wed. July 24, 2013 3:00 pm living room</u>

[Note: It was cool outside and Dave worked late on his car, so we passed on swimming. We also will skip Thursday (July 25th) swimming as we are going out to eat at the [Midland] Ponderosa buffet to celebrate the one year anniversary of my gamma knife operation (2nd brain operation) – July 25, 2012]. I have been working on this book this afternoon after I got back. We are getting into the heart of it now, with lots of editing, progress on the introduction and so on. I am about ready to spend extended times in the library [if necessary] and/or morning patio to try to recall events as best I can. There were so many to include. The day [Today] started out pretty routine. [I got] Up at 6:00 am to have coffee, rolls, let the birds out[,] and so on. I then left for the mall. I only did 2 laps and left a bit after 9:00 am, intending to work in [the Dow] Library again. I felt sleepy so I stopped at Burger King near the mall for a small coffee. I had some time to "kill" before the library opened anyway [9:30 am]. Their cash register [at Burger King] did not work so the cute girl I have talked to before knew me as a "regular" customer so [and] gave me the coffee for free. She is very nice [but young, unlike me]. I headed to the library and took the time to play my tinnitus [hypnosis] mp3 in the parking lot. It has been a cool, sunny day, just under 80 degrees as a high, but [it] feels mostly in the 70s. Dave is making progress on his KIA and tow bar. He is now out trying to mow the lawn and doing last minute chores before he leaves. He likely will go on another delivery when he gets the KIA ready. Mom sat [for the older lady] today then went shopping. I also got her some things at Walmart. I went there to pick up some more glasses [temporary] nose pads. I am trying to see if they will stick any better on the new silicon pads that are now on the glasses. I think I still need a very small lift in the glasses for clearer vision, especially with sunglasses on as the slight extra weight lowers the line of vision somewhat. In the mall and at Walmart, the field of vision that I commented about yesterday did not show up [appear as improved] as much and I still struggle to walk in the mall. Maybe I expected too much but the changes are so gradual! Well tomorrow marks the one year anniversary of my gamma knife procedure in Midland at the MidMichigan Medical Center. Right now, in honor of that, I am going to come up with something [fun] to do. The first thing I will do is take tonight and tomorrow off from journal [book] work. This will give me a break and honor the anniversary. I may buy those Seth books, have coffee in [at] Starbucks or something, I am not yet sure. Right now I am starting my break or "celebration" by stopping for a round of computer golf (yahoo!). We may try the pool later even if [there is] cool air outside. Last night the water was warm[,] about 78 degrees. It was refreshing. After [a] supper of chile dogs, we played dominoes. It was fun.

Thursday July 25, 2013 12:20 pm living room

Well, where to begin? [It was] Such an active morning. I thought I would get a few comments down while fresh in my mind. I just had a salami sandwich, chips and some cheese for lunch. It's bright and sunny outside in the 70s, a very nice day. Today is my anniversary (one year) since my "second" brain surgery. This was the gamma knife procedure here in Midland. In honor of that, I decided today that I would go easy on myself, with limited walking and journal [book] work. I am probably going to break those rules because that work has been so instrumental to my current life. I did put in two laps at the Fashion Square Mall in Saginaw this morning. I enjoy it there and as I have said before, I like to have coffee and hang out at the Barnes and Noble bookstore in Saginaw. I decided to do that today as I enjoy it and today is a day to do what I like to do. After the morning routine I headed out to Saginaw and got to the mall there around 8[:]00 am when they open up. I wore the "brain" shirt that Bob [my brother] and Marsha [his wife] got me [for Christmas], the dark blue one that says "I had brain surgery, what's your excuse?". It's always been one of my favorites. After my walk around the mall, I headed to the bookstore a little after 9:00 am. Going into the store a nice young lady [30s or 40s is now young to me, oh my!] held the door for me, noticed my shirt, and gave me a hug right at the door. It surprised me and I knew she was headed for coffee like me so I offered to buy her a cup. We started talking at the entrance [blocking everyone's way] then went to the coffee shop. I found out she is a 1st grade teacher who has the summer off and of all things her sister had 2 brain tumor operations also [as I did]. She [her sister] had the gamma [knife surgery] first, then [the] traditional [brain] surgery after [the opposite of me, of course]. She said her sister is making progress, which is good to hear, but [she] gets periods of depression and other mental problems. It was very interesting and it was nice to meet someone who listened to my story too. I felt as if I were talking to Anita, my speech pathologist, I had so much to say. This lady (and I was such a goof that I don't remember her name) [a bad habit of mine in not remembering a name when I first meet someone]--a note: she had me write down my name [for her at my suggestion] and I did it and I added a comment to her sister. She did not write her name and it was too awkward to ask [at that point..I can be such a "dork"]. Perhaps I will run into her again there, perhaps not. There was a big gap in our ages [as I mentioned]. She [is] probably 30-40 and me being 62 now. She also was heavily into church and religion mentioning a Bible study [class]. So it was probably not a compatibility match (as in the movies) [like I need that now], just an enjoyable talk. She was most patient with my slurring and my yacking about what has been going on in my life. After the coffee I let her get on with her day and I bought (finally) the Jane Roberts books [(she probably would think me a heathen, ha ha)] that I have had my eye on lately, as a reward and anniversary gift, you could say. I left for the Auburn [Branch] Library about 10 am so I could start [to read] one of these books. I read there until about 11[:]30 am and headed back. I changed [clothes], had lunch, entered this daily journal [written] comment and soon I will probably call [the] Ann Arbor [VA] to get them to redo my appointments for the next MRI and follow-up. They sent me a form [forms] (VA) saying the two appointments are set but on different days which will not do. Ann Arbor is over a 100 miles [away] and the VA no longer pays travel. Tonight we are going to [the] Ponderosa [buffet for a celebration]. Sandra will join us, very fitting since she was the one with me on the second operation. [An additional note: the teacher's sister was born on August 12th, the day of my 1st operation and my ex-spouse's birthday. It's just another interesting piece of information and to me showing how everything in life is linked [synchronicity] and there really are no coincidences].

Friday July 26, 2013

We had our buffet last night to honor my gamma knife anniversary. Not many people were there like [the] last time but the food was good. I managed 2 plates [this time] and desert and drank more water [than before]. Mom, Dave, Sandra and I were there. Steve was out of town, Amy was working. [Heather is in Colorado]. It was fun. We played some dominoes when back [at Mom's] then I had to bail out as I was tired (it was after 9 pm) and my right leg/foot was acting up again (very hot). I covered it, and as always, that helped. I read a bit more then crashed around 10 pm. I was up a bit early this morning ([I] got up around 5[:]30 am) and after my routine I left early for the mall, [I was near] Burger King at about 6:45 am. I played the tinnitus [hypnosis] mp3 at [Mom's] first to get from a "5" to a "3". Since I was way early at a little after 7[:]00 am I played it again [in the car and] then went over to Burger King and had my usual small coffee. It was an overcast, comfortable morning and I had my [car] windows down. I walked 3 laps in the mall and stopped at that to get over to the library again to work on this project. Today [while] there I just wrote down random memories of topics [that] I could use in my introduction [my "memory" pages I talk about in the introduction]. On the way back I stopped over at MidMichigan Medical [Center] and sat [parked] in the handicapped parking lot near the gamma knife clinic/radiation oncology department and wrote as fast as I could [about] topics related to my experiences there. After lunch I came up with an idea of creating separate "memory" files [papers or pages] listing these topics [or events that occurred to me] and then filed in with whatever I could remember. If this works then I hope it will make writing about the events much easier. I took a break midway to listen to a YouTube clip Dave sent me on Carl Perkins and Paul McCartney. It was very interesting. Dave is working on his car, Mom got back from working [sitting]. I will probably resume some more bookwork.

Sat. July 27, 2013 5:00 pm living room

Dave is working on his car, doing last minute things. He is taking an RV to Iowa, probably tomorrow sometime. He will try to pick up another at Elkhart, Indiana when he returns. He said he will not come back immediately after [he delivers] the first one. Mom is working in her bedroom and occasionally comes out. She is probably thinking about supper. I am on my purple recliner. My [right] leg has been hot all day and is flaring up again. I lift it up and down to try to get it to circulate, and that sometimes helps. I worked on a few "memory" papers, an idea I came up with to help in finishing this journal's [book's] introduction. It is still cool, too cool to swim as Dave said the pool was about 70 degrees. That's chilly. I went out to the Midland Mall this Saturday morning and noticed a return of clearer vision as a few days before. That may be breaking my way soon. The tinnitus was active when I awoke and I played the mp3 for it while I waited at the mall parking lot. I also played it at the Dow Library in the "quiet" room. This afternoon it's been suppressed but now as I write about it, naturally, I hear it. So I walked better, [and] saw better. I worked on the "memory" files at the Dow [Library] and at Mom's this afternoon. I read some also, watched some golf [on TV]. I will be off from walking tomorrow and as I get up early every day I most likely will take advantage of the cool spell and work on my book on the patio.

Sunday July 28, 2013 (3[:]30 pm living room Off day from walking)

[I] Woke up at 4[:]30 am. I played [my hypnosis] mp3 on tinnitus-- from 5 to 3 [level]. [I] Played Guided Meditation tapes [mp3s] on financial and physical [meditations]. I had coffee and a roll and went out on the patio to work on the book but it started to drizzle. This was about 7[:]30 am. I went inside to work and ended up working on the dining room table. Dave got up and changed his KIA oil. He has been mowing the lawn as he does not like Mom to do it at her age. He is doing last minute stuff before he takes off for Iowa later today or early tomorrow most likely. I worked quite hard on my "memory" pages and hopefully they will help me to finish the introduction. I am up to ["memory"] file 32. I plan to work extended time in the library next week [if necessary] to really make a dent in this project. It's nice to be physically able to do this. Well, I think I have done quite enough for one day. I have noticed slightly less leg pain today and a small improvement in swallowing ability. My writing is also more controlled. I bent down earlier to get the papers at the end of the drive, careful of my balance, naturally [this is much easier now]. I think I will unwind watching some golf [on TV], who knows maybe have a brew but not sure as I'm sure Dave won't have one before driving. I may play it by ear.

<u>Mon. July 29, 2013 (5[:]00 pm patio)</u>

I am now taking a break from working on more "memory" pages, short pages where I can put down memories on separate subjects that I still recall [from my surgeries]. I am hoping that these will make the finishing of my [book] introduction much easier. I am sipping on a "cheap" Michelob beer and after this entry [I] will browse the Golf Week magazine Mom ordered. It is still cool out, just reaching the 70s but for my choice, it's perfect. We had to stop using the pool as it got down to 70 degrees [outside]; it's probably colder now. Dave left late last night or early this morning on his trip to Iowa then back to Indiana for another RV somewhere. I spent most of the day working on this journal, as I mentioned. I am going to take some time off from mall walks and work all day on it until I can finish it up. It is tough but all writing is difficult and when your fighting your own brain at the same time, well let's just say that's lots of fun.

<u>Tuesday July 30, 2013 (dining table Wed. morning 7/31/13 7:30 am)</u>

I am catching up on this day's [written journal entry] from Wednesday morning, a day after. It was hectic and both Mom and I got back from the UNO restaurant at about 8 pm and just went to bed. We both read, Mom probably had her TV on. Dave called earlier around 5 pm and that's what probably helped wear us out. We had to make an emergency deposit for him so he could have money on the road. We have done this before but this time it was <u>very close.</u> The [Chemical B]bank drive through in Auburn closed in 20 minutes at 5:30 pm. I packed Mom's car as we were headed for [the] UNO in Bay City, a restaurant where we celebrated Amy's [Sandra, my sister's daughter's] Birthday (7/31). I push the [speed] limit to make it [to the bank on time] and Mom did a little front seat driving. She thought we would get a ticket. I knew otherwise [and that would take too long to go into] and [but I] knew we would be fine. We made the deposit with 10 minutes to spare[,] cutting it close. We both breathed a sigh of relief after, tried to relax and headed to UNO. It was a nice bar/restaurant. We were there last year for Heather's [my sister's other daughter's] Birthday. I drove then but it still is amazing to me that I could. This time [I have] much more balance, [and] control though [all is] not quite right. I still had [have] to eat slow and carefully. Both Mom and I had doggy bags for our pizza. I am staying here [to work at Mom's] and not walking for a few days. I am working on this journal [book] trying to put a dent in it. I am producing my "memory" pages and need the computer and printer. Hopefully, I will then go through the pages, write down additional scenes as they prompt my brain and "ideally" then [I] should be able to finish my intro[duction] to this book.

<u>Wed. July 31, 2013 (dining room table 4[:]30 pm)</u>

I stayed here [at Mom's place] to work again and did not walk [at the mall]. I got a lot accomplished and stayed [worked] at it slowly. I did take a break about 2[:]30 pm to mail Mom's bills in Auburn and to buy a few items at the Food Center there. Now I will take a beer and mp3 music break on the patio. I will then have a TV dinner for supper most likely and wind it down. I will stay here [at Mom's] another day to work early on the journal [book].

CHAPTER 8   8/1/13 – 8/15/13

Thrs. August 1, 2013

I spent another day working on journal [book] papers. Tomorrow I will do some shopping and banking since it is an early payday. I may go back early [to Mom's] to finish up the "memory" sheets.

Friday August 2, 2013 (patio 4:30 pm)

This morning I went to the laundromat on Waldo in Midland, the "Totally Clean". I have been there a few times now. I wanted to clean my bed comforters as they had not been done in 2 years. I used to do them all the time when I owned the machines [at my laundromat in Tennessee]. I was done a little after 9 am. By the way, I had some fairly loud tinnitus this morning so I played my hypnosis mp3 a couple of times first (around 4:30 am). I got up about 5:30 am, played with the birds, did my usual routine. After the laundry this morning I went to the little (Soldan's) bird (pet store) and bought some songbird seed and treats for my [wild] birds. I naturally stopped by the cockatiels there and whistled hello. I kept moving on but it was tough not to take them all back with me. I came back, fed the [my] birds, put away my laundry and spent the afternoon finishing typing my "memory" sheets. Tomorrow, while Mom sits [works], I will go on the patio and try to fill in any blanks or add new "memories" if necessary. I will probably do that Sunday too. Then Monday I will resume my walks and go to work at the library finally resuming the introduction.

Sat. August 3, 2013 7:30 pm living room

[It was] Another busy day. While Mom sat (worked)[,] I worked on the [this] journal, mostly editing "memory" pages. When Mom got back at 2 pm we both went over to Bob's. He was there taking a beer and food break. He had been working outside. Marsha [Bob's wife] was helping at a campsite [that] she usually does each year. Pat [Patrick] is taking Bob to a Tiger [baseball] game in Detroit tomorrow [Ben also went I found out later] so we wanted to wish him [Bob] a happy Birthday for this coming Monday the 5th of August. He said he was taking that day off to go to lunch with Marsha and to run errands. We had a nice visit and gave him some cards and Mom got him some gifts. We came back in an hour or so. I resumed work on this book and corrected [the] Journal_14 (July 16-31) [file]. I will proof edit it tomorrow then I will try to edit some more "memory" pages. All in all[,] it's coming along really well. I write this here in this journal entry because it describes a good portion of my day. I will wind down now and then do my nightly routine.

Sun. August 4, 2013 (3 :30 pm living room)

Today's big event is my stiff neck/back. I was dumb and propped up my head with two pillows as I do when I read [and fell asleep that way]. I guess I was tired. We went to Bob's[, as I mentioned yesterday]. I had a beer and then I took sleep and relaxation pills before bed. [As I say] I fell asleep with my headphones on and my head propped up so I have been battling a stiff neck all day. Despite that I have worked hard and finished [file] Journal_14 (July 16-31) and edited it. I then made hand corrections and additions all afternoon to the "memory" sheets. Next I make those changes to the [digital] files [on the USB stick and computer]. I will then try to merge them into larger [digital] files [my introduction files] and see how much of a story they make. Ideally then I will just have to smooth out the edges and I will have the "meat" of an introduction. This is probably more detail then you want to know but it's just me rattling in my journal as always. So [omit so] it's about 4 pm so I think it's "beer:30" as Dave would say. I may have some [beer] and watch some golf. Tomorrow I will resume my [book] work.

Mon. August 5, 2013 5:05 pm living room

There is [a] light drizzle out and its about 70 degrees. After the usual morning routine (I was up about 5:30 am) I went to Burger King. I did let the birds out for a short break [earlier]. I asked for a small coffee but they only had medium [cups] so I sipped on one [at the same price as a small]. That cute girl [that I have talked to before] gave me the coffee. She was busy with the morning headset. I sipped some [coffee]. The Asian guy with the greeter job at Meijer was there [as he is a regular]. I waved hello. I didn't think he saw me. I walked [later] at the [Midland] Mall but because I was off a week and I had some low [physical] biorhythms and I wanted to shop at Meijer for groceries and head [so I headed] back early (Mom was sitting). I walked only two laps then shopped for groceries at Meijer. I got back about 10 am and started working on my "memory" sheets. I did that until about 4 pm and took a beer break. It was drizzling so I came in [from the patio]. Mom is working in the front yard on some weeds. I will wind it down, have some supper, [and] watch some TV. I may get back early tomorrow again to work on this book.

<u>Tues. August 6, 2013 5:00 pm living room</u>

I played my [hypnosis] mp3 on tinnitus twice early this morning about 4:30 am when I awoke. I knocked it down to a 3 [level] or so and woke up, [and] did my routine. I wore the dark ["]brain["] shirt again. Some [people] noticed but most did not, as they were in their own routine or have seen it so much anyway. I came back after getting some computer paper at Target in the mall and some perch sandpaper covers at PetSmart. I worked on the "memory" pages from 10:30 am until now, about 5:00 pm. They are a slow, tedious thing but I think I can patch them together for the "meat" of the introduction to this journal [book]. Things get clearer daily at the mall, almost normal, but just enough off to still slow me down in walking and I also still have not achieved full energy yet. The leg remains hot but less so. Perhaps by the time I stop work on this book things will be normal and the book will only serve as a look into a <u>former</u> world I [once] inhabited. I can only dream!

<u>Wed. August 7, 2013 4:20 pm living room</u>

[I spent] Another afternoon working on my "memory" sheets. I walked 3 laps in the mall this morning. I then got some gas at Speedway and picked up some items at Meijer. I played a bit with my old cell phone, the Pantec Jest. I charged it 3 hours and it actually came to life. I wrote down contacts I had in the phone, Tennessee ones of course. I don't know my future plans yet. All I have to do is recover and write this journal and I will let the "future" take care of itself.

Thursday August 8, 2013 4:10 pm living room

I played the tinnitus [hypnosis] mp3 twice starting at 4:30 am when I awoke. I then played the financial and physical Guided Meditation mp3s. I did my morning routine at about 5:30 am when I got up. I played a little computer golf at about 7:00 am to 7:30 am. I went to the Midland Mall, parked at the outer [a farther away lot] for a change but stopped after one lap as I felt a sore right ankle. I guess it's a good thing that I can feel anything in that leg. I went over to the [Dow] Library at about 8:30 am and worked on my "memory" sheets on a picnic table. When they opened I worked until about 11:00 am [in the library] then [I] had a coffee. That [my swallowing] went well but I noticed that I was a bit unstable in walking. Sometimes it comes and goes. Either way I think I will only work on the journal [book] for a few days and hold off walking as my 2 year, 1st operation, anniversary is Monday. I will find something fun to do [on that day]. Mom has been getting good test results for her age in [on] her kidneys and general health so we both will likely go out Monday to Pat and Mike's [Jerry's] buffet [in Auburn]. Dave is still in California delivering [an RV] today and will be headed back but I don't expect him to be here Monday. Well I worked [on this book] not only at the [Dow] Library but here in the living room and I will likely continue that until I get them [the book] done. Next I will work combining all the ODT [Open Document Template digital] files into the introduction, also a tedious job.

Friday August 9, 2013

I stayed at Mom's today because of the sore ankle discovered yesterday while walking. I heard less noise this morning in my head. That's a good sign. I ignored it [anyway] and read a couple of Seth

[Jane Roberts] sessions [in my new "Seth Speaks" book] and played on the notebook computer. I then got up about 5:30-6:00 am. I did coffee, rolls, the birds as usual. I have been finishing the edit[ing] of my "memory" pages. I just got the first pass done in [on] all 109 or so of them [Oh my God, this book is getting so big!]. Tomorrow I will stay [at Mom's] to assemble them into larger [digital] files. I will keep everything in ODT format for now until I see what the printer [of this book] needs. I can then convert [them] if necessary [final submission needs to be in PDF format, which I can easily do in this "Open Office" software]. I am making great progress. After I combine the [digital] files then I need [do the] final edit [little did I know that I would be editing and proofing into November of 2013]. Hey Ma, look at me I'm a writer! or a writer "wanna be". I got an email from Cathy Lewis, my friend I had to leave back in Tennessee. She took Buddy, the male cockatiel at the nursing home[,] to live with her on [at] Rene's [the head nurse at the home, Cathy's boss] request. I am not sure what's happening there but I am glad he [Buddy] has a nice home. She [Cathy] is right, if I had been there I'm sure I would have a third bird. As I always say, somewhere that happened in some alternate reality .

<u>Sat. August 10, 2013 (4:00 pm living room)</u>

I have worked very hard while Mom has been out with Rose [her friend] today. I had to earlier (about 10 am) redeposit Dave's checks [check]. He didn't have it registered and Mom tried to deposit it earlier and it would not go through. We got a hold of him [Dave] in Arizona. He is on his way back from delivering an RV to San Diego. After Mom left around 10 am [to pick up Rose] I went to work and assembled all of the "memory" pages (all 109) into my introduction files. Next the whole thing [the files] needs to be edited [,as I have mentioned before,] and I need to make sure all of those files are in the introduction. It is tedious work but now I can see the light at the end of the tunnel and it's not the neurosurgeons pen knives [shining in my eyes]. I just got the mail, [and] did my check[ing account] register [balancing]. There were three magazines [in the mail] so I will now take my usual afternoon break as I have done so much [work] today. I will have much to be grateful for Monday [on my anniversary day] and today!

Sun. August 11, 2013

The tinnitus was a bit loud this morning about 4:30 am. I needed to use the [my] urinal [bottle] and woke up then. I imagine I got a good sleep as I probably conked out around 9-10 pm. Today after coffee I really made some progress on the book. I merged the "memory" pages into all the introductions [introduction files]. I am now doing the painful editing [job]. I have done about 20 pages (or "memories") so far. After I edit I have to check them off [a list] so that I make sure I have not missed one. Mom just ordered a pizza at the local [party] store [down the road] and I am going to get it. [It's] Good therapy. I will watch that front step as I fell on it yesterday getting a Powerball [lotto] ticket. Luckily I was not hurt but like everything it has been a learning experience. Well now I will take a break in honor of my 2 year anniversary tomorrow of the first and [most] major [brain] surgery. I may check out the Bay City mall early as we were near there when we recently went to UNO'S [restaurant and bar] to celebrate Amy's Birthday. After that I may wind up over to Barnes and Noble [in Saginaw] for a Starbucks [coffee]. I met that teacher on my one year gamma anniversary so you never know. One can hope. I will just be happy for the coffee and to browse the books. Jeez, I must be getting old!

Mon. August 12, 2013 (1:00 pm living room)

[It's] The big 2 year anniversary day!!! I'm still alive! Wow! And not a headache, or at least none like before, for two years. Other symptoms, yes, but damn, no headaches!! I played the [tinnitus] hypnosis mp3 2 times, got up, did the [my morning] routine, [then] headed for the Bay City Mall for something different [to do on this special day]. It's too far [to go there to walk regularly]. It's a small mall but clean and a good walk site but [there is] no bookstore or Starbucks there as in Midland so I will go back there [to the Midland Mall to walk]. I bought some "Batch 19" beer that Dave likes at Meijer [in Saginaw] and headed back. I had 2 pieces of pizza [for lunch] from last night (Mom ordered a large pizza from the local party store and I picked it up--good therapy) [, as I wrote before]. I did not fall on their front porch steps as I did a day or so [ago] when I got a lotto ticket. I was lucky and did not hurt myself [that day] and sure did not hit my head. I fell in [on] my bottom for a moment. A customer checked on me. I just was not paying attention. I know better now. Anyway [I] got an email from Dave that [said] he might be here around 4:30 pm. He wants to make it [this Monday] to go out with me, Mom, and Sandra to Pat and Jerry's buffet in Auburn to celebrate my 2 year anniversary. As I wait[ed] I cleaned the pool and even though I did not plan to, I will do some more book work until Dave and/or Sandra get here. I am wearing the pictured "brain" shirt that Sarah and Josh got me for this [special] occasion.

Tues. August 13, 2013 8[:]45 pm bedroom

Dave and I had some beers [this night]. I had an Alaskan Amber and a Kilt Lifter [that Dave brought back] from Arizona. I went to bed about 8[:]30 pm to enter in this log and wind it down. [We played] No games tonight. We had fried chicken [Dave and I] and some potato salad and coleslaw. I'm still full. I have been going through my journal seeing what I have done since my last speech therapy on July 15—so I will have something to talk to Anita [my speech pathologist] about this Thursday [during my appointment]. I am a little looped as those were strong beers. I went walking 4 laps at the mall [earlier] but [and] then [I] worked hard at the Dow Library and then at Mom's on the introduction to this journal [book]. I think I did intro_05, [and] 07 [files] today, a day of hard work. I have been thinking of continuing the journal past 8/15 but just not transcribing it yet [I eventually did stop making journal entries at the end of 2013]. I will think that over [some] more. Now I will stop and surf the [Internet on the] computer for awhile.

Wed. August 14, 2013 4:20 pm living room

I just finished editing and changing intro_08, [and] 09 at the Dow Library and back [at Mom's place]. [It is] Hard to keep it [the book] a secret but the "memory" pages technique has really helped [me to advance the completion of this book]. I hope to do the last of the intro[duction] Fri[day] and Sat[Saturday]. I have my speech therapy tomorrow morning in Saginaw. It looks like I may be able to do the rest of the Journal file 15 and then proceed with [to] the final edits of the whole book late August or into September. [It] Looks like we go to "press" in September or October, which is great. Vision was good at the Dow [Library] today as a worked. The coffee shop seemed sharper. [There are] Slow improvements as always but they continue.

Thurs. August 15, 2013 (7:45 pm living room)

We just had supper. Dave grilled [heated up] some leftover hamburgers and hot dogs on the grill. Sandra came over to eat supper. She had some dental work done and Steve was [is] still at his [their] cabin. The birds [my two birds] are squawking at all the commotion. I'm taking a moment to jot down some [written] comments in the [this] journal. I went to the Saginaw VA for my now monthly speech meeting with Anita this morning. I talked my usual drivel, but this time I prepared somewhat in that I went through my journal and wrote down the things that went on since my last visit in mid July. We did a few things. I talked about the pool, drinking beer, the Irish pub, my 2 anniversaries that went by[,] my gamma knife (1 year) and my brain operation, the main one in Tennessee, now 2 years ago already, hard to believe. Even though I will stop processing this journal into digital format on this Aug[ust]15th [today], I will likely still do a daily log [entry] out of habit and also because I may want to look at it or process it one day, who knows[?], maybe as a sequel[?]. I did no walk today. After the VA [appointment] I went to the Barnes and Noble in Saginaw for a latte [coffee] and browsed for an hour. I then headed to the Auburn [Branch] Library where I edited two files (intro 10,11). At

[Mom's place] in the afternoon I made the changes to file 10 on the computer but Dave wanted a beer break early so I stopped and we had 3 Alaskan beers on the patio until Sandra came over [Again, as mentioned earlier, I eventually stopped making further entries into my original journal in late fall of 2013].

Epilogue

First, let me thank you, my reader, for patiently reading my daily journal and my introduction story. I know it has not been an easy read and I noticed that I repeated myself several times while writing in the journal each afternoon or evening. For that I do apologize.

I wish I could have made this journal earlier, such as in 2012, but as I mention in the writings, I was not physically able to do so. Actually, I am very grateful to be finally able to share it with you and I am very happy to have been able to recall and to document these "memories". Perhaps, when all is said and done, this may be one of the greatest miracles of all, the fact that I could recall these events over two years later.

It is interesting to note, that out of habit, and to continue my writing therapy, as my speech pathologist Anita would say, I am continuing to make my daily entries in the journal, even past my chosen stopping point of August 15, 2013 [I did stop later in the year]. I chose that date [to end this book] as I wanted to get this journal out as soon as possible "into the world" and it was shortly after my two year "craniotomy" anniversary. I may or may not pursue a "sequel" to this adventure. If I do not, then this journal will still mean a lot to me, and someday I or someone else may look back and enjoy it. Again, I thank you all (ya'll) so much for your time.

As I write this and continue to edit it for publication, I sometimes just stop and reflect on how lucky an individual I really am. I am so grateful and appreciative of everything in this world, particularly as it slowly returns to me. May you also be grateful and a bit more thankful for the events in your life, now that you have shared some of mine. Thank you again for the honor of your time.

Index

1000 mg pill..11

12th of August, 2011..25

6000 mg..11

a few seconds to adjust..69

absolutely determined..74

abundance..248

abusive..70

acetaminophen..7, 11, 13

acoustics..98, 164

adjust to the real world..62

administrators..124

advance by "doing"..65

advanced rapidly..46

advancement...166, 225, 276, 277, 297

advances..138

air base..48

alertness..111, 198

alive and walking this planet..1

all saluting us...48

all went blank...37

allergic...57

alternating daily from right eye to left...53

326

always wave when I saw her..50

ambulance..18, 19, 37, 89

Amy..................................2, 3, 68, 211, 246, 247, 254, 287, 312, 315, 321

an error in my surgery..54

anesthesia..30, 102, 251

angle of entry into my throat...44

angled upward..75

Anita...3, 85, 101, 105, 106, 153, 172, 188, 195, 200, 201, 206, 214, 221, 227, 238, 249, 261, 272, 296, 297, 311, 322, 323, 325

anti-government...52

anything can spook the birds...81

applesauce..42

April...3, 42, 43, 51, 52, 53

armed guards..55

Arnold Palmer golf book...55

ask for food...25

aspirin..12, 18, 24, 28, 37, 89

at all hours now..81

at the end of the movie..69

ate at very regular times..39

awaiting word of my surgery...28

back to the world..32

ball game...163

ball got stuck	86
bankruptcy	33, 99
Barack Obama	34
bartered	41
baseball games	87, 88, 205
bazaar	29, 198
beer:30	317
Beethoven	145, 146
before the lights went out	27
belief	90
Ben	2, 180, 316
bend down	14, 66, 80
benign	25, 128, 152
Benton	7, 10, 11, 13, 15, 20, 23, 34, 50, 56, 59, 83, 86, 97, 119, 157, 192, 368
beret	116, 118, 265, 266
Betty	3, 132, 133, 134, 139, 180, 181, 253, 259
beyond disrespect	70
beyond insulting	70
big smile on my face	28, 36
big turning point in my life	54
Bill Gates and Microsoft	37
biofeedback	159, 188, 272

bird feeders..80, 199, 212

birds have such good ears..81

birthday he would always remember..51

bit of a talker...86

blabbed my life story..86

bland..14, 40, 44

blob...25, 238

blood pressure..12, 13, 15, 24, 159, 238

blurriness..138, 201

Bob................2, 67, 69, 85, 96, 247, 250, 255, 258, 259, 282, 310, 316, 317

Bobbie...2, 3

bobble..228, 234, 285

bobble head..213, 262, 283

bodily functions..26, 42

bookworm...77

boot camp..39, 55

bored her..49

boredom of the place...35

born to raise hell..124

borrowing cigarettes..56

bothered to look at my medical records..70

bottom getting hot...100

329

bowel..32

brain and eyes adjust...75

brain healing..72

brain is locking..306

brain limitations...90

brain lock...75, 98, 130, 141, 161, 239, 276, 281

break after every lap...79

break between loads...15

breaking all kinds of records..53

breathing a sigh of relief...43

brief messages..6

Brooklyn...2, 237

brother and mother stayed at my residence................................34

browse..107

brunette...26, 46

brushed my teeth..48

building up my confidence...88

bullshit..57

bureaucrat...1, 59, 71

burst out laughing..40, 46

business..7

busy now..35

cannot hear that well..70

cards in Benton...34

carnival...47

carry only one item at a time..64

cat scan..15, 16, 18, 128

catheter..30

Cathy...2, 11, 12, 13, 15, 16, 17, 19, 23, 26, 38, 47, 76, 80, 135, 166, 192, 254, 288, 320

caution getting in and out..126

Cedarville...68

cell phone...23, 38, 114, 115, 116, 141, 319

cell phone guy in the mall..115

cerebellum...31

Chattanooga...12, 13, 28, 86, 87, 88, 97

Chattanooga Clinic..15

check-out medicines...60

chirp in acknowledgment...81

choked..94

choking...103

chose my diet..35

Christy...9, 19, 20, 21, 22, 82, 212, 272, 286, 296, 303

classical music..97

cleaned up my bottom..32

331

cleared by default	33
Cleveland, Tennessee	11, 13, 33, 301
clipboards	40, 45
close to a stroke or death	15
CNA	15
coffee	107
coffee shop	93
cognition	306
cognition tests	45, 105, 181
Coke bottle	91, 185
cold war	48
coming loss of balance	9
communicate these stories	5, 6
competent to drive	74
conspiracy	52
constant headaches	10, 12, 28, 138
constant pain	12, 92, 151
continuing therapy	1
control my hands	5
control my left side shakes	6
control was returning	85
cotton	98, 110, 148, 182, 220

coughing	40, 44, 103, 258
could not bend over	10
could not read	76
could not remember	34
courtyard	43, 47, 55, 56
cover my right leg in the bed	36
craniotomy	2, 25, 30, 33, 102, 325
crickets	306
cryptography	49
Cup and Chaucer	93, 168, 212, 263, 276
curbs	119, 120, 168, 178, 183, 214
cut up into triangle shapes	32
CVS Pharmacy	307
daily increments	91
daily migraine headaches	6
daily walking therapy	83
dancing with girls	49
dancing with her boyfriend	47

Dave 1, 29, 33, 34, 35, 39, 49, 50, 51, 53, 56, 57, 60, 61, 62, 63, 75, 80, 87, 90, 94, 96, 97, 100, 104, 109, 113, 116, 120, 121, 124, 125, 129, 130, 131, 132, 133, 134, 135, 142, 143, 144, 147, 148, 150, 151, 152, 154, 155, 157, 161, 162, 163, 164, 166, 167, 169, 170, 171, 172, 173, 174, 176, 177, 180, 181, 182, 183, 184, 189, 190, 192, 193, 194, 195, 197, 199, 200, 201, 203, 204, 205, 207, 210, 211, 212, 214, 217, 218, 219, 220, 223, 225, 226, 227, 228, 229, 230, 231, 232, 233, 235, 237, 239, 240, 241, 242, 243, 244, 245, 246,

247, 248, 249, 252, 253, 254, 255, 256, 258, 259, 260, 261, 263, 264, 265, 269, 270, 271, 272, 273, 274, 275, 277, 278, 279, 280, 281, 283, 284, 285, 286, 287, 288, 289, 290, 291, 292, 293, 294, 295, 296, 297, 298, 299, 300, 301, 302, 303, 304, 307, 308, 309, 312, 313, 314, 317, 320, 322, 323, 324

Davenport	118
debts	33, 99
delayed reaction	78, 95
delusional	36, 38
delusions	34, 41
Dennis	3, 95
dental lab out of Tinker Toys	123
dependent on things to go just right	9
detached	161
determined to get better	64
Deva Premal	269, 290
device within my head	38
did not give up	74, 80
did not make waves	52
did not resort to the patch	77
difficult and agonizing months	74
difficult to talk	5, 102
difficulty walking	11
dirty laundry	7
dishonorable lawyers	33

disorientated	42, 84
DNA	94, 95, 96
do it "religiously"	83
doing everything by myself	12
doing it routinely	83
doing the right thing	1
Dolly Madison cakes	13
Doris	1, 6, 56, 128, 260
double image	72, 73, 74, 76, 77, 91, 129, 136, 140, 144, 155, 187, 214
double white line	74, 77
down to the bone	30
Dr. Chambless	2, 25, 26
Dr. Copeland	3, 67, 95, 123, 274, 275
Dr. Hrywnak	53, 72, 131, 187, 193
Dr. Janus	108
Dr. Orringer	3, 105, 108, 237, 239
Dr. Sills	2, 24, 25, 26, 50, 71, 91, 110, 307
Dr. Singer	3, 251
Dr. Valdivia	3, 108, 290
drinking fountain	44
drive there myself	104
driven in heavy traffic	77

driving range..109, 110, 191

driving skills..106, 108, 281

drove my mother down to Tennessee...2

dry heaves..14, 128

each and every swallow...44, 158

early rising..82, 186

eat very slowly...47

efforts on my behalf...1, 2

electric tension lines..167

elevation.......................................62, 66, 68, 69, 92, 98, 143, 165, 234, 278

ELO..246

embarrassed..41, 43

embolization...3, 31, 102

Emily...2, 6, 7, 178, 180, 217, 218, 258, 259

end of the world..61

endured 102

endured about two years...75

energy levels increased..54

enjoy life...79

evaluation meeting..59

exercise track..53

experimenting without a cane..78

exploded out of my mouth..94

expressways..106, 153

extremely slow..91

eyesight..170, 303

face was flushed..15

Facebook..6, 67, 119, 237, 284

fairy...243, 244, 263

faith that the eyes would correct..77

Falling Leaf..42, 52

false teeth..40, 44

fantasy...38

favorite books..297

fearless..65

feel my brain indentation..29

feel my hair..68

feeling of freedom!..61

fell hard into the wall..69

fell into a nearby recliner chair...9

fell to the floor..43

felt like a prisoner..40

field of loud crickets..182

field trips..48

fill up my Jeep..7

financial survival..10

fire escape stairs...52

first brain surgery..2, 31

flirt with a female office worker.................................60

flu shot...57

fluid pressure..28

flushed my sinus area out..13

Flying Tiger...263

follow-up visit...50

force both eyes to work...54

force out the words..168

forced to retire..33

foreclosure...33

forehead..53

four red screw marks...95

Fox News...52

Franklin..50

frequent trips to the restroom...................................51

fresh air..79

friends from Tennessee...119

from my viewpoint..5

fun reactions of people	85
fund raiser	73
funeral	123, 124, 275
gamma knife clinic	123
garage door	65
gave up on using it	39
gawkers	178
gawking	80
Gayatri Mantra	269, 289
get back in that bed	58
get out of bed myself	58
get this into writing	5
getaway weekend	56
getting lectured	52
giggle behind me	78
girlfriend	47
give her nuke codes	49
go back to Michigan to heal	61
Golden Corral	301
golf course	49, 78, 110, 117, 191
golf hacker	9
golf video game	87

good vibrations..2

got rid of my headaches almost immediately...28

grabbers...10

gradual daily improvements..65

grandchildren...2, 74, 242

grateful for my situation..1

grateful to have survived..6

great attitude and tons of patience..51

great news while I was waiting...24

Green Spot..125, 281, 301

growing rapidly...81

guards..55

gun turrets...55

gurney..37

had to bath me...41

hand dryers...64

handheld devices...113

happy just to be alive..55

hard for me to go back to sleep...81

hard of hearing...67, 123, 274

hard work...1, 7, 8, 66, 322

hardly able to walk..65

Harry Potter....76, 158, 159, 161, 162, 181, 183, 184, 186, 187, 192, 194, 197, 198

he was so "advanced"..39

head is full of cotton..157

head noises..111, 168, 205

head seeming to split..10

hear noises inside my head..11

hearing block..157

Heather...............2, 68, 203, 211, 222, 223, 247, 253, 254, 258, 259, 312, 315

held me down..27

held on to the laundry cart..14

hell or high water..80, 271

helmet..95

her normal nagging..58

here comes the "birdy" train..81

Hey, how's it goin, mon?..26

hieroglyphic..38

high tension line..112

high tension wire..156, 182, 306

hold me up..36

Home Depot..28

hot cayenne pepper..13

hot leg..79, 133, 273, 275 how not to deal with a new patient..69

hug the wall..83, 98

huge role behind the scenes..34

hugged the rail...88

human pin cushion...24

hummingbird..80

humor in most situations..40

hydrocephalus..30

hygiene..47

hypertension...12, 13

I did not hear sounds...222

I had brain surgery and all I got was this lousy t-shirt..............................85

I had brain surgery, what's your excuse?...........................85, 250, 295, 310

I'll see you in your dreams...35

ignore the signs...10

images finally aligned..74

images were double and blurry...36

in a tunnel...164

in his own world..114

in the center of my forehead...53

in the moment...40, 44, 103, 132, 148, 153, 158, 159, 165, 172, 189, 246, 264

in the right place at the right time...95

in their own world	115, 116, 141
incompetence at the VA	37
independent and forceful personality	12
inoperable	73
insane	145, 158
inside a magic carpet	35
insulting	59, 70
intense pain	14
intense pressure within my skull	10
interesting life experiences	106
intervened	16, 164
Irish Barber Shop	226, 282
ironic	25, 52, 61, 71, 86, 87, 125, 145, 229
ironies	86
irony	71, 78
Is he a doctor?	71
it had rapidly grown	94
it pressed up against my brain	119
it really did happen	48, 50
it took much bravery	77
it was her job	33
It's a Wonderful Life	4

Jamaican	26
James	3, 211
James Bond	35
Jamie	3
Jane Roberts	320
Jerry	3, 169, 181, 253, 259
Jessie	2, 26
Josh	2, 26, 85, 237, 293, 322
journals	126
jumpy over the dog	82
just be a customer	87
just out of my normal reach	58
just to get out of the place	42
Karaoke	49
kayak	7
keep my balance	52
keep my balance in the wind	97
keep things going	10, 11
kept my mouth shut	56
killing myself on my job	93
labeling yourself	85
lack of professionalism	70

lack of respect...59

lacked motivation to read..35

ladies around the bar..49

Lansing...113, 120, 368

Lansing Community College...113, 368

large mass..16

laser..38, 257

last minute mix-up..56

laundry buckets...14

laundry customers..8

lawyers..33, 99

laxatives..42, 43, 51, 52, 58, 89

leaning in one direction..51

learned to fix things..86

left eye prescription..76, 92

lesion..31

less of a "throttle" on my mouth...57

less shaking...229

let my mind escape...76

let the birds out for a break...82, 212, 308

levity to our routine..53

libraries..92

life in suspension...16

lift my right leg..87

lighthouse...100, 294

limbo...25

limit my head movements..90

line of soldiers...48

list of drugs..37

little pen lights..25

log puzzles...46

looked like I was over the limit..125

looked pretty bad..28

looking like some pirate...73

looking out the window..55, 86

looped..322

loss of left side control...10

lost it right there...63

lost my sheep..118

loud crickets..112

loud when the trains go by..81

love to read..12

loves clocks...63

lower floor library..57

made me laugh so much..63

made sure I got the medical treatment..34

magic..37

mail was all forwarded...33

maintain my balance..11, 52

make or break..64

male nurse...56, 57

malls are level and air conditioned..84

manifesting..138, 265

many pain pills...12

Marsha..............................2, 85, 247, 250, 255, 258, 259, 282, 310, 316, 317

Mary..50

mashed potatoes..40, 45

massive doses of acetaminophen..13

McMinn..7, 43

medications...38, 88, 89, 108

medicines..35, 42, 60, 89

mental adjustments..99

mental distraction..................................92, 111, 112, 148, 225, 234, 240

mentally ready for the swallow..44

microscope..26, 31

middle of a bad movie..49

MidMichigan Medical..67, 95, 123, 274, 312

migraine..6

mindfulness...158, 195

mindlessly surfing TV channels...35

minor grammar corrections..5

miracle...275, 325

miraculous...1

mobile phones..113

Mom..2, 3, 20, 21, 22, 28, 36, 39, 42, 56, 58, 62, 63, 64, 66, 67, 69, 70, 71, 74, 77, 79, 80, 81, 82, 86, 87, 90, 93, 95, 96, 97, 100, 103, 109, 110, 111, 113, 116, 117, 120, 121, 122, 123, 124, 129, 131, 132, 133, 134, 135, 139, 142, 144, 145, 148, 150, 151, 154, 161, 163, 167, 172, 173, 174, 177, 178, 179, 180, 182, 183, 187, 188, 189, 190, 191, 192, 193, 197, 198, 199, 200, 203, 204, 205, 206, 207, 210, 211, 212, 214, 215, 218, 219, 220, 221, 222, 224, 225, 226, 227, 228, 229, 230, 232, 233, 236, 237, 238, 239, 240, 241, 242, 243, 244, 246, 247, 248, 249, 250, 251, 252, 253, 254, 255, 256, 258, 259, 260, 263, 265, 267, 269, 270, 271, 272, 273, 274, 275, 276, 277, 278, 279, 280, 282, 283, 284, 285, 286, 287, 288, 289, 290, 291, 292, 293, 294, 295, 296, 297, 299, 300, 301, 302, 303, 304, 306, 307, 308, 309, 312, 313, 314, 315, 316, 318, 319, 320, 321, 322, 323, 324

Mom's shawl...74

Mom's yard..74, 109, 110, 240

more aware of my surroundings...58

more control..94

more independent..83

more physical control...44

more than pressure, mon!..27

more time to observe things..71

morning person..82, 83, 142, 203

morning routine..224

move along..101

Mozart...79, 145, 176

mumble..4, 70, 93

my decision nearly cost me my life...11

mystery meat..40, 44

nagging..58

Nashville TV...40

nasty ground meats..45

nearly every machine..8

nearly hitting an eye..62

nearly losing your life..80

needing to lift my leg every now and then..............................79

nephews..2

nerves..68

Neti...13

network..66, 267

neurologists...16, 25, 111

neurosurgeons...2, 25, 89, 320

never focus that eye...75

new environment..62

new phase of life..99

new set of perspectives..80

nieces..2

night nurse..39, 43, 58, 242

nightstand..62

no "brainer"..115

no obvious malignant features..31

no sleeping in..82

No way, Jose!..152

noises grew louder...11

noisy electrical device...182

not a vegetable...96

not able to be sick..10

not as shy...100

not everyone has the time to listen...101

not lay on my side..82

not thinking about it..84

nothing has grown back...96

nuked in a nice restaurant..61

oblivious to the world around them..113

obnoxious nurse..58

occupational therapist...46, 47, 112

Ocoee River...7

off all VA drugs...38

official permission..56

older than I was..44

older than me...54

oldest guys living there..56

on top of a desk..58

one eye at a time..53, 54

one final IV..27

one fortunate individual..126

one of the funniest things..63

one of the rare ones...73

one pair of glasses...63, 72, 247

one shower a week...59

one too many..78, 98, 125

one-man shop...10

only hit numbers..38

only one open entrance...88

open heart surgery...34, 96, 293

opportunity to drive..77

optimism..51

351

options were limited...61

optometrist..53, 72, 131, 187

orchestra...231

original thoughts...5

outgoing personality..100

outside the ICU..36

overcome...157

overcoming..256

Owosso...96, 104, 120, 235, 236, 237, 289, 297, 368

pace is very slow..91

par-3...9, 109, 191, 211

park and I go way back..79

park benches..78, 295

Pat and Jerry's..322

Patrick..2, 283, 285, 316

paying attention...48, 122, 159, 199, 246, 322

peep in their cage..82

people seem to be lost in them..113

Pepsi break...15

persevere...146

personality traits..56

PetSmart..318

phase it out	37
phase them out	89
physical abilities	23, 39, 40
physical condition	44, 64, 67, 77, 306
physical survival	10
physical therapist	3, 42, 43, 51, 53
piece by piece	26
pier	100
pinball	86, 229
plant by the VA	49
play the radio on the road	61
pleading with the doctors	26
plugged into machines	24
plumbing	1, 34
Ponderosa	132, 224, 247, 274, 275, 309, 311
poor cognition skills	45
positive attitude	60, 90, 238, 280
positive energy	51, 65
positive vibrations	126
potassium	24
powder	228
preoccupied	26

prep..27, 29, 30, 286

prepping..27

prescribed medications..88

presence...104

price gouging...117

prism lens..72, 129

prison atmosphere at times...54

probable...175

programmed computers..37

programming...66

progressive lenses..72, 129, 131, 140, 204

project outward...5

proper treatment...1

proud of my achievement...88

proud of what I have endured...85

psychologist...59

pull a string...41

punching that ticket..126

pushed the limit..88

put him in these briefcases and let's go..32

puzzle break...112, 239

Queen..63

questioned my own sanity..65

rafters..7

rafting companies...7

railings..97

raised up my body on the balls of my feet...............................107

ramps to the bridge...77

ran an old joke past her..45

rarely hungry..55

read a map..78

ready to tackle him..57

real world...55, 62, 86, 97, 100, 230

recovering in Michigan...6

recovery room..31

rectal exam...71

recycle...113

Red Eye...146, 198, 207, 215, 216

regrow...94, 96, 104, 237

regular progress..106

regular routine..82

relapse..196

rely on a shopping cart...11

remnant...3, 81, 94, 95, 96, 104 residential laundry..7

restroom looked very long..51

retired..247, 248

retirement...99

ring for help...43

river loads...10

river rafting...7

river rats..7

robotic device...38

rock the boat..53, 58

room for meals..39

Rose.............................3, 161, 183, 243, 244, 245, 249, 250, 251, 273, 320

rose up from lower left to upper right..91

rubber gloves...8

Saginaw Valley State...68

Sandra........2, 39, 68, 71, 72, 78, 94, 95, 96, 100, 104, 121, 131, 132, 134, 170, 185, 186, 187, 198, 200, 203, 211, 213, 224, 230, 236, 246, 247, 250, 254, 265, 280, 284, 285, 287, 293, 294, 296, 299, 302, 311, 312, 315, 322, 323, 324

Sarah...2, 85, 237, 293, 322

save the world for democracy...35

saving my life..2

scaling Mt. Everest...88

schedule for surgery..25

scrambled nonsense	38
Sean Connery	34, 35
seat in the shower	41
second brain operation	81, 123
second image	91, 202, 209
secret codes	49
see if anyone is paying attention	22
seizures	167
self heal	90
served promptly	82
setback	83, 178
several hundred pounds of laundry	7
shake too much	74
sharp enough to work on computers	66
sharper over time	92
she is hard of hearing	58
she left for lunch	24
she showed up in my life	12
short timer	53
shots in the stomach	42
showed up for the paycheck	58
showers	41, 42, 261, 293

shrink the tumor..28, 137, 216

sidewalks...78, 116, 117, 252

significant pressure..30

simply be a customer...86

sinus condition..12, 15

sinus treatment..13

sip slowly..108

sit down for the results...16

slanted..268

sleep aid...89

slight offset of eye images..90

sling them against the wall...40

slippery in the winter..65

slipping...10

slope..116, 253, 267

slow improvements daily..74

slowly sip...113, 224

slur. .5, 49, 59, 66, 83, 84, 86, 93, 105, 114, 126, 128, 161, 218, 219, 221, 259, 267, 290, 311

small daily improvements...5

small plastic bottle of water...44

smoke breaks...56

Smokey...9, 19, 20, 21, 22, 82, 262, 272, 286, 296, 303

Snickers..55

snow blowing..97

snow flurries...64, 65, 68, 86

so bright..27, 65

so many beers, so little time..113

Soldan's...316

some "real world" therapy..97

some bum going down the road...119

some of my energy back...35

somewhat normal...47

special diet...40

special drinking cup..40, 44

speech pathologist...105

speech-to-text...................5, 126, 139, 161, 267, 268, 272, 284, 285, 297, 305

Speedway...318

spell checking..6

spilled the entire cup of coffee...10

spiritual...147, 173, 265

spray..38, 257

squint...27, 28, 136, 157, 167

SSDI...33, 99, 109, 264

stagger like a "drunk"...83

staggered a little out of the bar..125

started to burn me..24

starting to wake up inside..58

stationary bicycles..42

stepped backwards...85

steroids..28, 137, 216, 306

Steve.....................2, 68, 134, 170, 185, 203, 211, 218, 247, 287, 296, 312, 323

still on the planet..27, 78

stole the money from my wallet...36

stop all reading..73, 77, 158

straight down my throat..43, 103

strain..55, 75, 128, 136, 140, 156, 202, 247

strength returning..47

stubbed my small right toe..9

stubborn...9, 11, 12, 16

stuck in my throat..44

stuck to my record...89

stumbled..295

summer breezes and smells...79

sure I could go...26

surprisingly good at it..52

surrendered...39

survivor...85

SVSU..68

swallowing problems...40

swallows...124, 282

swimming pool..63

swing with the remote control..9

symphonies...97, 98, 161

symphony concerts...97, 164

symptoms were getting stronger..11

take cover..60

talking with strangers...101

teacher's pet..47

technical knowledge..66

technician..16, 95, 123

tedious read...275

terminal..109, 123

testing sirens...61

tetanus..57

texted...113

texting...38, 116, 141

thankful that I wasn't hurt...43

that poor fellow..41

361

thaw........63, 102, 130, 134, 160, 167, 173, 178, 205, 208, 209, 215, 216, 229

the now..264

The Price is Right...46

therapists..3, 46, 53, 56

things need to be repeated often..67

thinking about it..84, 112, 145

time delay..69, 75

time now to tell mine...93

tire often...35

tireless individuals..1

to bed early..83

toilets...42

Tom.................................2, 35, 93, 178, 180, 212, 217, 218, 219, 232, 247, 302

too embarrassed to go back..87

Totally Clean................................87, 256, 265, 271, 273, 290, 307, 316

trained animals...40

transition...72, 225

transported me very roughly...37

trauma..137

Traverse Vision..300

tremble...119

triangular shaped..35

trouble focusing on people directly	157
trying to get help	39
trying to walk	42, 51
tube out of the top of my head	28
tubular, mon	27
tumor was not malignant	25
turn for the worse	8
turn on all the hall lights	39
turrets	55
TV "crawler"	76
twisted mind	57
two birds	14, 23, 323
two images did not line up	73
two images merged	77
two months to correct	54
two pairs of glasses	72
two very slow years	91
unbelievable incompetence	70
unbelievable tale	86
underneath one eye	62
University of Michigan – Flint	368
unknown tissue	16

unpredictable weather	63
up your nose	13
urge to go	51, 58
urinal bottle	58, 244, 308
urinating	26
use of her car	34
use their position to control you	57
used a waist belt	51
useless to me	39
using both eyes	54, 73
VA nursing home	48, 54, 59, 61, 164
Vanderbilt ICU	3, 24, 137, 216, 306
vending machines	55, 94
very embarrassing moment	32
very good physical therapist	51
very hard for me to speak	67
vibration	126, 137, 142, 236
vicious cycle	14
video poker	90
violent head pain episodes	13
vision "gap"	54
vision was going to be fine	76

visualization	110
visualize	151
visualizing	111, 258
vitamins and supplements	89, 201
waiting room	16, 17, 54, 55, 188, 272
Walgreens	298, 299
walk into the VA	50
walking at the malls	76
walking on ice	64, 198, 230, 284
walking therapy	4
walking up the bleachers	68
walks at the mall	141
wallet	36
wanna trade places?	27
want to get this story out	6
wanted to leave rehab	47
wanted to sleep	35
wanted to talk	24
wash their sheets and towels	7
watch me eat and swallow	45
watched a soccer game	79
watching snow blow	84

we cover them up at night	81
weird sense of humor	29
welfare state	41
well are you crazy?	109
well enough to drive	54
well here goes nothing	65, 68
well I never could sing it before"	46
went forward	65
what I wanted to do	66
what was going on in my mind	16
what's wrong with Daddy?	14
wheelchairs	39, 48
wheels on the bottom	62
white coat	12
white noise	144, 159, 160, 171
white tile on the floor	51
who was the President	45
wide silly grin	63
Williams Township Park	235
winning several events	47
wizarding	76
wooden house	62

Woods Memorial Hospital..15

wore a stocking cap,..56

work in the heat...11

working out for the best..8

world was so bright..65

would not need a ride..83

wrong left eye prescription..75, 156

wrote the debts off..33

x-rays..44

yawning...70

yell for help..24

you can't move if you wanted to..96

Zauel Library..107, 248, 249

About The Author

Charles S. Caylor was born in Owosso, Michigan on December 16, 1950. He grew up and went to schools in Michigan until joining the US Navy in 1973. He is a graduate from the University of Michigan – Flint with a BA in Psychology, Class of 1973. He completed the US Navy Nuclear Power School in California in 1975. He returned and lived in Michigan in 1979 after six years in the military as an electrician. He obtained his AA in Digital Electronics at Lansing Community College in the evenings in the 80s. He has extensive experience in electrical and electronic repairs and later became a computer programmer in Florida and North Carolina. He worked for companies developing and maintaining tax software. He became a self-employed business owner in 2003 in Tennessee where he purchased and ran the Benton Coin Laundry until "all hell broke loose" in 2011.